WHAT IS A UNIVERSITY?

A university is a place;

It is a spirit:

It is men of learning,

A collection of books,

Laboratories where work in science
goes forward;

It is the source of the teaching

Of the beauties of literature and the arts;

It is the center where ambitious youth
gathers to learn;

It protects the traditions,

Honors the new and tests its value;

It believes in truth,

Protests against error,

And leads men by reason

Rather than by force.

THIS BOOK IS PUBLISHED UNDER A GRANT FROM THE
MARGARET VOORHIES HAGGIN TRUST
ESTABLISHED IN MEMORY OF HER HUSBAND
JAMES BEN ALI HAGGIN

PHOTOGRAPH BY DORIS ULMANN

A UNIVERSITY
IS A PLACE···A SPIRIT

Addresses & Articles
By Frank LeRond McVey

PRESIDENT, UNIVERSITY OF KENTUCKY, 1917-1940

COLLECTED AND ARRANGED BY
FRANCES JEWELL McVEY

LEXINGTON KENTUCKY

UNIVERSITY OF KENTUCKY PRESS

1944

DESIGNED AND PRINTED IN THE UNITED STATES OF AMERICA
BY PRINCETON UNIVERSITY PRESS AT PRINCETON, NEW JERSEY

CELEBRATING THE SEVENTY-FIFTH ANNIVERSARY
OF THE UNIVERSITY OF KENTUCKY
AND HONORING THE PRESIDENTS WHO HAVE SERVED
THE UNIVERSITY
FOR THREE-QUARTERS OF A CENTURY

———

JOHN AUGUSTUS WILLIAMS, 1866-1867

JOSEPH DESHA PICKETT, 1867-1869

JAMES KENNEDY PATTERSON, 1869-1910

JAMES GARRARD WHITE (acting), 1910

HENRY STITES BARKER, 1910-1917

PAUL PRENTICE BOYD (acting), 1917

FRANK LE ROND MC VEY, 1917-1940

THOMAS POE COOPER (acting), 1940-1941

HERMAN LEE DONOVAN, 1941-

To the Sons and Daughters
of the University of Kentucky
this Book is Dedicated

Preface

THE articles and addresses in this volume, with the exception of two on Education and three on Taxation and Economics, have been chosen from those made by Frank LeRond McVey since he came to Kentucky in 1917 to be president of the University of Kentucky.

Born in Wilmington, Ohio, on November 10, 1869, the author spent his early youth in Toledo. At the age of fourteen he went with his parents, his sister, and three brothers to live in Des Moines, Iowa. Some twenty-odd years after his father had graduated from Ohio Wesleyan University, he entered that institution as a freshman. His mother had seen to his proper equipment for following in his father's footsteps by fortifying this young student with a Prince Albert coat and a derby hat along with more youthful attire. The year of teaching as principal of the Orient, Iowa, high school between his sophomore and junior years of college determined his life work, and a series of lectures on labor problems in his senior year at Ohio Wesleyan impelled him to enter the field of economics. He received his doctor of philosophy degree in economics from Yale University in June, 1895. At that institution he was deeply influenced by his instructors; especially by William G. Sumner, Arthur T. Hadley, Henry M. Farnum, and John C. Schwab. In the article on "Teaching as a Calling," he tells of his decision to enter his chosen profession rather than that of law or of the ministry, the vocation desired for him by his father and his mother respectively.

Immediately after receiving his doctorate from Yale, Frank McVey began to work for the Reform Club of New York, investigating in New England and elsewhere current monetary opinions. Those were the days of William Jennings Bryan and "The Cross of Gold." The young economist, preceding the Gallup Poll by many years, questioned a cross section of the population on their beliefs about Sound Money, Free Silver, and other economic controversial matters. Later that year he taught history at the Horace Mann School in New York City. The next year he became instructor in economics at the University of Minnesota, then assistant professor, and later professor.

In 1907 he was made chairman of Minnesota's first tax commission in which office he served for two years. Some of his experiences on the tax commission are told in the talks on "Taxes and the County Tax Commission" and "The Tax Commissioner, Yesterday and Today."

The University of North Dakota called him to its presidency in 1909. For eight years he lived and worked in North Dakota. Because of his organizing ability, he is known in the annals of that university as The Builder.

During these years Frank McVey had written books and articles; had lectured at various places in this country, in Canada, and at the Royal Frederick University in Norway (1912); and had been chairman and board member of various civic and professional organizations.

Ripened by experience in other institutions and states, he came in 1917 to Lexington as president of the University of Kentucky. Governor A. O. Stanley at that time described the new president as "A man of religion without bigotry, a scholar without pedantry, a man of business without greed, a diplomat without duplicity." "Turning the Page," the farewell address to the University at the June, 1940 commencement, shows in part his love for his adopted community and state and his never failing devotion to the University of Kentucky.

The president emeritus, retired from the exacting labors of university administration, studies, writes, lectures, paints, gardens, works on various committees, and thoroughly enjoys the company of friends and family. He rejoices in his two daughters and his son, his sons-in-law and daughter-in-law, and his six grandchildren, all of whom live nearby within a radius of a few miles.

In this volume omissions of addresses and articles have been necessary because of lack of space, because of loss of manuscripts, because of timeliness, because of the fact that many speeches have never been inscribed in their entirety from their outline form. From the notes, summaries, and memoranda on many subjects, the rather amazing versatility of the speaker is seen. "Printing," a discussion on the five hundredth anniversary of the invention of movable type; "Culture Patterns and Mental Health"; "The State and the Doctor"; "The University and the Press"; a statement to Greek citizens of Lexington; and discourses on foreign and domestic affairs are some of these. From the fact that the carefully prepared notes were never put into more permanent written form, the crowded days of the speaker can be judged, and also his attitude can be perceived that the words having been spoken had perhaps fulfilled their mission.

It is regretted that not one University of Kentucky "Between Us Day" or one "Christmas Convocation" speech can be found except in outline. "The Lost Century," in which reference was made to the inability of preserving present day records because of poor paper and nonpermanent ink, was quoted widely by the press, and many letters were received commending it; however, along with the penetrating talk on "The University As a Community," it must be omitted from this volume because these two addresses were not transcribed from their notes. So also some of the speeches on Kentucky, which show abiding faith in Kentuckians, deep affection for the state, and heartfelt concern for its welfare, were never written in completed form. Among these are "Turning the Corner in Kentucky"; "Kentucky, Beautiful Kentucky"; "Problems Before Kentucky"; and "The Dedication of the Tablet Commemorating Maxwell Springs."

An entire book could be compiled from the numerous radio addresses, only six of which have been used in the present volume.

Informal essays, book reviews, one of them a prize-winning review in *The Atlantic Monthly*, and various "whimsies" have been omitted, not because they were considered unimportant and nonrevealing, but because they do not synchronize with the book as a whole.

It is hoped that later the author will surely write an article, or perhaps a book, on some of the more humorous *Presidential Experiences*, brief notes of a few of which have been found. The questions that come to a president of a university are many and varied. They range from requests by parents for counsel in the matter of guidance of children and by children for assistance in leading their parents to demands for a "good-big-worded, fine-sounding name for a new darky orchestra"; from inquiries in regard to economic, political, and moral policies to the matter of correctness between "those molasseses and them molasseses."

The addresses in this volume have been gathered from summaries, from transcriptions made at the time of the talks, from copies of dictated speeches, and from some carefully written out discussions. The material has been arranged topically and not in the main chronologically. The subject matter has been placed for convenience in seven divisions of varying lengths. At the beginning of each section, a short essay or an excerpt from a longer work has been used to indicate the general theme of the addresses and articles that follow. The University of Kentucky; The Office of University President; The University and the State; Education in general, and College Education; Kentucky, and The Art Spirit; Economics; Democracy—Our Heritage; these comprise the seven parts. A list of the author's written works and an index complete the book. The divisions and the arrangement of the material within them may seem at times arbitrary; however, after being carefully considered, they are to me reasonable and logical.

Some short articles, a few greetings, and several brief discussions have been included purposely because of their special application to some question or remembered occasion or because of their interest to students, now alumni.

In editing these papers I have made no attempt to present a biography either temporal, mental, or spiritual, and no interpretations have been made. The articles and addresses speak for themselves and show the man of inquiring mind and of wide range of interests. Through this book Frank McVey is seen; educator, university president, author, economist, artist, citizen, friend.

He can be judged from this volume as fundamentally a believer in the value of real, many-sided education whether deriving from the home, the church, the community or from the school, the college, the university. His confidence in the "educability," the "infinite perfectibility," of human beings is unshakable. Cherishing all the sources of education, he is convinced of the importance of the state university. Through the discussions dealing with the university in Part III, his grasp of the tremendous implications and opportunities of this "service arm of the state" is clearly perceived.

In a convocation address at the University of Virginia on October 4, 1933, he said: "The life of the state and the continuance of civilization rest upon learning, research, and teaching. These are the very essence of a university. With all of its imperfections, the university is the mighty force for the prevalence of reason.

"Upon the university rests the obligation to maintain the standards of civilization, to guide the people by those standards, and to protect from vandal hands the institution of government so carefully wrought. These are difficult tasks that can be carried on only by enthusiasm and by constant emphasis upon the purpose of the university. If the state is to continue, it can do so only by the use of modern science, by careful organization, and by a knowledge of the problems facing it. The one agency the state possesses for these purposes is its own university. The state university serves the commonwealth when it gives to its students and through them to all the people a belief in the modern democratic state guided by knowledge and truth. Too often do we forget that civilization is something that must be constantly worked for.

"Thus the state university becomes a great factor in the life of the state. It explains, teaches, and expands the standards set up by civilization. It finds new knowledge, which it brings to the people for them to use in new ways. It protects and preserves the evidences of past civilizations. It trains the youth in the knowledge of these and teaches the creative life. But above all it shows the modern man the errors of the past and the snares of the future."

Trained as an economist, the author has deep interest in all phases of man's life and in the governments under which mankind lives.

His special avocational enthusiasm is for painting as one expression of the art spirit. The art spirit, he explains in a discussion of the meaning of art, is "a grip on life, a real understanding of things, their order and their balance; in it dwell harmony, form and beauty, and the ultimate expression of truth. The art spirit in its application means the removal of drudgery and the pushing aside of meanness. . . . We boast that we are children of God and we speak of the church as the house of God," he continues. "Yet, with the dignity and understanding such heritage should give us, we do not attempt to comprehend beauty and to incorporate it into our lives. Moreover the church we proclaim as the house of God may be ugly, not the beautiful place such a designation would indicate."

When Frank McVey went into the field of university administration from that of economics, many of his colleagues expressed regret at the loss of an outstanding economist. Nearly twenty years later Zona Gale was a guest at Maxwell Place, the president's home on the University of Kentucky campus. She had been talking with her host and had been looking at his paintings. Suddenly she exclaimed, "Now I know the answer!" She said that some days before she had been asked what she thought were the greatest present requirement and necessity in higher education. "I know now," she resumed. "The greatest need of universities and colleges today is to have presidents who can paint." The remarks of fellow-economists and of Zona Gale indicate not only the manifold interests of the man but also his sound attention to whatever he is engaged in doing.

In this preface I wish to acknowledge indebtedness to *School and Society* for permission to publish material that has appeared in that magazine and to *Popular Science*, the *Journal of Higher Education*, and other publications in which some of the articles have been printed.

I wish also to express gratitude to President Herman Lee Donovan of the University of Kentucky for his always helpful and ever encouraging interest; to Mr. Ezra Gillis for his help in finding some of the articles and in having many of them copied; to Dr. Thomas D. Clark for his valuable suggestions and wise counsel and for his time and thought generously given; to Dr. W. D. Funkhouser, Dr. Edward Wiest, and Mr. E. F. Farquhar, members of the Haggin Fund Publication Committee, for their evaluations of the material and for their aid in seeing it through the press. Appreciation is given to Miss Jane Nichols for assistance, in many ways through the years, which has enabled this book to be produced; to Miss Mary Hester Cooper for her help in verifying dates and statistics and in typing many of the papers; to Miss Mary Johnston and Miss Josephine Harrison for patience and ability in typing the manuscript.

Incorporating within its pages educational philosophy and practice, economic theory, and political understanding of an important era in the state and nation, 1910-1941, this collection will serve as part of the history of education and culture in Kentucky and the United States. It will be used perhaps as a reference book of the period covered. My hope is also that it will be a "memory book" for alumni, faculty, and friends who through its pages may recall occasions that will delight them to remember. The real reason, however, for my assembling these addresses and articles is that they mean much to me; in intellectual interest; in sentimental attachment; in reconstruction of past events and affairs; in awakening of the spirit; in presentation of economic concepts and democratic ideals; in realization of educational values; and in many other ways too subtle to express.

FRANCES JEWELL MCVEY

Shady Lane
Lexington, Kentucky
February 5, 1943

Contents

CONTENTS

CONTENTS

CONTENTS

A UNIVERSITY
IS A PLACE . . . A SPIRIT

PART I
THE UNIVERSITY OF KENTUCKY

The University of Kentucky

From the booklet, "Going to College," third edition,
November, 1935, "written, typed, and
illustrated by the President's Office, University of Kentucky."

T H E University of Kentucky is not only the buildings and grounds located in Lexington; it is not merely the faculty and the student body; it is all these and more. The University has a material form, but the real University is the spirit which has for its aim the growth and development of all of the people who live within the borders of the Commonwealth of Kentucky. The University of Kentucky numbers as its friends people of all races and all creeds, rich and poor, weak and strong, and it attempts to serve all people who call Kentucky, "home." The University of Kentucky has a warm feeling for the institutions that minister to the public good; it pledges its full cooperation to all organizations that are working for the goal toward which the University of Kentucky itself is striving.

To know the University of Kentucky, you must see it, you must catch the vision of its purpose and ideals. You should walk through the campus with its tree covered hills and look through the vista upon the graceful spire of Memorial Hall; you should visit the Library, the museums, the gardens, the University School in the College of Education, the Art Center, the Memorial Hall, the Astronomical Observatory, the Kentucky Experiment Station and Farm, the Engineering Laboratories, and the many other buildings well adapted to their use; you should meet its faculties and talk with its students. You will be proud to realize that to you as a citizen of Kentucky the University of Kentucky belongs.

The spirit and intention of the law creating a center of education by the state and for the state have been carried out effectively by the Board of Trustees of the University. In the University of Kentucky, a high moral and spiritual purpose exists. Here is fine determination to incorporate within itself the noble and worthwhile ideal of public education which is "the very breath of our national life," our state life, and our community life, the ideal that through equality of educational opportunity upon the campus of the University of Kentucky "the individual may climb to the place which his ability justifies him in occupying without having to meet obstacles based upon birth, wealth, and social position."

The University of Kentucky is engaged in a constant survey of its work and its purpose to the end that it may remain in the vanguard of those institutions which ardently desire the best in education. Yours is a splendid state university, worthy of the trust, interest, and cooperation of the people of Kentucky.

Turning the Page

Commencement address, University of Kentucky, June 7, 1940; published and distributed by the *Kentucky Kernel*.

FOR this the last Commencement on which I shall appear before you as President of the University of Kentucky, I have selected as the title of my address a phrase that in some measure epitomizes the occasion, "Turning the Page." In the reading of a book the reader turns the page and finds new words, sometimes new ideas, and possibly an admission to a great adventure in inspiration. The book continues from page to page to the end with continuity in the volume as the author moves on in his thought. In the life of a university many turning points arise, all of which fit into the whole of its history as the years go on. So now that we are turning the page to a new administration of the University of Kentucky, there is and must be in its life a continuity from one year to another.

As we gather here tonight for the purpose of conferring degrees upon a great group of students who have lived for a number of years in the University community, I am sure we are impressed with the large company who have come to see and to honor those who graduate at the University of Kentucky. Commencements at the University have grown steadily in the character of the occasion and in the beauty of pageantry that has been so carefully worked out by the committee in charge of the ceremonies.

Tonight the record shows that this ceremony of commencement is the seventy-third in the life of the institution, and in time it brings to a close the seventy-fifth year since the founding of the University in 1865. In a modest way this seventy-fifth anniversary is commemorated by our meeting out of doors under the canopy of heaven to confer degrees and to conclude in solemn ritual the academic year.

The history of the University of Kentucky may be divided into three epochs. The first was the epoch of union beginning in 1865 when the Department of Agriculture and Mechanic Arts was set up under the Morrill Act as a part of Kentucky University. This arrangement, which continued until 1878, was terminated by the bickerings and misunderstandings growing out of an attempt to combine in one institution the interest of church and state. The second period, known as that of the State College, extended from 1878 to 1907. In that time the College of Agriculture and Mechanic Arts was founded, and buildings were erected on the present campus. The city of Lexington and Fayette County gave the present site, which had been the county fair grounds, and funds for the new State College. In the year 1907 the University period began, and the name of the institution was changed to State University of Kentucky. During this generation the University has attained the form of an American university and has developed a university spirit.

What is a university?
A university is a place;
It is a spirit:
It is men of learning,
A collection of books,
Laboratories where work in science goes forward;
It is the source of the teaching
Of the beauties of literature and the arts;
It is the center where ambitious youth gathers to learn;
It protects the traditions,
Honors the new and tests its value;
It believes in truth,
Protests against error,
And leads men by reason
Rather than by force.

The essences of this definition are men of learning and a spirit that is free; books and equipment; earnest and eager students; belief in truth, protesting against error; and the leading of men by reason rather than by force.

Five presidents and two acting presidents have served the University during its history. The first, John Augustus Williams, presided over the affairs of the new educational infant just one year, resigning to become president of Daughters' College at Harrodsburg. Then came Joseph Desha Pickett, who after two years resigned to accept the office of State Superintendent of Public Instruction. Following him, the father of the University, James Kennedy Patterson, was in office for forty-one years. Henry S. Barker was president from 1910 until 1917. After him, I came and have been at the University of Kentucky, as you know, for twenty-three years. Thus, three presidents have held the office a total of seventy-one years. The two acting presidents were Professor James G. White and Dean Paul P. Boyd.

On the pedestal of the impressive statue of President Patterson is the sentence cut in the large polished granite stone, "He saved the seed for the next generation." President Patterson gave to the State College his strength and his ability, paving the way by wise guidance for a greater institution. Once when the State College was in dire straits, he loaned to the Board of Trustees his lifetime savings in order that the buildings might be completed. To the honor of the College, it may be said, the sum was returned; nevertheless, his was a generous act showing the extent to which the institution as long ago as 1882 had been molded into his life. At another time, President Patterson threw himself into the fight over the mill tax, a battle that threatened the very existence of the University. In many ways and at many times he fought valiantly for Kentucky State College.

When I came to the University of Kentucky in 1917, the United States had been in the World War for five months. The campus was a seething place where trucks churned up the roads, students marched and drilled, and recruited men labored in shops to learn skills that would be of value to the government in operating its war machine. As I turn over the office to my successor, the nations of Europe are engaged in a greater and more devastating war. No one knows what the outcome will be; no one can tell what will happen to the ideals and principles we hold so dear. It is indeed a time of uncertainty that brings a feeling of utter hopelessness, a sense of insecurity, to thousands of young people over the world.

They search for a source of guidance and of inspiration, and often they feel that they look in vain.

In the ancient world Alexander the Great saw no more worlds to conquer, and yet men lived to see his empire shattered. Napoleon held sway by force of arms over the larger part of Europe, but he too lived in his island prison to see men put their affairs in order. The world has a way of going on, and men continue to live and build and dream again. You who are before me will see a different world and a world of order. This may be wishful thinking; it is nevertheless true that slaughter cannot go on for long before people grow weary and the nations come to some agreement.

Here in our own land many ask what of the night? What of the watchers who look in wonderment on the world in which they live? Are there no more opportunities? Must one stagnate and die in hapless being? I can remind you that Thomas Jefferson in his day emphasized one of the fundamentals of democracy as an access to free land. Free land formerly was opportunity. The land of Jefferson's day was on the frontier. Free land in these United States is of the past. There are, however, frontiers today; new frontiers that are open to the adventurous, to the skilled, to the willing, and to the prepared.

There are the frontiers of science showing new vistas which call for able men and women. The whole social security movement must have trained personnel who will administer and guide the great social program that is slowly forming in this country. There is a new frontier in the application of the arts to living. This involves design, the use of color, new forms in everything, houses, buildings, machines, furniture, wall coverings, and textiles. Yes, new opportunities are before us.

Again there is a vast field of new things to be done that have never been done before, new applications of old principles to the meeting of needs. Whereas we have extensive developments in communication and transportation, in ideas and ways of living we are in the horse and buggy days. If one questions that statement, he has but to look at any town or countryside for illustration of how little we see the far-reaching results of the automobile or for that matter of the railroad. We do not know what these mechanical devices are doing to us; their effects upon population are only slightly understood. To look backward will bring no answer. The great task of this generation is to see the world in its possibilities and to comprehend clearly the trends and movements of the times. Bewildered, yes! But this generation must not be discouraged.

In the centuries gone by universities have served the peoples of the world, and in the days that are to come universities must serve to an even greater degree than they have in the past. Our own University has passed at times through difficult days, and hard problems will doubtless come to it in the future.

It is highly important that there should be an appreciation among students of the functions of a university in a commonwealth. Citizens of the state must understand the goals of their state university. On the alumni especially rests a heavy responsibility to realize what the University is and what are its ambitions. With the cooperation of alumni, students, citizens, the University of Kentucky will advance to the place it ought to hold in service to the state and in the affection of the people. The purposes of the university should always be within the framework of the state, politically, socially, and economically. The state university should study constantly the problems of the commonwealth and, by applying understanding to those problems, should be able to bring counsel and assistance in finding the right way. When this function of a university is recognized and utilized, the University of Kentucky will indeed hold a place in the lives of the people of the state, and support and prestige will come willingly and freely to it.

It is essential always that the principles of sound education shall guide the University of Kentucky. The University must be free and tolerant and hard-working. Fundamental appreciation of the arts and sciences as the basic phases of education needs to be maintained, although understanding of the vocational field and leadership in vocational education should be recognized. If we are to aid in the solution of the problems of the community, of the state, of the nation, of the world, and of human personalities, we must have real foundations in the accumulated wisdom of the past and in the best practices and precepts of the present.

In this city of Lexington where we are gathered tonight, I have lived for nearly a quarter of a century, and I have found it a pleasant and interesting town in which to reside. Through the years the citizens of Lexington have been kind and sympathetic. I like you, and I thank you. Since I have completed my majority as a citizen of Kentucky, I hope I may now be accepted as one of you. Kentucky is a beautiful state filled with interesting people who have learned to be friendly with each other for nine months of the year while undergoing during the remainder of the year emphatic political battles that engender considerable heat but result in no permanent blisters. Because it is a lovely state, I expect to continue to live in Kentucky, and I trust that I may be of usefulness in one way or another to this, my adopted commonwealth.

In these twenty-three years, the faculty and staff of the University have tripled in number. I have known most of them personally and can call by name nearly all of them. The University has by and large able associates. They have always been tolerant and co-operative. I am grateful for their help and sympathetic understanding during these years.

The Board of Trustees has given me great freedom in the administration of the University; the members have added much to the sound structure of the University through their advice, counsel, and judgment.

I would indeed be unmindful if I did not refer to the aid and comfort I have received from a fellow traveler, Frances Jewell McVey. She has contributed from her heart and mind to the welfare of the University and has made it her purpose in life. No one, more than I, knows how much she has meant in trying as well as in glorious days.

A university comes to have pride in the alumni who have passed through its halls. That is certainly true of our University of Kentucky. Scattered throughout the country, in foreign lands, and in many useful callings, the more than eleven thousand alumni of Kentucky have done well. Wherever I have met them, they have been cordial, sympathetic, and loyal. I am indebted to them for their support and good will.

Above everything else, a university is chiefly concerned about the students who come to its campus. Buildings and equipment are subordinate to their interests. The faculty and staff are brought together for their enlightenment. It is said a campus would be a pleasant place if there were no students—but that is the thought of a misanthrope. I have found the students of the University, the more than five generations of them, reasonable, thoughtful, cooperative. They have been helpful on many occasions. To you who have graduated in the past and to you who are graduating today, I hope your Alma Mater has given something that will stand you in good stead in the days that are to come. I bid you Godspeed, good luck, and a fair port.

Before me is a large body of students who are to have degrees conferred upon them and who are to receive diplomas from my hand. When the conferring of degrees is accomplished, it has been the custom for the members of the graduating class to take a pledge. In the pledge each of you who repeats it will realize that you are emphasizing honesty of mind, courtesy, belief in yourself and in God, and an obligation to work for the good of the commonwealth. The world is in sore trouble, and dangers are at hand. The present situation demands of all of us, and especially of those young people about to graduate, understanding and right action. It is a time when the need for real men and women is as pressing as at any time in our history. May each of you have courage, fortitude, courtesy, honesty of mind, wisdom, understanding. May to each of you come opportunities and joy.

What more can I say to one and all than that I have had a great time here at the University of Kentucky and a great opportunity! The University has grown in numbers and in usefulness because many people have contributed to its making and because the people of the state have come to know and value what the University may mean to the life of the people.

To my successor I bequeath all that may be good, happy, and helpful. I wish him as interesting a time as I have had. I trust he will have health, a good heart, a sound constitution, and a sense of humor. Equipped with these and professional qualifications, he can go far.

I come now to the last page of a chapter, not the last chapter, but one near the front of the book. I close the book, and I shall hand it to the new president where he may read in the first paragraph of the next chapter, "It was a beautiful sunny day, and all was harmony in nature. The minds and hearts of those who gathered to hear the opening exercises of the University of Kentucky in September, 1940 responded to the day. It was a good beginning of a new regime." May it be a successful one of glorious import to Kentucky.

The Spirit of the University

Inaugural address, University of Kentucky, June 4, 1918

ON THIS beautiful afternoon in June, I need not remind you that in another part of the world a terrific struggle goes on for world supremacy. The most serious period in the war is at hand, with the outcome in the balance. Today is a day for serious reflection, for the evaluating of present performances, and for the fearless consideration of the future.

The great war has placed new responsibilities upon all mankind; everywhere calls to service previously unknown are made, with emphasis upon leadership, causing those in authority to turn to education and educational processes to meet the situation. When the United States entered the war in April of 1917, the army and navy received substantial reinforcements from the colleges and universities of the country. These reinforcements have, however, been swallowed up in the demand for leaders, and the cry is for more and more to fill the vacancies.

In the civil life of the nation under war conditions, the same demand appears. Calls for materials, for equipment, for supplies, and for services of all kinds have forced the use of the draft to fill the positions created by the war. The women of the country have come forward in increasing numbers to assume their responsibilities, and singularly enough we have discovered that their capacity can be utilized far more extensively than was supposed. In the same way in which women have answered the claims of other times, they are responding now with faith, hope, patience, and mercy as contributions to the needs of mankind.

Out of the conflict the conviction grows that the result of the struggle will depend on intelligence and brains. Other things being equal, the most resourceful people will win in the final analysis. But it is not enough that we should have intelligence; it is essential that we should have trained intelligence. So a new emphasis has been placed upon the greatest resources that a nation possesses, namely its brains, and in this connection the colleges and universities of the country have come into larger importance as they attempt to train leaders and to guide intelligence.

May we inquire at this point, what is a university? Many definitions have been given. One declares that a university is a collection of colleges; another that it is a place where everything is taught. On this occasion I venture to formulate a definition of my own which in some measure covers the salient features of the others. A university is a place where the youth of the land may be trained in the higher arts and sciences and taught the ideals of national life. It is certain that there is at present a new concept of a university and that the students, perhaps before anyone else, have grasped the import of this new ideal. The students have suddenly learned that the university is a vital force and not merely an abiding place. The faculty, too, have come to a recognition of their increased responsibilities; they realize that they must be not only gentlemen, scholars, and teachers but that as members of the university faculty they should be imbued with a real sense of responsibility to the life of the commonwealth. Thus a new conception emerges which regards the university and the college as a necessity, as something which the nation must have, if the leadership which is so essential to the practice and continuance of democracy is to be provided.

The story is told of a man who, speaking of educational institutions in his town, said, "We now have two universities and we have just cut the logs for the erection of a third one." In Kentucky we have passed beyond that way of looking at things. The University is no longer a competitor but a cooperator with the other schools and colleges. For a considerable part of the University of Kentucky's history, such results as have been accomplished have been mainly through the energy and persistence of Dr. James K. Patterson, president from 1869 to 1910. His contribution to the life of this institution centers about the university idea and the placing of the university in substantial form through the medium of the state government. His administration unified the University and made of it a consolidated institution.

The meeting of the legislature in the winter of 1918 was the beginning of a new era for the University. The General Assembly recognized the government of the institution, established a substantial and continuous appropriation for its support, and enacted the required legislation to cooperate with the federal government for the conduct of education in the state. These were large achievements. The legislature, encouraged by the hearty support of Governor Stanley, passed legislation necessary to place the University upon a satisfactory basis. With such legislation making an essential contribution to the University's affairs, it is possible for the friends, the alumni, and the people of the state to look forward to an increased usefulness in meeting the needs of the commonwealth.

Not attempting today to outline the program of the University for the distant future and yet wishing to indicate what may be immediately before us, I desire to call your attention to some of the things which the University expects to do in the next year or two.

First, I may say that the University of Kentucky is in the war. The service flag which you see contains 823 stars, each representing a son of the University who has entered the service of his country. From the senior class of 1918, thirty-seven are either in France or in training in this country, and many of the others have arranged immediately to enter into war service. On the campus the Reserve Officers' Training Corps has been organized during the year, and many men have been given instruction in military science. Courses have been provided for women in the field of domestic science to take care of the changes made necessary in home life, and it is expected that during the coming year provisions will be made for the instruction of women as nurses and secretaries. During the summer Red Cross courses will be given, and a course will be offered to women desiring training in drafting. A very considerable change has been made in the College of Agriculture, which recognizes the necessity of keeping men in college; and this year a short course will be offered beginning in October and ending in April. The Division of Agricultural Extension in close touch with the requirements and urgencies of agricultural work in the State is ready to undertake any enterprise that will be of advantage to Kentuckians at home or at war. The University proposes this coming year to add to some of the departments and courses of study particularly in the fields of art and design, music, economics, sociology, and the sciences.

During the past year additions to the faculty have been made in the professional schools, placing emphasis upon the creation of leadership. The University hopes also to enlarge the library by increasing the number of volumes. Since various departments depend upon the library almost exclusively for their research and laboratory material, without an adequate working library they are limited and hampered in what they can do. It seems desirable also to encourage the founding of a museum as soon as possible. Kentucky is indeed rich in art and historic objects, but as things now stand there is no place in the state where these materials can be brought together and protected. Certainly, the University offers satisfactory location and utilization of such artifacts.

The spirit that should animate the University is the scientific spirit. That spirit is one of thoroughness, an attitude that should pervade the University in working out the essential things in university life. With that purpose is the obligation to insist that the student shall do his work thoroughly and accurately. The University must be at liberty to go its way, free from political domination whether for party or for individual interests. The spirit of tolerance must pervade the University in order that the largest service may be given to the state and to the nation.

To the alumni of the University may I say that they can be of great help in upholding these ideals. With this viewpoint of thoroughness, freedom, tolerance and with the true spirit of democracy, we can build a real university.

To the colleges of the state may I pledge the attitude of the University of Kentucky toward them as one of cooperation animated by the spirit of good will. The University desires to maintain a graduate school to which the graduates of the colleges of Kentucky may come with increased confidence in the work done at the University. In this sincere spirit of friendship and cooperation and in the recognition that there is work for all of us, the University of Kentucky and the colleges of the state may render service and do their part in the present situation.

Nothing is more evident than that the old days are gone; the pioneer stage is past, and the comparatively simple conditions which confronted the greater part of the country in other days have changed to complex problems. Added burdens have been placed upon the colleges of the land in meeting the larger obligations of education. Only in the recognition of these increased demands can the University face honestly its responsibilities. The state has given evidence of a new interest in the University, and the University must in turn be worthy of this consideration. The University, moving forward to meet new times and new needs, will do well to keep the traditions of the past, so dearly beloved.

It is in this spirit that I present to you today, very briefly to be true, some of the hopes and ambitions of the University of Kentucky, and it is in this spirit that I have accepted the call to the presidency of the University of Kentucky. I look to you for sympathy, for support, and for substantial help. With these generously given, the University can do its part in the building of the Commonwealth of Kentucky.

The Teaching of Evolution in Kentucky

At the meeting of the Kentucky General Assembly in 1920, bills were introduced to prohibit the teaching of evolution in tax-supported educational institutions in the state. The president of the University of Kentucky through the press, through speeches before both houses of the legislature, through assistance from educators inside and outside the state used every legitimate means to bring about the defeat of these "anti-evolution bills" with the result that no such law is on the Kentucky statute book.

A Letter to the People of Kentucky:

In view of the many statements, the confusion, and misunderstandings that have arisen relative to the bills introduced in the Legislature providing for the prohibiting of the teaching of evolution in the public schools and institutions of higher learning supported by taxation, it seems desirable that some direct comment should be made.

I have an abiding faith in the good sense and fairness of the people of this state. When they understand what the situation means and when they come to comprehend the motives underlying this attack upon the public schools of the state, they will hold the University and the school system in greater respect than ever before. Although apparently the proposed legislation prohibits the teaching of evolution in the public schools and educational institutions maintained by the state, the attack is narrowing itself more and more to one upon the University.

As president of the University of Kentucky, I desire to say as emphatically as possible that the charge that there is teaching in the University of atheism, agnosticism, and Darwinism (in the sense that man is descended from baboons and gorillas) is absolutely false. No such teaching is carried on in the University. Moreover no member of the staff of the University attempts directly or indirectly to modify, alter, or shape the religious beliefs of students.

The University, however, does teach evolution. It is, in fact, bound to do so since all the natural sciences are based upon the theory of evolution, and failure to teach evolution would mean elimination of courses and textbooks relating to astronomy, botany, bacteriology, biology, geology, and zoology. The students in the University as well as in the normal schools and high schools would have to go elsewhere to get instruction in modern sciences. What this means does not seem to be generally appreciated; in truth it means that Kentucky would be shutting itself off from all contact with the modern world as a consequence of such an attitude on the part of the commonwealth.

Most of this discussion is due to lack of understanding and lack of knowledge of what has happened in the world of science.

What is evolution? Evolution is development; it is change; and every man knows that development and change are going on all the time. Evolution is a great general principle of growth. It is that idea that development goes on during long ages under varying influences of climate, surroundings, food supply, and changing conditions. It is the belief that the earth was formed ages ago and has evolved gradually and slowly. Today man is known to have lived on the earth a long time; to have evolved from lower conditions to the one he occupies now. Science has brought to our knowledge some conception of the greatness of the universe. It has made clearer than ever before that God works through law and that men are to use their God-given minds in order that they may learn more of the power and glory of God as manifested in His works in the universe.

Many theories of evolution are held today. The man, therefore, who attempts to put in one phrase all the views regarding the development of the earth and states that evolution is comprehended in the slogan, "man is descended from a monkey," is simply betraying his ignorance and his lack of analytical mind.

There is the scientific theory of evolution; there is the theistic theory; there is the materialistic theory; and there is the so-called Darwinian theory.

The scientific theory of evolution seeks to determine the historical succession of various species of plants and animals on earth. It tries to arrange them according to natural series of descent. "This theory," it has been said, "is in perfect agreement with the Christian conception of the universe for the Scriptures do not tell us in what form the present species of plants and of animals were originally created by God."

The theistic theory of evolution regards the entire history of the world as a harmonious development brought about by natural law. This conception is in agreement with the Christian theory of the universe. God is the Creator of heaven and earth; if God, therefore, produced the universe by the creative act of His will, its natural development by law implanted in it by the Creator is to the greater glory of His divine power and wisdom.

The atheistic theory of evolution maintains that the cause of the world's development was material and that through the process of law the development of the universe has proceeded to its present form.

The theory of Darwin placed special emphasis upon the survival of the fittest, upon sex selection, upon hereditary influences in present day forms of life. The men of science have found that Darwin's theory, as important as it was at the time of formulation, does not explain the new facts that are being discovered from time to time. Darwinism frequently stands in popular usage for all theories of evolution. This use of the word rests upon a confusion of ideas.

The foremost thinkers everywhere, religious and scientific, have accepted the idea of evolution. The testimony of many men throughout the world is given again and again that there is no conflict between the theory of evolution and the Christian view.

If this be true, manifestly then legislation of this character is unnecessary particularly when the principles of it are already safeguarded in the public school laws found in section 4368 of the Kentucky Statutes. But more than this, such legislation is exceedingly dangerous in that it places limitations on the right of thought and freedom of belief. If the history of America has stood for anything, it has stood for freedom of belief, freedom of speech, and tolerance in religious matters. The Constitution of the State of Kentucky found in Section 5 of the Bill of Rights reads as follows:

No preference shall ever be given by law to any religious sect, society or denomination; nor to any particular creed, mode of worship or system of ecclesiastical polity; nor shall any person be compelled to attend any place of worship, to contribute to the erection or maintenance of any such place, or to the salary or support of any minister of religion; nor shall any man be compelled to send his child to any school to which he may be conscientiously opposed; and the civil rights, privileges or capacities of no person shall be taken away, or in any wise diminished or enlarged, on account of his belief or disbelief of any religious tenet, dogma or teaching. No human authority shall, in any case whatever, control or interfere with the rights of conscience.

Adherence to the Bill of Rights means that such legislation as is proposed at the present time is unwise and unconstitutional.

The weakness of the position of those who are backing these bills is shown in the fact that the first bill provided for prohibition of the teaching of atheism, agnosticism, Darwinism, and evolution and attached fines of from $50 to $5,000, a prison sentence of from ten days to one year, and revocation of the charter of the institution. The second bill eliminated prison sentence and reduced the fines to a bracket of $10 to $1,000. The third bill is merely a declaration against the teaching of anything that will weaken or undermine religious faith of pupils in any school or college or institution of learning maintained in whole or in part in this state by funds produced by taxation. It provides no penalty but that of dismissal of teachers giving such instruction. Provisions to safeguard religious freedom already exist on the Statute Books of Kentucky as indicated above.

In closing, I may say that the University has an unusually fine body of students. The morals, ideals, and spiritual attitudes of the students cannot be excelled anywhere. The Y.M.C.A., the Y.W.C.A., and other religious organizations are active and well supported. There is absolutely no reason for this attack upon the University of Kentucky in the guise of the anti-evolution bills. When finally analyzed the bills will be shown to be really an attack on the public education that is maintained and supported by the state.

(Signed) FRANK L. McVEY
President, University of Kentucky

The Aims of the University of Kentucky

A UNIVERSITY is generally distinguished from other institutions of higher learning by the fact that it is made up of several schools or colleges unified under a single administration and having certain objectives in common. It is further distinguished from the college by emphasis on graduate teaching and its necessary accompaniment, research. The university differs from the college by the character of its equipment, the variety of its courses, and the professional standing of its staff. The university must have for the achievement of its purposes library facilities, laboratory equipment, and personnel beyond that normally found in either the arts and science college or the teachers' college that operates as a separate unit. These provisions are essential to its graduate and professional teaching and its research program.

A general indication of the objectives of the University of Kentucky may be stated in terms of the three principal functional divisions of a fully developed university. These are teaching, research, and service.

Teaching is the most apparent obligation of a university. The university shares in substantial measure the instructional offices of the liberal arts college as well as of the undergraduate teachers' college. In addition it has certain teaching functions peculiar to itself, most of them having their origin in the graduate and professional character of much of its educational procedure. This professional character of the University of Kentucky is observed in the College of Law, College of Education, College of Engineering, College of Agriculture, College of Commerce, as well as in the College of Arts and Sciences and in the Graduate School.

Among the most important additional teaching purposes may be enumerated: development of leaders for positions in governmental administration including health, welfare, education, finance, highway engineering, and other technical operations; education for leadership positions in social service, business, agriculture, industry, law, teaching, engineering, and other liberal professions; training research workers for various fields of scholarship and professional activity; instruction of those who will engage in the interpretation, in more meaningful terms, of the content of civilization and knowledge.

Perhaps all of these types of teaching objectives except the last are obvious without explanation. The process of interpreting civilization and human knowledge involves such activities as the preparation of textbooks which will make learning easier, the making of addresses, and the writing of articles and books designed to convert the technical language of the scholar into the common language of the people.

Research is the function of the university that most clearly distinguishes it from other institutions of higher learning. Usually research is carried on by the scholars on the staff of the university and by graduate students preparing for the vocation of professional scholarship. Libraries, laboratories, and museums are needed to aid those engaged in research.

In the matter of *Service*, the state university should so integrate itself with the life of the community as to render its influence a pervasive force throughout the state and itself an indispensable partner in all aspects of social betterment. In general, achievement of the service aim of the University of Kentucky follows the principal lines of aid in solving public problems as for example: educational problems presenting themselves to a given public school unit; financial or administrative problems pressing upon a particular city, county, or state department; cultural problems of all varieties arising in civic groups particularly in relation to their public activities; problems of the day in agriculture, commerce, industry, and social welfare. The University, moreover, by means of extension activities and by cooperation with the press, interprets for the public the results of its research and teaching.

The aims of the University of Kentucky are listed in general above. Thus is the University, through the extent of its purpose and the variety of its activities, necessarily differentiated from the arts college or teacher training institution. In founding the University, Kentucky's purpose was to give to the people an arm of the state that would engage in the education of the people; in the investigation of their problems in industry, business, government, agriculture; and in the maintenance of the means and sources of knowledge through laboratories, libraries, and museums. All the purposes of the University of Kentucky look constantly toward the advancement of the people's welfare.

The University of Kentucky

Summary of address given in 1926

IN THE various reports on education, Kentucky is written down as a laggard in the procession of states. This position is confirmed in many minds by the statements concerning illiteracy and the calls for money for the support of the mountain schools.

The plea for help in the conduct of education in the mountain districts of Kentucky is a true one, and help is much needed. This district is cut off from the rest of the state by the lack of roads, but the mountain district is not all of the state, and the conditions prevailing there do not exist in other parts of the territory that stretches four hundred miles from the Big Sandy on the east to the Mississippi on the west. Kentucky has made real progress in the past ten years, in fact, astonishing progress when statistics of the last decade are compared with those of previous years. It must be remembered that Kentucky did not establish a public school system until a few years before the Civil War. Her neighbor on the north, Indiana, started a public school system in 1816, and the University of that state celebrated its one hundredth anniversary two years ago. During the years 1861-1865, the devastations of war fell upon the South, destroyed its property, cut off the flower of its manhood, left discouragement in its wake, and smothered the states in debt. Such facts should be remembered in judging the southern states because they go far in explaining the position of the South today; they make the educational standing easily understood.

The heritage, too, of the private academy and college held sway in the minds of the people for a hundred years and kept them from embracing the idea of a great public school system complete from kindergarten to university.

Today in Kentucky there are 550 high schools on the accredited list of the Department of Public Instruction with 50,000 children in attendance. The colleges of the state number fourteen, enrolling 9,000 students of college grade. Of the fourteen, the public institutions of higher learning are the University of Kentucky, the four state teachers' colleges, the municipal university at Louisville, and a normal and industrial Negro college at Frankfort.

The story of the University of Kentucky runs parallel to that of public education in the state. In most of the states the passage of the Morrill Act in 1863 marked the beginning of the state universities. But in Kentucky the administration of the funds provided by that act was turned over to a privately maintained institution, which for fifteen years continued to give the instruction and to expend the appropriation made by Congress. The interest of the state in the arrangement languished; however, not until 1878 was the State College of Agricultural and Mechanical Arts established as a public institution. The public support was meager indeed, and the State College went on its way slowly gathering momentum until in 1907 the name was changed to the State University of Kentucky. The addition of a College of Law to the Colleges of Arts and Sciences, Engineering, and Agriculture had caused the change in name, but the University still was one in name only not in fact. In 1917 the institution became the University of Kentucky.

During the years that have passed since that time, the University has grown in student body, in usefulness to the state, in organization. It is composed today of seven colleges and schools: Liberal Arts, Agriculture, Engineering, Law, Education, Commerce, and the Graduate School. The list of the agencies of the University is not completed with the enumeration above. The Kentucky Agricultural Station with its farm at Lexington, the Substations at Quicksand and Princeton, the many demonstration plots, as well as the widespread activities of the departments of Agricultural Extension and University Extension, must be included if something of the work of the University of Kentucky is to be understood. Little by little the University has been brought closer to the people and has become an increasing factor in the life of Kentucky.

Less than twenty years ago, in 1908-1909, there were 546 college students enrolled in the University. At that time the entire staff including the specialists in the Agricultural Experiment Station numbered eighty-five. The enrollment of students in residence in 1924-1925 was 3,004. Of this number 155 were resident graduate students. During the summer session of 1925, there were 992 students enrolled, and the Extension department reported 1,021 students doing work by correspondence and study classes. Meantime, the staff of the University has reached the figure of 178 administrative officers and teachers, and Experiment Station experts and persons engaged in Agricultural Extension number 168. The state, with this development, has materially increased its support and has provided for additional buildings on the campus. The University has now reached a period of rapid growth, which measures in no small way the changes that are taking place in the progress of education in Kentucky.

What the University of Kentucky has done for the commonwealth that founded it cannot be measured in years or in facts alone. The 30,000 students who have attended it have filled important places in the state and nation. During the World War the University trained 3,000 men for the service, sent 1,200 of its alumni into the ranks, and mourned the loss of thirty who gave their lives to the nation. Today the University looks forward to new usefulness through interpretation of the great facts of science to the common life of the people and through the maintenance of the light of knowledge within the borders of the state.

The University of Kentucky

Summary of commencement address, University
of Kentucky, June 6, 1932

T H E story of the state universities in the United States of America is an amazing and magical one. In it are inspiration, pioneering courage, adherence to a great idea, and persistent struggle to maintain that idea. That the people of the United States should establish universities is evidence of their belief in the safeguarding of democracy by means of education supported by the states. Through the early days of statehood, the ideal has been pursued until every state in the Union has a university with the exception of three, Massachusetts, Rhode Island, and Connecticut; and these have state colleges. The state university was first established soon after the creation of the Constitution. North Carolina and Georgia each passed legislation providing for a state university in the last decade of the eighteenth century. In the second decade of the nineteenth century Indiana began its university. The University of Michigan was established in 1839, and other states under the influence of the Morrill Act inaugurated institutions in the sixties. Since then, state after state has found it desirable to establish its own university.

In our own commonwealth the people have been working nearly one hundred and fifty years to inaugurate and maintain a public university. This century and a half have seen reverses, misunderstandings, and conflicts with accompanying delays in the development of the university idea. Five distinct periods are to be noted in this history: the beginning period in 1790 to 1858; the breakdown of the combination, 1858 to 1865; the University under church and state, 1865 to 1878; the Land-Grant College, 1878 to 1907; the University, 1907 to 1932. As a state institution of public education, the University of Kentucky has had a history of fifty-five years; as a university, it has had a history of twenty-five years.

Kentucky might have had one of the earliest of the state universities if the purposes of the Virginia Legislature had been followed. In 1780 before Kentucky was a state, the House of Burgesses appropriated land for a public seminary west of the Alleghanies and set aside 8,000 acres of escheated lands. Two years later 12,000 acres more were added to the grant. After Kentucky became a state, sums of money were voted by the General Assembly to buy books and equipment for the institution. A school had been started in 1789 near Lexington; ten years later this school was combined with Kentucky Academy, and the Transylvania Seminary was united with it. A rapid succession of Presbyterian, Baptist, Episcopalian, and finally Disciples presidents followed through its history. Under the leadership of Dr. Holley from 1817 to 1827, Transylvania University advanced rapidly; its progress, however, was disturbed by religious controversies. Beginning as a state institution, it gradually lost its public contacts and became a private college.

In 1856 the offer made by the trustees of Transylvania University to turn over the institution to the state was accepted by the Kentucky Legislature, and an appropriation of $12,000 a year was voted for its support. Unfortunately, two years later this appropriation was withdrawn. Bacon College, established at Danville in 1836, was three years later moved to Harrodsburg. Its activity was suspended in 1850, and John G. Bowman, a graduate of Bacon College, undertook to found a school to succeed his Alma Mater. He obtained a charter from the legislature in 1858 and created Kentucky University. Some progress was made, but the main building was burned in 1864. Meantime, the Morrill Act had been passed the previous year, and Bowman brought together Transylvania, the new Land-Grant College, and Bacon College at Lexington as Kentucky University in 1865. The new institution had in land scrip 330,000 acres. Bowman had collected $112,000, and there was an endowment of $200,000. The new institution, in spite of necessary readjustments caused by the War Between the States, started under fairly favorable auspices; it had a student body in 1869 of 764 from twenty-five different states.

The system under which the new Kentucky University was established combined state and church. It was a public institution united with a sectarian organization. Doubts soon arose, controversies developed, and the Agricultural and Mechanical College as a member of the University was handicapped from the beginning. The matter reached the legislature, and a report was made by the commission appointed in 1878 unanimously recommending that the union of the colleges be dissolved. In the legislative statement given at that time an important comment is that "the State Agricultural and Mechanical College shall forever remain a State institution free from all ecclesiastical entanglements or control. The establishment and success of the State College are matters of great and common interest to the people of the whole State, and that College should be the pride and aim of every citizen having the future prosperity and welfare of the commonwealth at heart."

After almost ninety years of the pioneer and war periods, during which time attempts were made to develop public higher education in Kentucky, the new State College began its career in 1878. It grew slowly, it was faced by controversy, and its rights were attacked in the courts. Valorously here President Patterson rendered perhaps his greatest service to the College in preparing a brief, setting forth the fundamental principles of higher education.

With the establishment of the Law College in 1907 the State College became the Kentucky State University; in fact we may say that the University of Kentucky as a university began its history in that year. The new university had to win its legal status, to learn its functions, to respect scholarship, to engage in research, and to accept responsibilities beyond its walls.

In 1918 the legislature recognized the larger function of the State University and gave it an increased part of the mill tax. Later, the legislature added a part of the inheritance tax and made more generous provision for the institution's support. The University began to enlarge its libraries, equip laboratories, and engage in research. Now it stands the University of Kentucky, recognized at home and abroad as an institution of merit and position. Today it has 4,000 students in its seven colleges and schools, three experiment stations, a great system of agricultural extension, and libraries of 130,000 volumes.

The University of Kentucky has had a unique history. Its story is wound through and through the fabric of the state. The heritage which it possesses today was gained through a long struggle. It had a bad start; it was handicapped by misunderstandings in regard to education. Now it is free to do a great work. It had first to escape from religious entanglements and factional contacts. Today it is free from political domination, and the people of the state recognize its interests.

As this commencement period closes the academic year 1931-1932, the University finds itself faced with financial difficulties. These have arisen, not because of mismanagement and extravagant expenditure, but because of national and world economic conditions. The University hopes, nevertheless, for the best, hopes to be understood, and hopes to be a great factor in the life of Kentucky. It works for the state at all times. It is in fact a part of the state set up by the people and tested again and again through the years. It has now reached a point in its history where it should do its best work. The University is a beacon light to the people. It is a great force for the prevalence of reason. In these days of complex and difficult financial problems, it may help materially in the educating of students and in bringing to adults everywhere the principles of government and the growth of science. The University of Kentucky desires to aid in the solution of the problems of Kentucky and to assist in the giving to the state the benefits of high citizenship through the spread of moral and intellectual enlightenment.

The University of Kentucky

Fifty Years Ago and Today

Comments on fifty years of the University of Kentucky
written for the Fiftieth
Anniversary Edition of the *Lexington Leader*, May 1, 1938

In 1888 the Agricultural and Mechanical College of Kentucky had a student enrollment of three hundred and twenty-six; in 1938 the University of Kentucky, the educational outgrowth of that early institution, recorded a registration of three thousand, five hundred and thirty-seven students for the fall term. Thus, from a small beginning, the state's largest institution of higher education has enjoyed a growth worthy of the hope and trust of those educators and citizens who have contributed to its development through half a century of progress.

Today in reviewing the history of the commonwealth, of the city of Lexington, and of the institutions which have survived the past fifty years, one is interested to read of the Agricultural and Mechanical College of half a century ago and to measure by the years the increase in size, in enrollment, and in service from the state institution of that time to the University of the present.

In 1888 the Agricultural and Mechanical College of Kentucky granted a degree to its first woman graduate, one of a class of five to receive diplomas that year and one of fifty-one graduates since the establishment of the College. Including the mid-year graduating class of 1938, ten thousand, one hundred and fifty-nine students have graduated from the University of Kentucky. The June, 1938 class will include approximately four hundred and twenty-five candidates for degrees.

The University of Kentucky of today meets the needs of the youth of the state with a resident teaching staff of two hundred and seventy-two. In 1887-1888 there were eighteen faculty members on the staff of the Agricultural and Mechanical College and of these only one was a woman. President James K. Patterson was professor of Metaphysics and Civil History at that time. The remainder of the staff consisted of Dr. Robert Peter, emeritus professor of Chemistry and Experimental Physics; John Shackelford, professor of the English Language and Literature; James G. White, professor of Mathematics, Physics, and Astronomy; A. R. Crandall, professor of Natural History; F. M. Helveti, professor of French Languages and Literature, who also served as secretary of the faculty; John H. Neville, professor of the Latin and Greek Languages and Literature; M. A. Scovell, professor of Agriculture and Horticulture and director of the Experiment Station; J. R. Potter, principal of the Normal department and professor of Pedagogy; Dillard H. Clark, First Lieutenant, U.S.A., commandant, and professor of Civil, Mechanical, and Mining Engineering, and Military Science; Walter K. Patterson, principal of the Preparatory Department; William Prewitt, instructor in Latin and Greek and assistant in Preparatory Department; J. Lewis Logan, assistant in Preparatory Department; Mrs. Lucy B. Blackburn, matron and assistant in Preparatory Department; Alfred M. Peter, assistant professor of Chemistry in Experiment Station; James A. Yates, tutor in Mathematics; David A. King, professor of Practical Mechanics; and M. L. Pence, assistant in Preparatory Department.

At that time the Board of Trustees of the Agricultural and Mechanical College consisted of four members. They were Judge William B. Kinkead, Lexington; ex-Chief Justice B. J. Peters, Montgomery County; General Don Carlos Buell, Louisville; and Hon. W. H. Wadsworth, Mason County. The present Board of Trustees of the University of Kentucky has fifteen members, and the governor of Kentucky serves as chairman of the board.

The Experiment Station was established during the year 1887-1888; until that time there had been on the campus only five buildings including the greenhouse. These buildings were the present Administration Building and White Hall (the Old Dormitory), the first two buildings to be constructed; President Patterson's home, now being used as a woman's building; and the commandant's house, which has been torn down. The greenhouse, also long since destroyed, was located near the spot where President Patterson's memorial now stands.

Students who attended the college in 1888 did not have the choice of making their own schedules or of determining their own midday meal hour, according to the minutes of the faculty for September 14, 1888. The object of the meeting of that faculty was "to fix a suitable hour for drill"; and "after consideration, different hours having been proposed, it was decided to have drill from one to two P.M. and dinner at two P.M."

The minutes of that early faculty are often interesting. One record, dated October 1, 1888, reports the case of two cadets who were absent from quarters without leave, having gone to the opera, and who were, "in consideration of their bad record as to conduct, dismissed." It is difficult to imagine such strict discipline in comparison with the extracurricular freedom which is granted present day students. However, even that early faculty was not so strict as to disregard a plea from one of the two students for readmission, and the minutes of October 5, 1888 granted reinstatement to one of the cadets.

The Agricultural and Mechanical College of Kentucky, established in 1878 as a separate institution from Kentucky University under which organization it had functioned since 1862 as a department, was only ten years old in 1888. It boasted its original holdings of fifty-two acres of campus and an additional forty-eight acres in the Experiment Station plot which had been acquired in 1887 with the establishment of the station. In 1938 the University of Kentucky has ninety-four acres in its main campus and six hundred acres in the Experiment Station at Lexington, a forest reserve and subexperiment station of fifteen thousand acres at Quicksand in eastern Kentucky, and a subexperiment station of six hundred acres at Princeton in western Kentucky.

So, like nearly everything men undertake, the half-century has seen a great advance in the development of the University of Kentucky. Particularly has this been true in the past ten years for during that time the student body has increased, the staff has been enlarged, and numerous buildings have been erected. In the last two years seven new buildings have been added to the plant of the University. Today the total value of real estate, buildings, and equipment of the University of Kentucky amounts to $7,000,000.

The University of Kentucky has come into a larger relation to the state through its experiment stations, agricultural extension, university extension, and the various bureaus established for the purpose of rendering service to citizens. It has made marked contributions to the commonwealth. Today the University of Kentucky consists of seven colleges, an experiment station at Lexington, subexperiment stations at Princeton and Quicksand, a great agricultural extension organization, university extension activities, and bureaus of business research, government research, school service, and publicity. The University has encouraged organizations that are helpful to the state, such as the Public Health Service and the Municipal League, to become associated with it.

One of the marked developments that has taken place has been in the library. Fifty years ago the College Library was at its beginning with meager equipment and few books. In 1917 the University Library contained in all twenty-six thousand books. Today the volumes number two hundred and fifteen thousand, exclusive of the nearly one thousand periodicals and newspapers, making it the largest institutional library in the state and the seventh in the South.

All of these figures and many more indicate something of what is happening at the University of Kentucky. Needless to say, the newspapers of Lexington through their cooperation have aided materially in the development of the University and in its increased prestige in the state. With pleasure, therefore, the University of Kentucky extends to the *Lexington Leader* hearty congratulations upon the completion of a half-century of service and wishes for its management continuous growth in good works.

The University of Kentucky Library

Foreword in pamphlet issued at dedication of Library,
University of Kentucky, 1931

THE University Library has emerged from a place and has evolved into a factor. As a place it housed the books of the institution, and occasionally bold, adventurous students entered the doors. The college library of yesterday had its good points, but now the library has come into an added importance as a part of the instructional purpose of a college. Teaching has gone beyond the textbook. It is in fact a process of direction. The student gathers his materials, works with books and maps, and by the help of his instructors formulates his ideas and viewpoint.

The present day library is no longer a depository alone. It is also a collector of books, an advisor of students, and a director of study programs. It is in truth the center of the university's intellectual life. As such it must be alert to the teaching and research needs of the university. Everything in print and manuscript form assumes a new importance for books are made from reports, articles in newspapers and periodicals, speeches, and manuscripts. The glory of the library staff is found in extending opportunities and materials to student, teacher, and scholar.

Now that the University of Kentucky has a fireproof building for the care of books and manuscripts, it can hold out loving hands to the gifts with which devoted friends may intrust it with the assurance that the gifts will be well guarded and intelligently cared for. It can also serve as a place where the books of earlier times lost in garrets, attics, and forgotten cases may find a home and a new usefulness in their availability to student, teacher, and scholar. The possibilities of the University of Kentucky Library are great indeed. It must have increased funds for maintenance, for larger staff, and for books. These funds will come as the value of the library to the University, to the community, and to the state is realized in the days ahead of us.

Memorandum on the Making of Gifts to an Institution

(1936)

T H E first thing which a donor has in mind in making a gift to an institution is the continuity of his gift. How long will it be preserved, and what are the chances that the institution will continue to carry on its purposes and functions over a long period of time?

As I envisage a state university, it will have a life as long as the state. The list of state universities which are now more than a century old is a considerable one; the University of Kentucky, though comparatively young, has been in existence for seventy-five years.

As the years go on the state university will become more and more important to the people of the commonwealth because the people will need the interpretations of social movements, the knowledge and understanding of scientific investigations and discoveries, and the benefit of trained personnel to carry out the purposes of the state. Moreover the state university, because its financial support is not dependent upon the ups and downs of interest rates and upon the changing value of endowments, can have constant growth and improvement. It is obvious that the numbers of people in a state who become vitally interested in the university continually increase and that the evergrowing groups of alumni have the purposes pretty well in mind.

A further consideration on the making of gifts should be in regard to the solidity of management that results from the corporate form in which the institution is organized. A determined effort to separate the University of Kentucky from political interference and to make it the institution of the people of the state has been manifested.

One may be sure that by the state itself buildings will be kept in repair and funds will be provided for the increased staffs that are needed by the university. In consequence, a donor may look to the utilization of his gift for the specific objects for which the gift is made and not for purposes other than those that he had in mind. At the University of Kentucky it is quite apparent that new buildings will be required and ought to be provided for in the near future. The state will necessarily have to make appropriations for buildings for instructional use; additional activities may have to wait for other means of support.

There is a need at the University of Kentucky for a museum building to house the materials which are already collected and which, because of lack of space, cannot be properly exhibited. Many people would be willing to send valuable objects and artifacts to the University of Kentucky if on the campus was a fireproof building where they could be safeguarded and exhibited.

A building for exhibitions of art objects and paintings as well as for quarters for the Department of Art is urgent.

The University should have added residence halls to provide lodgings for men and women. The demand for such buildings increases constantly with the growth of the student body.

[35]

An administration building in which the various departments of business and administration of the University can be given adequate space should be built.

The College of Commerce, which has grown rapidly in the last few years, ought to have a larger building to provide laboratories, recitation rooms, library, and offices for this important phase of education.

Other buildings are likewise needed for the social sciences scattered as they are around over the campus in the older buildings.

Aside from investments in buildings, the University of Kentucky could use a large number of scholarships to be awarded to students of promise to help them in their education. The demand for scholarships which the University is not able to meet grows every year.

The University needs a fund to provide an income for the purchase of books and art objects; the first to increase library facilities, and the second to provide a good, permanent, growing exhibition.

Many other suggestions for the use of gifts come to mind. This memorandum, I hope, will indicate in a general way the enduring usefulness of any gift that might be given to the University of Kentucky.

The University of Kentucky Builds

Address to businessmen of Lexington, Kentucky, and to alumni
of the University of Kentucky, 1937

W H E N a businessman undertakes to erect a building to house his mercantile operations, he wants first of all a plan that will fit his needs and that will make it possible for him to carry on his business as effectively as possible. He is interested incidentally in the ornamental side of the building. In addition he would like a fireproof building, a well-lighted building, and a building that is ventilated and air-conditioned. He wants a building with modern heating and lighting, and particularly he desires that the cost of maintenance will be low and that obsolescence will be as near nothing as possible.

To get these essentials he must inform himself in regard to the latest developments in lighting, ventilating, and construction and must use the best and latest materials. His desire is to secure an honest building that is planned to meet his requirements, that is made of the best materials to be secured, and that is good-looking in proportions, color, and design.

New processes and devices that are far ahead of ordinary building practices are available today. To take advantage of these is often difficult because we all go along in ruts, using time-worn plans and methods. Some of these new devices are steel sashes, doors, and partitions; new ventilating and heating methods; roofs that are effective and yet do not put an undue load upon the structure.

Many people find it difficult to understand that the western world has passed into the third great stage of construction. The first method is from the Greek, the so-called classical architecture; the second is the Gothic; and the third is the modern, which today utilizes present day materials and designs. If builders are to construct their buildings by the modern method, it follows that the architecture must be paralleled by the materials that are used. Modern architecture recognizes this important fact and therefore is attempting to emphasize simplicity, precision, and basic proportions. If the materials of the twentieth century are to be used honestly for what they are, then the form of architecture must be synchronized with them.

The program of building at the University of Kentucky is endeavoring to keep these truths in mind in the hope that it will be able to secure buildings that are better lighted, more fully fireproof, and more competently heated and ventilated than those that have been erected on the campus in the past. Moreover, it is believed that the cost of maintenance will be reduced by using modern materials in a modern way. So many are the new inventions and discoveries in regard to lighting, heating, ventilating, use of materials, and so forth that the present day builder has an obligation to see that his building is thoroughly adapted to its use. A university is surely the indicated place to employ these results of research.

The University of Kentucky has never had an adequate central heating plant. The little plant in the middle of the campus took care of six buildings. The ivy-covered chimney was a landmark to be held in memory, not to be kept as a useless relic on the campus. The other buildings were heated by individual units, nineteen in number. Some of these plants carried as many as three buildings. Consequently the first undertaking in the new building program was a central heating plant and with it an extended underground system of heating mains.

The second building is a Law Building, now about two-thirds completed. It is being erected near the University Library and is of the same material and of the same color of brick. The design is fundamentally based on classic principles though modern in effect. There will be no cornices since these do not add to the effectiveness of a building and do increase the cost of maintenance. The building when completed will be, in the opinion of those who have the construction in charge, satisfactory both in appearance and in use.

The third, fourth, and fifth buildings are additions to the Engineering College group. The old buildings have been removed with the retention, for sentiment's sake possibly, of a part of the original Mechanical Hall. The sixth building is a Student Union Building, long desired by the students as a center for their various social activities. This structure is located between the Alumni Gymnasium and Frazee Hall and is being built at a cost of about $230,000. The last project under this arrangement with the Federal Government is a Biological Science Building to be located on Graham Avenue west of the Men's Residence Halls. Containing recitation rooms and laboratories, it is to be three hundred and ten feet long and three stories high with a central eight story tower. All of these buildings will be modern in architecture and in materials used. Another project has been carried on in the enlargement by one-third of the Experiment Station building on South Limestone Street. The cost of this entire construction program will be about $1,300,000.

The present building plan of the University of Kentucky which has been under way for the past year and a half is now approaching completion. This project is financed under the PWA by a grant of

45 per cent coming from Federal sources and the balance from University funds. To match the Federal grants, funds were secured by the issuance of bonds on a 3½ per cent basis for a period of thirty years. The University therefore is obligated to pay interest and amortization charges on the $634,000. The University in the last ten years has built $3,000,000 worth of buildings with little or no direct cost to the state. Including the buildings in process of construction, the assets of the institution amount to $7,000,000, an increase of approximately $5,000,000 in twenty years.

Many other buildings are needed on the University of Kentucky campus. Among these are a Home Economics Building, a Woman's Residence Hall, Residence Halls for men students, an adequate Administration Building, an Art Building, a Music Building, and a Museum. The University of Kentucky has answered only a part of its needs. It must continue to build.

The University of Kentucky's Contribution to Rural Life

Radio talk over WHAS on the Country Life Program, sponsored by the University of Kentucky, May 13, 1935

AGRICULTURE, the great basis of life, plays an important part in the growth of a people. Relatively, as the march of the machine has proceeded, agriculture has declined in the production of the national income; nevertheless, it continues as a fundamental part of the economic and social life of the nation. Agriculture has from the first been more than an industry. It has included living, a philosophy, and a social order. To think of it in terms of a business is to overlook the larger import that it carries in the life of a people.

The phrase, rural life, indicates a distinct way of living as contrasted with the urban life. The two have been regarded as separate and in a measure opposed to each other. By degrees the lawgivers, economists, and philosophers have come to regard them as complementary. No great city can exist without an abundant hinterland that is prosperous and that is occupied by a happy people. Such being the case, more attention is now being paid to the welfare of the agricultural group.

Unlike many enterprises agriculture combines home, land, place of business, and means of support. Industry, conducted on a large scale, separates the home from the business, the man from his tools, and the family from its food supply. In some measure agriculture has imitated industry, and farming has followed the procedure of business. The farmer has lost sight of farming as a mode of life and has disassociated man and tools, home and land, family and food. Really to separate farming from the family and family life is, however, impossible. Therefore, the household in all its relations through school, church, and community, as well as in the matter of crops and cattle, must be considered in a comprehensive discussion of rural life.

In agricultural procedure emphasis is placed upon one phase by one group, upon another phase by still another group, with a resultant organization of this and that part of the industry. One group stresses soy beans, another sheep, others wheat, bees, and legumes. All are important, but the overemphasis of any of them makes the trees stand out over the forest. A rural life program not only must bring the parts together and balance them in one great procedure but also must present the life itself as the reason for the parts.

This is the purpose that the University of Kentucky has in sponsoring the Rural Life Program in cooperation with the Rural Life Institute. Farming is a mode of living. It is not a business alone but the welfare of a family group that lives on the land. Thus the social philosopher, the economist, the minister of the Gospel, the school master, the public officer, the merchant, and others are vitally interested in cooperating with the farmer. For sixty years the University of Kentucky has had no mean part in the agricultural development of the state. At the beginning that interest was directed largely to better crops, better farming, and better marketing. All of these are relatively significant in themselves; their true importance, however, depends on their contributions to real country living. The changing years have laid a heavy hand on rural communities and have disturbed the old order that prevailed even thirty years ago.

Yet rural life offers opportunities of actual living that are superior. These are worth keeping. But, unless intelligence of a high order untangles the twisted skeins, decline must continue. Such intelligence is to be found in the rural areas among the farmers, the farm women, the ministers, teachers, and business people. At the University of Kentucky are specialists who have given time, much study, and energy to the rural problem. Here exist two groups who should work together in earnest effort to understand these regions and who should then formulate methods of procedure by which something can be done to save this vital part of the national life. The University of Kentucky serves the state. It has no other purpose; hence what it can do in this most important matter is to offer its teachers and investigators to help in getting at the facts and in instituting a program. The University of Kentucky wants to see prosperous country churches engaged in Christian teaching. It wants to see good schools, well-cared for children, happy households, and effective farming. These things cannot come without a material foundation, it is true; and on that foundation must be built a splendid, well-rounded rural life. To the end that they may be accomplished the University of Kentucky hopes to be of utmost assistance.

The University of Kentucky Station at Quicksand

Published in *Mountain Life and Work*, January, 1934

In a bowl, surrounded by hills broken by the North Fork of the Kentucky River and the Quicksand Creek, lies Quicksand in Breathitt County. Once a noisy, dirty, busy place, it is now a quiet mountain village held together by the University of Kentucky station, known as the Robinson Substation. The span of years that separates the two scenes barely reaches a full decade. Much has happened to bring so great a change to pass.

It was in 1920 that the Mowbray-Robinson Company completed its sawing of logs and making of flooring. The timber in the forests had been cut, and little remained to hold a commercial enterprise in its location when the raw material upon which the industry relied was nearly exhausted. Employees left their wooden shacks when the end came, and the town dwindled from 1,500 to 300 people. The great saw mill stood stark and strong, its huge stack marking the burial place of a dead industry. A sprawling lumber yard flanked the mill on all sides, while railroad tracks crowded with cars and engines cluttered the space toward the north. At the south end of the area the big flooring mill filled with machines, belts, and pulleys was silent. Between the saw mill and the flooring plant on the other side of the railroad sat the village with its stores and ramshackle houses. The whole was a scene of confusion, dirt, and disorder.

However, the two men who operated the plant had a picture in their minds of what the region needed. Now that the lumber industry was gone, something should take its place. The University of Kentucky was asked to accept the site of the plant and 15,000 acres of cut-over land for the purpose of establishing a station where agricultural experiments could be carried on and where a social and economic program could be developed. The Board of Trustees of the University accepted the gift and asked the Kentucky Legislature to appropriate $25,000 annually to support it. This was done, and the station began its work.

The first task was to clear the ground of all vestiges of the lumber period. It took two years of hard, grinding work to complete this task. Several of the buildings were retained for residences, club house, and auditorium. The switching yard was leveled and covered with a spread of blue grass. Trees and shrubs were planted. The place with its natural background of hills is pleasing to the eye. The mills gone, Quicksand is now known as the home of the Robinson Experiment Substation.

The program of the University of Kentucky for the new work at Quicksand was a simple one in the beginning: first, to develop a mountain farm that would be an example to all who saw it; second, to survey the forest land, to cut fire-prevention paths, and to make an inventory of the timber; third, to bring into the region with their headquarters at the station a county agent, a home demonstration agent, and a forester. Behind this group of workers, keeping a constant hold on tact and good will, was a policy of helpfulness and careful consideration of the needs of the people.

The farmer at the end of the first year produced a great corn crop. Other products of agriculture were raised, grass and root crops were planted, orchards were started on the hillside, and poultry houses were built. As a result the station swung into a full program in the short space of three years. At first the work of the station was looked upon with scepticism and in some instances with suspicion. As the days went on the good intent of the University and the friendliness of the staff became evident, and the "Universalists," as they were called by the local people, were accepted.

A program of any institution must be developed slowly and by experience. The station, in order to better the agriculture of the region, traded tested seed corn bushel for bushel and also swapped eggs of purebred fowls for the product of the scrub chickens of the farmers in the region. There has been a resultant betterment of crops and poultry. These activities were carried on along with experiments in checking erosion, planting of grasses, and the distribution of small fruits. As the interest grew, the station had many visitors who asked practical questions about farming, building, cooking, health, and other matters.

It was eight years ago that the first fall festival was held at Quicksand. This was before the Highway Commission had embarked upon an extensive campaign of good road building in this region. The people came on foot, on mule back, in wagons, and in an occasional automobile. The premium list with prizes of $1,500 brought out a considerable exhibit of farm products. This exhibit was supplemented by showings from some of the mountain schools and from many homes. The festival has been continued from year to year with increasing interest and attendance. The most recent, held in September, 1933, brought a large crowd who came over greatly improved roads in automobiles and trucks. The event has become an institution.

To the staff, which at first consisted of superintendent and farmer, were soon added a county agent, a home demonstration agent, and a forester. The county agent ranged through the large mountain area, talking with farmers, helping with the 4-H Clubs, and encouraging the schools to interest their pupils in the program of farm betterment. The home demonstration agent visited homes and schools, organizing groups of girls in clubs and bringing the women together in local circles. The forester undertook the survey of the forest area, opened fire lanes, made inventories of the timber, and stimulated interest in his work by exhibits at the festival. The station as a part of the University of Kentucky called upon the staff of experts located at Lexington for advice and assistance in many projects.

By the growing confidence in the staff of the station and through the increasing appreciation of the fact that the University of Kentucky had no axes to grind, the station has materially added to its effectiveness in this mountain area. Located in the center of the Kentucky mountain region and looked upon as neutral ground, it has been used more and more as a place for meetings of different kinds. The Homemakers to the number of ninety-seven gathered there from nine counties. District leaders of the 4-H Clubs came from twenty-eight counties. A 4-H Club camp for mountain boys and girls is held at the Quicksand farm annually. The station has been the scene also of the annual encampment of farm women, whose program continues for a week. Farmers gather every now and then to hear talks and see demonstrations of work done, and there are many meetings of clubs and of church societies from nearby towns and communities. Just recently the regional conference of Mountain Workers, attended by one hundred people, met at Quicksand in a two-day session.

A very definite policy animates the work and purposes of this outpost of the University of Kentucky. That policy may be stated in a few words: to do those specific things representing the duty of the substation; to do those things that cannot be, or are not, done by other agencies; and to cooperate with existing agencies, public and private, in carrying out a program of helpfulness. So the station does not expect to develop a school of agriculture, to engage in public health work, to build roads, or to superintend school teaching; the members of the staff of the University do expect, however, to cooperate in every reasonable enterprise having as its purpose the development of rural interests. One of the greatest functions which the station can exercise is to find out the facts about the mountain area and to formulate the problem. No simple formula can solve the difficulties of this region in an overnight discussion. To that end a good deal of money, time, and ability has been spent in gathering material about population and about the resources and the social and economic life of the people. On an understanding of these depends the success of future work.

How important this gathering of information may be is not always fully recognized in the conduct of religious, educational, and industrial enterprises in the mountain area. In the long run an institution, church, or school will go up or down with the area. It is necessary to know what is happening to populations. Is the population increasing or decreasing or remaining stationary? Is there a possibility that a self-sufficient economy can be maintained, or has the basis of such an economy disappeared under the forces of modern life? Can any considerable industry be established in the absence of transportation that leads out to real markets? What basis is there for subsistence farming along with the mining and lumber industries? To what extent can the local communities support schools, and what amount of aid must the state give to establish a fair degree of equality in public education? These are sample questions that confront every worker in the field. Effective expenditure of money for educational, religious, and industrial development depends upon the answers. Looked at in this way, the station at Quicksand with the University of Kentucky guiding and managing it should be a serviceable cooperative agency for every community and for every educational and social factor engaged in the effort of advancing the standards of living in the mountain region.

The University of Kentucky
Listening Centers

Written for radio presentation over C.B.S. from Cordia, Kentucky, at
the installation of the Listening Center, May 3, 1937

T H E art of broadcasting implies the coordination of two factors;
first, the broadcaster, and second, the listener. With either element
missing or imperfectly adjusted to the other, a successful broadcast
is impossible.

For more than eight years, the University of Kentucky has
utilized the fifty thousand watt clear channel facilities of station
WHAS, the outlet of the Columbia Broadcasting System in Louisville, for the dissemination of educational, agricultural, musical,
and cultural broadcasts. During these eight years, almost six thousand such programs have been presented, and much interest on the
part of listeners has been manifested. Assuredly the broadcasts have
been a potent force in stimulating the mental life of Kentucky.

In some parts of Kentucky eight years ago, radios were few. The
programs broadcast from the University on nature, language,
health, agriculture, government, and a score of other useful topics
were not heard in many districts because facilities were not there.
How to establish and use these facilities was the question that the
University of Kentucky hoped to solve.

The University of Kentucky, like most state universities, must
meet heavy financial demands for resident instruction. Such things
as the purchase of radios for isolated points, however worthy,
could hardly be included in the customary budgets. A solution
seemed to exist in the use of old, discarded battery sets from
owners who had no further need for them. Soon the University of Kentucky radio workshop was filled to overflowing with
radios manufactured between the years 1921 and 1925. A few of
the better battery sets were repaired as well as possible, and the
University's director of radio work went forth to make a few in-
stallations. The first center was established at Cow Creek in Owsley County under the supervision of Reverend Albert Tull, a
pastor and community center worker. The following day Listening

Center No. 2 started operation at the Carcassonne Community Center at Gander, Letcher County. The results, based upon the quality of the radio sets placed in these and a few other centers and upon the enthusiasm with which the programs were received, were all that could be desired.

However, it became evident shortly that battery sets that had fulfilled their usefulness many years ago in the more populous areas would never serve efficiently today in isolated locations. Modern up-to-date sets with a high degree of amplification, good tone quality, and low battery drain were demanded. Thus cash donations to the system became necessary if it was to survive. The various service clubs of Lexington lent a helping hand. As information about the University of Kentucky Listening Center system spread, donations began to come from other sources. Bankers, presidents of business concerns, magazine editors, and others sent sums of money sufficient to equip a number of centers.

Today the University of Kentucky has twenty-four Listening Centers in eastern Kentucky in the counties of Knott, Leslie, Breathitt, Harlan, Letcher, Floyd, Martin, Magoffin, Owsley, Johnson, Wolfe, and Estill. Most of these are equipped with modern receiving sets, although perhaps seven need better receivers. In addition, applications are on file from fifty other points, most of which will be equipped with radios as funds become available.

Operators of the University Listening Centers have come from many callings; some are ministers, community center directors, school teachers, general store owners, postmasters, and farmers. These people are sincere, highly respected citizens of their communities who believe in the worth of radio as a means of improving their local situations. Daily a score or more of those who dwell in the various communities gather at the Listening Centers to listen to news broadcasts, broadcasts of a direct educational nature, farm programs, musical presentations, children's hours, and entertainment. The enthusiasm of these audiences for this comparatively new instrument of enlightenment is great.

The future of the University of Kentucky Listening Center system in eastern Kentucky is a matter of interesting speculation. Already through the cooperation of the Kentucky offices of the National Youth Administration, a young lady has been employed who will act as project supervisor for eight of the centers. Current event clubs, children's groups, health clubs, and other community groups will be organized to listen to germane broadcasts several times each week, with each listening period to be followed by a stimulating discussion period under a competent leader. People living near the Listening Centers will be given special encouragement to go into the centers and attend the broadcasts, and a wider dissemination of information about programs will be attempted. Thus the coordination urgently needed between the broadcasters and the listeners for the successful utilization of the programs is furnished by the Listening Center operators and by the project supervisor.

The Radio Listening Center system is an interesting and a unique undertaking. At this time on behalf of the University of Kentucky, I want to thank the friends in all parts of the United States who have rendered material and spiritual support in the development of the Listening Center idea.

ODK and the University

Radio talk over WLAP in connection with the
twenty-fifth anniversary celebration of ODK, December 2, 1939

W H E N universities and colleges open in the fall of the year, great numbers of students gather on the campuses for registration. In most of these institutions there are various tests and examinations through which the freshmen are compelled to go. The purpose is to find out something about the abilities, capacities, and attitudes of the entering students. A majority of them belong in the middle groups. Above and below these are other students, about equal in number.

Many students who come to colleges and universities have hazy ideas in regard to college education. They know that they are to go to college for four years at the end of which time, if they have done fairly well, they will receive a degree. The great possibilities, spiritual, intellectual, social, and physical, that are to be found in the institution are only vaguely comprehended. It takes, therefore, one to three years for the student to orientate himself and really to come into an understanding of the purposes that brought him to the campus.

To facilitate the early recognition of the objective of higher education, university administrations have been setting up in recent years personnel bureaus, guidance offices, brotherhood and sisterhood schemes, with not always successful results due perhaps in large part to the fact that the approaches are from the administrative angle rather than from the student viewpoint. An association such as ODK has great value to a university because of its ability to enable incoming students to grasp the real meaning of the opportunities that are before them.

Among students a large number of organizations that have all sorts of ideas behind them develop in a comparatively short time. Some of them are interested in the welfare and advancement of the university or college; many are purely social organizations. Some of them apparently have the idea of heaping honors upon their members without regarding their obligations very seriously.

Into institutions of higher learning has come an organization that asks, "What can ODK do to help the administration in the problems that confront it?" This is something of a new slant, and many administrators regard the question with raised eyebrows. The relationships that have been developed in various institutions have depended upon the wisdom and understanding of young men who are members of the organization and the attitudes of the administrative officers towards them. In some institutions administrative officers began to apply little tests to find out how successful this cooperative spirit would be and how enduring was the interest of ODK. In most instances ODK has been found worthy of an ever increasing importance in the affairs of the institutions.

Perhaps the greatest problem the college has to solve at present is to enable students to understand the purposes of education and to appreciate the institution's manifold relations with students, faculty, alumni, and the public. If ODK is to progress in the future as it has in the past, it should attempt to aid in the solution of this problem. I am sure that the organization is to be more and more useful. ODK is well-led, has high ideals, and will bring significant contributions, I believe, to every institution in which it is established.

The Student's Creed

Read before a joint meeting of Y.M.C.A. and Y.W.C.A.,
University of Kentucky, March 9, 1919

I BELIEVE in God; in His Son, the great Master; in the state under whose protection I live; in the University of which I am a member; in my fellow man; and in myself.

I believe that religion is essential to my spiritual welfare, that it is the spirit of the fathers expressed in good deeds and noble aspirations, and that it will keep me free from that which smirches the soul.

I believe in a clean body and the domination of the mind over the physical.

I believe in education, in the training of the will, and in the application of reason to individual and public problems.

I believe that the economic life of the state and of the individual must be set to right principles and high ideals. I believe the laborer is worthy of his hire and honest endeavor should leave no debts.

I shall work and play in the spirit of right living. I pledge myself to the welfare of those I love, to the University, and to the state, knowing by such action that I can do my part in the higher purposes of life.

Greetings to Students of the University of Kentucky

In *Kentucky Kernel*, September 17, 1937

FOR seventy-two years young men and young women have been coming to the University of Kentucky to enter college in September of each of those years. A larger number than ever are here now. I am wishing for each student a great year of which he will be proud as he reviews it at the end of the session. That there may be a spirit of friendliness and of good will in all our dealings through the months of our working together is my desire for all of us at the opening of the seventy-second session of the University of Kentucky.

Greetings

In K. Handbook, issued by University of Kentucky
Y.M.C.A. and Y.W.C.A.

W H E N the recipients of this K. Handbook come to the University of Kentucky, they are enrolled as members of a fraternity of letters. Membership in the organization places obligations upon each of them. Those obligations are to be a real gentleman or a real lady in all relations, to work at studies, to play enthusiastically, and to profit by the sojourn in the University. The recipient, the faculty, and the president are engaged in a true partnership to advance the interests of each owner of this book. The responsibility is not on the book but upon the holders of it. To them I extend good wishes that they may meet their obligations and thus create for themselves a splendid year at the University of Kentucky.

Welcome to University of Kentucky Homecoming

In Kentucky Kernel, November 23, 1937

H O M E C O M I N G D A Y this year has been designated as Thursday, November 25. This is the day that the University of Kentucky plays our honorable and friendly rival, Tennessee. On that day, the office of the Secretary of the Alumni Association will be open in the morning; a tea will be given at Maxwell Place to all alumni immediately following the game; and in the evening, there is a dance in the Alumni Gymnasium.

[51]

In behalf of the University of Kentucky, I extend to all alumni and friends of the University a welcome on this occasion. It should be a day of thanksgiving from many points of view, for the progress of the University, for its great body of alumni who have contributed much to the welfare of the state and nation, and for the opportunity to serve in the highest sense of that phrase. With grateful appreciation, therefore, I welcome the alumni of the University of Kentucky to the campus on Thursday, November 25, 1937.

To Students and Faculty of the University of Kentucky

In *Kentucky Kernel*, Christmas Issue, 1937

T H E staff of *The Kentucky Kernel* have asked me to extend greetings to the student body and the faculty of the University of Kentucky in connection with the holiday season, and I am glad indeed to meet the request. The closing week before the holidays has been one of unusual weather, making it difficult to get to classes and to move across the campus from place to place. I appreciate the patience and cheerfulness with which students have made the best of conditions and have attended their classes as far as possible. This shows something of the pioneer spirit.

I wish for all the students and staff of the University of Kentucky and their families, wherever they may be, a pleasant and happy Christmas. May this Christmas mean the joining of kindred spirits and the interchange of kindliness and love so that families may be united and greatly pleased over their reunion.

The spirit of Christmas is not made by the exchanging of expensive articles but rather by good will and affection. It is in this spirit that I wish all a very happy time during the holidays and a return after the New Year to the University of Kentucky in excellent health and dispositions.

Christmas Greetings

In *Kentucky Kernel*, Christmas Issue, 1938

CARRY to your homes for all who dwell therein the good wishes of the University of Kentucky. May this holiday season mean more to friends and relatives than usual because of the return of goodly sons and lovely daughters. For yourselves, I wish a pleasant and interesting time interspersed with rest. The real spirit of Christmas is yours to make a part of yourselves.

The Great Alumnus

A Greeting to All Former Students of the University of Kentucky

THE great alumnus is the one who rejoices in the advancement of his Alma Mater and does not mourn for the old days. He has a kindly memory for those days and looks back upon them as something to be cherished and as a happy part of his life. If he is a great alumnus, he knows his university cannot stand still. New faces must appear in the faculties, new buildings must be built on the campus, and changes must take place in the curriculum and in the procedure of his college. His university must be a contributor to the life of his time as it was in previous generations. It is the spirit of the place that becomes dear to him. The spirit of learning, of work, of ideals is after all the true quality of a university. The great alumnus is ever ready to say a heartening word for his Alma Mater, to encourage it in the work it is doing, to believe in it, and to regard it as a force for the best things in the life of his country. The university not only needs the time and resources he may give to the solution of its problems but also requires the faith he has in its work and its purpose. This latter contribution any alumnus can make. If he knows his university, loves it, esteems it, has faith in it, the great alumnus will contribute mightily to the upbuilding of his Alma Mater.

The Alumnus and the University

Radio talk over WHAS to the alumni of the University of Kentucky,
Louisville, Kentucky, April 19, 1930

ALUMNI have, I suppose, never thought of themselves as problems, yet from a university's point of view they present grave and serious questions. They graduate and are scattered to the four winds; some live in their own state, others in neighboring and distant places, and a few in foreign lands. Their Alma Mater wants to know where they are, what they are doing, and how much they are adding to the world's store of righteousness and knowledge, its wisdom and its wealth. Also, what do they think of the education they received at their college? How has it fitted into life, and how has it made for richer living?

The answer to the first question is not an easy one to find. Letters asking for addresses are laid aside for long intervals or never answered at all. The poor alumni secretary struggles to keep up his file of names and addresses and hopes to get enough material to issue a directory once in five years. He is usually disappointed, but the few alumni answering may be a blessing in disguise because, if all answered, he might be confronted by the cost of a printing bill he could not meet. Now and then the alumni in a community, brought together by the drawing power of mutual interest, form a club that for a time fairly bursts with institutional pride and loyalty. The club soon passes into complete silence if there is not some individual alumnus who takes upon himself the burden of organization and the work of keeping the club going. When alumni get together, the exchange of news and the talk of old times may hold the group for a considerable period, and possibly permanently, but in most instances something else is needed. That something else is the lifeblood of the university; it is the purpose and results of education.

I have often thought the reason for alumni's being so enthusiastic about athletics is that they do not know much else of what their Alma Mater is doing. Perhaps institutions have been neglectful in not giving to alumni the plans and difficulties of the institution.

Alumni would undoubtedly be interested in the changing problems that are constantly presenting themselves in the field of education and that will vitally affect the children of the next generation. Just now there is an emphasis upon new methods of admitting students to college. This new procedure is an attempt to add to the university's educational effectiveness. How do these changes in educational procedure concern the alumni? How can the institution find out? Only by telling the alumni, explaining what such changes mean, and indicating the results that are hoped will come from them.

Alumni of an institution ought to have an intellectual life; they should in fact be interested in intellectual matters. Sometimes there is a reaction against study after four years of college. Moreover, the main concern of the young person is often in making a living and in establishing for himself and his family a certain amount of economic security. The alumnus for a time may drift away from the intellectual life but, if he has received a real education, sooner or later he returns to it. He measures life and its rewards by a different rule from the one that he might have had without his years at college. At any rate the college faculty hopes, and the state which has maintained the university expects, that the alumnus will contribute intellectually and spiritually to the solution of individual and public problems.

In my recent journey around the state I have met and talked with a good many alumni of the University of Kentucky. I found them an interesting group coming into increasing importance in their communities. There are now seven thousand graduates of the University of Kentucky and five times as many former students who have attended the University a year or more. About three-fourths of the graduates have received their degrees since 1917. This means that seventy-five per cent of the graduates range in age from twenty-two to thirty-seven years. They are young and are just entering into places of consequence. If they have the truly intellectually and spiritually educated way of regarding life and if they carry into their occupations and activities the sense of service, they should be a decidedly helpful influence in molding the state. Many of the older men and women who are graduates of the University of Kentucky have made honorable contributions to society, and some of them have made notable additions to civilization itself.

I have been much interested in what students now at the University are doing. The stories of their accomplishments are varied and colorful, filled with courageous attempts to carry on and win intellectual attainments for themselves. In the classes and laboratories instructors tell me that there are more serious attitudes and greater efforts to work than have been noted in many college generations. The students of today are earnest and purposeful. Undoubtedly this is a reflection of conditions and living among the people as a whole. It is in fact what might be expected. The student is asking as he has never asked before just what are the real values of his education. The University should endeavor to make plain to the student the results to be obtained from his college course.

I believe sincerely that a student of a state university has a real obligation to his Alma Mater and to his state. Too often he thinks of his education as a matter of right, a something that the people owe him. The people have realized that they need forward looking, intelligent, and educated young people to help build the state; they trust these students to work to that end. Here are a relationship of the highest order and a trust that is noble and expectant. The alumni of a state university are bound to recognize this trust and to accept it. Such relationship places a great responsibility on them; first to act in the best interests of their community and their state, and second to give to their Alma Mater love and affection that will now and then take the form of material goods.

The alumnus can always speak a good word about his Alma Mater and defend it against hostile and unreasonable criticism. He can insist that its welfare shall be given fair and honest consideration when it comes before governmental agencies. He can learn its great purpose and can, when the opportunity arises, speak of its worth to the state. He can assist in maintaining loan funds with which to help deserving students. He can, when he wins this world's goods, devote some of them to the extension of the University's work. He can interest those who have books, manuscripts, and valuable historical materials to give them to the University Library. Because the University will live as long as the state itself exists, he can justly urge these things. He can call the attention of promising young people to the educational facilities maintained by the people of Kentucky for their education. The alumnus can in fact be a missionary of public higher education who through his own acts and words adds to the glory of his Alma Mater. The alumnus should be proud of his Alma Mater; it has won the right to his loyalty and good will, and it requires for its full accomplishment that loyalty and good will.

The University can make its claim for such affection on one basis only, and that is service. It must serve the students who come to it and the people of the state who have supported it through the years. You as alumni give your thanks not to some donor but to the people of the commonwealth, who have made the University of Kentucky possible.

Four Men in Books and Life

Convocation address, University of Kentucky,
September 24, 1925

DURING the summer I became acquainted with four men who interested me very much. Two of them were found in books and the other two in life. Those in the books were Sir William Osler, whose biography prepared by Dr. Harvey Cushing tells of this noted scientist and physician, and Lord Byron, depicted as *The Glorious Apollo* by E. Barrington in her interesting but not deep novel of Byron's life. These two men stood at the antipodes in everything but genius. One of the men I became acquainted with in life was Otto Swanson, now seventy-seven years old, who had led a hard pioneer life and in his later days had ripened into a philosopher and kindly person looking upon life with tolerance and sympathy; the other was a young mechanic, expert in the care of gas engines, honest to an unusual degree, skillful, and delightful to meet.

I think it is worth while looking at these men more specifically. Sir William Osler came from a family of preachers. His father and mother left England in their early twenties and settled in the backwoods of Canada where they built a church and developed a community in which their spirit constantly appeared. In their home were books and pictures and the evidences of intellectual life. The country in which Osler spent his boyhood was a frontier land. In his young life he came under the influence of two unusual teachers whose interest was in the field of natural science. With his background of family life, with the incentive that he had from his teachers, he laid the foundation of his career.

The second man made known to me in the books was Lord Byron. Although he came from a family of noble lineage, nevertheless his was a poor heritage. A dissolute father and a harridan of a mother with constant bickering and lack of home life gave him his background. Blessed with an unusual genius he came to be the first poet of his time. But genius without character left him at the end of a short life discredited and disreputable in his last days.

The Swede I have spoken of, Otto Swanson, came to America when he was thirty years old and found his way to the forests of Michigan where he worked hard and struggled from morning to night. He finally built for himself a small competence and created in his person a character with honesty and industry as his guide.

The young mechanic evidently was thrown in contact with tools early in his boyhood. With little education he, nevertheless, constantly pried into the mysteries of mechanics. His integrity, perseverance, and industry coupled with his curiosity about mechanics have made him trusted and honored in the community in which he lives.

In considering these four men we see certain similar elements in their development. They all possessed industry, they had a goal which they desired to reach, they had perseverance, and they had ideals. With the exception of Byron their ideals were the ideals not only of thoroughness but of character as well. Osler was one of the great scientists of his time, and Byron was a great poet; the other two men are forces in their own community.

In his comment upon the early days of his life, Sir William Osler stated that the corner stone of the foundation of his career was work and the pleasure he had in doing it. He added other fundamental attitudes which he developed in his life; namely, the art of detachment, the virtue of method, the quality of thoroughness, and the grace of humility. The art of detachment means the ability to isolate oneself from the pursuits and pleasures of the world. The whole history of man has been the story of his struggle against idleness. By nature man is a loafer, and, when he lives in a city of some size, the necessity of the art of detachment is more important than it is in a smaller town. There are so many things that divert attention, fill the mind, and take time that only the man and woman who are really able to isolate themselves accomplish great results. It is hardly necessary to say anything about the virtue of method except perhaps to emphasize the point that, unless one has method in what he is doing, in the proper distribution of his time, and in the way of approaching the objects that he is dealing with, he is bound to lose much of the value of his effort. The world wants thoroughness and a high quality of it, but one must know what thoroughness is before one can attain it. The grace of humility is the capacity of a person to keep himself in his place, not to be overstimulated by success, and to remember that there are attainments that he has not yet reached.

All of these qualities which Sir William Osler emphasized in his life are conquering forces which open the door to opportunity. He had a very unusual heritage, his heart and mind were clean, and he had a religious viewpoint that made his life sweet and worth while. Almost all failure is due in the long run to the lack of moral autonomy. By moral autonomy I mean the power of self control, the ability to act right and to see right, and the obligation to keep oneself clean in mind and body.

Of these four men Byron was the failure, great as his place in literature is. He had no moral stamina, he had no discipline, he really had no character. Gifted, attractive, he had noble impulses spasmodically; these impulses would too often be diverted by self-indulgence and unevenness of purpose. He was deflected from a high viewpoint to the lowest and most disreputable attitudes. He stands out in marked contrast to the three other men of this study.

If one were to pick four men from the student body, one could tell after some observation what they are likely to be throughout their lives. If they have industry, thoroughness, humility, ideals, although they may not reach the great heights of fame, they will be useful members of the communities in which they live. A man with loose morals not only is a danger to himself but to those around him. The injuries which one receives on a football field or in an athletic contest are usually repairable; time and nature and the skill of physicians will most often effect the cure. The scarring of the soul through the formation of habits of idleness and through a let down in morals is not so easily cured. Shiftlessness in mind and intellect may develop through heedlessness into an unbreakable habit. The self-disciplined person through his own determination can make any good habit or break any bad habit. The shiftless person lacks the power of self-discipline.

During this week the new students who have entered the University of Kentucky have been subjected to a series of intellectual tests for the purpose of ascertaining their ability and of measuring their capacity. Ability is something with which we are born; although the University can not create ability, it can teach us how to use such ability as we have. The application of the principles suggested by Sir William Osler, thoroughness, honesty, concentration, humility, industry, will bring great results. In one's student days as all through life, it is worth while to hold to a goal, to have something toward which one is striving. We learned as a consequence of the World War the use of the word objective. We now have objectives of financial drives; we have objectives of programs; and the student, also, can have an objective.

At the University of Kentucky are two learned societies, Sigma Xi and Phi Beta Kappa. These emphasize scholarship. The new student who comes to the University of Kentucky may well make

scholarship his goal. With scholarship should be associated courtesy in all of one's relationships; the effort to grow physically,
mentally, and spiritually; the holding to religious ideals and the
development of a religious point of view; and the bringing in of
artistic appreciation in order to add beauty to living. It must be
said in this connection that the appreciation of art, painting and
sculpture, music, and literature can only be had after one has
cleared his mind of the lumber of misunderstanding.

To return now to the four men with whom I became acquainted
this summer! Three of them were real men. One of them reached
the realm of distinction with a blemish on his name for all time.
One of them was a great scientist and physician. The other two are
humble citizens doing their duty in their own walks of life. Character, environment, heritage, and education enabled Osler to bring
to the world his gifts of healing.

The lesson to the student in all of this is that he cannot get
something for nothing. The world is a firm task master and demands arduous labor. Work without method and plan is unavailing. Many men work hard, struggle, get nowhere, and become
irritated with fate because of their failures. They lack concentration, they have no method, they do not put their minds on what
they are doing, and they are not thoroughgoing. Therefore the student must add method and concentration to hard work. Humility
and sympathy he must also have; humility in his accomplishments
because, no matter how great they are, they are necessarily small
in comparison with the world's intellectual and spiritual needs;
sympathy for other folk and their causes.

So we come to the end of this address. The University of Kentucky gives to the students an opportunity to spend their years
here among "the best that is known and thought" in science, in
literature, in art, in life itself. The students determine whether
they will spend their time among the best or among the fairly good
or among the shoddy. College education is a cooperative enterprise
between the institution and the students. Without determination
on the part of the students to get the best, the University can do
little. With determination on the part of the students to do their

work well with method, thoroughness, concentration, humility; to be courteous and sympathetic and understanding in all their relationships; to grow physically, mentally, spiritually; to develop appreciation for the beauty and truth of life; with this cooperative attitude on the part of the students, the University of Kentucky can accomplish an almost infinite amount for the students themselves, for the state, and for the nation. The University can provide the spring and keep it clear, but it cannot make the students partake of its water.

I beseech you, therefore, to keep the high ideals that you had in mind when you came to college. I urge you to employ the art of detachment, the virtue of method, the quality of thoroughness, the grace of humility. Moreover, I beg you to remember that a life without religion, even if it is successful in this world's goods, is a barren thing.

To the New President from Past Administrators

Part of the inaugural ceremony of
President Herman Lee Donovan, University of Kentucky, May 6, 1942

IT IS a privilege to stand today in the presence of this large company, gathered to see you, Herman Lee Donovan, inaugurated as the sixth president of the University of Kentucky, and to speak for the presidents of former days.

During the existence of the University of Kentucky, eight men have held the office of president; three as acting presidents and five as permanently appointed, the latter serving seventy-three years in all.

In the seventy-six years covered by the work and administrations of your predecessors, the University of Kentucky has been the shifting scene of increase, of decline, of rise, of progress. Going through many serious periods of difficulty, discouragement, scarcity of operating funds, indifference, and sometimes bitterness, the University of Kentucky has, on the other hand, constantly grown in usefulness to the state and has found therein a responding loyalty. It now holds a place of influence, of respect, and of affection in the minds of alumni and of many citizens of Kentucky.

During these years under the direction of the former presidents, a considerable amount of property has been acquired by the University; the campus has been enlarged; farm lands and forests have come into the possession of the institution; buildings have been erected; libraries and equipment have been maintained. These will be materially augmented in the years ahead. Moreover, greater support and additional means of carrying on the University will come to you. All your predecessors would join me in the hope that these added resources will be available.

The history of the past presidents and the contributions that they have made are now laid in your hands in order that the noble purpose of the University of Kentucky may be continued.

It is a place of responsibility, this position of president, as every man knows who has actually borne the burdens through the heat and cold of the days and years. But it is an interesting office with its obligations and duties. The holder of it has many joys along with many difficulties; he has much opportunity, some influence, and even at times a little power.

All who are here today know that you, President Donovan, will guide wisely, will build soundly, and will help courageously the University of Kentucky in its every ideal and design. All are happy in the prospect of a long and well-directed administration. Your predecessors, presidents of the past, would join in rejoicing in this prospect and, were they here with me, would extend the right hand of fellowship to you.

The presidents of past days would place their benediction on her who is closely associated with you in this enterprise, Nell Stuart Donovan, and would extend their good wishes to her for happy living at Maxwell Place. By her charm, by her graciousness, by her wise outlook on life, she has already won the hearts of those who love the University.

That all may be well with both of you is the message from the presidents of other days.

For myself, I wish you, President Donovan, great happiness and great success in leading the University of Kentucky to new heights of service.

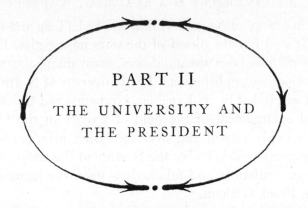

The University and the President

Prepared for the inauguration of President Frank Graham,
University of North Carolina, November 11, 1931

EVERY now and then a new university president is inducted into office. The event is fraught with interest, with possibilities, and with hopes: with interest because the people of a state are concerned about educational opportunities open to them; with possibilities because there is an expectation in student body, faculty, and alumni that the new incumbent will bring to the institution an inspiring leadership; and with hope that the expectations so aroused may actually take form and come to pass.

It is assumed that a university president will be many things, such as teacher, administrator, speaker, wise counselor, advocate of good causes, and go-getter exciting the admiration of all. Manifestly, it is impossible to be all of these. He must of necessity make a choice. In my opinion, the university president of these days must be a thinker and a student of educational problems. He must, therefore, have relief from many duties, exacting details, and harassing time-taking interviews. The university president of today, if he is to lead, must see as far ahead as possible so that shoals and rocks may be avoided. The university is a complicated organization that goes along as it fits into, and directs as well, American life. Its leadership must be wise if the university is to realize its goal.

The University of North Carolina has had a long and honorable history. It is in fact the oldest of the state universities. During its history there have been ups and downs, many disappointments, and many glorious accomplishments. The University of North Carolina has been wisely led by its Venables, Grahams, and Chases. In the successful enlargement of the field of activity of the University and in its richly earned and ever increasing prestige, the South has taken great pride. Today the South and the nation may well extend congratulations and felicitations upon the inauguration of President Frank Graham.

I am charged with the pleasant duty of extending these wishes to the new president and to the University of North Carolina on behalf of the colleges and universities of the South. That your administration, President Graham, may be happy, progressive, and effective is the wish of all your colleagues throughout the South. May the University and the citizens of the state give you every assistance so that contentment, peace, and good will accompanied by scholarship and effective leadership may go with you and the University of North Carolina.

The Office of University President

Published in *The Quarterly Journal*
of the University of North Dakota, April, 1920; reprinted by the
University of Kentucky, July, 1920

THIS discussion of the office of university president is from the viewpoint of the present rather than from the guesses about the future. It is confined to a present day consideration of the presidential office and will endeavor to set forth, in what must necessarily be a brief form, some of the more conspicuous elements of the problem. The presentation is sure to emphasize certain phases that may be regarded by some as important, to minimize much which may seem important to others, and to leave untouched some things which should be included. As the writing of the paper proceeded, the end seemed far away in the multitude of subjects that should have been added to the list for discussion, but the very limits of type and space have crowded out many of these topics.

Starting with the small college in which the duties of president in the modern sense were nominal, the office has developed into one of power, influence, and enormous responsibilities. As it now exists the office of university president represents an evolution which in time will be modified by the democratizing of the government of university affairs. A number of years ago a well known university president said: "The office of president has become an impossibility." In enlarging his remark he went on to say that the demands, details, and requirements were so great that no one man could fill them. Such an officer must be an eloquent speaker, a good mixer, a business expert, an educational student, a scholar, a guide and inspirer of students, a leader of people, and a prophet and seer as well. When the matter is put in such fashion, there is no doubt that none but a superman could meet all the requirements of the popular imagination.

The student of education from a foreign country gathers some strange ideas about the office of university president in America. This official in this country has no counterpart in other lands. He is appointed by boards of trustees often without any suggestion from faculties, though in recent years committees have been created by such boards with representatives of faculty and alumni upon them. That the results of cooperative selection are more satisfactory than those obtained by the old system remains a question still to be solved. In accordance with the modern spirit of cooperation seen in every large organization, certainly a mixed committee of trustees, faculty, alumni brings to the selection of a president a variety of views that materially widen the scope of the inquiry. There is, on the other hand, the possibility of checking out men by the test of individual prejudices until in the final group only those are left who have found their way into the list by negative virtues rather than by positive qualities.

Fifty years ago men of ministerial training because of the emphasis upon Christian education were almost invariably chosen as the heads of institutions. Occasionally this custom was modified by the selection of men of scholarly attainments in other fields. A quarter of a century ago the economist in view of his training in business organizations was the choice, and now in more recent years the trained educator has had more vogue. Such training is desirable; but the qualities of intelligence, scholarship, tact, patience, good sense, robust health, and moral courage still predominate as the fundamental requirements.

The progress of an educational institution, however, does not rest upon any one man. By virtue of the problem and the bigness of the things dealt with, one man is unable to accomplish much alone. Cooperation of board, faculty, students, alumni, citizens, and president is the ideal and the only producer of great and far-reaching results.

Because of this strenuous business of being a president, the office belongs to the extra hazardous occupations. An examination of the tenure of the official life of the presidents of the seventy-two institutions on the Carnegie preferred list shows eleven years as the average length of service, leaving the occupant at the age of fifty-three without a position and in the language of the street, "all dressed up with no place to go." What the figures would show for the institutions of the whole country cannot be stated, but undoubtedly the service period is even shorter.

The more courageous and determined a president is, the more he is sure to make enemies. Friction and misunderstanding accumulate in the course of the years so that few men live officially beyond the short period of service mentioned above. Yet there is nothing more disastrous to the growth of an institution than frequent changes in the chief administrative officer. The new president is received with acclaims of praise; these die down during the second year as a matter of course; and in the third year many are sure that a mistake has been made in the administrative head. If the president lives through this crucial period, he is likely to go on for a number of years until the accumulations of policies and decisions bring up a new batch of oppositions. Whether he will pass through this period or not will depend upon his ability to give and take and upon his patience and tact. Strange to say, the opposition is more likely to arise from the antagonism of his colleagues and a few alumni than from any other source.

Dissatisfaction in salaries, failure to secure promotion, lagging of public interest in the institution, and the inability of athletic teams to win victories make up the category of many a presidential tragic story. This is rather a sorry list for educational policy is not included even as a minor item. However, where one president gives up his task on account of differences in educational theories, ten find themselves outside the pale because of these irrelevant factors. Occasionally disagreements with trustees are referred to as the cause of trouble, but as a usual thing these discords have found their sources within the institution itself or among the alumni. More often the confidence of trustees in the president of their choice is carried to the extreme of standing with him sometimes against needed reforms and of using their combined power to put down any offender who may speak for larger freedom in academic matters. A better day is at hand without any question as a result of the appreciation of the joint relationships of boards of trustees, presidents, and faculties.

All universities have certain elements in them which, while variable, nevertheless enter into nearly every problem of an administrative character. These are governing boards, faculty, students, alumni, the public, and the plant; they crowd into the consideration of money, public interest, and educational policy.

Under the American plan of university government, the board of trustees is the directing agency, appointed in public institutions by governors or even legislatures (sometimes elected by the people of the state as in the case of the University of Illinois) and in private foundations by the governing bodies themselves. In many instances the alumni have membership on the board, but almost without exception the faculty is represented by the president alone; his official position, in the minds of most university men, prevents him from acting as deputy for them. The European university goes to the other extreme and gives all control to the faculty. It is true, as in France and Germany, that the ministry of education passes on final appointments and on the budget of the institutions. There probably is no institution in Europe that has the multifarious duties to perform that are placed under the direction of one of our larger state universities. It is but a natural result of our system of government that the boards of trustees should be granted wide powers. In time no doubt this procedure will be modified by a larger representation of faculty members and by the realization that various matters rightfully must be left to the decision of faculty groups.

The ideal type of board has been discussed in many books and papers. In actual fact boards of trustees differ from those with three members to the legislative bodies of seventy-five or more constituents. Probably a board of seven to nine is the best size for real effectiveness because larger boards develop speechmaking and create cliques to the marked interference with university policies. In a large board no committee can feel any confidence that its recommendations will carry, and university policy is at the mercy of shifting opinions in such an audience.

On the other side, boards of control as set up by some of the states in the government of their public institutions drift into financial and purchasing agencies, leaving the policies of the institutions almost wholly in the hands of the presidents. For an interim a wise man may do well, but the tendency of the board of control to lump the educational institutions into one group brings about a failure to distinguish the larger university function from that of the normal or industrial school and leads to a mediocre development of university ideals. Besides these considerations, boards of control are apt to emphasize policies that are actuated by a viewpoint that has no sympathy with university ideals. The university in their eyes is a part of a system. Purchasing becomes the great purpose of the board, and the real object of leadership in human thought and human values is submerged in the emphasis upon the business side alone. The trend of such concentration of authority seems to be subsiding; certainly no great advantage has been shown in the board of control idea over the government by a board of regents cooperating with other institutions and the state department of education. There is one exception to this statement from the legislative standpoint that should be emphasized, and that is the opportunity the legislature has to deal with all the institutions through one board. In the crowded days of a legislative session this is an important point.

The selection of members of the staff is in one sense the greatest work a president can do. However, his many duties make it increasingly difficult for him to see candidates, and this assignment is more and more intrusted to heads of departments and deans. That this function should be given over to faculty committees has been proposed. When such an arrangement has been tried, delay has often resulted due to a variety of opinions that are difficult to harmonize. Sometimes, moreover, departmental heads have been known to choose men of inferior caliber and mediocre attainments in order not to jeopardize the status quo of the department. All selections are subject to ratification by the board of trustees. No president of wisdom would consider picking members of the staff without consulting department heads and deans. As commerce and trade hold out large rewards to able young men, the university is being hard pressed to offer inducements in opportunity and salary that will in any event attract able men.

In order that this great responsibility of selecting the proper teaching staff may not be slighted, certainly the office of president must be relieved of many of the burdens that crowd upon it. Only by constant travel, corresponding with other institutions, and attendance upon the meetings of scholars, can a president really do his duty within the confines of his ability in recruiting the university staff. Even if the deans and department heads are given liberty of selection, yet conference of the president with his colleagues in all the steps taken would appear to be wise and advisable. Also it must be kept in mind that, although the nominations come from the department heads through the deans to the president, the final selection must be by the president if a uniform program of educational progress is the goal to be attained.

Since business has found in college faculties new hunting grounds in the matter of employees, every university has felt the competition for its men. High cost of living, on the other hand, has dimmed the light of many a scholar with the result that he has reluctantly gone over to the commercial field for the substantial gain in salary that he expects to use in holding up his standard of living. Increased cost in maintaining the college plant has been another factor that has added to the heavy load and the difficulties of the university president. The future does not hold much comfort.

Depletion of staff might not be a matter of such great concern if there were fair hopes of making good the loss; however, the virile men of graduating classes are not working in preparation for teaching, and the supply for the places now vacant in many a faculty is composed of mediocre men who want more pay than the former abler incumbents received. A further decline is noticeable in the general culture of the younger men seeking university positions. There are many exceptions to a statement of this kind, but no university president can be oblivious to a situation that is more or less patent to the observer of present day trends. The bolder and more aggressive types of young men and young women are finding their way into large business enterprises and into more lucrative professions.

The faculty is the heart of the institution. In their hands must rest the shaping of curricula, matters of discipline, and the every-day conduct of the institution. This means organization, and such organization ought to be comprehensive enough and democratic enough to encourage the help of every member of the staff.

A great deal of the conflict between presidents of institutions and faculties has been due to a few causes. The foremost cause of discord, perhaps, is the absence of clearly stated rules of organization that set down definitely the relationships existing in the complicated organization of a modern educational institution; second is the lack of tact and frankness in the dealings of men with each other; third is intrigue and the failure to cooperate, arising out of misunderstanding or ambition; and fourth is fundamental differences between the president and faculty groups, growing out of variances in policy.

A well worked out plan for the functioning of an institution coupled with good will and ability will remove practically all of these difficulties. A project of this kind places the legislative functions regarding courses, students, and the general conduct of the academic side of the institution in a faculty body made up of professors and assistant professors. This group by committees can coordinate opinions and apply the wisdom of the institution to its work, thus bringing about a cooperative feeling throughout the institution. If along with this legislative group there is an administrative body meeting frequently, the problems of the institution are constantly in review by everybody concerned. To make such a plan a success, complete frankness in submitting to these councils all university matters whether great or small must be habitual.

Necessarily the board of trustees passes upon the financial business and appointments. The relations between trustees and faculty and the relationships within the faculty must be cordial and mutually trustworthy.

The right to teach and speak as one thinks is the essence of academic freedom. Along with this right, however, are to be placed tact and good sense on the general principle that the blunt edge of a wedge does not split much wood. A good deal has been said on this subject, and numerous cases have been brought to the attention of the public in the last ten years. Nearly all of them contain errors of judgment on both sides due to the failure to take up the matter before it reached the critical stage. With provisions in the university organization to hear in full the evidence in such cases, there is little likelihood of a university going far wrong in the conclusions reached. Unfortunately a great many cases of the implied infringement of academic freedom arise out of the ventures of university men into fields where they are not fully familiar with all the material. They are thus led to make public statements that cannot always be supported. A university is not a place for propaganda but rather a place to find out, to study, and to reach conclusions. When these processes of thought have been followed, men have been free to express their views because they are thoroughly supported by facts.

The organization of the American Association of University Professors has already done good work in insisting upon the real facts in the cases it has examined. With closer knowledge of the situation, it should be a helping agency in eliminating a lot of the nonessentials from many of the academic freedom cases as well as in establishing certain ethical standards. The right of a university professor to leave his chair after a two weeks' notice is claimed by a few men in faculties as wholly within their privilege because the university is great, and they are only one. On the other hand, when a university calls for a resignation with several months' notice, the claim is made sometimes that the dismissal is due to failure to meet the view of the president or of the board of trustees. So academic freedom comes in as a part of the controversy. Fortunately this sort of case does not arise very often, but the American Association of University Professors can render a real service if standards of ethical relation can be established as the basis for the action of members of faculties and of governing boards.

Three matters, now much discussed, are being brought to the fore by men interested in increasing the prestige of the faculty. These are the budget, appointments, and salaries. In a large institution the budget consumes much time in the making. Although the more people are consulted, the more time is required; nevertheless, so important are the financial phases of education that it is essential that departmental needs should be given fullest consideration. The usual method of preparing a budget by having the dean of each college present the departmental statements to the president has the advantage of acceleration, but it leaves everybody in the dark in regard to relative grants made to the various colleges and departments.

The review of the budget by the deans and president before it goes to the board of trustees works toward a levelling up process but does not bring into the consultation the larger body of the faculty. Certainly, a committee from the faculty might be brought into touch with these mysteries; and probably, as a step toward larger understanding, the budget might well be read in entirety to the faculty body before it goes to the board of trustees. A debate upon the budget would undoubtedly upset the work of months and result in more hard feeling than the present organization of university democracy could well stand. Unfortunately the universities are manned in part by those who have no large university viewpoint but are overly impressed with the greatness of their departments, and even more of themselves, and with the futility of a lot of others. Many of these difficulties will be obviated when men who are preparing to teach in colleges and universities are required to study, along with their special lines of interest, the history of education and particularly of university administration.

What was a rather minor matter under pre-war conditions has come to be the all absorbing question. Practically every institution is trying to secure the means of increasing salaries in order to make them at least equal to those paid before the war. This is being done by alumni contributions and by larger appropriations from state legislatures. There are, however, two ways of dealing with the general salary problems; one is by establishing grades of pay, and the other is by paying according to merit. The first is the easier to administer and on the whole produces more satisfaction to the faculty group; however, it fails to provide for the exceptional man who cannot be fitted into such a plan.

As soon as the grades of pay method is departed from, and only a little time elapses before it must be, the administrative officer who then must decide on merits is subject to criticism on his decisions that some men are better than others. Placing this difficult question in the hands of a faculty committee may relieve the president from some embarrassment, but in time the committee is pretty sure to involve its members in endless controversies with those who are not recommended for more pay and higher position. Such a plan was tried in one of the larger institutions, and after many meetings the committee, reporting that they were unable to agree, asked to be discharged. The problem was just where it started, in the hands of the president, and where it is bound to rest under the American type of university organization, unless salaries are fixed by the board of trustees on the basis of grades and on certain periods of probation before promotion takes place. No boards can know well enough the individuals on a teaching staff to devise salary schedules that will be satisfactory. When they do make the salary schedules, the factory system of pay is likely to be the outcome.

One of the great temptations, always present, that a college president faces is the allurement of plant and campus. Without doubt, there is an effective and energizing psychology in fine buildings and beautiful campuses. They may, however, be over-emphasized when the expenditures on them reduce salary funds, curtail research and library opportunities, and limit the more important purposes of the spirit. Yet it is essential to plan for the future. No college president of the past twenty-five years can be charged with planning too largely. More often his projects have been too small, and he has thus hampered the continuing growth of his institution. It is here that the wisdom of widely experienced business men on the board of trustees, combined with the training and experience of a high grade architect, renders valuable service for the institution.

The designing of buildings is really a difficult matter. Instances of the failure of constructions to fulfill their expectation for a reasonable period of years are seen again and again. The unit building, susceptible of enlargement in many directions by well planned additions to the original structure, meets many of the difficulties encountered. Moreover, the cluttering of campuses by small buildings is avoided, and departments are held in closer physical groups.

When education was young in the land, the college president knew the students of the institution. Now the dean of men and the dean of women know the students whereas the president is absorbed in a round of speeches, conferences, and details. It is unfortunate that this is the case. The best he can do is to meet occasional groups and appear before the students' assembly from time to time. Because of the increasing size of institutions, the personal relation between presidents and students is bound to vanish as a university presidential function. To lose touch with the student body is a serious matter that leads to misunderstandings likely to result in breakdown of effective administration. This difficulty can be met to some extent by conferences with student leaders at luncheon periods or in the president's office or home and by "at homes" for the larger groups in the president's house. The presence of the president at student affairs shows the right attitude and goes a long way toward the establishment of appreciation and understanding.

With the exception of a very few institutions, the alumni interest in their Alma Mater cannot be spoken of as vital and alive. The struggle for position and fortune in his earlier days after graduation takes up the time and energy of the alumnus with matters far removed from the problems of the institution from which he graduated. This attitude may now and then be modified by the cries of Alma Mater for help. His occasional visits to the campus do not carry the alumnus much beyond the days when he was in college. Unless he is associated with education, he is apt to look at the institution as it was in his day.

Most of the efforts to organize alumni spirit have been rather meager in their success. The reason can be found in lack of organization, lack of funds, and lack of appreciation of institutional problems. The lack of organization and of funds has been made up in many instances by the university's assuming the responsibility. Lack of enthusiasm is due to the passage of years and the failure to bring the alumni into actual touch with the university's real problems. Many alumni reunion dinners are formal and dampening to the spirit because of the absence of a real purpose so far as the alumni can see. Without question, the ardent interest alumni take in athletic matters may be definitely traced to the fact that the football team can be seen and can be rallied around whereas the actual needs of Alma Mater, her ambitions and ideals, are never presented to the alumni in graphic form.

In athletic affairs alumni interest may sometimes be highly detrimental especially when the name of Alma Mater is tarnished by the use of alumni money to strengthen athletic teams. When such methods are followed, university authorities are often in the dark, and a great scandal may develop before they are aware of it. Alumni have no intention to do injury, but their zeal may lead them to overestimate the value of "a winning team." Victories secured in such ways are not worth having, and the demoralization to college ideals is far-reaching.

It would be unfair to leave the matter here. Alumni are a part of the university; they are in fact torch bearers, and they reflect the influence and power of their Alma Mater. That there could be a vast improvement in education not only in college but in communities where they live, if they would give utterance to the faith that is in them, can not be doubted. The university and college alumni of America could make this country what they choose if they would implement their claims to leadership.

The outer office of a university president in a city of some size is filled each day with people who wish to see him about everything under the sun. On the telephone he answers all sorts of inquiries, from the illiterate who wish to know which is right "them molasses or those molasseses" to matters of importance involving questions of government, business, and social affairs. Book agents come to secure endorsements, solicitors ask for funds, elderly ladies seek employment, visitors come from far and near; all of these sometimes seem to swamp the people who ought to see the president about university matters. Unless he is blessed with a secretary of great tact, wisdom, and ability, his time is taken from university and public affairs that should receive the most careful consideration. His office should be equipped with effective personnel, an infallible filing system, card indexes showing the daily movements of student population and the complete history of every member of the staff, and a library consisting of the latest educational reports.

Above all, a university president must have time to think; this valuable time is something the average incumbent of the office cannot get unless he has more determination than most to pass by many of the calls made on him. The weaknesses of the presidential office under modern conditions are its deficiency in getting into closer contact with students and its failure to bring to bear upon university problems the full capacities of the incumbent. Freedom from details may perhaps help the president to correct the latter weakness. However, retirement to secluded spots now and then may be the only way in which he is enabled to think and thus to re-create his abilities.

The essential elements in the successful administration of the presidential office are patience, tact, good sense, and knowledge. The president must provide initial leadership, and this means sympathy with all plans for advancement within the confines of financial support. He cannot sit in his office as a kind of umpire between the contending factions of a university faculty. No factions should exist in a university; complete understanding and brotherly outlook from the educational towers of the university should prevail.

No one can be more conscious than the author of the many omissions in this consideration of the office of university president, and of the inadequacy of the discussion on topics that might well take as much space as the article itself. Education is in great jeopardy in America. The progress made in the last few years will be lost if the heavy financial burdens continue. Moreover, farseeing leadership must be available if the dangers that always touch the reorganization process are to be avoided. For this work the universities must have presidents of vision, of wisdom, of understanding. Whether the burdens of the office will permit any man who may be called to a presidency to see into the future is an immediate question of far more importance than is generally conceded.

Administrative Relations in Colleges

Address at the inauguration of President Herman Lee Donovan, Eastern State Teachers College, Richmond, Kentucky, October 26, 1928; published in *School and Society*, December 8, 1928

BEHIND the hard and pedantic title of Administrative Relations in Colleges is a great sea of romance on which have sailed the barks of learned men in the quest of knowledge for youth. The story of colleges and their administration goes back many centuries and parallels the history of government, business, and religion. This story in its details would cover many pages, much controversy, a large number of failures, and numerous successful enterprises; it would at the same time show the effort to throw off the trammels of tradition and the struggle to push aside the heavy hand of privilege.

Three phases of one problem in administration adjustments are to be discussed here. The first has to do with the place of a board of trustees in the American college; the second in contrast concerns itself with the functions of a college faculty; and the third deals with the relationship of administrative officers to boards and faculties. The contention which is upheld is very brief. It is likely to pass unnoticed. To formulate it is to accept it, though in practice this theory is by no means the prevailing one in the government of American colleges.

The theme can be stated in the following form: boards of trustees and faculties are cooperating factors in American education, and administrative officers are their executive agents. The members of the board of trustees are in fact the directors of business affairs, the guardians of money, the planners of building enterprises, and the protectors of the legal rights of the institution, of its staff, alumni, and student body. The faculty has its function in the formulation of courses of study and in the establishment of legislation for the control of its own affairs and for the government of students. The administrative officer by virtue of his office and his relations to the board and the faculty is an executive agent for both. In this triple relationship none assumes arbitrary powers but all work together, each in his respective field. That such understanding of functions moves toward progress has been seen in some of the universities in the United States of America in contrast to the failure of other institutions of higher education in our land to hold and develop the spirit of learning under an arbitrary and despotic institutional government.

The university in Europe had two beginnings; one of student origin, the other founded by the masters. In neither was there a board of trustees. Students gathered in some city and there established their own institution with the courses, texts, and rules worked out by them. The lecturers were employed by the students and subjected to student regulations in the matter of hours and of tardiness and in the manner of instruction. Great crowds of students came to the university towns, paralleling in numbers those in attendance at the largest institutions in America today. The University of Bologna was a university of scholars; the University of Paris an institution founded by masters. The student guilds later selected their own rector and made the governing regulations. In the passage of time student autonomy and student control broke down, and bodies of governors were appointed by the state. Since the church with its great power was interested in these educational movements, here and there the university came under ecclesiastical control. Thus the colleges ceased to be voluntary organizations of scholars and came under the government of state and church.

In this country Harvard College was founded in 1636 with the title of fellows and tutors for the governing board. It was a resident government. In the later controversy over ecclesiastical matters the control was taken from the teaching group and placed in the hands of an absentee government. Since 1800 no faculty member has been elected a member of the board of fellows of Harvard University. In 1693 William and Mary College, a body corporate, had a government designated as president and masters. Yale began in

1701 under an ecclesiastical board when ten clergymen were given the authority to establish a college. A new provision of government was enacted in the Princeton charter in 1746 whereby a company of non-scholars with full power was authorized to organize a college.

Harvard College at its beginning was in line with European experience with groups of teachers their own governors. Because of difficulties of ecclesiastical import the lay board, often meeting away from the college town, came into existence. The absentee government required a representative in the person of a president who would have more authority than the presiding officer of a body of scholars. As the absentee lay board could not know the problems in a personal way, the members kept in touch through the key man, the president. It was natural as this system spread through the educational institutions, both old and new, that marked differences of functions for the lay board and the faculty should develop. The American type of college president associated with the lay board was soon engaged in administrative duties and enmeshed in details. The faculty's function was confined to teaching duties. As this system of government got into swing, the board of trustees, coming into possession of all authority, determined by virtue of that power the educational, financial, and administrative policies of the institution.

In the course of two centuries of educational history in the United States of America, the management of higher education moved a long way from the European system. Certain advantages arose from the American method of government of educational institutions. Unity of purpose in the conduct of the institution developed with the concentration of policy and administration. In large measure this centralization under boards of trustees accounts for the rapid growth of colleges in numbers, in support, and in material equipment; by enlisting the interest of lay members of boards more abundant financial support accrued as a consequence. There are, however, disadvantages in the subordination of educational policy to financial and administrative interests, which weigh heavily at times upon the ambitions and hopes of faculties. In our

American system unfortunately the authority of the teaching group is reduced to a much lower place in influence and standing than that occupied by the staffs of European universities.

The college faculty likewise has passed through many changes in its development. In the early history of educational institutions in this country it was both a debating society and an administrative body. Its members discussed educational problems, adjusted student courses, and determined the nature and extent of disciplinary matters when students came before the group for disobeying the rules of the institution. As colleges grew in size and organization, the number of students increased, and the faculty found difficulty in acting as an administrative body and also in dealing with individual cases of misconduct as they arose. It, therefore, moved more and more in the direction of a legislative group, establishing principles and creating rules and regulations for the conduct of courses of study and for the administration of student matters. With this development the administrative officer came to be a representative of the faculty group and its executive agent in carrying out legislative enactments.

Where a faculty has an indefinite and hazy place in institutional organization, a wobbly type of legislative organization results. When the acts of the faculty can be vetoed by the president or by the board of trustees, this faculty as a group falls to a low estate with no power and very little interest in the general problems of the institution. Thus the written constitution of an educational institution should set forth clearly the rights, power, and authority of the different governing groups in the organization. The faculty should be something more than a traditional body engaged in routine educational matters. It should in fact be the group that determines educational policy. The faculty having these responsibilities and powers is self-respecting and is deeply interested in the affairs of the institution, in the personnel of the staff, in the courses of study, and in the general purpose of the college or university. Since the faculty in its relation to students possesses the most important role in institutional organization, its position, integrity, and rights should be fully recognized in a constitutional provision.

In the larger institutions the faculty remains a college organization, and the legislative affairs of the institution are considered in a senate which is composed of representative membership from the various colleges. This senate has some control over the colleges in their courses of study and general policy. It also passes regulations applicable to the institution as a whole and has the obligation to develop unity of action and to define the purposes of the institution. As an organization the senate is wholly legislative. It is not an administrative body, and in consequence the administrative officer comes into the possession of authority and executive power.

One of the important problems which confronts every institution is the establishment and maintenance of a budget system. A budget is an orderly presentation of the financial affairs of an institution and has for its purpose the planning of income and expenditures. In its creation the heads of departments, deans, president, and the board of trustees have a part. The senate as such does not possess authority or power of budget making. This, however, is an anomaly, and the senate as the representative body of the teaching group ought to have something to say through a committee or by group action in the important matter of budget making. There are many difficulties in carrying out this democratic attitude. Disagreements are sure to arise on the allotments that are made to different departments and to the various objectives of the institution. A resultant disruption of good feeling is likely to ensue. In the present status of colleges and universities the question arises whether the institution should preserve its essential unity or should adhere to a principle that might for the time being work havoc in its progress.

At present and for that matter for some years past the organization of colleges and universities has followed very closely the corporation development in industry; that is, a board of directors selected for various reasons and representing different groups determines the policy and works out the general line of expansion for the institution. In such a system with absentee members of the board constituting the controlling government, the executive officer is entrusted with large authority; and he and his colleagues are bound to take the necessary steps to carry out the policies, whatever they may be, of the board. The staff of the institution is employed upon the recommendation of the administrative officer. The functions and the work of the institution are likewise determined by the executive. Where this system is used in its fullest sense, the college becomes a one-man institution with the faculty having only an incidental part in its conduct. Without doubt the American system of college administration has led to concrete results, but many of these have been accomplished at the expense of the spirit of democracy and at the price sometimes of educational ideals.

If the educational purpose is to be emphasized over the financial and building program, the faculty, instead of being subordinated, will be looked upon as a body of experts engaging in the development of educational processes and attempting to provide courses of study that will meet the changing requirements of modern life. The faculty will in fact become the agency in the institution through which the educational policy is determined and administered.

When the view is taken that the administrative officer is a representative of a board of trustees whose members are living in various parts of the country, then that officer is likely to place his emphasis on the business side of the institution and neglect its educational purposes. But if the view is accepted that the executive officer is to carry out the purposes of the two groups, board and faculty, then a different place is given to the educational functions of the institution. The president in the second instance administers educational policy as well as finance and business. If he regards the board of trustees and the faculty as the formulators of policy, he ceases to be an arbitrary officer acting as a kind of educational despot and becomes instead advisory and administrative in his relationship to these groups. In fact, his position in a well organized institution in which both faculty and board of trustees have definite and important governing roles parallels more and more that of the cabinet officer who is subject to the rule of opinion under a parliamentary government.

Unquestionably the functions of boards of trustees are being materially modified in these days. Many institutions have delegated to the boards the financial obligations and have provided that all educational policies must be determined by the teaching staffs. A movement back to some of the earlier attitudes and the European methods of university and college government is to be seen in this country. In the process of building and fund collection, the lay board is greatly needed. In the modification of instructional methods, the faculty's importance steadily increases. The business and financial policies of the institution on the one hand and the educational policies on the other hand are the distinct functions of the two groups.

Under the European system both functions are carried on by one group, the faculty; however, in this country we have not yet reached the conclusion that it is possible or desirable to place all responsibilities, financial and educational, in the faculty. It is quite essential that the two groups whose relationship and attitude materially affect the life of the institution should be brought together. The secrecy of board meetings is passing, and in many institutions copies of the minutes are now distributed to the members of the faculty. Other groups, such as the alumni and sometimes faculty, are being represented on the board of trustees. The time will come when surely members of the faculty and possibly representatives of the student body will be found in the membership of the institutional board. Meantime there might very well be joint committees and joint assemblies of board and faculty for the purpose of bringing together the two groups. Certainly a board of trustees cannot administer the affairs of an institution without knowing rather clearly its educational ambitions. And, on the other hand, a faculty cannot understand the difficulties attendant upon financial matters unless attention is called to them in a vital way.

Undoubtedly, in this country we are entering upon a new stage in education. The larger and more important emphasis is now being placed upon educational principles. With this shift in view, the president becomes an advisory officer with executive functions. He is particularly charged with the development of mutual esteem and respect between the board of trustees and the faculty group. The European university lacked the advice of men of affairs; the American college has too often failed to avail itself of recommendations of the educational group associated with it. Neither is a happy situation. The combination of the two, with the recognition of the rights and abilities of both, is productive of sound and far-reaching results. When this association is effected, in times of stress and difficulty and in the prosperous days, the American college can progress in the true spirit of learning. The college in its government as well as in its teaching must recognize the unity of purpose, the demand of the democratic spirit, and the cooperative character of education.

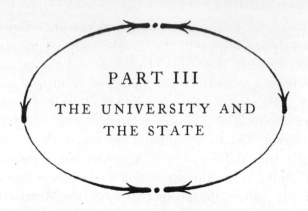

PART III

THE UNIVERSITY AND
THE STATE

The University and the State

LET US CONSIDER a few simple steps to be taken in the present development of the state university to bring it into closer relation to the problems of the commonwealth. The first step is the frank recognition of the research function of the university and the acceptance of it by the state in the appropriation of funds for such purposes. This recognition would stimulate and centralize the more or less sporadic attempts at research now being made in state institutions of higher learning.

The second step is to use the various departments of the university to aid in the solution of the problems of the state. The distinctly statistical functions of the state should avail themselves of help from the department of economics in the university. In the field of political science the experts in government can be used to assist in the forming of legislative programs, and graduate students should be apprentices in state departments. Many of the problems of a state tax commission are pure problems of economics; the department of economics is in a position to assist materially, and the school of mines has the data and knowledge of mining taxation that can be of great assistance in dealing with the many difficult questions arising in the valuation of properties. A list, long and impressive, can be made of the possible opportunities of cooperation between the state university and the state government to the benefit of both.

The enthusiastic acceptance of the worth of a university as a factor in commonwealth building is bound to come. There is no other conclusion. These steps taken in the near future will materially enhance the value of the university as a working agency in the state. And when that is once done, the university can enter into the important purpose of fact finder and mediator. It will then in truth be one of the means by which men may find a path through the world chaos that threatens to overcome them. There must be a light to show the way to men who, being so busy with the affairs of getting and begetting, cannot look to the stars for guidance. The university, considered in this larger sense, is the real leader by which a people's progress may be directed if the people of the state but will it so.

The Critical Attitude of the Public toward Higher Education

President's address to the National Association of State Universities, Chicago, Illinois, November 12, 1923; published in *School and Society,* August 30, 1924

An examination of the topics treated by former presidents of the National Association of State Universities indicates a rather close adherence to the purpose of the association marked by a tendency to follow a strictly academic viewpoint. Consequently, the discussions have dealt with finance, state legislatures, boards of control, the status of professional incumbents, the function of the university, relative advantages of liberal and technical education, salaries, tenure of office, and so on indefinitely. Naturally, every presiding officer desires to leave on the minds of his hearers an impression of versatility, wisdom, and ability to deal in English with the intricacies of this well-trodden field; I am, however, taking the liberty of presenting a topic new to the programs of the association—"The critical attitude of the public toward higher education."

Unless the members of this Association have had their heads in the sands of oblivion or contrariwise extended into the clouds of fancy, of which no state university president has been accused, no one here can be ignorant of the increasing criticism of higher education that has arisen in the past five years. University education has always been under the fire of critics, but the comments made by them were in the main well intended and not so destructive certainly in character as they are at the present time.

Today the criticism is more scathing and the indictment more severe than was the case in days gone by. John Henry Newman commented on Oxford in the fifties of the past century, and our own Doctor Rice discussed college education with keenness and insight. Ten years ago Birdseye made an examination of the educational system of the country that resulted in uncomplimentary conclusions. Within the biennium numerous magazine articles, books, and brochures have appeared that refer to the universities as antisocial, a point never raised by the more academic critics of the past. The full import of this charge is not to be measured by the usual considerations that one may have in mind about the views of some socialist writer or speaker. That is not in reality the essence of the charge, though it may contain some of the elements. Rather it is a declaration that the colleges do not make for good citizenship and that they have been carried away by a gross materialism which is reflected in their management, lack of scholarship, snobbish tendencies of student life, the false ideals of athletics, and the divorcement of the essentials of culture from the curriculum.

"How could it be otherwise," inquires one writer, "when Main Street has gone to college and College Avenue belongs to Main Street? The universities have been Babbitted," he wails. All that Babbitt means in his littleness, his smug patriotism, and his adherence to the conventional standards of a well-meaning but uncultured, untrained, and ill-educated group have been carried over by sheer force of circumstances into the universities. This critic further says, "The standards of instruction, conduct, and management of the universities through the capture of these institutions by big business methods and great undigested student bodies have been changed from the cultural purposes of the founders to those of materialism determined by the requirements of the age."

Two contributions to *Civilization in the United States*, a publication by thirty Americans, discussed the matter in destructive comment. Upton Sinclair in characteristic manner has launched a sensational attack in *The Goose Step*. In fiction Scott Fitzgerald went the limit in *This Side of Paradise*, Mr. and Mrs. Montross called the turn in *Town and Gown*, while William J. McNally in *The Barb* and Paul-Jordan Smith in *Cables of Cobweb* added fuel to the flames.

" 'Behold!' they may shout," paraphrases John Anderson in an article, *The College on Main Street*, " 'American education is a trade-marked product fitted to the youth of the land like ready-made clothes. It is a mechanical contraption adjusted to the owner with the least personal inconvenience and guaranteed to operate on

level pavements at a minimum of discomfort. Parts are interchange-
able at any wayside station and upkeep costs are nothing at all!' "

The pamphleteers, novelists, and magazine writers might be
pushed aside if it were not for the tone and character of discussions
emanating from sources worthy of serious consideration.

"I don't know what the matter is with education," said Secretary
of War Newton Baker, "but something is. I doubt if there has been
any time in my life when education is as undervalued and in as
great disrepute as it is at the present moment. . . . If we (referring
to the Army school) can in addition be educational philosophers
and develop a system that educates men as well as technicians, our
work may well be improved and absorbed by the other educational
institutions and may finally lead to a departure from the system
and theory which are now somewhat in disrepute."

More recently an exchange professor from England who had
spent two years teaching in American universities summed up his
experience in an article under the title of *American versus English
Universities*. Professor Zimmern, the author of the article, is as you
know an educator of international repute and an economist and
publicist. He held the Woodrow Wilson Professorship of Politics
at the University of Wales, 1919-1921, and for the past two years
he has been in America investigating and teaching in our universities and colleges.

The frank words of this impartial observer of American higher
education may be regarded as unbiased and worthy of consideration
for the reason that what he says is free from the superficial and
sensational views of many of the fiction and magazine writers. Accordingly, I am taking the opportunity to present his discussion in
considerable detail as having a bearing on the topic I am trying to
discuss.

"The great difference between British and American university
administration," writes Professor Zimmern, "is that English universities are controlled by scholars along lines of administration
which, however much open to criticism in details, have been evolved
to meet the special needs of institutions of learning, whereas in
America universities are, on the whole, administered by business

men along lines which are assimilated, as closely as the differences of function and circumstance permit, to the organization of a business enterprise. And as, in the nature of the case, the assimilation cannot be complete, there is necessarily something unsatisfactory about American university organization which affects the prestige of a university career in all sorts of subtle ways.

"Nevertheless the fact remains that the business man put in charge of an institution of higher learning is undeniably in a false position. His training and outlook inevitably drive him to apply forms of thinking and to favor policies which, however sagacious in business, are wholly unsuitable to education; and the greater his sense of responsibility and his anxiety to make a success of his trusteeship, the more calamitous are his policies likely to be. A business man is no more competent to run a university than a scholar to run a bank or a factory. The business man is trained to look for 'efficiency,' for a smooth-working organization, for definite and measurable results, for a valuable and imposing plant, for the outward and visible signs of 'success.' The scholar, who knows that his standards are not of the crowd, is concerned not with quantity but with the quality, not with the mounting curves of statistics but with the spirit working in secret places, not with the piling up of buildings but with the transmission of living ideas. No doubt universities, like churches, need buildings and equipment and cannot dispense with the services of the sons of Martha skilled in these matters. But business ability should surely be kept, as it is at Oxford, in its natural place, which is that of advising rather than controlling the directors of university life and policy. . . . No one has set forth the ideal of the scholar's life more eloquently and persuasively than Emerson in his Phi Beta Kappa address on *The American Scholar*. But the eighty years and more which have since elapsed do not yet seem to have made scholarship truly at home in the American university."

Mr. Zimmern estimates more directly the presidents themselves: "I do not say that presidents of this type do not exist in America. I have indeed met one or two, both in the east and in the west. But they are the exception, not the rule. The typical university president, whatever his scholarly attainments in the past, seems to have drifted into the position of being the traveling salesman of a body of business trustees, or, in the case of state institutions, the lobbyist skilled in the defense of the interests of his enterprise. Ready to pack his bag and dash into his sleeper at an hour's notice, he spends his time at conferences, at alumni banquets, at the celebrations of allied institutions—anywhere but in his own library and among his own faculty and students. In more than one institution, after waiting to see the great man after his return to his alma mater from a business journey, I have found him so overwhelmed with fatigue that he could hardly keep his eyes open."

Mr. Zimmern, in commenting on the lack of scholarship, states that from his observations university appointments go mainly to those who have blunted and narrowed their scholastic interests by soul-destroying research. Nor is there truly intellectual independence in the universities, due to lack of understanding among those in authority as to what intellectual activity actually implies. Until emphasis is placed on real teaching, the universities will only be such in name.

I turn now to a very different type of writer whose contention is that the universities have been taken over by big business, body and soul. In an elaborate book of nearly five hundred pages, which you have all read through curiosity or because of a sense of duty, Mr. Sinclair piles up damning evidence, as he thinks, of the prostitution of the universities and colleges of the land to the support and propagation of capitalism and its spirit. This book has had a far more extended reading than I supposed until I began to make inquiries. All the cases of academic freedom, disgruntled instructors, unwise trustees, familiar to those who have been in educational work during the past thirty years, are set forth anew. The book in its cumulative piling up of evidence carries to the uninitiated a full amount of conviction. And because of its seeming adherence to the truth, it cannot be ignored. Wherefore, I am presenting in brief form the contention of this writer.

"The key to educational control in America is to be found in Wall Street in the interlocking directorate. . . . Since men die, new generations must be trained for the agencies of capitalism."

In his study of boards of trustees he asserts that trustees are identified with big business.

"The president of an institution is therefore selected with this purpose in mind. With such control and with such purpose there can be no liberalism especially in economics and sociology. Class ignorance, class fear, and class repression are written over the modern curriculum at Harvard as at all other American universities. The great universities are run on the lines of an army, rigid, precise, and formal. The training of many prominent university presidents was secured in Germany where they got the military spirit in education. The consequence is in every issue involving a conflict between the people and special privilege, the universities and colleges are on the side of special privilege."

Without intending to weary you, for to me this viewpoint is highly interesting, I am proceeding to another phase of Sinclair's discussion.

"All university influence," he says, "depends upon keeping up a pretense of freedom. . . . The students are taught to think but they are not thinking the right things. . . . I have not been able to find a single one of the great American universities which is truly free. . . . A college professor is not a citizen in Pennsylvania any more than he is in Illinois. . . . They, the professors, have no tenure and no security save the kindness and good faith of those who hold the purse strings and rule their lives. . . . The college professor must do what the laboring men are doing—agitate, educate, organize."

The remedy for autocratic university government according to Sinclair is to place large faculty representation on boards of trustees. To bring about a change in the purpose as well as the government of American colleges and universities, he would urge that something drastic be done. A strike of faculties against the present system of control and direction of higher education would bring about its collapse and the reorganization of higher education.

With this summary of quotations from *The Goose Step*, I turn to the satirical comments of the editor of the Chicago *Literary Times*, who says in a recent issue: "Professor Meiklejohn's effort to convert Amherst into an un-American institution has come to an end. The good professor retires from his task with the conviction, if he is half intelligent, that higher education in America must consist of the business of contributing high falutin' phrases to interpret the conceits and dogmas of the yokelry.

"With this conviction no one can argue. It would be deplorable, and we mean it seriously, for a nation to pretend to one set of notions in its political and social life and to allow its universities to go harloting after another set of notions in its intellectual life.

"The American university is a distressing anomaly in the life of our country. It is tolerated chiefly as a symbol of prestige to which all good citizens aspire and as a formal haven from the enveloping industrialism of the age. Unfortunately education is a dangerous force with which to trifle. It stirs questions and curiosities and philosophical skepticism in the minds exposed to it. Questions, curiosities and skepticisms, in the Republic, are offenses punishable by exile, incarceration and social ostracism.

"The only way in which to circumvent this paradox is, of course, to make the American university a non-educational institution. This the dozens of university presidents and thousands of university trustees and donors have accomplished to a marvelous degree. It is possible for an individually intelligent man or woman to survive in a university. But the handicaps are rather difficult."

To all this might be added the comments of more conservative writers in the *Atlantic Monthly, Century, Scribner's,* and *North American Review.* All of them point out defects in the system of higher education in this country and deplore the machine type of education that they are convinced is in existence in our universities and colleges.

Another class of criticism should be brought into this review of public attitude. It is wholly different from the one so far discussed and has its foundation in backward looking and obsolete theology.

Regarding the universities and colleges as responsible in more than a considerable measure for a drifting and declining church influence in the life of the nation, the fundamentalists have issued the challenge against modern science and have lifted high the banner bearing the phrase, "Back to the Fundamentals." The doctrine of evolution, upon which science has built its structure, literature has found its inspiration, history the key to progress, and man a hope for the future, comes in for attack and repudiation. Modern instruction in any field of learning is evolutionary in character. By the very nature of growth it must be so. Nevertheless, four state legislatures have passed bills or resolutions forbidding teaching of evolution in public educational institutions, and as many more state legislatures have given serious consideration to the contentions of the fundamentalists. With this effort to secure legislation to hamper thought and teaching, much criticism of the colleges and universities has been made to the effect that they are un-Christian and irreligious.

There is the criticism on one hand that institutions of higher education are conservative, capitalistic, and dogmatic; on the other that they are radical, irreligious, and material in thought and teaching, tending toward socialism. Both opposing camps agree that they are materialistic, but each defines materialism in its own manner.

Another critic is found in the Commission on Advance Program among Student Associations. In its recent report this commission states that the purpose of the commission is to facilitate the release of spiritual energy resident in the school life of today. "This purpose," the report says, "is clear recognition that great resources of spiritual power—purity, sound thinking, redemptive love and sacrifice—lie dormant within the lives of most students. . . . Education in the United States should be guided by a clear conception of the meaning of democracy. It is the ideal of democracy that the individual and society may find fulfillment of each in the other."

To that end the commission regards health, command of fundamental processes, worthy home membership, vocation, citizenship, use of leisure, and ethical character as the ends of education. To accomplish these the commission feels that it will be necessary to make a radical transformation in educational theory. And unfortunately, says the commission, "the higher institutions of learning in which the Y.M.C.A. functions will be loath to accept these new American educational doctrines and very slow to practice their demands."

Up to this point I have made only casual reference to the criticisms that come from organizations like the American Civic Federation to the effect that the American colleges are honeycombed with socialism in their economic and sociological departments. Nor shall I endeavor to discuss this angle of the matter except to call to mind that university economists and sociologists in the past decade have shown a clear understanding of social principles and a high patriotism ready to serve their country.

To concentrate all of this criticism and, if possible, to classify it are quite necessary. In order to assemble the points made in the conglomeration of criticism from many sources, I am grouping them under five heads: first, the administration of universities and colleges is autocratic and capitalistically controlled; second, ideals, if they exist, are not carried over to the student because business concepts rather than scholarship rule the thought of the institutions while religion is forgotten or given a second place; third, the supervision of the student life in health, housing, and amusement is largely neglected; fourth, instruction is given by poorly paid, spiritless teachers who have lost their freedom as citizens and as thinkers; fifth, facilities for instruction are unequal to the task of education, and the whole system of higher education is overrun with a vast horde of elementary students.

Part of this indictment is true. The problems that arise in the functioning of higher education cannot be so simply stated as they have just been put or as they are generally outlined by critics. These problems are more intricate, more subtle, and more difficult than they are usually thought to be. They are in fact a part and parcel of the growth of the country. Large numbers of students result from the educational policy of free instruction to all; inadequate facilities are due to this rapid growth and to the lack of public understanding in regard to the demands in dollars and cents that the policy of free education entails. A great deal of what is complained of in the business attitude of administration officers arises from the burdens placed on them. A cursory review of the duties performed by any state university reveals the truth of this statement. I have reference to police functions, public health laboratories, chemical examinations of industrial products, and many other burdens that are laid upon such institutions by legislative act. Moreover, confusion in the mind of the public in regard to the university and its functions forces administrative officers into publicity and propaganda that take time from the scholastic work of the university.

Without doubt the American universities have their faults, but their presidents and faculties are perhaps more keenly aware, and certainly more eager for a solution, of the situation than are any of their critics. Extended health programs are being developed in the institutions; religious instruction is more emphasized than at any other time in the history of public education; administration, in so far as autocracy ever really existed, is rapidly changing to a wider and more democratic basis for government of university affairs. But these signs of progress do not answer nor do they solve the difficulties.

Undoubtedly freedom of teaching, emphasis upon scholarship, development of research, and the enlargement of democratic government in the university are all bound up in the purposes of a university. Until these are clearly understood not only by presidents and boards of trustees but also by faculties, by students, and by the people who support the institutions of higher learning, criticisms will continue and confusion will grow.

With these purposes and criticisms in mind I raise the following questions. Are the universities alive to the problems confronting them, or are they merely engaged in the process of making themselves going concerns? How far have the universities and colleges been guilty of emphasizing machinery instead of truth, knowledge, and the spirit of self-development? Do they really wish to grasp, formulate, and expand the realities bound up in all life whether expressed through science, history, the arts, or religion?

Is it not time for this Association, in fact is it not a great opportunity given to us, to issue a statement of the meaning of the universities in American life? Such a declaration should emphasize the real purpose of institutions of higher learning, the motivating ideals of the men who guide them, and the essential contributions that are being brought constantly to the people of this country by the universities.

Obviously and undeniably the greatness of a university depends upon the spirit that prevails in its faculty, student body, and governing board. The principle of truth in teaching and research cannot pervade a university unless its purpose is understood. Here is the weakness of the situation. Engrossed in details of administration, hampered by the educational system prevailing in America where elementary students are thrown into university life before they can grasp its meaning, the institution drifts along without the unity of purpose that it should have and without a clear vision of its goal.

The state university has a duty to the people in solving the problems of a state; it has an obligation to teach the youth who come to it; and it has a task to perform in the search for new knowledge. In the very existence of a state, progress is woefully limited because of prejudices, heritage, inefficiencies of education, and the lack of development of the arts. These cannot be ignored. So much more then is it necessary that the objective of a university in the social organization should be clearly understood. The proclamation setting forth the meaning, value, and purpose of the university should be given to the world not tomorrow but today.

Financing the State University

Address to the National Association of State Universities,
Chicago, Illinois, November, 1933

IN THE September 2, 1933 issue of the Detroit *Free Press*, the Chairman of the Board of Regents of the University of Michigan has much to say in an interview about the increasing expenses of operation of the University. The tenor of his remarks is paraphrased here. Gradual accretion of costs can be met by fees from students and receipts from taxes; even additions to capital amounts in the form of buildings and equipment may be taken care of by direct appropriations in the biennial sessions. These receipts, although covering the ordinary advancement of the University, cannot provide for the betterment of instruction, the employment of higher type men, the payment of larger salaries, and the addition of libraries, all of which are essential to the making of an outstanding institution. The alternative seems to be, from the point of view of this board Chairman, that the Board of Regents must call for gifts to be used at the discretion of the Regents if the University of Michigan is to meet the demands made upon it for the best in the field of teaching and research.

To attain the best in the field of teaching and research is an ambition that every institution cherishes, but the means of reaching this goal through private beneficence raises a number of fundamental questions which it is my purpose to consider.

The questions raised in the statement of the Chairman of the Board of Regents are important. Does this opinion indicate a defeatist attitude toward the future of the state university? Has, in fact, the state university reached the limit of state financing? The answer to these questions may be approached first from the negative side and then in a more affirmative way.

Although demands upon education have grown steadily in the past twenty-five years, the state has at the same time been called upon to finance many other activities that are essential to the welfare of the people of the commonwealth. The unfortunate dependents who are afflicted by disease or limited mental capacity as well as the delinquents who have committed crimes against society must be taken care of; and, with the growth of scientific knowledge of human deficiencies, the equipment of an earlier day is no longer sufficient. Consequently, requests are being made from year to year for larger sums of money to maintain penal and charitable institutions and also to add to their capital structure.

We may turn to the public schools, in which the state is endeavoring to uphold a fairly equitable standard throughout the commonwealth. These requirements, in view of the variant needs, must be met by an equalization fund. Those interested in public education believe that the public schools of the state can be brought to a fair standard of effectiveness only by the utilization of such a fund.

An added demand has appeared in some of our states in the form of pensions for mothers and the aged. The community has not fully sensed the importance of this new social obligation. It is only as the technique of management is understood and developed that the system commends itself to the voters of the commonwealth. But without a doubt provisions for mothers and old persons will become a charge upon the incomes of the different commonwealths.

In another field the progress that is being made in the construction of new highways because of modern motor transportation will fall heavily upon all divisions of the state. This item of road construction is perhaps the largest in the state budget, and accordingly, even though special taxes are levied, it places a heavy burden upon the state, county, and township.

The expenditure of income by institutions is being placed more and more under restrictive legislation. Budget commissions have been created in many of our states. These commissions direct the formation of legislation to be presented to the assembly. No one can have objection to this procedure providing it is based upon a knowledge of the problem. Too often the budget commission reaches its conclusions upon the basis of political considerations rather than on the basis of merit. Again the legislature leaves the budget commission without adequate clerical assistance so that the commission exists in form only and is in reality an obstacle in the way of satisfactory legislation. Also some of the states have created boards of control in whose hands all the financing, purchasing, and building are placed. Boards of control can buy some commodities, such as coal, lumber, brick, and insurance, at an advantage when the purchasing is concentrated in one body, but the tendency in such boards is to make a showing at the expense of quality; it is in fact very much to be doubted that they make any great saving to the state if all factors are taken into consideration.

Looking back at educational institutions thirty to fifty years ago, we realize that very little provision existed for the care of students or for the maintenance of satisfactory clerical staffs. Today much more is done for the student in every way than was done in the past. His health is watched, his mental status is studied, and an effort is made to provide direction of his affairs through the creation of personnel departments. The number of persons serving the institution in clerical and administrative matters constantly increases. The cost therefore of operating and administering an institution of learning is much greater now than it was formerly.

What has been said thus far in this discussion has been negative in showing the increased expenses and demands upon the state; there is, however, another side to the picture. Certainly all that has been written in books, periodicals, and papers about the growth of wealth in the United States has some meaning. In the period from 1917 to 1922 the wealth of this country rose from $186,000,-000,000 to $320,000,000,000, an increase of 72 per cent. If more recent years are taken into consideration, the economists are telling us the national wealth has reached $400,000,000,000 and the income $90,000,000,000. We are spending for higher education $483,000,000 or approximately $4.00 per capita. Meantime the per capita wealth has increased in the neighborhood of $1,000 since 1912. Has higher education grown so much more rapidly than the increase in the wealth of the country?

The method of financing educational institutions by some of the legislatures is that of direct appropriation not only for construction of buildings but for their maintenance as well. Each two years the institution comes to the legislature for an appropriation to meet its requirements. This method has the advantage of keeping the needs of the institution before the people. In other instances taxes are levied which are paid directly to the institution through the collecting agency, and such taxes are expected to meet the entire requirements of the university. In a third case the institution is maintained by appropriations and by the receipts from fees in the form of fertilizer fees, feed fees, royalties, and the like. In general the appropriations, as well as the receipts from taxation, for the financing of state educational institutions come from the direct tax, known as the general property tax, upon real and personal property.

Sooner or later the states will enlarge their taxing basis especially in view of the change in the form of wealth. Students of taxation have often pointed out the inadequacy of present tax methods in dealing with the new types of wealth, and unquestionably in time provision will have to be made to obtain income from these sources that are at present largely neglected.

Four types of available taxes are rarely converted to the securing of income by the states. In the majority of cases they have not been employed, with the exception of the tax upon gas. For the past sixty years the tax upon incomes has been used by the federal government and by some of the states, but most of the states have found its collection so difficult that little revenue has been produced. The difficulty of administering the tax is being overcome by a better understanding of it and of the technique of the government. New York and Massachusetts have had an income tax for many years, and in North Carolina its reorganization has been so successful that $8,096,000 were secured for state purposes in the past year. The use of this tax in view of the change in the forms of wealth will be invaluable, and the important thing to be kept in mind is the study of its administration not only by the state but also by university departments of economics.

The estate tax, known as the inheritance tax, has been called a satisfactory form of taxation by all students of taxation. Receipts from it relieve the general body of the state from the burden of increased taxation; and, with the present law providing that inheritance taxes levied by states are given 80 per cent credit on the federal tax, no adequate reason can be found for discontinuing this form of taxation. The argument for its use in the educational field is very strong. Certainly the receipts from this tax should not be diverted to paying current expenses but should go into capital investments. For some time there has been a strong lobby in Washington working against this tax; if the law is repealed, the financial condition of the states as well as of the nation will be demoralized and disorganized.

With the pressure for additional income, the states have looked about for other resources and, following the example of the federal government, have given some consideration to luxury taxes. The suggestion has been made that the states take over the federal tax on the admission to theatres and movie shows; however, so much opposition to this has arisen, and the problems involved in the final payment of the tax are so great, that very few of the states have gone into it. Much the same can be said about a tax on cosmetics. These are looked upon by legislatures as luxuries and unnecessary, but practically one-half of the voters regard them as necessities. So there remains the tax on tobacco, particularly cigarettes. Eight states now have taxation of this kind. Such a tax brings into the treasury of Tennessee $1,250,000 annually. The special session of the legislature of Tennessee increased the tax on cigarettes to four cents with practically no opposition. What the result will be remains to be seen, but unquestionably tobacco is a fruitful source of possible taxation.

The directors of higher education in this country missed an opportunity when they failed to obtain a part of the taxes upon gasoline for educational purposes. This tax is distinctly popular. It is regarded now as belonging to the highway commissions of the various commonwealths, and it undoubtedly will be needed for the development of motor transportation systems.

The agitation for increased financial support has raised fees to a high point in certain instances, especially in privately endowed institutions. But the raising of fees involves the development of loan funds for the larger number of students who are to be assisted in getting an education. Without doubt, the time will come when public institutions will have to levy higher fees and call upon private individuals to supplement these fees by the establishment of loan and scholarship funds. Another source of revenue is the levying of a special fee upon every student in the university; this method was followed for a short period by the University of

Washington to establish a building fund. The amount so collected, if set aside, might meet many an emergency.

In the operation of the modern state university, many business activities which require the attention of administrative officials have come into an important place in the organization. Although the receipts from book stores, commons, dining halls, residence halls, athletic games, and so forth swell the gross income, impress the public with the enlarged resources of the institution, and may in time under good management actually add to institutional resources; yet these activities call for increased staffs and enlarged administrative machinery and are not in their final analyses supposed to be making money. Moreover, the administrative officers may be deluged with financial cares that are only incidentally educational.

Whereas added burdens press upon the state universities as going concerns, a movement is now under way in the formation of junior colleges that may make for some simplification in organization. The state university will be raised to real university status; however, a heavier load will be placed upon taxpayers in financing many small junior colleges, and the university may be farther removed from the people.

All of these matters are important. In reality the future of the state university and its adequate support depend upon the concept of the university held in the minds of trustees, faculty, and the people. The call for adult education and the increasing requirements of modern life for scientists, teachers, administrators, and skilled persons in many fields point to the need of greater universities.

Not less but more support will be forthcoming surely as the universities serve their purpose and the people realize the value and the necessity of education. The increase of wealth in this country justifies and certainly will require a payment beyond four dollars per capita for all higher education in the United States. In truth, the growth in educational resources depends first of all upon the work done in the universities in teaching and research. Increased support will come to the state universities when the purposes of university education are formulated and when those purposes are made clear to the people. If the universities fail, the failure will be because they have not been able to make their message impressive enough and because their vision has been too small.

The Registrar and the Next Step

Address to the American Association of Collegiate Registrars, Cincinnati, Ohio, April, 1934; published in *Bulletin of the American Association of Collegiate Registrars*, July, 1934

WHAT I am attempting to say this morning is not a summary of all that has been said by the preceding speakers but rather an indication to you of the next step, as I see it, in the office of the registrar and in his relation to two problems.

The registrar stands as a kind of outguard between secondary education and higher education. He has had an extensive development in the last fifteen years; during this time he has moved from a bookkeeper and a guardian of records and grades to an officer who is really interested in educational procedure and who has more material in his possession for study of academic processes than has any other agency or any other group in the field of education.

What is he going to do with this material? How is he going to use it?

The tendency must be more and more, I believe, in the direction of applying these records and documents to the purposes of research. The office of registrar should have among its personnel a research man, associated possibly with the college of education, in order that not only the usual business may be carried on but also helpful and constructive study of the material, too often locked up, may be made. Because in the record books is the story of what is actually happening in the field of higher education, intensive attention must be given continually to those data in the registrar's office if we are to know what to do, where we are going, and when we may hope to arrive.

Problems are apparent in the field of secondary education itself, and problems are present in the relations between the secondary schools and the colleges and universities in the matter of certification and admission of students. An enormous expansion of subject matter has developed in the high schools. In some degree the schools have copied the college courses, making it embarrassing often for the colleges to build or to modify their procedure in the fields in which secondary education has already perhaps given superficial pre-views.

Moreover, secondary education has lost ground with the public in the last half dozen years. If it is to regain that favor, it must make a restatement of the courses which it offers in the public high schools and in the private secondary schools. It must check an expansion that has reduced the effectiveness and the efficiency of the work which has actually been done by the pupils in the high schools. It must work on its own, not on college, courses. A great many teachers in high schools, coming from their master's work or their doctor's work in a university, transfer all that they have been doing in the graduate field to the classes that they are teaching. The result is that with somewhat reduced statements of the courses that they have had, these teachers follow the same lines, the same general ideas, the same viewpoints that were taught to them in the university.

There must be a restatement of these courses, not on the basis of college needs or necessities, but rather on the basis of the problem which faces the secondary school. And the reselling of the secondary school to the public becomes a necessity because of loss of confidence in it. You have seen the attacks upon the high school, emphasizing the fads that have been developed. After all, a presentation of the content of secondary education will have to be made from the point of view of the group with which it deals and of the part which it plays in the social order.

These are general statements, always easy for pedagogues to make. They are noted for being able to tell the world that it ought to be reformed, but the question of telling it how it can be reformed is a very difficult process. Secondary education as it stands today occupies a highly important position in the whole field of education; it must rest upon the idea of doing a particular thing for the youth at that particular time, in a new environment, and under new conditions. The expansion which has taken place, it seems to me, must be arrested, and emphasis must be placed upon what might be called fundamental courses.

When we turn to the group of students in the secondary field who are entering college, the situation there is changing rapidly, bringing in additional problems. The registrars of our country have set up a neat system of admitting students and of recording their grades in their archives. It is a very neat system—there is no question about that—and it works well from the point of view of accounting. But a registrar who is alive to his opportunities will not abide by that kind of procedure just because it is convenient. I think he must come more and more into the general trends of the present time, namely, the admission of students into college on the basis of ability to do college work. And such a basis of admission will mean that a lot of the things that we are now asking in the way of so much English and so much mathematics and so much science and so much social science will be put aside as really the accounting method of getting into college, and in their place we shall attempt to bring about the acceptance of students because of their abilities and interests.

Dr. Ben Wood was here the other day, and I presume he talked to you about certain phases of this problem and gave you a great deal of material about it. I notice on the program other speakers who probably moved somewhat in that direction. You have, I think, a new basis for admission of college students from the secondary schools which is likely to come into a procedure and a method in a comparatively short time. At present they are admitted upon fifteen units, the old Carnegie Units; we are finding, however, that these units do not really search out the abilities that we want in college students. So the tendency must be more and more toward asking the high schools to cooperate in finding the best students in their graduating classes in order that they may go on to college, not on the theory that they have done a certain number of units of work, but rather on the grounds of their ability and of their interest in college work.

There is very little use in sending a boy to college simply because he wants to go if he has no literary or scientific interests of any kind and if he is not concerned about books or learning. The lengthening of adolescence by four years is a delightful thing; but, from the point of view of the college and of the student himself, the question of ability and interest should come first.

Under this new procedure, the high school would send the student's record to the college. This record would indicate not only the kind of work which he had done but also his scholarship, his attitude, and his activities.

His scholarship would include, of course, his interest and ability. His activities would show his relationship to his fellow students and his manner of working in cooperative arrangements and cooperative organizations. His attitude would have to do with his approach to social ideals, with questions of his integrity and good sportsmanship, and with his honesty of mind and honesty of purpose. All of these would be included in his record. The student, therefore, instead of coming to college as he does now with a record showing that he has done this, that, and the other thing in special topics, would come to college with a record that would show his ability, his interest, his activity, and his relationship to his fellow students. And when he was admitted to college on that basis, we should have a student who would be acceptable to the college. Certainly the interest that would be aroused in that student, as a consequence of the new attitude of the secondary school and of the college, would result in very beneficial effects and influences upon the boy.

Now what is the relationship of the registrar to all of this? I should say that he can stand in the way of a procedure of this kind by insisting upon the old type of record and the old type of admission, that he can hamper the movement very considerably by his attitude. When the members of a faculty determine on a mode of conduct, necessarily the registrar will have to comply with it; on the other hand, you will always find in a faculty certain conservatives who, strengthened by the office of records, can make impossible the bringing about of hoped for results.

So the registrar's office must necessarily move in the direction of more careful study of the records with which it is dealing. It must make the attempt to formulate from the study of those records new attitudes and policies because in general the administrative officer of an institution, on account of the multiplicity of duties that he has, must rely upon the work which is done by his colleagues in the study of educational problems. If the registrar's office has a trained research man or a research woman in its organization studying the problem from the point of view of the institution and of the high school, it may make a great contribution to the present period in education. In this epoch, education must adjust itself to the changing forms of government, of political organization, and of social life. To arrive at even a fairly happy solution of these challenging and changing forces demands constant study because nobody knows the drift and nobody can foresee the final harbor that we are going to reach. The only way that we can keep in contact with present day tendencies is by constant study, and the agency through which much of that study can best be done is the registrar's office.

The registrar who is equal to the opportunity and who has a sufficient amount of knowledge and understanding of the technique of statistics and of educational policy to make these needed contributions, I believe, will occupy a much larger place in the guidance of educational policies than he has had in the past. Because of the marked change and increased scholarship in the field of the registrar's office, that office will come into added importance in analyzing records and in bringing about forward looking purposes in the colleges. Such is the next step for the registrar.

The Superintendent of Buildings and Grounds

An Outline of His Responsibilities and Duties in a Modern Educational Institution

Published in
The Educational Business Manager and Buyer, December, 1930

T H E professionalizing of college staffs goes on apace. Not so long ago a clever young woman looked after student records; a professor gave part of his time to the library; laboratories were just exhibit places; the college doctor and nurses were unknown; and the business office received fees and endowment income and spent the money by order from the president of the college or university. Now purchasing is a difficult and special task, and accounting has become a guiding agency for the administration of the college. Along with these developments which indicate the progress made in educational facilities, the superintendent of buildings and grounds has come into his own and is rapidly reaching a professional status.

The office of superintendent of buildings and grounds has grown in the last twenty years from a janitor, gardener, and man of all work to a position of major importance. The old college plant needed little attention, comparatively speaking, except cleaning and maintenance of buildings and campus lawn. The remarkable betterment of college architecture, the improvements in sanitary arrangements, the enlargement of heating and lighting facilities, all of these with their possible breakdowns and their always requirements of repair have demanded a trained and experienced man to look after the ups and downs of the institution's physical equipment.

In my day as a college student, the student body was allowed to shift for itself both on and off the campus. There may have been advantages in such a regime; however, possible tragedies of illness, cold recitation rooms, draughts, and the closing of the college for a few days in time of heavy weather occurred frequently. Moreover, modern requirements of comfort and the equipment of libraries, offices, rest rooms, dispensaries, living rooms, swimming pools, and laboratories with many kinds of machines and motors have complicated the occupation of maintaining a college plant and have made that operation a business in itself. This fact is gradually being recognized by college boards and executive officers; along with other officers of health and administration, the superintendent of buildings and grounds is being given his rightful and respected place in the university staff.

What does the superintendent of buildings and grounds do? The answer to this question will throw some light on the duties of this new department in the college organization and will also give a basis for the discussion of his duties. The list cannot be complete nor is it given in the order of importance. Since verbs expressing the activities will give a picture of the doings of this officer, here are listed some of the things he or his organization does: employs, cleans, gardens, repairs, paints, mends, builds, estimates, selects, plans, draws, disciplines, watches, observes, listens, transports, confers, records, orders, collects, catalogs, inventories, analyzes, experiments. The list might be indefinitely expanded, but the main activities are covered by these twenty-four verbs of action.

What has the institution in the way of grounds, buildings, and equipment? Where are the roads, telephone wires, sewers, water connections, and heat lines? Even today few institutions have data covering these matters. The superintendent of buildings and grounds starts his office with a campus map showing topography, location of buildings, roads, and all service connections. Such a map cannot be made over night for it requires accurate data on all the locations. Campus planning is superficial indeed unless the data on these matters can be supplied by the institution when the plan is made. Quite often the board of managers forgets the cost of making connections with service lines, and the money for a building is exceeded because the service connections have been overlooked. In this respect the superintendent of buildings and grounds supplements the work of the architect and is a potent factor in making the building a going and habitable structure.

Following the mapping of campus and grounds, he has the problem of inventory. In some institutions this falls upon the business officer, but it might well be one of the duties of the superintendent because he is in close contact with buildings and their contents.

The superintendent, at any rate, must keep an inventory of supplies for janitors, building materials, lamps, towels, and so on. He must watch the market for his materials so that purchases may be made advantageously.

And as a buying officer he must keep on hand catalogs of all the manufacturing and jobbing concerns that deal in the materials required. Such a catalog collection to be of any use must be arranged and must be kept up to date. His office is visited constantly by agents and representatives of business concerns far and wide, who take much time and an infinite amount of patience. His real problem is one of conservation of his time; otherwise he is harassed and hindered in his daily duties. The study of catalogs is a matter of importance to the institution because a careful and keen superintendent can save a great deal for his university or college by watching the changes not only in prices but in the types and character of materials.

The buying of coal is an example of what this statement means. To most people coal is coal. As a matter of fact, coal varies greatly, and the buying of it scientifically by tests not only saves wear on furnaces but lowers costs of transportation, reduces ash handling, and produces more heat units. The superintendent of buildings and grounds, therefore, should have the help of the chemistry department in analyzing the coal. His records, moreover, should show what every furnace is doing and who are the most efficient firemen. Of course, he knows how many square feet of radiation he has to heat, and he learns where the careless professors reside who open windows and leave lights on. His records must show the costs of operation and be comparable from year to year so that he may know the expense of heating each building.

Staffs come and go, though some that ought to go stay on and become college characters! The success of a department of buildings and grounds depends upon the reliability, honesty, intelligence, and hard working qualities of its staff. Besides the superintendent, the staff for an institution of average size might consist of an assistant, a clerk, a night watchman, a plumber, a boss carpenter, an electrician, a gardener, janitors, and laborers. These men and women should be selected with great care, and emphasis should be placed upon intelligence, honesty, and physical condition. The institution should provide liability insurance, grant a vacation of at least a week each year, make provision for illness, pay a living wage, and retire the worker at the age of sixty-eight on a small pension. In the office of the superintendent should be kept a record card for every employee on which are listed name, age, nationality, color, job, residence, wage, length and effectiveness of service.

The wise superintendent will bring his staff together several times a year to talk with them not only about their work but also about possible accidents, about methods of cleaning, about guarding the property of the institution, about the reports they should make, and even about the purposes of the college. Problems of discipline will arise now and then. These vary from carelessness to drinking and stealing. The atmosphere of the institution will permeate the staff in time, and, as the staff gathers morale, such lapses grow less frequent. Patience and understanding, accompanied by firmness and by clear, definite instructions, create loyalty and good will. Many a superintendent has failed because he is hazy and indefinite in his orders. Written orders posted on bulletin boards meet this difficulty in part. A booklet containing general instructions and stating the obligations of employees might clear up a good deal of friction because the employee then knows what his duties are and what he can rely upon.

In the older days very few institutions had night watchmen, and none of them had any police system. The automobile together with increasing student bodies, larger campuses, and greater buildings has made what was a minor problem a really difficult situation. Watchmen must be chosen after much thought, given clocks, and required to cover certain stations and to make a daily report on temperatures, on open windows, on unlocked doors, and on other matters seemingly unimportant but nevertheless indicative of what is going on during the dark hours.

In the daytime the grounds' police have to deal with traffic and parking. There are strangers to be directed with courteous comment. Meantime the superintendent must study his road and walk scheme, hoping that he can make improvements that will reduce the noise of traffic and keep motor cars concentrated at two or three points. The faculty may rule that students are not to have automobiles, but this law seldom solves the problem, and the superintendent has the traffic question before him all of the time. Each campus differs from others so that the solution in one case does not help much in solving the problem elsewhere. To expect a seventy-five dollars a month man to be a good night watchman and the ordinary laborer to become a day policeman is to hope for the impossible. Modern living procedure has placed a police problem on the college, and the wise superintendent recognizes it as such, trusting that his president may see it too and make suitable provision in the budget.

Fire protection has advanced considerably under the pressure of insurance companies and the advantages of co-insurance. Not only must the buildings have water connections in case of fire, but apparatus must be able to approach buildings on hard roads. The superintendent, who should be *persona grata* with the local fire department, must furnish the chief with a map of grounds and plans of buildings.

Like all other campus dwellers the superintendent of buildings and grounds is beset by the temptation to organize a staff that will do everything, that will be housed compactly, and that will enable him to expand the functions he hopes to take on. What shops ought his department to have and how far should they be expanded in making furniture, setting up boilers, steam fitting and plumbing, painting, grading, carrying on construction and architectural planning? I do not know that any one can say offhand just how far these activities should be engaged in by the superintendent of buildings and grounds and his staff; the warning though should be given that a drifting policy regarding these things may prove to be very expensive to the college. The reason for this statement is to be found in several facts: first, an organization may be too large for the college and may maintain a staff that cannot be profitably employed; second, the oversight of many activities may be more than the superintendent and his office can take care of; third, the cost of production may be larger than careful buying and effective contracting can provide. The answer depends upon local conditions and the size of the institution.

It is to be doubted whether the buildings and grounds organization should attempt to do architectural work in the planning of buildings. The training of the superintendent hardly fits him to undertake such work, and the high grade professional architect can produce better looking and more convenient buildings than any department of buildings and grounds. The employment of a permanent architect who shares office with the superintendent is seldom satisfactory. All of this does not mean that the superintendent of buildings and grounds, especially if he is a good engineer, should not be in constant communication with the architect, keeping him in line with the problems of the institution as a whole. It is quite desirable that the superintendent's office should supervise construction, taking over this function from the architect. The average building supervisor employed by the architect is apt to let construction proceed and then report on the defects after the material and work have been put in place. The superintendent of buildings and grounds as the direct representative of the owner has a greater responsibility and far more pride in the excellence of the construction. His relations with the contractor are on a solid basis since he is the owner's representative.

When students are housed in residence halls, the college undertakes the responsibility sometimes to earn an income on endowment but more often to provide better housing facilities than can be had in the town. Whatever the purpose, the erection and management of student halls add to the burdens of institutional administration. Sometimes the men's residence halls are placed under the military department if there is one connected with the institution; but more often they are managed by a separate staff under the dean of men supposedly independent of, but always falling back on, the superintendent of buildings and grounds. In any event he must look after the heating, lighting, and care of lawns.

The cleaning of the buildings is placed in some colleges upon his organization, and he may be called upon to hold down the lid when the populace that inhabits them gets out of hand. Should the matrons of halls be under his organization since they are primarily engaged in keeping the buildings clean and well directed? Or should the whole matter of discipline and care of buildings be located with the deans of men and women? If the purpose of a buildings and grounds organization is taken into account as it must be, then discipline and everyday management should be left to the deans' offices, and the superintendent of buildings and grounds should be given the responsibility of keeping up heat, light, lawns, and repairs. In any event, the line should be clearly drawn to avoid constant confusion and to prevent much going back and forth to settle problems over which no one seems to have any authority.

Colleges as a general rule pride themselves on the appearance of their campuses. The lawns and ivy covered buildings inspire many a poem dedicated to Alma Mater. Chance does not make beautiful campuses. It is true that some campuses have more natural beauty than others, but all of them must be planned, thought about, worked over, and loved if the grounds are to continue attractive. A first class landscape architect can lay out the grading and planting scheme and can do the initial work; the institution itself must go on with the ideas in connection with its own general plan. On the staff of the superintendent should be a gardener, and the superintendent himself ought to know that round flower beds or star shaped embellishments have no place in campus landscape plans. Adherence to the planting design is fundamental, and diversion from it by occupants of some of the buildings who have planting ideas or by the superintendent himself brings confusion and ugliness. If the campus is large enough, the college may undertake the maintenance of a small nursery where may be grown the larger portion of the shrubbery for building and walk landscaping. The laying out of walks and roads is a problem that may well test the wisdom of Solomon in these days of traffic. There is no rule except to hold the number down and to make them as broad and as convenient as possible.

Among the important things that the superintendent of buildings and grounds must analyze and must show in his records as the results of experimentation are cost and reliability of various kinds of coal, paints, plasters, roofing and materials of all types, and methods of cleaning. The cost of cleaning is an increasingly expensive item in budgets. To hold this sum down and yet to get efficiency are matters for great vigilance which require the careful selection of staff and the use of the best soaps, cleaners, and scrubbing machines.

The records must show the cost per square foot of floor space and the varying uses to which buildings are put. Comparisons from year to year will yield valuable information as a guide to the best results. Although creditable manufacturers are usually careful about the claims they make for their products, still the use of them under different circumstances shows a variety of performances that require careful inspection and study if the institution is to get the most for its money. What paint will do under weather conditions must be tested. Radiator valves, steam pipe coverings, gaskets, and all the long list of technical materials are under constant observation. The results must be tabulated, and the records kept if the accuracy of conclusions is to be something more than a matter of memory.

The budget question looms large in the problems of the office. It is a question that carries with it difficulties and much bookkeeping if it is not made clear to the buildings and grounds department as well as to every other department in the institution. General repairs on buildings are chargeable to the budget of the building. This appears to be understood by all concerned, but the various changes and repairs for departments may be charged to the budget of the superintendent or may be chalked up against the department. In addition, unexpected expenditures, often small but necessary, leave the business man of the institution wondering what to do about them. The bickerings over matters of this kind consume a good deal of time of well paid officers. The main thing is to know what the plan is. The budgets of departments may carry repairs within the habitation of the department, or the changes may be charged to the building. Perhaps it is fairer to charge such costs to the departments because comparison of expenses from year to year will then include all the items of departmental costs. The budget of the superintendent of buildings and grounds, therefore, would include the main items of repairs but not small expenses of the departments. If such is the plan, the office of the superintendent must have a copy of the budgets for all departments in which such allowances have been made.

The patience of Job has been regarded as the acid test of human ability to withstand annoyances of all kind. The superintendent of buildings and grounds has need of this attribute. He is called on to do almost everything from the trivial to the important. His telephone rings constantly carrying requests and complaints from every part of the campus. These matters must be attended to promptly and good naturedly if the campus is to be a fairly happy place. So equanimity of mind and heart is an essential quality. Honesty is a fundamental requirement. The office is subject to many temptations and is in a position to secure commissions and gratuities from salesmen and contractors if it is in the mind of the superintendent to take them. Such a course is disastrous to any officer who allows himself to go in that direction and will sooner or later bring disgrace upon him and break his professional career. Seldom does this happen, and it is an honor to the professional standing of the superintendents of buildings and grounds that this is the case.

Many are the burdens, and long are the hours that the superintendent carries in his daily routine. A weak man, physically, is not equal to the many calls made upon the holder of the office. Good health is indispensable.

Sympathy for his staff and his colleagues, comprehension of the goals of the university, understanding of men, and a sense of humor are all necessary for the person who would fill adequately this important position.

Professional training is essential. The old-fashioned superintendent of buildings and grounds can hardly cope with eccentricities of motors, machines, valves, meters, contours, balances, and mathematical calculations of stresses and pressures. This new calling requires the trained engineer who has had experience in the practice of his profession. Modern plants of colleges and universities are complicated and intricate. The demands of the students, the professors, and the public grow every day. The sanitation of buildings; the beauty of grounds; the heating and lighting of rooms, offices, and laboratories; the protection of property; the maintenance of structures against wear and decay; the care and beautifying of grounds; all rest on this officer who should be accorded an honorable place in the staff of an institution of higher education.

Research as a University Function

Summary of address to the
Kentucky Chapter of the American Chemical Society; published in
School and Society, June 21, 1919

THIS discussion of research as a university function may well be begun by the Socratic process of asking questions and by making definitions. The first query, "What is a university?" has been answered thousands of times, and the dictionaries give at least three different answers. One of these says that a university is a collection of colleges; another defines it as a group of scholars organized together in search of truth; and the third combines the two suggestions contained in the others and defines a university as, "a group of colleges in which scholars are gathered for the purpose of presenting and finding the truth." With this definition of a university before us, we may ask, "What are its functions?" The first of these is commonly stated to be teaching; the second is the carrying on of research with intention of adding to knowledge and the extending of knowledge by publication; the third deals with the gathering of material in libraries and museums for the purpose of illustrating the progress of civilization; and the fourth is the service to the state. As it is the second function in which we are interested, I turn again to the definition of research for the purpose of abstracting from it some ideas of the meaning of this much used word.

Research is called a diligent, protracted investigation requiring studious inquiry. The Standard Dictionary says, "It is a systematic investigation of some phenomena . . . by the experimental method of discovering facts or coordinating them as law." In these definitions there are certain words that need to be brought out and to be emphasized, "diligent, studious, and systematic." However, if only the elements of diligence and system are essential in research, then the persistent individual without imagination or ingenuity would be put down as the greatest of the mighty. Above all diligence and systematic study, the chief requirements in modern research are imagination and ingenuity. University men are so impressed with the necessity of research that too often the form is taken for the real essence of such activity. As a result of this mistaken exertion a type of investigation has developed that throws on to the educational world much expended effort in the matter of useless publication.

In research what is worthwhile depends upon the selection of the problem. If the person who attempts to select the problem does not know the field, he is bound to come to disappointment; particularly is this true in the case of young workers. Every graduate committee knows that this happens many times with the result that a year's work must be thrown away. Along with the selection of the problem the research worker must have absolute honesty of purpose. Any man who attempts to disguise the facts or pull them around to a previously determined theory is bound to do harm to science and to education. Research requires honesty of purpose and loyalty to the science in which one works. There must be some comprehension of the problem with a clear determination not to force it or to compel it to come within the scope of a limited discussion. It is essential then that the man who undertakes research shall be honest with himself, with his science, and with his problem.

Nor is it necessary that all research should be practical. The history of science is full of surprises, and many an insignificant problem in the realm of pure science has turned out to be a great principle capable of vast values. In fact, most of the great dis-

coveries of the world have been made without any purpose of applying them to some practice. True wisdom, therefore, prompts
the student engaged in research to remain in the realm of principle,
to search for the fundamental, and to abide by the laws of science.
He must also be willing to apply, wherever it can be done, the
harrowing process of elimination and to throw aside the experiments over which he has labored long and hard if they are found
not to comply with application of principle. In the laboratories
and work rooms of science, principles have been applied to practical problems, and mere guesswork has been put aside as the honest
way to a conclusion. Hence, it would appear that research bears
hard indeed upon the man who is insincere and who is impatient of
sound work and of thoroughgoing methods.

It has been fairly well shown that there are very few men who
possess both the power of teaching and the capacity of carrying on
research; yet a very close relationship exists between teaching
power and ability to find the truth. In our graduate schools, the
man of research, though he has no desire to teach, can find a con-
genial atmosphere of study. His interest may not be in the students,
in which case he should be given an opportunity to attempt to
arrive at the goal of his science. Nevertheless, the fact remains
that good teaching depends upon the constant refreshment of the
man who is engaged in it. Just as soon as he begins to feel jaded,
to look upon his material as old, and to come into a feeling of tolerance with his accumulated notes, that man is on the road to poor
teaching and to loss of power. Teaching is a great force and, like
everything else, it must have materials; if these materials are not
supplied by constant additions, teaching will lose its inspiration.

The teacher who has not been able to carry on investigation and
research is, moreover, likely to be at the mercy of any kind of educational faker who may present some new scheme or some new
consideration in the intellectual field. This has been illustrated
more than once in the visit of book agents to college communities.
A man in the field of science would never think of buying a book
with little or no standing in the scientific field; but the man who
is unacquainted with history or literature will buy many a book

that should not have a place on his library shelves because he has no testing standard. Furthermore, the teacher without interest in research may become so hidebound and set in his own world that his mind is not receptive to new ideas and discoveries.

The same sort of thing applies to the teacher who, having little or no knowledge of the modern methods of investigation and research, finds himself unable to apply that discrimination of judgment which makes good teaching and which produces intellectual interest in students. As I have observed the development of faculties and the presentation of educational work in classes, I believe it is essential that every teacher should have a problem to work upon—a problem that will keep him fresh in methods of procedure and make him a bigger man as he goes on with his study.

One of the disasters against which the university must be on its guard with zealous care is a tendency of teaching bodies to become mediocre. This tendency can be prevented by the injection from time to time of new personalities of high grade in faculty groups and by the fact that every member of a faculty has before him some worthwhile problem in his particular field. As he touches the fountains of knowledge anew, he feels an inspiration that is constantly added to and magnified. In his teaching work this inspiration is felt by both the teacher and the students.

Research therefore, to my mind, is one of the great important factors in university life. It assists the university in carrying out one of its reasons for being; and also, because it is the basis of good teaching, research is verily the life of the university.

The University and the Development of Agriculture

Address at the inauguration of President Lotus D. Coffman,
University of Minnesota, May 15, 1921;
published in *The University and the Commonwealth* by the
University of Minnesota

NOTHING is more pathetic in the history of education than the early attempts of institutions to comply with the conditions of the Morrill Act as they were understood in the early seventies and eighties of the last century, unless it is the pristine efforts of psychologists to drag their subject from the "science of the soul" to the higher land of a real analysis of human functions. Without any guide, for there was no science of agriculture, the early builders of these institutions established schools in imitation of those already existing and set up courses of study that were closely akin to the secondary schools of the time. In order to impress the public with numbers, the emphasis was laid upon the type of school that would appeal to the many. Content with this view of their functions the agricultural colleges of the land for the first twenty years of their history drifted along with little or no instruction in the field of agriculture as we know it today.

With an occasional exception, the great patrimonies of public land were sold for a mere song, and the proceeds filtered away in the construction of ugly buildings devoted to the housing of departments of language, mathematics, and the other highly respected subjects of the old-fashioned curriculum. The teacher of agriculture was faced with a difficult task since science failed to provide him with the data required for satisfactory instruction.

The establishment of the experiment stations in 1887 had an immediate influence in widening the vision of, and adding new content to, the courses in biology, physics, and chemistry. Coming as they did when the Central West was passing from small grain agriculture to diversified crops and animal husbandry, the experiment stations had a marked effect upon the teaching in the universities and colleges associated with them. Nevertheless, time was required to enlarge courses of study and to bring the standards of teaching up to a college level, not to mention a university plane. Only during the last twenty years, therefore, has the university idea of research found its way into agricultural instruction.

Meantime agriculture as a great industry has forged ahead, bringing problems to the state universities faster than they were able to solve them. So rapidly has this movement gone on that it threatens to outrun the financial and administrative capacity of the state universities and agricultural colleges to deal with it. In addition the rural delivery, the consolidated schools, the agricultural press, and other agencies have raised the standard of country life and created a clientele among the farmers of the land who may safely be counted as more progressive and intelligent than any other industrial group. This in itself widens the problem and forces upon the state universities and agricultural colleges the necessity of really doing research and giving instruction of an unusually high character to meet the needs of the people.

Within the memory of all of us, agriculture has passed from an individual status to an industrial one demanding business organization, careful statement, and application of scientific principles. That such an evolution should have taken place in so short a time, now that we review it from present day vantage ground, was to have been expected. Looking forward to the next twenty-five years, the universities can not have any excuse for failing to meet the situation. If the scientific principles then known could have been applied twenty-five years before they were, the advance in national prosperity would have been almost unbelievable. It appears, therefore, that the obligations of the universities to the fundamental industry of agriculture are compelling, necessitating the application of vision, courage, and knowledge to the problems of today.

It is not necessary to insist that agriculture is the foundation upon which rests the welfare of a great industrial people. Although that fact is accepted, it might be well to emblazon on college walls the words of Daniel Webster:

The cultivation of the earth is the most important labor of man.

Unstable is the future of a country which has lost its taste for agriculture. If there is one lesson of history that is unmistakable, it is that national strength lies very near the soil.

Such statements do not solve the problem of the university's relation to agriculture; they only tend to bring it out in bold relief.

The time has come, however, for the administrative bodies of the state universities to grasp the full meaning of Daniel Webster's comment. That they have not, I think, can be fairly well demonstrated. With a few exceptions the agricultural colleges are somewhat isolated parts of the university organization. The emphasis upon the needs of expanding professions has brought many problems to the universities in the form of greater plants and new schools of law, medicine, engineering, and education. Also the constantly growing student bodies have clogged the machinery of administration and directed the attention of university heads to housing, welfare, and construction to the possible neglect of agriculture. When this is said, it is not to be understood that no progress has been made but rather to be deplored that the development of agricultural courses and of investigations has not kept pace with the growth of the industry or of the universities themselves.

I do not go so far as to say that there is a crisis in agricultural instruction today, but I know that we are close to a period of depression if not actually in it. Obviously the universities are by no means keeping pace with the needs of the industry in the presentation of scientific data and the teaching of principles. An inquiry among those best informed on the status of agricultural extension will disclose the somewhat general impression that agricultural extension has slowed down all over the country. Although good results are being obtained, they are not fully commensurate with the time or money expended. This condition is due first to the lack of well-trained men to fill the positions created by the Smith-Lever Act and second to the absence of scientific data needed to supplement the work in the extension field. The informational course of instruction has all but spent itself, and the extension worker finds that he needs scientific data of a specific character if he is to enlist the interest of the farmer.

Both the training of men and the explanation and accumulation of scientific data are university functions of the highest order. The first of these requires a staff of able teachers, highly skilled and thoroughly acquainted with modern problems. Such staffs are a rarity due to the drawing of able men into government and managerial positions at salaries higher than the universities pay. The result is a dearth of men for the positions in agricultural teaching including the extension field. The second, the accumulation of scientific data, is quite as important. It was the intent of the Hatch Act to make the experiment station research organizations capable in their staff and equipment of dealing with agricultural problems in a really scientific way.

Much valuable work has been done by the stations and is being carried on by them today; nevertheless, there is a gradual dropping back in agricultural research among the agricultural experiment stations. This disturbing situation is the result of insufficient support. Up to 1914 the states increased the funds so designated to meet the federal appropriations, but since then they have not added to the aggregate amount despite the difference in purchasing power of the dollar in 1914 and in 1920. This failure to appropriate for the experiment stations may be accounted for in the new demands upon state legislatures through the Smith-Lever Act, vocational education, and the federal roads expenditures. The old story of the hide is applicable; there is just so much of it, and, when used for shoes, it cannot be made into a coat to keep out the wind.

Another incubus rests upon the stations and their work in the form of police and regulatory duties that take the time and energy of directing officers. Many of the stations look after the regulations of seeds, feeds, fertilizers, drugs, the licensing of creameries, the keepers of bees, the planters of orchards, and the sale of nursery stock. All of these are worth doing, but, when saddled on a research institution, they act as the Old Man of the Sea on the back of Sindbad, the Sailor. The list is not completed with this recital. On the other hand, the agricultural colleges so closely associated with the stations find that the station men can be used for teaching oftentimes more extensively than is desirable for the best work in the colleges or the stations. So the research work is hemmed in by lack of funds, regulatory and police duties, and teaching functions. Thus the source of agricultural information is clogged, and the whole system of instruction is affected, by the conditions existing in the research field.

Nor am I certain that agricultural education is received into the full fellowship of the university faculties. This is not due to intention but to a lack in appreciation of the problems of agriculture. Moreover the other faculties feel that, because agriculture strongly emphasizes the practical, it must of necessity lose sight of the principles of science. Certainly agriculture must have all that physics, chemistry, and biology can contribute if it is to meet the problems with which it is confronted today. It needs, however, the sympathetic appreciation of its difficulties by the chemist, physicist, and biologist and the willingness on their part to assist specifically in the work of instruction from the agricultural point of view.

It is not to be assumed that agricultural colleges, organized separately, are solving their problems more easily. I am sure the history of agricultural education has demonstrated the error of that view. Agriculture as a science and as an industry needs the university idea applied to its problems with sympathy and vision.

With this statement of the situation within the university, we may turn to the agricultural conditions in general. I have already called attention to the existence of a highly intelligent farming population, intent on the whole in bettering their condition and improving the industry. The change in world markets since the signing of the armistice has intensified the economic situation and made the farmer keener than ever to secure an adequate and satisfactory disposal of his products. He is turning now to real business proposals, based upon sound principles, for relief in a highly difficult situation. Political devices have been found wanting. He is anxious to secure the benefit of the advice and help of trained economists who can direct him in the organization of the sales side of his business. He has learned that the local efforts to suppress production have no bearing on the markets of world commodities, such as agricultural products; hence the farmer is calling for leadership, organization, and information that will make it possible to create for agriculture a modern industry replete with banking, marketing, and transportation facilities. The problem is enormous, but it must be solved if the country is to rest upon a sound industrial basis.

Other problems are pressing for solution in addition to the great one of market organization. The perishable products of the farm are too often lost by lack of transportation and by delay in harvesting due to weather conditions. Such losses spell disaster, but dehydration or distillation with comparatively little difficulty might be used to save food products or to utilize damaged crops for the manufacture of spirits.

Again the destruction of animal parasites would be a boon to the cattle industry, but little progress has been made in this direction. There is likewise a great need for new light on the problems of breeding, but the animal husbandry experts stand in about the same place that they occupied fifteen years ago. All of these matters are really laboratory questions to be worked out by careful research methods requiring the university point of view.

Perhaps no other effort would bring as great results as the issuance of information at regular intervals on the supply and prices of agricultural products. The government has established bureaus of information that send out the news regarding the condition of certain crops, but the farming industry is not well equipped with price information. The consequence is that the farmer acting on meager news or on instinct fails to get the results that the better organized and equipped manufacturer and business man obtain.

In most industries brands and standards are well established, but outside of wheat and cotton this is not the case in the sale of agricultural products. In the South a long discussion went on during the fall months with the purpose of securing cooperative action in cutting down the acreage of tobacco. But no agreement was reached due partly to distrust and partly to the need of a money crop. Since then the discussion has turned to better grading and marketing methods for tobacco. Progress is hampered by the lack of information and extensive knowledge in regard to the tobacco industry. A solution can be worked out and probably will

be, but it is necessary to have the cooperation of economists, bota-
nists and plant experts, the press, the farmers, and the buyers of
tobacco.

What I am trying to intimate is that the university has in this
problem, as well as in others, a real duty to supply the technical knowledge. Foresight on the part of the universities of the
states where tobacco is raised would have provided this information when it was needed; but the very restrictions upon experiment stations in the lack of funds and in extraordinary duties in
many fields have acted as checks in the presentation of the information now so greatly valued.

It appears then that agriculture cannot be developed through
short periods of time because the problems of the industry are of
long time, extending over decades rather than years. The work
which has been done is largely in the nature of marking out short
time problems. In fact most of the research now carried on in the
universities is conducted by the laboratory man who has set himself
a definitely narrow problem that touches here and there the fringe
of agriculture. This procedure is undoubtedly necessary, but the
wider aspects of agriculture must be grasped by the university
in order that the research may be conducted as a whole and not by
the piecemeal plan. Without doubt the future development of
agriculture depends upon the sympathetic cooperation of the university in organizing the scientific work as a group problem. That
the university will take over agriculture or conduct the business
side of agriculture is not to be thought of; however, the university
must provide the scientific data for the uses of agriculture at the
time when such data are needed.

Agriculture is in a constant flux; it never stands still. The soil
changes with every crop, and the population moves and shifts
as the agricultural basis of national life is modified. The university must be ever on the alert to ascertain the effects of the forces of
nature on this great industry and to bring to bear in solving its
problems the resources of the departments of botany, physics,
chemistry, biology, economics, and history. In the matter of agriculture the state is indeed the campus of the university. Satis-

factory results cannot be obtained by the present method of individual efforts and problems in the laboratory. Agriculture must be considered in its entirety, and its needs must be studied. Research should be definitely organized to meet the immediate demands of demonstration agents in the field, to answer the requirements of courses of study in the colleges, and to develop unknown resources that will anticipate the conditions of the future.

The University of Minnesota was pioneer in agricultural instruction and research. The work of men like Hays, Green, Snyder, Haecker, and Boss was outstanding in plant-breeding, creating of new varieties, and development of the creamery industry. For some time now, Minnesota like the whole country has been so busy with extension that research has been neglected. Accumulated knowledge has been drawn upon, and the new sources have not been investigated. Upon the university rests the very clear duty to restore the experiment station to its real function, to enlarge its vision of the great service that can be rendered to agriculture, to raise the instruction to higher efficiency, and to recognize that the training of men for the field of agricultural research is one of the greatest tasks that a university can undertake.

Cooperative Industrial Education

Summary of speech to the
Institute of Meat Packing, Chicago, Illinois, October 22, 1924

O N E of the most interesting and significant discoveries in modern times is that of education by industry. Recognition and acceptance of the principles involved require careful consideration of the possible outcome of a cooperative relation between the two since this relationship implies a probable modification of the ideals of education and a marked change in the administration and objectives of industry. That both may be greatly benefited by cooperation is undoubtedly true. Since neither the idealism of the one nor the practical results of the other must be materially altered, industry should recognize completely the ideals of education and those in charge of education should accept the practical viewpoint of industry. It is truly refreshing that a conference such as this, initiated by industry, is considering the question of cooperation with education. Plans presented heretofore have been almost entirely from the academic side.

The rapidly increasing growth of industrial organization has created an immense demand for executives and scientists who have an educational background. The old system of developing the executive through individual experience has lost its effectiveness because, in the passing of the man, nothing was left for the organization, and consequently a rich heritage of experience did not get into the training process of the industry. In addition, the rule of thumb has gone, and an industry stands on a scientific basis both in its management and in its production.

Cooperation in education and industry has been tried in various colleges and universities. One of the most noted is the University of Cincinnati plan. This scheme was developed for the preparation of engineers. It had as its basis the need of, and the difficulty of procuring equipment by the University. Under this plan the student spends a period of his time at the University and another corresponding period in the industry. Without doubt, this method brings real engineering problems for solution to the classroom, it places the student in touch with positions, and it enables him to earn while getting his education. On the other hand, it has disadvantages in that adjustments and rearrangements must be made several times each year and the college course is lengthened to fifty-five months. Nevertheless, it is regarded as a successful experiment.

In some of the industries, notably in electrical engineering, apprentice schools have been established for college students. Although these schools have had a marked influence in developing their students, they should be actually more closely related with the college course. In communities where industry flourishes extensively enough to call for a number of apprentices each year, courses have been maintained in high schools in cooperation with shops and factories. The difficulty here again has been in obtaining supervision over the factory instruction. Other plans have been tried in the way of continuation schools which provide instruction for persons working in the industry during the day.

The proposal to establish an institute to be supported by the American Packers Association is an attempt to unite the elements of cooperation in college, continuation schools, and research.

In these various arrangements the word, "cooperative," is used to describe a method of providing courses for colleges and schools in association with shops and factories. Most of these projects have had in mind the aid that can be given to the students through their earnings as apprentices and also the reduction in expense of equipment in shops and laboratories. These plans only incidentally touch business organization.

For cooperation to be effective, it is necessary to unite the ideals of education with the purposes of industry, but the difficulty is that a given educational institution can take on only one or two industries at the most. The institution is not sufficiently financed and is not large enough to enable it to cover many industries. Moreover, if any widespread cooperation is to exist between business and education, the plan necessarily will have to be restricted to the cities and towns where such institutions exist. The question of the instruction of lecturers and teachers of industrial subjects in this cooperative plan must be answered. These must be trained also in the business of teaching.

Cooperative industrial education encourages students to enter vocations and gives them a knowledge of the requirements and needs of industry that nothing else can give. Such teaching plans ought to be supplemented by the creation of fellowships and scholarships both by colleges and research laboratories. No limit can be set to the possibilities of this relationship if sympathy and understanding exist between the university and industry. Unquestionably the principles of education should assert themselves in the instruction that is given, and the function of the university itself should be clearly apprehended and understood by industry. Upon the university must rest the necessity of appreciating the problems of industry. These are really the bases of cooperation in the plan of the Meat Packers Association. There is good ground to hope that the foundation now laid will develop into an effective method of instruction.

Education in Relation to Industry

Address at annual dinner of the
Southern Division of the American Mining Congress, Louisville, Kentucky,
March 17, 1931; published in *Kentucky Progress Magazine*, April, 1931;
reprinted in *Kentucky Alumnus*, February, 1932

IN THE MINDS of many, I have no doubt, there is no specific relationship between education and industry. If, however, I can show that the two are closely connected, I shall be satisfied with the opportunity and the occasion.

Let me ask you to think of a definition of education. When the word is used, what is in your mind? What associations does it bring up? Does it suggest a process closely related to life and one which concerns you during all your days?

To some people education is the acquirement of a mass of knowledge, and in their opinion that man is educated who knows a great many things. The old definition of science was a body of classified knowledge; this definition of science is no longer accepted by the scientists themselves for it is as old-fashioned as the early automobile appears to modern users of that form of transportation.

Another group thinks of education as precepts and axioms which the student learns for the purpose of guiding his own conduct and behavior. In the accumulated wisdom of the world the supposition is that there are enough precepts and axioms to guide us in what we do, and the acquirement of these is education.

There is, however, another view which looks upon education as an evolving process. Education might be defined as the growth and development of the inquiring mind. If this view is accepted, education is not the accumulation of a great mass of knowledge or the memorizing of precepts and axioms; it is rather an attitude that has to do with the acquirement of an intellectual curiosity. Science in relation to this view of education is not classified knowledge but a procedure, the technique and method of dealing with problems in every field.

If, then, education is the development of the inquiring mind, it has a very definite relationship to industry because industry today is confronted by vast problems that are scientific, economic, social, and technical in character. The solution of these problems can only be gained by placing the facts for analysis before the inquiring mind. In that way progress is made, and every new step in the sphere of industry has a foundation upon which to rest.

This country of ours has passed through interesting material progress. Waves of population have swept across its plains and mountains; the frontiers have rolled westward, one after another, until the last frontier is gone. In that pioneer period lasting almost to the close of the nineteenth century, the problems were largely in utilization of natural resources for refinement of method was unnecessary. But now a great many difficult and serious questions have arisen in the field of industry. It has been found that physics and chemistry, biology and geology, all have contributions to make to the scientific phases of industry. In fact, industry depends upon what these physical sciences are able to develop. It is hardly necessary to refer to the progress that has been made in the radio and the chemical industry, to say nothing of many others that improve and increase only as the factors that are involved are scientifically understood and studied. Competition between groups as well as between nations has brought the trained man into an important place in the field of industry. Corporate organizations have built vast laboratories in which scientific men labor to find out those things that will be of value to their business enterprises.

But modern problems of industry are not limited to the contributions which are made by science; they carry over into economic and social fields as well. This statement may be illustrated by reference to the question of transportation. We have built many roads in this country; nowhere is so extensive a road system to be found as in the United States. To say, however, that we have solved the transportation problem is to claim more than anybody is willing to accede. Even the character of roads and road-building is not yet determined. And, when the movement of traffic is considered, there is much confusion of thought concerning it. We are just now entering into the matter of interstate control of motor traffic. All of this means that it is necessary to find the facts and then to analyze them in order that we may come to our conclusion. This is the scientific method.

The illustration might be further extended by reference to problems of organization, of marketing, and of salesmanship. The recent depression in this country shows very clearly that much is to be done in the field of banking; rural banking, for instance, has in a large measure broken down, and we have yet to build up a satisfactory system of financial assistance to agriculture. Along with the questions of marketing and salesmanship, the heavy costs of getting the products to market militate against higher standards of living and against happier conditions among the population.

In the social field many adjustments are to be made. We have just begun to work with employment insurance. The country as a whole is much agitated over unemployment and over the difficulties which follow in its train. Old age dependency is another factor. Industry is confronted, therefore, with social as well as with scientific and economic problems. What are we going to do about these matters? All of this discussion brings up the subject of education. The inquiring mind is needed to pry into these problems, to look at them, to get the facts, to analyze them, and to come to conclusions. Then in turn these conclusions must be tested by experience, must be reformed, and finally must be used in establishing any procedure.

In what I have said thus far it appears that many social, legal, and economic problems confront the different states in this country. Theorizing about them will not get us anywhere. Half-baked proposals will not solve difficulties. The first step is the finding of the facts.

In every state with four exceptions, there is a state university. Such institutions were established by the people of the commonwealth to carry on certain functions. One of these and the one most obvious to everybody is the instruction of the youth that gather upon the campus of the institution. Little by little new activities have been added. Provisions through acts of Congress and the state legislatures have made the state university an important agency in experimentation and the organization of agriculture. The function of studying facts, however, calls us beyond this point of agriculture. A state university should be and generally is a free agent. It ought to be the institution to which the people may look with confidence for the finding of facts and for their interpretation.

The administrative duties that are placed upon courts and upon state, county, and municipal officers are so great that they have no time to work at the fundamental facts underlying many problems. Yet the solution of these problems depends upon the knowledge of the facts and the understanding of them. A state university ought to be the agency through which the people of the commonwealth can come into the knowledge of the truth about resources, economic problems, and social questions. In many states something of this sort has been done, but in the long run much more will have to be done if we are to deal with the difficulties which confront us.

Mr. Herbert Hoover several years ago gave as the reason for the unprecedented advance of industries in the United States the fact that college graduates are recruited into the industries. These men have contributed new attitudes and on the whole a higher type personnel than could be obtained from any other source. Industry, complicated as it is today, needs the products of education. It needs the inquiring mind. Many of the present problems which confront industry are not like those of the nineteenth century; they are social problems the solution of which requires the gathering of information, the analysis of it, and the testing of the conclusions by extended experience.

The University of Kentucky has maintained for some years a College of Engineering. The purpose of that college is not so much to develop technical men as to lay a broad foundation in order that, when the student graduates, he will have discipline, training of mind, and an attitude of curiosity toward the problems with

which he may be confronted. This school has been highly successful in placing its graduates in industries, but unfortunately the vast
majority of the students must find their employment outside of
the state. In other fields the University of Kentucky prepares men
and women to enter industry as well as the professions, but those
who are trained in chemistry, physics, bacteriology, and so on must
go elsewhere for their occupations.

Kentucky is confronted by numerous problems. The progress
which we shall make in the future depends upon our understanding of these problems, and the understanding of the problems
rests upon the gathering of the facts and the analysis of these
by the inquiring mind. The University can be and is of assistance
to public officials and to members of various callings throughout
the state; it should be looked to more and more often in dealing
with questions involved in the welfare of the commonwealth and
of the citizens. In the nineteenth century to get along fairly well
without technical knowledge was possible, but in this century technical knowledge is the foundation of development and growth.
The inquiring mind must be put to work upon our state problems,
social, economic, legal, and technical. This is education in use. It is
the answer to the relation of education to industry.

Questions Before the Southeastern Conference

President's address to the Southeastern
Athletic Conference, University of Louisiana, February 9, 1934

THE Southeastern Conference meets today for the second time.
The first year of its history has passed with little more to be reported than the adoption of organization plans, the making of
schedules, and a few decisions about charity games.

The purpose in the creation of the new Conference was to reduce the number of members to a more workable group contained
in a smaller geographic area. Another purpose was to place the
direction of athletic matters more directly under the management

of the presidents of the institution members and by such action to secure an understanding of the problems confronting the Conference and of the procedure followed by the members.

The appeal addressed to the several universities when the new organization was under consideration was for progress in athletic matters. Rumors then in circulation were to be carefully sifted, and necessary reforms were to be inaugurated. With that in view the presidents of the institution members met in Atlanta and adopted a constitution and by-laws. Taken as a whole, these measures showed some advance particularly in the eligibility rules and in the administration of funds for the aid of students.

Nevertheless, it is difficult to find out what is happening. Every member of the Conference, it is alleged, has violated eligibility rules and has failed to report in full the use of funds to help students interested in athletics. An inquiry from my office to each president brought replies from every member except one. These replies vary much in frankness; however, taken rather broadly the general attitude is that no faculty committees administer any funds that are specifically used for athletic purposes. Yet the rumors still persist. For my information and your amusement I have listed the different methods that are said to be followed in this association to assist student athletes.

In making this list of assistance procedures used by members of this Conference, I am not attempting to identify the institutions with specific activities or to bring charges against the group as a whole or against any of its members. I am merely attempting to formulate the procedures as they have come to me by conversation, newspaper comment, and some correspondence. My purpose is to set forth the different schemes followed in this Conference in "taking care of students" who participate in intercollegiate contests. This support is maintained by three distinct agencies: the institution, itself; the alumni; boosters' clubs and other organizations.

The various methods of carrying on institutional support direct or indirect in the subsidizing of individuals on athletic teams may be classed as four in number. The first consists of the giving of straight scholarships to athletes usually with some academic requirements. These scholarships are always described as having no relation to the matter of athletics and as being granted on the basis of merit and ability. The second type of assistance comes from the granting of jobs, more or less arduous, on the campus of the institutions and the obtaining of employment for promising athletes in industrial plants or public enterprises. The third is concerned with provision for the lodging of students who have places on athletic teams. The maintenance of these dormitories and lodging places in gymnasiums and elsewhere is provided out of institutional funds, by gifts, or from athletic receipts. The fourth method consists of actual money from activity fees used for the support of athletics in general. This fund is often administered by a faculty committee and is used to provide tuition, room, board, and books. More fortunate institutions have sometimes from cooperative stores large receipts which are divided among many activities.

So much for the institutions themselves. There may be other methods which have not been brought to my attention, but in the main I think the list above covers them.

We turn now to alumni activities. These are difficult to ascertain. Alumni are solicited for funds by a committee for whom the authorities of the institution have no direct responsibility. Individual alumni may make provision for some promising boy to come to the university. Obviously, little can be said on this score in one way or another. Funds obtained from alumni may be administered by members of the faculty or by an alumni committee.

Another agency, boosters' clubs, has no connection with the institution. These may be chambers of commerce or specifically organized boosters' clubs. They solicit funds and distribute them directly to the athletes. The procedure is even unknown to the university, and the methods followed are concealed from the athletic authorities. The dangerous phase of this method of subsidizing athletes is the collection of funds by outside agencies and the distribution of them by individuals who have little real knowledge of the institution.

How far these procedures are followed in the Southeastern Conference is as well known to you as it is to me. Rumor is probably considerably exaggerated, but undoubtedly one or more of these practices may be found in every institution.

At the last meeting of the Southern Association of Colleges and Secondary Schools, a resolution was passed calling upon members of the organization to give certain information concerning students who have places on the football teams. One of the problems which confronts this Conference is so to conduct its affairs both as a group and as individual members that criticism from the outside may be reduced to a minimum. The only way that such criticism can be avoided is to abide by the regulations of the Conference not only in the letter but in the spirit. The institution members should give to these regulations the benefit of the doubt when a question about a situation arises; in fact, the rules should be adhered to strictly and should not be put aside for any individual case. Dubious procedure in athletic matters surely means lowered morale on the campus. The maintenance of ideals in the student body not only in times of victory but in times of defeat is all important. This fact should always be kept in mind.

I am quite certain that in the long run intercollegiate athletics as a separate organization in our institutions will result in a breakdown because of difficulties with coaches and the persistence of the question of policy and procedure. Sooner or later those institutions that have not already done so will find it necessary to place intercollegiate athletics under the department of physical education. If intercollegiate athletics become merely professional contests, then they stand on the same basis as the professional games which are developing rapidly. In the public estimation, the professional organizations can defeat the colleges. Eventually all athletic contests of our institutions must be made a part of the educational organization, and the coaches must become members of the faculties not merely as figures but as actual participants in their meetings and their policies. This means that the old type of coach will give way to a man of larger vision and of greater appreciation of the educational problems involved in athletics.

Our institutions need to widen the basis of student participation. The use of money for the support of individual athletes would be materially reduced if the enthusiasm of large bodies of students to take part in games was encouraged. Athletics would then be developed because the students really wanted to play. The pressure to recruit would in a large measure be removed.

In regard to recruiting I have a specific suggestion to make: an institution, upon hearing that a representative of another institution in another state is attempting to line up high school football players, should call the attention of the president of the offending institution to the alleged violation of Conference rules. Although the result may be a denial of any infraction, the fact that the query has been made will at least insure caution. If all institutions would refuse support to athletes out of the state, the interstate commerce now going on would be reduced to a minimum.

The problems before this Conference, other than matters of a technical character relating to scouting and recruiting, are largely questions dealing with the enforcement of eligibility rules and the subsidizing of players. What can be done about them?

There is no doubt that little can be done about scholarship requirements unless the institutions themselves maintain and enforce the regulations. I urge upon all the fullest cooperation with, and the careful upholding of, the rules of the Conference.

From the replies received from the institutions in answer to the question about scholarships and grants, it is quite evident that the Conference regulation does not cover the problems involved or that the institutions do not know what is being done by some agency or persons directly or indirectly associated with them. I can but urge that presidents really find out what is going on in the support of student athletes.

The first step in solving this problem is to get the facts and look them squarely in the face. Whatever the methods used, an institution is finally held responsible for them. It is far better that all support of every nature be given over to a faculty committee to administer than that outsiders should be engaged in the practices now rumored to prevail. Can this body be frank and honest about these procedures? I have some hope that it can. The fact that the question has been raised may be a beginning.

The subsidizing of athletes has been closely related to debts incurred by athletic councils for the construction of stadia. To bring large attendance, victories must be won. The box office has pushed for receipts, and receipts depend upon winning teams. In some measure the heavy pull of stadium debts has been removed so that now these institutions are free from old pressures. Is it possible for institutions to play games with teams that come naturally from the student group rather than from recruiting and subsidizing? Has the time come when the members of the Southeastern Conference can disarm?

The University as a Social Agency

Memorandum on the Function of a University

THE University as a social agency becomes in practice a corporate body with rules for its conduct and government. The state creates the corporate body because its citizens believe the results of university operation will aid society in its government, advance the social order, help citizens to enjoy a larger life and assist them to perform their functions as voters, workers, leaders, homemakers, and as human beings. Therefore, the university endeavors to provide general, professional, and technical education so that these ends may be attained.

The importance of general education in the so-called higher fields of learning is great indeed. As a matter of fact, general education must be integrated with the whole of life. In a machine society, the product of barely a century, the problems are immense and extremely difficult. Thus, general education cannot be blocked off in sections but should give the student in the higher schools some conception of the social system in which he lives and of the part he is to play in it; the schools should help him to adjust himself when called upon to begin his career as worker, citizen, head of a family, and social being.

Professional education assumes new proportions in these days of a complicated society. The rule of thumb training of an earlier time that supplied the legal practitioner and medical man is not accepted today; long and thorough courses of study and practice are required by an exacting society. What is true of these professions is true of the others, such as the ministry and teaching. Hence, expert teachers are required, libraries are needed, laboratories have become fundamental, and accordingly larger sums of money must be expended if society is to be well served by her professional men and women.

Our age is called a technical age. It is largely a product of applied science, hence the technician. His training becomes an important part of an educational program. Machines cannot be kept going and new ones made without the technical expert. Because the education of this expert is something new, society, becoming aware of his importance, is beginning to understand the expense involved in the process of making the technician.

But technically trained and professionally prepared men and women, because they are citizens with responsibilities to the commonwealth, the nation, the world, must understand the social order in which they live; for this reason, general education as well as special training must be theirs if proportions and relationships are to be kept and adjusted.

Unquestionably, the university fills an absolutely essential place in the social order. It has done so for centuries. Today the university is not something that may be dispensed with. It is a part of the very life of a people. The way in which it fills this place rests upon the teaching done, the research carried on, the preparation of students, the attitude of the administration, and the support given to it.

As an educational and social institution, the university must touch the various sides of the commonwealth. There are things to be done which fall naturally to it, such as the preservation of libraries and museums; there are many activities that come out of federal and state laws, such as the maintenance of experiment stations and extension services for the people in rural areas. These services are what they are today mainly because of the fact that they are required by legislation. In addition, special groups call for extension services, such as women's clubs, teacher groups, commercial boards, and industrial and technical organizations. Now the demand for more extended adult education programs has become so decidedly vocative that the university is compelled to answer this call.

The need for visual educational facilities is growing at a rapid pace. Schools and the Civilian Conservation Corps are asking for sound films to assist them in the educational procedure. It is natural that such organizations should look to the university for guidance as well as for help in providing films for instructional purposes. The public school administrator must seek this service from the state office of public instruction or from the university. In either instance, a central organization and expenditure of funds are involved.

More and more, state, county, and municipal governments turn to the university for aid in the problems that face them. These problems extend from the form of government and legislative drafting to matters of taxation, police administration, and traffic direction.

As the intricacies and complexities of modern life are better understood, the demands made for help increase until the university is confronted with the question of what to do and how far to go. Administrative officers are holding back from, rather than pushing into, many of these fields that are opening so extensively and so rapidly. Under the conditions of limited plants, staffs, and finances, institutions are compelled to decide upon their major functions.

The lack of comprehension of the new demands and of the great tasks and opportunities before it may result in the university's failure to assume its rightful role with the consequence that the growth and best development of society may be hampered. Undoubtedly the university recognizes the impossibility of lending support to all of the many proposals that are made. The answer appears to be wise selection of interests and sincere cooperation between institutions in order that research, book collections, instruction of a highly specialized form, and various activities may not be duplicated. Because no one institution can meet all of the calls for service that are being made, universities in regional areas are attempting to coordinate their efforts and opportunities.

Finally, it may be said that the concept of education in the popular mind makes little or no distinction between quantity and quality production; institutions are expected to give quantity education on a quality basis. For a century the view has been held by the group in the higher educational field that this quality-quantity ideal can be reached. Recently attempts have been made, not only in thought but in action, to make the distinction as evidenced by special classes for large numbers in a particular field through extension courses and the general colleges. To meet ever increasing demands and to answer many social needs, the university has been forced to expand its staffs, administration and teaching, sometimes to the detriment of the quality purposes of the university. Clarity in regard to the function of a university in an educational system is sorely needed. A university, in the matter of teaching, must concern itself with vocational education; general or cultural education, including what is termed adult education; scientific preparation for research or professional careers; and professional education.

In the development of professional and scientific education, the university is carried into many activities such as hospitals, clinics, experimental stations, child institutes, psychopathic analyses. Why does the university gather so many of these social agencies to itself? The answer is that society has no other instrument to which it may turn to use in meeting its urgent requirements. The university, therefore, continues to expand and in expanding may, because of insufficient funds and because of lack of comprehension on the part of the university staff, tend to make all of its educational offerings quantitative rather than qualitative.

The university is ever ready to be of greater service to the state. Through its faculty, library, research laboratories, the university can be of untold value to the commonwealth. If the people insist that the university meet all their demands in a thoroughgoing, wise, and intelligent manner, then they must in turn be prepared to answer the requests of the university for financial support.

The Practical Value
of Higher Education in the State

Address to the
Council of Associated Alumni, Richmond, Virginia, 1927

FOR more than three centuries Virginia has been a great factor in the contribution of men of genius to the life, growth, and administration of affairs in our land. In this respect the state has stood in the front rank in American commonwealths. But Virginia did another thing that affected the history of the Ohio Valley. Possessed of a large hinterland acquired by royal grant, discovery, and conquest, she gave to the new nation the area from which has been formed a number of the states of the Central West. With such a record Virginia should earnestly strive to keep up her contribution of men and of knowledge to national and state life. From the very beginning her people have had high regard for education. Now they are asking if perhaps certain constituent elements in the development of a state have been overlooked. This meeting, therefore, has been called for the purpose of considering the important matter of the assistance which higher education can bring to the state's welfare and progress.

Consideration of the subject assigned to me is not to be made in the form of a debate between those who attend college and those who receive their education through experience, nor is it to be a discussion of the relative merits of public and endowed education. It does not concern itself with the coeducation of men and women. But it does have to do with education as a factor in the advancement of the commonwealth.

The story of nations and states points out rather clearly that there is a relationship between national growth and educational opportunity. "The educated mind," says one, "is the greatest producing agency in the world without which resources are so much useless material." Every land has its natural resources of climate, soil, waterways, minerals, animals, and plants; out of these by the application of the human resources has come a great mass of artificial or capital wealth such as is found in water power, manufacturing, agriculture, commerce, railroads, banks, homes, churches, and schools. The human resources, the men and women, create the artificial out of natural resources. Only from this cooperation can we have living and homes and industry, and develop law, order, justice, education, and art.

The type of education which exists in Islamic countries is one of memory and of rote. The same is true of education in China where the official classes have developed a high degree of mental discipline devoted almost wholly to the studies of the classic sages and philosophers. These countries have failed to see the importance of applying the inductive principle of reasoning to their problems, and consequently they have continued to live in the same pattern without that development of better living which is found in western lands. Education must be concrete. Since hand, mind, and eye must touch the actual problems, the process of observation, study, experiment, and conclusion comes to be the method by which discoveries and knowledge are made human possessions.

On January 7, 1927, an important and interesting thing occurred. It was the accomplishment of telephonic communication between London and New York by radio. That event is typical of what is happening today. In marked contrast it stands out when compared with the science of a hundred years ago. New problems are arising everywhere, and there must be new knowledge brought to their solution. Thus the chemists told us within the month that the making of liquid coal is approaching realization. What an effect such an event will have upon manufacturing, transportation, and the whole technique of production! With the increase of these problems demanding insight and investigation, men must receive advanced types of training in order that they may be equipped to solve the complicated questions of modern civilization.

Our forefathers who came to the colonies on the Atlantic seaboard were able, ambitious, and effective men. Those who made their way into the wilderness were men of bravery, strong and vigorous, but their needs were simple. A man with a rifle and an ax and a few tools could accomplish wonderful things. He built his home, made his furniture, erected schools and churches, and constructed bridges over streams. The problems which confronted him were relatively elementary. Books and papers were luxuries and not necessities. These conditions are past; today with the world closer together than ever before and with population steadily increasing, the technique of modern life has grown so enormously that improved training is demanded of men to meet the present requirements.

Thus the countries that have recognized the importance of education as an element in national growth are those that have progressed. Scotland, poor as it is in resources and agricultural lands, has produced a mighty race of men who rule everywhere. The Scottish people have always advocated education, and in proportion to their means they spend more upon it than any other country in Europe. Old Bishop Grundtvig in 1847, having seen the fundamental need, established seventy People's High Schools throughout Denmark. The effect upon the peasantry of that land was such as to make them among the world's most intelligent people.

For a nearer example of the workings of this principle, let me call your attention to Kentucky and Indiana. These states of almost the same area have populations that differ in number by about a half million. Kentucky has two and a half million people, and Indiana has three million, but the assessed values of properties in the two states vary enormously. Though the natural resources of Kentucky are much the greater, Indiana has more than twice as much wealth. Certainly the fact that Indiana established a state university a hundred years ago, set up a public educational system before 1800, and created a technical school in 1874 must have some bearing upon the evaluated property in these two commonwealths.

Another instance of this principle of the effect of environment and educational facilities upon the growth of a people is to be found in that rather interesting book, "Who's Who in America." The statistics derived from such a source are not wholly satisfactory, but they do give something of a slant indicative of the present day drift of things. In the 1926 edition there are 24,278 names. Of this number 77.36 per cent are college graduates, 5.85 per cent are high school graduates, 8.38 per cent are persons who had common school education, and 7.13 per cent received their education in seminars and similar educational institutions. In other words, whereas about one per cent of the entire population of the United States are college graduates, three-fourths of all of the names listed in this book are graduates of colleges. A further examination of these interesting data reveals the fact that in five southern states there are 2,303 names. Virginia with 706 names has almost a third of this number; 419 live in Tennessee, 385 in North Carolina, 283 in South Carolina, and 510 in Kentucky. But there are 1,975 persons listed who are residents of Ohio, 2,129 of Pennsylvania, 2,050 of Massachusetts, 3,565 of New York, and 914 of Indiana. Unquestionably the reasons that five states above the Potomac and Ohio Rivers have more than one-half of all the names in the book and the five southern states have slightly less than one-tenth of the names are in the main these two facts: first, the northern states present greater possibilities for obtaining an education; and second, they furnish more opportunities for the profitable use of training after it is completed.

It may be worthwhile to inquire into the difficulties under which the South labors in this matter of education. Although it is impossible in the narrow compass of an address of this kind to deal with all of the phases, there is one which should be pointed out. The history goes back to the English Poor Law of 1588 and its administration in the colonies. This Poor Law Act required every parish in England to take care of the poor by the levying of rates on property. The law was carried to the colonies as a matter of course; however, a little later the problem of educating the children of the colonists arising, the practice of levying taxes for the poor was widened to apply to the supporting of schools.

In Massachusetts Bay Colony, the court decided that the Poor Law Act applied to public education and, in consequence, that all property was subject to a levy for the maintenance of such instruction. But in Virginia the opposite interpretation was made, and it was declared that the only public schools supported by public taxation were those to provide for indigent children. As a result the New England States began to develop their school systems almost immediately, whereas in Virginia, Tennessee, Kentucky, and other southern states public school systems were not organized until the middle of the nineteenth century. Then the Civil War interrupted such growth as they had made, reconstruction followed, and public education was left behind in the movement of affairs.

Likewise in the organization of colleges, New England led in the creation of Harvard in 1636; of Yale in 1701; of Brown, Dartmouth, Williams, and Bowdoin before 1800. In Virginia from 1693 to 1819 William and Mary College, Washington and Lee University, and the University of Virginia were established. In the earlier history of these Virginia institutions, no great public school system existed as a foundation for the colleges. Therefore these colleges did not have the close relationship to public education enjoyed in some of the other states until about the beginning of the 1880's. Meanwhile Virginia had established the Polytechnic Institute and the Military Institute and later had begun a normal school system.

Undoubtedly Virginia could support public education in a larger way than is now done; the evidence points to that conclusion. By ranking the states according to the facts of the federal census, it will be found that the Old Dominion is nineteenth in true value of property, seventeenth in banking, twenty-first in income tax, forty-third in the tax rate, thirty-first in the cost of state government, the same in the support of state educational institutions and in the percentage spent for education. A very much newer state, a state of the Middle West admitted to the Union in 1846, is twenty-third in size, thirteenth in population, twenty-sixth in manufacturing, tenth in banking, tenth in true value of property, twenty-first in the cost of government, ninth in the general property tax levied for state purposes, sixth in the state support of colleges, and first in school attendance. The people of that state believe in education and, recognizing its importance, have provided a support as much in advance of their ability, judging by the statistics, as Virginia is behind in her ability to maintain education.

At present in the states of the Union a great program of education, of transportation, of distribution, and of production is under way that was undreamed of even a century ago. With the passage of years this program becomes more complicated, necessarily so, because of the changes that have taken place in state, national, and world life. Accordingly, there must be an active agency to develop the human resources, to point out the way, and to discover the means of dealing with modern conditions. For the commonwealth to use science and knowledge in its enterprises and in the living of its people is a matter of necessity, prudence, and statecraft.

Without any question an institution of higher education under the maintenance of the state can bring great values to the commonwealth that supports it. Many are the stories that show these real benefits. You recall the Babcock Milk Separator created in the Agricultural College of Wisconsin and the part that institution played in the development and guidance of the dairy industry that is today the largest in the whole United States. The agronomists of Minnesota produced new types of wheat and corn, the School of Mines of that state was of assistance to the Tax Commission, and various departments of the University there have dealt effectively with problems of industry. The value of the work done by schools of medicine is beyond calculation. These are merely instances of what is happening. The state in this twentieth century is under the pressing obligation to supply the trained men and women who are needed for the future; school teachers, ministers, lawyers, doctors, engineers, farmers, business men—all of them, citizens learned in their callings and intelligent in the questions of government—these and many more must be produced for the future.

For two thousand years there have been universities, but only in the past half century have such institutions been closely associated with the lives and problems of the people. That kings and rulers should have recognized now and then the importance of learning was remarkable; on the other hand, that the people, when they had evolved a democratic form of government, should establish the state institutions of higher education was necessary. They believed that the public colleges and universities had the significant functions of teaching the youth and of maintaining libraries and museums where the products of study might be collected and the relics and records of civilization be protected against the decay of time. In this age of ours, research, the search for new truth, becomes a university function and the most important duty of higher education. Publication of the results attained naturally follows in these days of the printed page. The need of adult education reappears in new form, calling upon the college to go beyond the campus to the people who want and require the knowledge of today. Thus four great functions are performed by the public institution of higher education: (1) teaching, (2) maintenance of libraries and museums, (3) research, and (4) the carrying of knowledge beyond the doors of the institutions.

The group gathered here under the auspices of the Council of Associated Alumni is interested in forwarding the greatest enterprise which the state can carry on—that of education. A low type of higher education means in the long run a low type of state. Modern conditions require study, knowledge, investigation, and the use of that knowledge. Unquestionably the people of any state would be enthusiastic to advance as rapidly as they possibly could a system of higher education, if they but had a vision of its accomplishments. The duty of this group of Associated Alumni is to come honestly and ardently to an understanding of the meaning of education in modern life and to carry the message to the people. It is a great cause and a great necessity. If I have been instrumental at all in pointing out the way, I am honored and proud.

A Philosophy for Today:
The University as a Protector of Civilization

Commencement address, University of Cincinnati, June 15, 1934

OUR universities as protectors of civilization must have a philosophy. Moreover, the need is great to point out to the students who come to them the value of education in making life more worthwhile and therefore in building a people who uphold the arts, believe in science, govern themselves well, accept spiritual growth as an important part of life, and look upon living as a human achievement.

The two universities, the University of Cincinnati and the University of Kentucky, are engaged in providing both education and training; the first that through the higher things in life men may find larger enjoyment, better living, and more satisfactory government of their affairs; the second that skills may be brought to great effectiveness in dealing with the needs of a people. Education and training are not the same thing. The difference lies in that education presupposes a wide knowledge and background of human interest as expressed in history, literature, and science; and training indicates skills that have been developed through experiment and drilling. In the future surely every man or woman should have not only skills but also all the education of which he or she is capable. The larger the number of a population with intellectual interests, the greater that population is likely to be in its outlook and attitude on matters of state. In this is comprehended much of the philosophy of education. It is my purpose to enlarge on this point.

Werner Sombart, distinguished economist of the nineteenth century, pointed out a highly important and significant thing in the development of Europe. That this weighty fact had not been noticed before is beyond belief in the present time, but evidently it escaped the writers and thinkers until recently. Sombart showed that the entire population of Europe in 1800 was 180,000,000, and just before the war in 1914 the population of European countries had risen to 460,000,000. Europe, having increased faster than America in population, was faced with the exceedingly difficult task of absorbing these masses of people into the traditional culture. In this statement is the essence of modern European history.

Under the old regime of the eighteenth century and prior to that time, the leaders of the day attained their places by appointment or by birth, and the heritage of Europe which had been built up slowly through the years was held together by a comparatively small group of men in the fields of government and science. The French Revolution was something more than the overturning of a class. It was the rise of the common man and the development of liberal democracy. Therefore the widening of the rights of men coupled with technical knowledge tripled the population of Europe in a century and brought the pressure of the common man against the old regime. Thus is raised the problem of this century: liberal democracy based on popular education must proceed hand in hand with the growth of technical knowledge.

The forces which are making this modern world are scientific experiment, industrialism, and liberal democracy. These have been gained by man through a long struggle of organization, slow growth of knowledge, and the development of technique. The contributions have been made gradually through the years. The question which arises now is: will the common man take for granted the accomplishments that have come in recent years and concern himself but little with the real fundamentals of civilization? Such civilization as we have is based upon invention, construction, organization, and learning. Do these stand out sufficiently to be recognized and accepted by the modern man? What we have today is based upon the will to live in common with restrictions, standards, and courtesy as the bases of justice and reason. The foundations of liberal democracy can only be maintained upon the right of all to express an opinion whether it be the opinion of the majority or of the minority.

The present age is characterized by the presumption that it is superior to all other times, and it looks upon the past with some contempt. In consequence it loses the norms and standards on which past ages have laid much stress. The man of today regards himself as capable of creating anything, but he is in doubt as to what to create. Although we have more means, more knowledge, and more technique than ever before, the world drifts because the mass man, feeling himself sufficient, does not know enough about the processes of civilization and the long and painful road to reach the heights.

Is there a tendency for the great multitude of men to give over their leadership of democracy to demagogues? In Europe are to be seen evidences of the way in which the mass man is likely to act under pressure. Resolved to impose his opinions whether right or wrong, he accordingly favors direct action and the setting up of a dictator who will carry out his purpose. In Fascism and Hitlerism appears a new type of man who will not give reasons and who is not especially concerned about being right but who is interested in imposing his opinions and beliefs. Such an attitude is to be seen in the United States now and then, in the Farmers' Strike in Iowa, in the Milk Strike in New York, and in other evidences of mass action.

In the world of today is needed the truly steadying influence of an agency that links the past with the future and that knows unquestionably how fragile is the flower of science and how necessary it is that learning be fostered. The vital part of the technical development of industry is pure science. The vital part of liberal democracy is education. Both of these live and have their growth in the university. The hope and expectation for liberal democracy and its continuance depend upon the maintenance of support through the agencies of the press, the pulpit, and the school; but behind these will be found the university, which must keep the foundations of modern learning and of modern science as broad as possible.

Such an institution serves the state by explaining, inculcating, and expanding the standards that are set up by civilization. Through the study and research in present science come many techniques and new methods for the advancement of the people. The university is engaged in protecting, preserving, and collecting the evidences of past and present civilizations. It must train the youth in the knowledge of these things and teach him how to find the truth. The university is engaged in teaching creative life; and upon such an institution rest, perhaps more than on any other thing, the continuance, the growth, and the development of social well-being. It brings learning, scholarship, and discipline of the mind to the problems of the day.

This crowding of men into the social organization has brought many problems. The machine has created miracles in the production of goods with a resultant breakdown in the price system. Although the universities continue to teach and carry on research, their knowledge and discoveries are not used fully in our society by government or industry. Moreover, there is going on before our very eyes the creation of a state within a state. In my own lifetime that amazing spectacle has taken place as a consequence of mass production, huge populations, and the inability of the old types of governments to deal with the problems produced by new conditions.

I was brought up on the doctrine of laissez faire. Competition was the soul of business, and the purchaser was presumed to look out for himself. In those days we were taught that we should save in order that we might have money, which is power, and the essence of success was financial. It was declared again and again, that the successful would push the inefficient off the road. So business and industry pursued their own way.

It was not long, however, before numerous problems arose which required some control and direction by the government. The state found it necessary to insist upon the regulation of public service organizations. So little by little were developed the Interstate Commerce Commission created in 1887, the Anti-Trust Act in 1890, the Clayton Act in 1914 giving trade unions freedom from conspiracy, and the Seven Sister Acts relating to the Federal Reserve and various financial matters. With the World War, mass production was pushed to extremes, and the country produced more than it could use. We are all familiar with the breakdown of the distribution system and the closing of the banks about a year ago.

That the let alone policy would have to be modified had been clearly revealed. The government was pushed into extended systems of regulation, as shown in the NRA and various other devices. Now we know, as we never knew before, that knowledge and understanding are required to conduct a modern state. We have found out something about the weaknesses of government; how many of its parts are obsolete, and how many of them function effectively. We are beginning to demand redress from the inadequacy of our police system, the ineffectiveness of the courts of justice, the bungling of business by county governments; and we are seeing the drift now toward city management, regional organizations, and state planning.

Added organizations are made a part of government, but these cannot work without the human being who is both trained and educated to guide and direct. Organization is not all because the importance of human life is to live up to its possibilities. There is need to emphasize success in being a human being. It is necessary to cultivate the power to live and to utilize ability in living. Unquestionably loveliness of life must be fought for just as anything else worth having. The student owes an obligation to the state because, through its agency, the social organization is maintained. The student today must have a philosophy of life which incorporates not only his own position in the world but that of others. He must place a new emphasis on the value of tolerance. Cooperation must become an essential part of his attitude. He must be honest in mind, diligent in action, and he must develop his spiritual resources if he is to be a real citizen.

This modified social state that is upon us requires a conversion of the citizen from his old view founded on the let alone procedure to one from which he looks at the state as constituted of all of us. Some of us carry out the will of all of us for the common good. The citizen of the social state that is forming so rapidly must bring to it a social conscience, a better knowledge of government, and a willingness to throw his lot in with the socially good.

Verily a great task faces the next generation, a task which will demand the finer qualities of mind and heart. From college and university the student should come with an ethical and spiritual regard for the needs of his fellow man. Education means discipline of mind, an attitude of tolerance, and a willingness to work for the general good. The state has a right to expect these benefits, and the needs of society require them. They are the alternative to mob action and mass impulse. Democracy rests upon understanding, and understanding rests in turn upon education, education that will be broad enough to supplement training and to make the welfare of the people the primary purpose in the mind of the educated man.

The University and a Philosophy

Summary of address at the celebration of the twenty-fifth
anniversary of North Dakota Alpha Chapter of Phi Beta Kappa,
University of North Dakota, March 9, 1939

IF ONE is to judge the needs of the day from the discussions in faculty meetings and educational convocations, a primary demand is for an educational philosophy. In search for such a philosophy, I ask you to look with me at the viewpoints of a half dozen men, who have lived from the middle of the fifth century before Christ to the present time. These men taken as evidence of the thinking of their times are Plato, Roger Bacon, John Henry Newman, Matthew Arnold, Thomas Henry Huxley, and Robert M. Hutchins. The latter might be quite surprised to find himself in a list of this sort, but I am justified in including him because his educational philosophy is now being widely debated.

Conditions in Athens were disturbed in the middle of the fifth century B.C. Deficiencies existed in the education then prevailing; much that went by the name of learning was mere quibbling, and little progress was made in the settling of questions. Socrates, introducing the method of inquiry, tested the answers by severe logic before he reached his conclusions. In all that he said, he maintained the view that "vice is ignorance and knowledge is virtue." Plato took the learning and procedure of his mentor and carried them farther, removing verbal fallacies from the pathway of progress. This may be regarded today as one of the greatest of human achievements. He emphasized knowledge against opinion and affirmed that the power of the mind could lead people toward greater perfection. Because to him human improvement rested upon the power and supremacy of the mind, Plato, himself, arrived at the highest place in the cause of wisdom and inspiration.

In the thirteenth century flourished at Oxford a learned man, Roger Bacon, who is now regarded as the real father of science. Bacon held that the attainment of all knowledge is through science and that man is brought to God through knowledge of the external world. Thus mathematics and experimentation are indispensable. The first is the key, and the second the only basis of certainty.

John Henry Newman, an Oxford teacher and later a cardinal in the Catholic Church in the nineteenth century, emphasized the ideal of a gentleman and Christian. Thus a cultivated, intellectual man becomes a useful man. The importance of Knowledge in relation to Learning, to Professional Skill, to Religion, Newman emphasized.

Living at the same time as Cardinal Newman was a remarkable man, Matthew Arnold. He was an inspector of elementary schools for thirty-five years and professor of poetry at Oxford from 1857 until his later days. He believed in the public system of education and even there emphasized the standard, classical Greek view. He was an apostle of culture and maintained that it was desirable to know the best that has been thought and said in the world. He stood out against the emphatic view of Huxley that science was the most important part of education, and pointed again and again to the need of a knowledge of humane letters to establish a way of living and to instruct for beauty in life and conduct. He believed that as science developed and grew more expansive in its teaching, the study of the liberal arts became more necessary to the world than ever.

Thomas Henry Huxley, a contemporary of Newman and Arnold,

had risen to great heights as a student of biology. He asserted that, since Plato's world is not ours, Plato, scorning trades and handicrafts, possessed no conception of a great industrial community; moreover a modern industrial society will and must shape its education not according to Plato but to its own needs. If a handed-down education does not fit the situation, the modern world will drop it and try another. Huxley declared advisedly that if life were a game of chess, we would learn the rules. Also he held the view that science is a part of a whole, and the larger part. Nevertheless, he believed that liberal education was the desired goal to be arrived at through the understanding of science.

So the battle has raged back and forth with, I think, increased emphasis upon science as the center of education. It is here that Robert M. Hutchins, President of the University of Chicago, comes in. I assume that he is not opposed to science as such. He gladly admits that a knowledge of science is needed for culture but declares that literature has contributed most to the development of mankind. He wants students to know what the great books contain. He, however, does not go back to Plato and Socrates as founders of learning, although he insists that they and other scholars of all ages are necessary contributors to education. President Hutchins maintains that the trivium and quadrivium are essential to education in these days as they were in medieval days. The first includes grammar, rhetoric, logic; the second, arithmetic, music, geometry, astronomy. It may be pointed out, however, that, in the days when this program of education was set up, the subjects in the trivium and quadrivium included all of the knowledge of the times.

In his consideration of a university President Hutchins introduces a number of interesting educational processes in the undergraduate college. These are to be found in the development of the comprehensive examination, shorter courses, and the orientation of the student in science, social theory, and literature. The idea of the great books and the procedures referred to are being tested now in the University of Chicago.

That a university should have a philosophy of education, a distinct objective, and a spirit that will inspire it and its students is highly important. In these days of emphasis upon professions, vocations, and various trainings, to formulate a philosophy is difficult, let alone to develop and use it in a consistent way. But it is fundamental that a goal should be erected in order to know the desired course to follow. The philosophy must have a broad basis if the wisdom of the past is to be kept for us. What is the part that liberal education is to play in the university? Can the cultural subjects live in the atmosphere of vocational and professional training and continue to give their values to the enlightenment of a people? That is the essence of the university problem.

At this particular period of university history, it is essential that the cultural subjects shall be strengthened in order that the colleges of arts may not fall to the level of service colleges but on the contrary may become leading agencies that have as their end the extension of beauty and intelligence. The Society of Phi Beta Kappa is particularly interested in supporting this view. The founders of the society and those who have accepted membership through the years have steadily held to the ideal of a liberal education as a basis for further specialized training and as a foundation for a happy and useful life.

May I wish for you and for the University of North Dakota "an increased spiritual activity, having for its characters increased sweetness, increased light, increased life, increased sympathy." And may you continually strive "To render an intelligent being yet more intelligent, and to make reason and the will of God prevail." In these words of Matthew Arnold you have the basis surely of a philosophy for a university.

The High Obligation
of the Land-Grant College and University

President's address to the National
Association of Land-Grant Colleges and Universities,
Washington, D.C., November 18, 1935

GENERAL GEORGE WASHINGTON, shortly retired with many honors from the Army of the Revolution, sat on the wide porch of the mansion house, gazing over the broad expanse of the Potomac. Far away he could see a schooner coming up the bay. As the ship drew nearer, he recognized the vessel as the one he had dispatched from his wharf the day before with a cargo to England. He hastened to the water's edge and strode out on the long dock to hail the master of his ship. The General learned that the vessel had been turned back by the Marylanders, who wanted a tax on vessel and cargo. The indignation of the General knew no bounds. Similar incidents had happened before when commerce passed over the borders of one colony into another, and many exporters were wondering what was to be done.

It is sufficient to point out that the meeting at Annapolis in 1786 was called to remedy the situation that had so irritated the General. When the gentlemen gathered in Old Town, the problem appeared very much larger than a question of trade. It, in fact, extended to many phases of colonial and intercolonial relations. Since the greater wisdom of the Annapolis group saw the implication, a call was issued for a meeting at Philadelphia in the hope that a wide and permanent basis for the relations of the thirteen states might be provided. The result of the meeting was the Constitution of the United States, the outcome of the deliberations of able, brave, and conscientious men who were trying to solve the economic, social, and political situations confronting them and the states they represented.

Our Constitution, now almost one hundred and fifty years old, was thus the direct consequence of many intercolonial problems. The trade between the states was badly hampered by colonial laws and regulations causing difficulties, international threats, and embargoes. When the Constitution was adopted after a lively debate in every part of the new states, Congress went to work to create uniformity of trade regulations, to provide for a currency and banking system, to levy taxes, and to set up the judicial system specified in the document.

Nor have these governmental devices enacted by the early law-makers continued down through the years without many changes; some of them are at present markedly different from the original plan. Through the years the banking project of Hamilton was put aside. A period of chaos followed with a national banking system emerging during the Civil War. The same story can be told about the currency of the country. The national land policy wavered back and forth, resulting in the homestead act which was, after all, a means of meeting an unemployment situation. The War Between the States through force of arms effected an adjustment of government policy; it settled the matter of slave and free labor economics and determined the relation of the states to the federal government in so far as their allegiance to the Union was a matter of dispute.

Since the epoch making period of the War Between the States, many other affairs of vast importance have been before Congress. Wider and wider the range of interstate commerce spread over the nation. The railroad wars of the seventies, eighties, and nineties forced the regulation of rail and water traffic by federal authority. The difficulties of banking created a strong demand for legislation resulting in the federal reserve banks. And now a situation produced by organization of corporations and the sale of securities has brought the government to a rather stringent regulation of brokerage houses and stock exchanges. The chaos of the oil and coal industries indicates, with no doubt in the minds of those who know what is going on, that the government will be called upon by the operators themselves to interfere and regulate the methods of doing business.

I have taken examples from our history here and there. Many other instances could be cited where modifications in law and in procedure have been made. Our national life is full of just such

things. The commerce clause in the Constitution has been interpreted from time to time to meet the changes that have arisen in
industry and business. If there is one thing certain in the history
of our people, it is that a definite trend can be clearly seen in the
enactment of law and the interpretation of courts to build a financial and industrial system that has been of help to the large organizations. The huge industrial structure developed by this trend
reached its greatest dimensions in the first quarter of the present
century. So large did it become that it began to break down in vital
places partly on account of its own size and partly because of the
failure of management. The climax of the system seems to be at
hand, variously prophesied by our seers and prophets to take place
in another decade. The results of our industrial and financial building based upon a century-old concept of social organization are facing a crisis. This will be not in the form of a bloody revolution
but rather in alterations that will fit the organization to modern
requirements. To adapt law and organization to our needs is inherent in the genius of our people.

The center of this change is found in the word, "control." Industry and business build their structures on the foundation of
control by industry and business. The notable economic and political phenomena in this past century have been the increased part
government has in business. It is assumed by some that government has gone into business because it has a predilection to do so.
As a usual thing, businessmen are averse to such action on the part
of government. An analysis of the century's happenings certainly
discloses that government has gone into business because it has
been compelled to do so. The continued and bitter rate wars between
carriers forced the creating of the Interstate Commerce Commission. The oil producers' controversies, the coal industry's troubles,
and the difficulties of the public utility business, to cite but a few
instances, have pushed the government to the taking of a hand in
business. From every village, city, and state come cries for help.
"Regulate this," "Operate that," are the demands and implorings
that go up to the state and the federal government. Many urgent

pleas are for the purpose of trying to save some broken down enterprise, such as railroads, banks, cooperative marketing schemes.

It will appear to anyone who studies the field of human endeavor that much of the machinery of modern life has become governmental. The process by which this transition has taken place has been going on for a full hundred years. The explanation is not so far to seek when it is put in the formula of a student of the corporate organizations. "If business is essential to life, business will be conducted by private enterprise if possible; if it can not be so carried on, then it will be operated publicly." To state the matter specifically: if finance does not meet the needs of the country as it is organized, then it will be reorganized and a new system set up that will meet the needs of the country. Such has been our history, and there is no reason to suppose that the trend will cease.

This being the case, two alternatives are open to the people of the United States of America. One is the pathway that leads to centralization, enlarged government functions, and the acceptance of a nationwide organization. The other is decentralization with many scattered regions and isolated units, each seeking its own justification and endeavoring to build an economy of security even though it may be one of scarcity.

There is no single method that will fit every situation that arises. We should try the procedure that seems wise and prudent with no theory of a despotic state before us as a guide. The system in this country has been one of absorption of business when necessary, which absorption has been brought on by the great forces of an organization which seems unable to furnish the requirements of modern life. I have already indicated how this process goes on. It is apparent to all who read and note the changes that are taking place. The government is asked to assist. Reluctantly it does so. Setting up a control of the business that is being assisted necessarily follows. Now that the government has begun the assistance of railroads, who can doubt that government ownership is on the way?

In the mere process of our economic life we shall be compelled to keep certain businesses going because they are necessary. Since the private owners have allowed them to slump, the government will be forced to revive them and to take them over. These situations can be met by Congress without developing extreme centralization. To a degree, money and credit as essential to the life of the body politic will become a very necessary part of the public business. There are grave dangers from such action, but these dangers can be avoided. A policy of meeting situations as they arise from time to time will carry the nation into larger business. There will, of course, be room for private enterprise, but the public needs which are greater than any private enterprise can meet will be met by a government organization. The recognition of the trends and the needs of our time by a people, working under the law, who revere the rights provided in our Anglo-Saxon parliamentary government should enable us surely to deal with problems as they come up without resort to dictatorships, whether fascist or communist.

What are the tests of these tendencies that are apparent to the economists, political scientists, and political seers? In his report to the president of Columbia University, Dean Roswell C. McCrea, of the Columbia School of Business, said as stated in the daily press: "These tests are reasonably clear: what forms and methods will yield the largest national dividend of goods and services at lowest cost in resources and labor, with the largest practicable individual freedom, both in choice of work and in choice of goods, with the widest possible employment under conditions of security of reasonable livelihood? In a more centralized form of government," Dean McCrea said, "there will be three areas; first, that of direct government control . . . in the railroad industry and other public utilities; second, that of partial government control . . . highly integrated industries such as automobiles, coal and milk; third, the professions and highly individualized forms of work. There will be areas of comparative freedom for individual enterprisers whose effort and planning will be focused on localized performance, with few functionaries in the offing other than tax gatherers, statistics garnerers, and statistics providers. Certain other areas may well be assigned to direct governmental handling. In any case, the area we have entered is one of search for new adjustments of sphere of action between business and government."

I have quoted this statement from a dean of a great university in the largest city of the land to indicate that I am not setting up a straw man to be knocked down by a sentimental statement of social trends. Are we not all agreed that an era has ended and we are now on the way to new experiences, new adjustments, and new relations? America moves essentially in the direction of absorption of private enterprise when, and only when, a necessity arises which cannot be met by the existing organization. The process of decentralization no longer goes on. The drift is all in the other direction with the elimination of separate and isolated units.

The country has moved in the century toward centralized industrial organization and a more concentrated form of government. We may look for the gradual disappearance of small counties and the development of larger administrative areas. Tax systems, both state and federal, will be coordinated to provide revenues without the burdens of double taxation and the annoying practices of revenue collections by duplicate machinery.

The purpose will be to seek those forms of government and industry that will yield the largest national dividend at the lowest cost in resources and labor. With this process, it may be said, the citizen will seek the greatest possible individual freedom as well as reasonable standards of living and economic security for himself and his family. The object is the one expressed again and again in American life, the betterment of the common welfare. In the words of the preamble of the Constitution of the United States the purpose is "to promote the general welfare."

To meet this desirable goal requires more and wider knowledge, a broader efficiency of mind and hand, and the acceptance as a common faith of the need and value of the higher life. Here is an educational program that involves a clear understanding of our own history and of the effect that industry and government have had upon the progress that we as a nation have attained.

I have reached the turning point in my address. Perhaps I should make clear that this summary of our industrial and national life is to establish in your minds and in mine the framework in which the labors of the immediate future are to be undertaken.

Certainly there are numerous questions to be answered and many relations to be adjusted. It appears to me that one group of agencies must bear an increasing part and responsibility in meeting the problems of the immediate future.

Forty-eight institutions have been established under the provisions of the Morrill Act. Nearly three-quarters of a century have passed since the first of the land-grant colleges opened its doors to students. In that time a vast change has taken place in the function, purpose, and effectiveness of these institutions. It is true that the concept of these institutions in their early history was largely that of trade schools; but gradually with the widening of opportunities and the increasing demands for educational advantages the land-grant colleges have expanded in equipment and facilities as well as in understanding of the problems before them. Many of these problems have been confined to production, cultivation of the soil, engineering, and the material tasks that pile up in a rapidly developing country.

Today Americans are brought face to face with a great climactic turn of events. The forms of government and many of the methods of industry at present prevailing are those of a simple organization functioning in a limited scientific and economic world whereas the nation is confronted by a wholly different need from the one that existed even a quarter of a century ago. This being the case, it is important to understand the objectives of the land-grant colleges and the problems that they must meet as the nation comes to the crossroad of national drifts.

Through the years the land-grant colleges and universities have reached the status of an actual arm of the state. Although not fully recognized, this relationship has been established; the flowering of it, therefore, into a helpful factor in government and social organization is but a matter of time. The salvation of the people is knowledge. Knowledge, however, must be truth and not propaganda. Colleges and universities established by the people as an aid to the whole purpose of democracy thus become an agency of democracy. The people will rely more and more for unbiased fact and analysis upon the devoted men and women of the universities who are wedded to the truth and are eagerly working on the problems of the commonwealth. These institutions may enter into a new and amazing relation to the people; they may become the interpreters of the very essence of common welfare and the guides to higher levels of living. Many responsibilities go with such an opportunity.

First of these is the teaching of the youth who finds his way to the campus of the state university or the land-grant college, in order that he may be alert and curious in seeking the intellectual life. It is essential that he shall have ideals and live up to them so that the values of life may have meaning. In a new time his use of leisure will make or mar the future of the social order in which he lives. It is important that he shall know the best there is in the intellectual inheritance of the race. The student, if he is to contribute to better government, must be imbued with the standards of popular rule, knowing its possibilities and its weaknesses. Teaching must go forward in the spirit of freedom without propaganda. It is a great responsibility requiring the very best of the teacher.

In addition to this first task of teaching are many others. The careful study of problems to the end that there may be wise action requires the presence of scholars and experts trained scientifically in the knowledge of the day. This is fundamental to the progress of a modern society. One example may be used to illustrate the point of my statement. The trends of population are basic considerations in making plans for the future. Are we to have a stationary population in the course of twenty-five years with a predominance of age over youth? The query itself raises many issues that are of untold importance to industry, education, and government.

What the social scientist needs are facts and still more facts. When careful and intensive study can bring these to light, then the future may be fairly seen. Systematic gathering of materials in the form of documents, reports, and publications must be made so that the student will have them at hand for his investigations. The sciences have a vast undertaking before them which demands highly trained men with extensive laboratories equipped with instruments and materials. And again there should emerge from these institutions a body of young men and women capable of carrying on the tasks of government and the requirements of business and society. Not only must they have training but they must also have ideals and a deep understanding of the common welfare.

In the last analysis the land-grant colleges and universities should be a source of knowledge on which the people of our land may rely with confidence and with certainty. They must speak the truth and act truthfully. They are in fact through their research and extension services the people's means of finding their way. The people therefore must insist at all times that these institutions be free from political interference. Nor are the leaders and teachers of these colleges and universities to jeopardize their functions and their places in the social order and the political government by partisanship and narrow prejudices. It thus appears that the land-grant colleges and universities have come into a great responsibility and an amazing opportunity.

Was there ever given to any group a function so wide, so important, and so filled with destiny? Were there ever placed upon any human institutions such responsibilities and such privileges? These are shared with privately endowed institutions founded by wise men. But in so far as the people have created the land-grant colleges and universities, just so far is there a direct obligation to serve the people, and this obligation cannot be set aside or forgotten.

Our history has been one of adjustments from the days of colonial troubles and controversies to this very hour. Sometimes we have been forehanded, sometimes almost too late, and sometimes the opportunity to meet the situations arising has gone before we discovered it. There are more agencies today with which to work, but there are also more problems. As in the past we shall have to adapt, change, modify to meet situations. The high obligation of the land-grant colleges and universities is to serve the nation intelligently and wisely in this time of change, as the national trends reach their climax and charts are made for the future.

If General Washington were seated on his wide porch this afternoon of November 18, 1935, looking across the noble river from his Mount Vernon estate to the distant dome of the capitol of a great people, I am sure he would join us in the prayer: "God give us the vision, the strength, and the wisdom to do our part honorably and well. Amen."

The Man and the Building

Address at the dedication of the Agricultural Building, University of Tennessee, November 13, 1937

IN THE dedication of this building a man and an occasion have been brought together. The man is more prophetic of what may happen in the future than is the building.

The man lived as a boy on a farm; his boyhood days, his studies in agricultural schools, and the work which he did in graduate fields, all these gave him a real foundation for the work to be done later. He served an apprenticeship in Louisiana where he rapidly made a place for himself as teacher and investigator. With a gift for making friends, he won appreciation for the work he was doing and steadily widened his influence by the results that came from his use of science, his common sense, and his administrative qualities. The only future possible for a man thoroughly grounded in and devoted to his work was that he should go on as scientist and administrator into larger usefulness. So he became Director of Extension, then President of the University of Tennessee. Now he is a member of the Tennessee Valley Authority. Here his knowledge of the people and of agriculture has been of immense value to the purposes of the Authority. Into all these relationships he has carried with him a love for the land, a concern for the people, and a belief in agriculture as the true bases for the understanding of community, social, and industrial life. Like a missionary of old, he has gone up and down the realm preaching this doctrine.

The building which we are dedicating today is a material thing. It may be nothing more than a warehouse where equipment is placed, materials accumulated, and men come and go. It may instead be a temple filled with the spirit of learning and the wisdom of experience which flow out from the building to all who come in contact with it. In this building experimentation and the accumulation of knowledge will go on year after year, and here students will be taught. But if this Agricultural Building fulfills the hopes that are raised in us today, it will also be a temple where spirit directs and guides, and whence the fruits of the spirit emanate.

Ours is called an age of science, and rightly so. We are dazzled by the amazing results that come from research. We see great production in every field and real progress marking the movement of time. In agriculture much has been done to improve the breed of animals, to provide the rotation of crops, and to hold insects in control; but in all these things there may be an emphasis on agriculture solely as a business. When it is thus looked upon, much has been lost. If agriculture is to hold the place that is hoped in the life of the nation, love of the countryside supported by song, legend, and poetry must be inspired so that men may wish to stay on the land because they are endeared to it. Sincere belief in country living must be justified. Throughout the nation must be demonstrated the blessing that rural life brings to the home and family, and the reservoir of vitality it furnishes to the nation. Scientific research should be employed in all phases of agriculture; in production, in distribution of products, in better living, in more adequate housing, in community organization, in government, and in education.

The agricultural colleges established under the Land-Grant Act of 1862 brought into existence an educational agency that has had an amazing history during these seventy-five years. In the earlier days of this story these colleges had to find their way, and naturally they imitated those institutions that already existed. After the early years the colleges entered upon a period in which great emphasis was placed upon vocational pursuits. In this last third of these seventy-five years the scientific side has received support and has been followed ardently. The information gained from research has been carried far and wide by the great supplementary agencies set up under the federal law. Finally, the results in the matter of living that have come from well-conducted agriculture have received attention.

But in all of this teaching, the spiritual values of agriculture seem to me to be lacking. So far as I know, there is no agricultural college that presents a history of agriculture, none that teaches the literature and art of agriculture, none that emphasizes sufficiently the pride that people may have in the countryside. This problem of bringing to agricultural leaders, and through them to the people, a spiritual conception of country life is altogether as important as scientific endeavor.

The University of Tennessee stands today in a strategic position. It is in the very central portion of the Tennessee Valley area where a great social experiment is being carried on. What is this experiment to be? Is it to be an economic demonstration only, or is it to lift the people to higher levels of living and to better citizenship? Necessarily, the basis of life here as elsewhere is economic; however, the Tennessee Valley experiment can have permanent influence only if with the economic basis it combines spiritual understanding and values. Harcourt Morgan has always held this ideal.

In accepting this building today the University of Tennessee has acknowledged an obligation to protect the building, to keep it clean, and to use it. In naming this building, Morgan Hall, the University is assuming a further responsibility, that of making the building a temple of learning in which will be taught a synthesis of science and living and where will be shown spiritual values as both a means and an end of living. Stemming from the man for whom the building is named, an indwelling of ideals should result in the people who work in it and in the people who benefit from it. The trustees, faculty, and alumni have this grave responsibility upon them. In conferring this honor on Harcourt A. Morgan, the University of Tennessee assumes this sacred obligation which must be fulfilled not only for itself but also for the state as well.

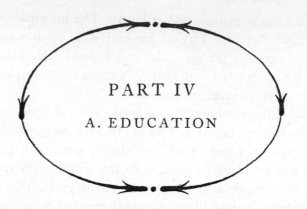

PART IV

A. EDUCATION

Education

EDUCATION is something more than learning; it is in reality using the mental faculties to sift, to organize, and to bring to a conclusion the facts and ideas presented to them. Thus the educated person has such control over his mind that there is an orderly process of thinking with a resultant answer to the problem that is before him for solution. Education is, after all, a matter of discipline; that is, the rule of purpose over mind. One's thinking apparatus can be held to a job if one is really educated. The emphasis is too often, however, placed upon the procedure rather than upon the purpose or objective of education.

Much is heard today about education. Discussion in regard to what education is supposed to do for all who are exposed to it continues unabated.

Those who believe in the interest philosophy assert that one learns about that in which he is interested. Others declare that education is acquired by conning a thing over and over. This is the philosophy of reiteration. Such statements are merely indicative of a process. Education is the control of mind over the thought and action of the individual. The result, which is the test of education, comes from hard work and constant holding to a purpose. Going to school or college will do something for almost anybody; education, however, issues as the result of the will to learn, the determination to think, and the application of the spirit to high ideals. Thus the educated person is one who has his mind and body under discipline, discipline that brings his mind to high thinking and his body to sound living.

The process of education goes on every day from the cradle to the grave. It is essential that what is acquired each day shall be good and have value. Formal education (the education of the schools) is the means by which students are brought in contact with the tools of knowledge, the heritage of the race, and the usages of the society in which they live. If education in schools and colleges is to be significant and far-reaching, effort on the part of students and cooperation on the part of teachers, parents, administrative officers, and the community are basic requirements.

The Purposes of the State in Maintaining an Educational System

Memorandum on the Goals of Education in Our Democracy

THE tendency of most of us is to take things around us for granted. Thus, government, industry, education, and even life itself, as we know them, appear to be matters of fact and evidently, so far as we are concerned, will probably continue forever. Many of us go through the primary and secondary schools, and some of us may even graduate from the state university, without asking any questions in regard to the relationship of the state and the public schools.

Why does a state maintain an educational system and what is the purpose of the individual's education? Speaking in the large, education is a process for preparing human beings for life, and the aim of American education is to produce a definite American social order in relation to a definite world order.

Through education the democratic state tries to provide the means by which each individual may do his best. The democratic state endeavors to develop a people sound in body and mind, an informed people in the plan, purpose, and objectives of the state. It wants to have a people who know and understand their great racial inheritances. It desires a people of integrity who believe and respect the truth. It wishes a people who through their skill and industry will make a livelihood that will result in comfort. It hopes for leaders who have an obligation to duty and to truth in all the relations of life.

Education is a lifelong process. In order to hurry the procedure, instruction through the ages has been given by the elders. Consequently, to think of education as solely of school and college is to give it too narrow an interpretation. Of the 8,760 hours that make up a year, children spend not over 1,000 hours in school; therefore, during the year many other influences are brought to bear upon the pupils. I am saying this to indicate that the tendency to insist that formal education, both public and private, is entirely responsible for the development of young people is erroneous. The schools cannot be held wholly accountable for weal or woe because the other social agencies such as family, church, and community have their functions in ascertaining conduct and motives to an even greater extent sometimes than have the schools.

The goal of formal education in our democracy is set forth above in the purpose of the state in maintaining an educational system. Because the citizen ought to know something of the national life and the part he should play in it, the student who goes to college should be enabled to understand cultural backgrounds including a knowledge of racial heritages. The student ought to comprehend the social order and appreciate the government which administers the affairs of society. In college and in school he should come to an interpretation of procedures and attitudes in the practice of democratic usage. Because of the welter of confused ideas, group propaganda, and ignoble purposes, the student in college and the citizen after college are in danger of not being sufficiently well-grounded to distinguish the shoddy from the real; therefore, a knowledge of fundamental principles and a comprehension of the trends of civilization are vastly important. The understanding of the economic conditions and the social forces at work today is absolutely essential in order that the true processes of democracy may be aided and not thwarted and that the greater good for the greater number may be attained in an orderly way.

The student should learn to adjust himself to people and to institutions. In his heart and mind he should establish a feeling of tolerance for people, for attitudes, and for ideas that are different from his own. He should appreciate the worth and the necessity of courtesy and good manners. A fine sense of values should enable him to recognize the place where adaptability on his part should cease; through "application of ideas to life" the student should know with conviction that at times life must be adjusted to his own ideals. Moreover, the maintenance of health and well-being for himself and for society is an important consideration for the student in formal education.

In pursuing his studies through the use of books, libraries, and laboratories, the student incidentally develops skills that are valuable to him in this day of reports and statistics; he acquires the great gift of concentration; and he learns, among many by-products of formal education, discrimination and proportion. In the attainment of these goals the educational institution guides the student by assisting him in personal and social adjustments and in occupational objectives.

Such are the purposes of the state in maintaining a system of education. The individual may have reached his own standard of education and not have obtained mastery over the conditions of life. We call that individual educated who has used his ability to think, to see, and to accept the truth; who understands and readily uses the opportunity and material given by and produced by the society in which he lives; and who maintains himself in the social order. Education thus becomes a life process and does not end with the four years of college. The individual must apprehend the meaning of civilization and must be master of himself and of his environment to the end that he may live a life equal to his capacities. Education to be effective and forceful cannot be separated into parts. It is a whole. Consequently, the attitude of the state toward education materially affects the individual and the state as well.

Since the future of democracy rests upon the wisdom and well-being of the people, the school and college in cooperation with the community, the church, the family, and the home are potent factors. In maintaining an educational system, the democratic state hopes constantly to increase in the people intelligent understanding, right living, unselfishness of attitude, and the appreciation of the dignity of human life.

What Is Education?

Commencement address; published in *School and Society*,
September 4, 1915

IN MANY a college dormitory hangs the cynical mandate: "Do not let your studies interfere with your education." No truth is supposedly contained in this statement, but behind it is a considerable philosophy based upon the very wide difference between instruction and education. The latter is the epitome of all the processes which a society has adopted for realizing the ideals which are approved by the race; the other has to do with the definite means and methods used by a particular institution for the purpose of accomplishing certain ends.

The separation of the two, instruction and education, has brought criticism from all sides. Those holding the brief for education in the larger sense rail at the adherence to disciplinary or merely technical subjects; they call for a wider view and larger tolerance and ask ardently for a blessing of the spirit and an adaptation to world needs. The believers in instruction as synonymous with education are demanding more of the practical, less of the "mere nothing," and more of the things that touch life. Accordingly the schools and colleges are asked to train mechanics, engineers, men in fact who know something that can be turned into dollars. From this adherence to instruction are developed vocational theories as varied as the advocates of their merits. A third group of prophets are heard in the land, who in loud tones declare both are wrong; they maintain that education does not educate, neither does it train men. Moreover, they believe that the schools fail to meet the demands made upon them, that they are unsatisfactory and sometimes actually useless in the industry of the world. Millions of dollars are in consequence wasted, and time is lost to thousands of young people in their struggle for wealth.

Nevertheless today for the purpose of receiving instruction in exchange for time, the greatest capital resource that man holds in his possession, eager young people come from far and wide to the portals of the temples where sits Education amidst books,

papers, and apparatus. What means he who says there is no education worth the while? How comes it that the men who have served
as priests in the temples no longer chant the same hymn? Through
the land dissension arises as to the worth of that which the institutions of education are giving to our sons and daughters.

In my attempt to present in a paragraph the importance of my
message, I may have inadvertently overemphasized the differences
of views now raised as to the intellectual and moral values produced by what we call education. Be that as it may, it gives me the
opportunity, of course self-made, to present on this occasion what
education means to me. Education may not mean the same thing
to you unless, after I have finished this discussion, you discover
that our ideas on the matter coincide.

To achieve education, you will agree with me, we must per-
chance have instruction. In considering the process of instruction,
we perceive that each brand, whether commercial, scientific, literary, has come to place special emphasis upon the part wrought by it.
Through specialization of instruction, eyeglasses are no longer
fitted to the general view but may be made for astigmatic sight.
The whole man never appears; it is always the overdeveloped
or undertrained man who is thus exhibited as the visualized product of education. But should the truly educated man come into
view, those who pause long enough may be able to gather from
looking at him just how far or how near they have come in their
endeavor to create this desired product of the educational process.
Time, however, separates the work and the product. Laboring in
the field, the teacher plants the seed. The youth who watches or
better still labors by his side, after a passage of years, gathers the
harvest, be it tares or grain. Anxiety as to the results of his product
and fear that he is out of touch with the times cause the teacher to
take count and to pause to ask which way. If he is not wise and farseeing, he is almost certain to move from one purpose to another,
emphasizing some new phase of education at the instigation of
some new leader in an endeavor to square his work with the requirements of the present.

The nation has moved forward in every way during the last half century. The problems are more involved, intricate, difficult, and even dangerous in comparison with those of the earlier and simpler days of our forefathers. The burden placed upon schools from kindergarten to college is heavier than ever. Through the land a noticeable loosening of home ties has taken place; parents command less authority and at the same time have fewer standards of action. Temptations have grown apace whereas religious convictions have become conspicuous by their absence. Meantime, the amount of knowledge demanded of the candidate for any position has materially grown in its breadth and intensity. The top of the ladder is farther from the ground, and the crowds at the bottom are larger in number than they were a quarter of a century ago. The gap thus opened by the great industrial, social, and moral changes in the social order is filled only in so far as the school attempts to do it. With a heritage of this kind and a problem so large confronting him, the educator of today sees new light at the very time that the critic of school, college, and university refers in language as varied as his feelings to the inadequacy of education and of its real purpose. Many of these criticisms, it is true, are from men within the walls and are therefore a hopeful sign rather than otherwise.

As the centuries have gone by, men have presented various theories about the training of youth. These, when collected and reduced to groups, may be enumerated as theories of discipline, acquisition, utility, unfoldment, adaptation. The first of these is familiar to every educator and to most of the youth of the land. In its essence the emphasis is placed upon the value of doing because of the effect upon mental powers. In its cruder form, the holder of this view maintains that mind is mind and all the faculties present in the adult are to be found in the child; therefore, through discipline and training, power and efficiency can be developed. Under this concept, the subject is of no special importance; it is the power that counts, later on to be used in some problem quite remote from the matter originally studied or in a changed environment that has taken place.

To acquire knowledge has been regarded as the *summum bonum* of the human intellect for through such acquisition the mind is freed. Like many other purposes it in many instances defeats its own ends by becoming merely formal without relating the knowledge to the action and conditions of the individual.

The third view, that of utility, places the emphasis upon the idea of winning from men and nature the means of maintaining life. Carried to its logical end, the emphasis is placed upon material utility without much regard to the finer things of sentiment and sympathy. Life is to be enjoyed by possessing the material means necessary to such enjoyment.

Against this crass view of education is the doctrine of unfoldment. By degrees, the child's mind is "unfolded so that its faculties are spread to the light," and out of this development comes the realization of the purpose in creation. Self-expansion to heights of reason, unknown in the earlier days of childhood, brings to their full power later on the faculties possessed in embryo. In this view, things are striven for on account of themselves; beauty because it is beauty; reason because it is reason and the highest form of intelligence. That such a theory of education produces results is evidenced by the writings of Froebel, Hegel, and other philosophers. From the individual's point of view, always though there remain the old questions of practical contacts with life and the ever pressing needs of the hour in meeting daily and hourly problems.

Another theory of education to which has been given the designation of adaptation is still to be considered. Adaptation is not a doctrine of utility in that man is interested solely in the work of securing bread for his sustenance but rather a belief in man as an integrated being who, because he is related to the world in three ways through his social, religious, and physical nature, has some end in view for every act. Everywhere it is observed that man has used his powers to adjust himself to the world. Under this concept there are no eternal values; all are relative, shifting, and changing as the truth of relationships becomes clearer.

This theory might be expressed in a slogan: Adapt yourself in order that you may adapt the world to your needs. The insistence upon the study of world experiences is but half of education;

the knowledge that the world may be adapted to the man is the other and more important half. The teaching of truths already known is supplemented by the discovery of new truths. In these words we have the essentials of adaptation. But why adaptation? In order, in the words of the hedonistic philosopher, that pleasure may be increased and pain lessened. Discredit rests upon any hedonistic theory which emphasizes the Epicurean view of pleasure; in the meaning of the modern philosopher, pleasure is the object of life in all fields of activity, and in the highest sense perfect adaptation would yield perfect pleasure.

Issuing from the jungle of the hedonistic theory of education with the materials provided in the five views presented, I shall attempt to construct an educational philosophy with which I hope you will at least in part agree. It may be presumed that the advocates of any of the above views will maintain that they are inclusive of the others and that the designation of them by the terms they emphasize forces the proportion of the relation and gives undue weight to a part rather than to the whole of the theory. To know in fact what pleasure is and when it can be realized necessitates standards of beauty, of truth, and of action. Acceptance of this point gives a place to what have been called eternal values and impresses discipline as well as gradual unfoldment in the process of adaptation. Obviously otherwise, we should fall into the errors of the Epicurean. Pleasure alone, even in the highest sense, can hardly be regarded as the basis of all human action.

The *summum bonum* of human existence becomes a series of ends which are the most desirable and the most capable of pursuit at the time. Among these surely is the welfare of our fellow men as well as of our individual selves. No consensus of opinion can be gained in regard to any one end of human existence. A theory of education which emphasizes one phase of human relations or brings to bear an undue insistence upon certain functions can hardly provide the broad basis required for the modern training of youth.

What then *is* education? In its essence, education is the creation of an attitude of mind which is characterized by fairness, openness, and willingness both to receive, and to undertake the search for, the truth. This means the possession of capacities by which to judge the truth: a disciplined mind; acquired knowledge; the power of adapting, and of being adapted to, the community in which one lives. And to all these must be added the salt of determination. Education is not only the epitome of all the processes adopted by a society for realizing the ideals approved by the race but also the desire for discovery, the intent of adding to the world's store of knowledge, and the ability to discard the unimportant for the essential. Education must bring with it a spirit of tolerance, a breadth of view, and a readiness to accept with cheerfulness the duty of the day whether it be work with hands or brain.

What are the elements practically stated that constitute education? I should put them in this order; the right attitude toward facts, appreciation and sympathy, imagination, leadership, the spirit of service.

A fact is a real state of things; it is not belief or opinion but a thing in the actual world, agreement or disagreement with which makes a proposition true or false. Its importance is great as evidenced by the statement of Challis that "A law is a grouping of observed facts." In his lay sermons Huxley declares, "A world of facts lies outside and beyond the world of words." So too says Bain, "The basis of all scientific explanation consists in assimilating a fact to some other fact or facts." The attitude then which men take toward facts makes them tolerant or bigoted, broad or narrow. How to weigh evidence, to sift the true from the false, is not only a matter of knowledge but of character. Ability to wait until the evidence is all in constitutes an important part of justice as well as of the formation of opinion and judgment. Inference as an art is attained after long and careful study of facts, but inference based on guesses is nothing more than shrewd suspicion. In government, in business, in the professions, dealing with facts is fundamental.

The college instruction that passes by the need of careful adherence to fact, clear distinctions of truth, and frank statement of results misses possibly the most important function of education since many other elements, some even of moral injury, are tied up with these failures. Slack recitations and slovenly statements are the breeders of half truths, quibbling decisions, and shambling and weak-kneed positions on important questions later in life.

A rare gift is appreciation. Here again is an attitude of mind backed by knowledge since appreciation requires the separation of the gold from the dross. It is, in the dictionary sense, the act of estimating the quality of things and giving them their due value. To do this requires sympathy, the common feeling of humanity. Bentham says: "In a good sense it (sympathy) is styled benevolence, and in certain cases philanthropy, and in a figurative way brotherly love; in others, humanity; in others, charity; in others, pity and compassion; in others, mercy; in others, gratitude; in others, tenderness; in others, patriotism; in others, public spirit." If we accept half the meaning of sympathy laid down by Bentham, education does not reach full fruition without it since the relations of men to each other are fundamental in society. The fellow feeling inbred in a democracy is born of the appreciation of what men cooperating together have done in government and industry. Without appreciation and sympathy, aloofness, snobbishness, and aristocratic notions are developed which prove actually detrimental to government.

We turn to the third element in education, imagination. That you are "seeing things" is no longer a disqualification even for business, providing the objects seen finally spell dollars! As a matter of fact, it is through the medium of imagination that the initial and essential functions in every branch of human development have their origin. The picture of the thing to be must be humanized, related, and made akin to life before it can be born; and this is the part that imagination plays. Hence, science, literature, and art stir the student to picture for himself the bigness of things and encourage him to peep over the wall that surrounds him into the beyond. If discipline only is the object, then is the spirit of the thing studied reduced to a minimum, and the net result is the old Biblical saying, "Much study is a weariness of the flesh." Imagination is potent; it marks the difference between the plodder and the seer, between the digger and the empire builder, between the statistician and the poet. It saves us from mere oxlike treading of the path about the mill. It is the feature most difficult for instruction to make a part of education.

As the world grows in population multiplying the complications of human government, there is an increasingly imperative demand for leadership. Because of the nature of its being and the reasons for its existence, the college ought to produce leaders. The college furnishes a place in which men act, in which work goes on, and in which credit is given very much as in the so-called outside world. If his training has been worth while, the student has received preparation and development not only in mere mechanical matters but in changing, complex, and difficult affairs.

Associated with leadership must be the spirit of service. Without this, society will have built and directed great educational enterprises to little purpose. The world needs men capable of moral and mental leadership, the former quite as much as the latter; men who have large thoughts beyond selfish interests. Colleges have in the main supplied the leaders; they will always continue to do so, though the efficiency of the education furnished and its adaptation to life will determine the real strength and greatness of this leadership.

And now we may return to our query: what is education? The answer has in some measure been given. It is training, wide and comprehensive; it is not, however, confined to school and college since life is a process of education. Nevertheless, upon the college and the university is laid the obligation to direct the course of education through the personality and character of their teachers. The maxim of these teachers should be: "The men and women passing through our hands must be trained to do the world's work, to know what that work is, where it is, and how to do it. Knowledge of facts, appreciation and sympathy, imagination, leadership, and a spirit of service are needed for this accomplishment."

The university tries to do three things, represented by the college, the professional schools, and the graduate courses of instruction. It endeavors in the first to give a broad outlook on life, in the second to teach specific methods of doing things, and through the third to improve procedures and to increase knowledge. Since these three phases constitute education, they are present in life; and unconsciously every boy or girl, every man or woman, influenced by the educational processes found in life itself, carries them on in some measure.

Realizing that it is always difficult to define spirit, we can appreciate the overemphasis on routine, the reliance on method and husks rather than on substance and fruit. Hence the smart saying, "Do not let your studies interfere with your education," has much to sustain it if we interpret studies to mean routine instruction only and education to mean the development of the mind and spirit in knowledge of facts, appreciation and sympathy, imagination, leadership, and spirit of service.

Emerson has said: "The great object of Education should be commensurate with the object of life. It should be a moral one; to teach self-trust: to inspire the youthful man with an interest in himself; with a curiosity touching his own nature; to acquaint him with the resources of his mind, and to teach him that *there* is all his strength and to inflame him with a piety toward the Grand Mind in which he lives. Thus would education conspire with the Divine Providence. A man is a little thing whilst he works by and for himself, but, when he gives voice to the rules of love and justice, is godlike, his word is current in all countries; and all men, though his enemies, are made his friends and obey it as their own."

The instruments that we as a people have established to bring about this great end are the public-school system, the colleges, and the universities. To designate a secondary school as the people's college is to emphasize an incomplete training as complete. Reduction to this view means a lowered standard of life everywhere since knowledge is the way to progress. Each year sees a material growth in the efficiency of the colleges. The rapid development of problems calls for new leaders with larger tolerance and greater culture. The colleges and universities only can furnish them. On Commencement Day, therefore, we should well give thanks for what we have received, and also we should pray fervently that strength and wisdom may be granted to our institutions of learning for their work in making men and women ready for the responsibilities of life.

Teaching as a Calling

Address at Ohio Wesleyan University, March 29, 1920; published in *School and Society*, June 12, 1920

TEACHING is in the limelight at the present time. Many things are said about it that are discouraging and disconcerting to those who contemplate undertaking it as a calling. The objections that existed before are now reenforced by the economic conditions to be found everywhere.

The superficial attitude of many toward teaching was presented in a statement of a smart paragrapher in a recent newspaper who said, "Some do, others teach." Again, in one of our national magazines appeared an article on the "Third Sex," referring to professors in colleges and universities. When such belittling viewpoints are to be found widespread throughout the land, the individual who thinks about teaching is quite likely to listen to the query, "Why teach when larger money is to be had in other things?"

Of course, it goes without saying that the emphasis upon money throws the whole discussion out of balance for teaching is fundamentally a matter of service not of money. Because the intellectual and spiritual welfare of the nation is bound up in this matter of education, the problem of teacher supply becomes one of immediate concern. In fact, unless the national teaching staff can be constantly recruited, there is bound to be a decreasing efficiency in the population.

Every young man or young woman is compelled to face the choice of a calling. Even where he is subsidized by wealthy parents or in the possession of a fortune, it is necessary to spend time in some way. Accordingly, under our social scheme, an individual choice in the matter of a vocation must be made. That the success of such a calling is limited by the ability and training brought to it is plainly apparent. The student is faced in the first instance with the necessity of choosing between industry and a profession. But there is still another distinction that can be made. Practically all of the human race can be divided into three groups; those who are motor-minded, those who are sensory-minded, and those who are a combination of the two. The motor-minded individual has by native endowment or by habit a peculiar preference for motor and kinesthetic images in memory, dreams, or thought processes, whereas the sensory-minded person has the sense of general perception. Sometimes these two types of mind are combined; even then one or the other is apt to predominate. Consequently, the selection of a calling in conformity with the type of mind that the student possesses is a fundamental requirement for the success which he hopes to achieve.

There are various lines of endeavor which require motor-minded types for their successful development. Among these are manufacturing, inventing, engineering, the military calling, and surgery. Even in this last instance, surgery is largely a matter of the application of physics, and the laws relating to it, to the patching up of the human body. However, the student who is inclined towards the law, ministry, the various social endeavors, the work of the artist, teaching, or even salesmanship is likely to be successful if he possesses what is known as a sensory type of mind.

The student should endeavor to know himself in order that he will not make the mistake of entering a calling which requires a different kind of mind from the one he possesses. Careful analysis of his own qualities is necessary with such advice as he can obtain from other people who are trained in the field of vocational guidance. It is hoped that, having made a thorough study of his ability and qualifications, the young person who comes within the group which can make a success of teaching will consider seriously that calling as one of great opportunity.

I think it is not going too far to say that civilization rests in no small degree upon the teaching through the school, the church, the home, and even the factory. The process of teaching has been carried on from the beginning of animal life, one generation instructing the other by example and later by example and precept in the essentials of life. Civilization and education, therefore, are bound together in the strongest kind of relationship. The great architects who have constructed notable buildings from the days of the pyramids up to the present time have been trained men. No poetry of any distinction has been written by an ignorant person. The paintings that have gone into the galleries were created by men who were taught by the masters under whom they served their apprenticeships. It is the teacher who carries the torch of civilization, and because of this fact teaching is one of the distinguished professions of the world.

No other profession to which men can devote their time presents as great possibility for molding opinion. The work of Socrates lasts until today. His successor, Plato, has left an indelible stamp upon generations. In more modern times we have Ruskin, Agassiz, and others who have had a marked influence upon the present generation. But besides this noteworthy factor of molding opinion, an opportunity for fruitful scholarship is found in teaching. Any one who has tasted in a small degree the delight and interest of doing something well that adds to the world's knowledge knows what this means. If you turn the pages of the nation's history, you do not find on them the names of manufacturers and contractors, important as their work may be; but you find the names of scholars, teachers, ministers, writers, artists, and statesmen.

The teacher is brought into contact with youth. He feels some of its inspiration, its open-eyed wonder, and in addition he meets the great fundamentals of the world as science has revealed them. His thought touches the high points, and he has an interest that carries him through the days and the years. Other advantages to be had by the teacher are leisure time, long vacations, and interesting people with whom he becomes acquainted.

I often recall the remark made by Professor Laughlin to me some years ago; after he entered the business world, he said, the realization suddenly came to him that, while he was teaching, he had been paid to do the thing he most wanted to do. There are, of course, disadvantages in the calling of teaching just as there are disadvantages in any profession. These, however, center largely around the matter of salaries; at present teaching is confronted with serious economic questions. The teacher moreover is supposed not to understand public affairs; but, as far as I can see, he is more likely than the average man to be in touch with the proceedings of his community. He is usually called upon to assist in all matters pertaining to community life.

That anybody can teach and that no real preparation is necessary for the business of teaching have been too prevalently believed. Yet I think it can be clearly stated that the man who has a thorough preparation of a professional character will prove to be of more value to his community and the institution which he serves than one who does not possess such an experience. Certainly a knowledge of the errors and development of education through the centuries is worth while. This study of the history of education is just as helpful as any other type of history and is quite as likely to mold the viewpoint of the student as economic or political history. Both histories are essential, and one should not be substituted for the other; however, the man or woman who is to engage in teaching ought to have a clear conception of what has been done in the educational field.

In addition, he should have a knowledge of educational administration with all of its difficulties and problems. We are now finding that finance is important in the administration of educational enterprises. We also know that in order to find out what is happening in an educational system, it is necessary to examine carefully the statistical information that has to do with that educational process. All these, however, are necessarily in addition to a thorough knowledge of the subject matter which the teacher is undertaking to teach. Enthusiasm for his subject, thorough training, interest in his students, together with information concerning educational procedures, make a satisfactory teacher.

Perhaps it will not be out of the way for me to relate briefly something of my own teaching experience. Between my sophomore and junior years in the early nineties, I undertook to conduct the destinies of a small school in a western state at a salary of $45.00 a month. My enthusiasm for the work was such that, if this large payment had been taken from me, I should have gladly continued to teach. When I returned to college and listened to Dr. Slocum's lectures on labor problems in the United States, I felt that I had solved two questions; one in regard to my calling, and the other concerning the specific subject that I should undertake to teach.

After graduation, I went away to a university for advanced study, and I found my field and my opportunity. Upon completion of this work, I entered as an instructor in the Teachers College at Columbia for a brief period and secured a viewpoint of professional training that would not have been possible in any other way. So, I had received certain benefits through these events: first, the determination upon the calling; second, the necessary preparation for it; third, some experience in teaching; and fourth, professional training in the field of education. With this background, I have continued in educational work, purposely refraining from giving it up or entering other occupations, because it seems to me to possess enormous possibilities for usefulness, contentment, and real happiness.

Teaching is too great a profession to trifle with. The man or woman who enters into it ought to undertake teaching with a clear understanding of what he is doing. No one has any right to toy with the precious human spirits that are to come to him under our educational system. And certainly no one has a right to enter a calling of that kind without the training necessary to make it possible for him to appreciate the problems with which he is confronted. My hope and expectation, therefore, are that the men and women before me who are thinking of teaching will decide upon their vocation deliberately and will make the necessary provisions for definite training and experience in the work.

If I were advising young men and young women regarding the matter of a profession, I should specifically say that there is no better time from the point of view of opportunity to enter a calling than at the time when people are leaving it and looking for chances in other directions.

The man or woman who enters teaching now and who has a fair

amount of training is apt to go forward very rapidly. More than that, the public has been aroused to the necessity of better pay, and a marked change has taken place in the last few years upon this point. In the large schools, the salaries now range in secondary work from $1,200 to $4,500; and in the administration side of public instruction, the salaries extend from $2,000 to $18,000. Naturally there are very few openings at the higher figures, but many positions are being filled today in the field of superintendent of public schools at $5,000 to $8,000. In the college and university sphere, the professorships extend from $1,500 to $8,000. Harvard University has now placed professorships on the basis of $5,000 to $8,000, and Yale has done the same thing. Other institutions all over the land are endeavoring to raise the salaries of professors. In the administration side of college and university work, the salaries range from $3,000 to $18,000, many college presidents receiving from $5,000 to $10,000. In fact, there seems to be a dearth of men in the field of college administration, and many institutions at this time are looking for presidents and deans.

Teaching really offers a considerable opening to those who have the qualifications and preparation for it. The war showed new possibilities in the realm of education. It brought out points that had been overlooked by educators themselves. The difficulties with which the nation is confronted verily emphasize the fact that our educational facilities are not adequate for the opportunities which are before them.

In a book by Professor C. Hanford Henderson on the subject of "What It Is to be Educated," the viewpoint of education is put in this way:

To the outsider, to the man not taking part in the game, education may easily seem a very drab-colored enterprise, a mixture of monotony, naughty boys, and ultimate disillusionment. But, to the man who participates in the game and puts his heart into it, there is not in all the world a drama half so interesting, half so exciting, half so important as this veiled drama of education. As a present act, it engages all his faculties and resources, all his knowledge, skill, love, insight. He can never bring enough equipment to the task. And, as a world process, it is a determining factor in the future of the race, that part of destiny which we hold in our hands.

It is well said that the teacher holds a part of human destiny in his hands. Like a god, he touches the destiny of individuals, but too often he has little realization of the vastness of the adventure. The teacher indeed is the bearer of the torch of civilization, and the man or woman who enters teaching with that ideal is bound to live a happy life based upon the fundamental reality that he is doing a great service.

Graduate Work in Economics in Preparation for Teaching

Published in the *Journal of Political Economy*, January, 1917; reprinted

PERHAPS it has been forgotten that the organization of a real department of graduate instruction as a part of university work in America is less than fifty years old. The evolution of this sphere has been from college foundations toward a larger and wider development of instruction of a graduate character. The original objective of the courses was to fit the candidates for degrees for teaching positions. This purpose, however, is no longer the controlling one in graduate schools for new demands are being made upon them for experts in technological fields and in municipal, state, and federal governments. These schools have been nonprofessional, emphasizing culture and learning as their great objects. Adherence to this broad purpose has clouded the vision of the men who guided them when they were challenged in terms of community life. Men have not been prepared to do distinctive things.

Too often the teaching has emphasized "my" theory and "my" development of a specific line of work, not so much for the purpose of instructing the student, as for the purpose of developing a book to be presented to the public later on. In the graduate departments emphasis has been placed upon the doctor's dissertation, perhaps too much so in that the holding to specific lines of work tends to narrow scholarly interests and to limit the sources of knowledge to which the candidate for the degree looks for his preparation. It certainly aids in circumscribing his range of vision and has a tendency to develop a pedantic point of view. In holding this view I do not wish to be considered as opposed to good thesis work. In truth, I think the graduate student should be tested out in research methods more than he generally is when limited to his thesis as the means of showing his ability to get facts and coordinate them.

The purpose of graduate work stated broadly is to "emphasize discerning judgment and develop critical estimation of the essential significance of facts and principles." The colleges and universities look to the graduate schools for the men to fill teaching positions. Since this really is the largest demand made upon the schools, it is surprising that two things in particular should be taken for granted. One of these is that anybody can teach, and the other that economics is such a narrow subject that a man who has had courses in the department of economics ought to be able to cover any point in the field.

The viewpoint of economics has been and still is social. But each day sees a larger and larger body of students calling for training in business. Now the viewpoint of business is not in the ordinary sense social; although business is of important social value, the attitude of many business men is primarily acquisitive with profits spelled in large letters. This call for help must be met, and in order to meet it the graduate schools must do one of two things; either let go, or take hold. If they propose to let go, then the colleges of commerce succeed them with a decided loss of the graduate and perhaps the social viewpoint. If the graduate schools propose to take hold, then there must be a distinctive recognition of this need and an intelligent attempt made to meet it. At present business procedure is not a science; even the facts are not at hand. But this deficiency makes the problem just that much more a work of graduate character.

The weaknesses of the present products of graduate schools in relation to their preparation as teachers can be stated in this way: first, the overemphasis on specific lines of work and an insufficient grounding in the theory of the subject; second, lack of knowledge regarding the elementary principles of teaching and the organization of material for purposes of teaching; third, deficiency in comprehension of modern educational principles and the adherence to procedures of instruction that have been repudiated by modern psychology; fourth, the lack of understanding of the purpose and organization of colleges and universities; and finally, a failure to make community and business associations that relate the individual and his subject to the life of the community. Put in another form, the obstacles in the way of those candidates for degrees in graduate schools who expect to teach are these: first, too meager information regarding subject matter; second, inability to apprehend clearly methods of presentation; third, absence of an understanding of educational relationships; fourth, small valuation of community life and community connections as a part of training.

In regard to the first point, the graduate student must specialize along some one line over and above the elementary courses that are ordinarily offered in the study of economics. The breadth of interest that now exists in the case of economics makes it necessary for every graduate student who wishes to be a master of some specific line to specialize in a particular field. Yet this specialization can be carried too far for general teaching purposes if it is done at the expense of broad understanding. Consequently, the teacher should have a broad and liberal background of culture and particularly a wide knowledge of both political and industrial history. In other words, his specialization ought to follow upon the development of a considerable body of knowledge rather than precede it; however, there seems to be a tendency for the candidate for a doctor's degree to plunge into special lines of work before he has secured the larger vision and background.

If I may put it more specifically, the man who is a candidate for a teaching position in the field of economics ought to have the undergraduate courses in sociology relating to the ethnological development of people and the general principles of social organization. In addition to these he should know the political and industrial history not only of his own country but of England and

Europe as well. After he has obtained these (and I am taking it for granted that the language requirements have already been met), he may now undertake specialization in his own subject. Certainly his elementary economics should be followed by courses in money and banking, financial history, and economic history; and then upon these should be developed a very extended and thoroughly organized course in the advanced theory of economics. The tendency of modern instruction seems to be to pursue the false gods of descriptive material and thus to lose sight of the essential groundwork of theory.

The second difficulty I have referred to is lack of knowledge regarding the principles of teaching. That this statement is clearly true of practically all of the younger men who enter the field of teaching can be readily confirmed by reverting to our own experiences. Most of us had to find our way gropingly and sometimes after bitter experiences when it came to the elementary phases of instruction. The visiting of college classes has emphasized the deplorable lack of organization in recitations and lecture material especially as they are presented by the younger men. Sometimes such failures take the line of wrong emphasis upon subject matter, and sometimes there is a great deficiency in the science of questioning. I have come to the conclusion that these difficulties are due not so much to a want of knowledge of the study material as to a defect in understanding educational principles.

Most of those teaching today were brought up under the doctrine of formal discipline, and we were told that it was not so much the content of a course as it was the manner in which it was presented. Accordingly, courses of study that had memory tests and required a good deal of drudgery to do the necessary work were looked upon as disciplinary in character and good for the soul of the student who undertook them. The psychologists of the present day tell us that the content of a course has more to do with the effect and influence upon the student than has the general character of the subject or the severity of the training. We have also learned that the development of a specific quality through the mastery of one field, such as languages, does not carry over into the field of a subject like economics and that a man may well be a high grade student in French and German without reaching any particular distinction in the sphere of economics. This means, then, that adherence to the idea of formal discipline, the making of a subject hard and difficult, does not necessarily result in successful teaching.

Now a young man entering a college department for the first time with little or no probation as a teacher must find his way through various trials and tests into successful teaching. He therefore uses his classes as clinics and as material upon which to experiment. In the course of two or three years he may come forth pretty well purged of his earlier notions and may through his experiences develop into a teacher of considerable ability.

I have referred also to the relationship of the instructor to the college or university. Our universities are in a transitional stage without any question, and they have been hampered again and again by the failure of the teaching staff to understand clearly the movement of modern education. Every faculty meeting is witness to the truth of this statement. Within faculties, clashes constantly arise between the modern viewpoint of education and the older procedures. The young man who enters an institution of learning without some idea of the history of education is handicapped for the best work he can do there. My experience has been that in the smaller institutions not less than two years are needed for the newcomer to obtain what might be called a knowledge of the inherent methods and processes, and in the larger institutions three years would probably be nearer the measure of time. It certainly would seem desirable then that candidates for positions as teachers in institutions should have some knowledge of the background of the profession to which they belong; yet the graduate schools have practically omitted any requirement of this kind for the candidates whom they are recommending as members of college faculties.

If I may proceed still farther, I should say that in the smaller communities where many of the colleges and universities are located a constant demand is made upon the men in the social and economic departments to deal with community problems. These problems vary all the way from matters that are of local concern to those that are state wide in character. And more than that, the presence of various types of opinion in such a community means that discussion and wise guidance are always desirable. The young man who enters such a community is called upon at once to take part in helping to solve some of the problems. Too often he is very poorly prepared for any such relationship. In the first place, he has no knowledge of the meaning of community organization and has little understanding of the part which it plays in the whole scheme of society. The result is that his work as an economist is militated against by reason of his failure clearly to understand community action, and moreover his opportunities for service are hampered because of the lack of such understanding.

His attempts to guide business men along practical lines sometimes come to nothing on account of the teacher's inability to understand that the science of economics emphasizes the social organization and does not in its broader aspect deal with the detailed principles of business. The wise teacher of economics has the rare opportunity of perhaps inculcating in the business men of the community the attitude that business is a social enterprise rather than a wholly profit making endeavor. Instruction, therefore, in the principles of business and social organization is highly important for the teacher of economics.

In view of these difficulties and requirements I should say that there ought to be a sharper distinction between the various groups of persons who expect to enter the different realms of labor in the economics vineyard. We might classify these as first, the teaching field; second, the field of the expert; and third, the field of the publicist. The expert is associated with the work of some commission, like the tax commission, or some business enterprise; and the publicist enters upon journalism, the lecture platform, or the sphere of literature. If this distinction were made, it would be possible to ask the candidates for teaching positions to come to their graduate work with some preparation in the processes of education.

I see no reason why the graduate school should not ask those who propose to teach to take at least several courses in the department of education prior to their entrance upon graduate work. These courses among others ought to be educational psychology, the history of education, and the development of college and university organization as shown in this and other nations. It would be desirable also that potential teachers should be required to take a seminar course in the methods of the recitation. When they go out from the university, they will not then be compelled to use a great deal of time and strength in adapting themselves to the mere machinery of their problem but may actually have some knowledge relative to methods of presentation that will be of value to the institutions to which they go.

Again, the matter of community connections to which reference has been made could be assured through the utilization of opportunities for actual contact with some practical problems. I see no reason why the student who is spending three years in a graduate school should not employ part of the time in some state department or some division of municipal government or in some industrial enterprise. It is true that he might not get from these various phases of outside activity all that he would hope for; however, as the relationship between the graduate school and these different organizations was developed and a clearer understanding of their purposes came to both sides, a valuable influence would be brought to bear upon the graduate student in dealing with the actual problems.

One of the difficulties with the present system of theses is the danger of emphasizing mere mechanical methods of investigation. The collecting of a bibliography and the gathering of a certain number of notes and putting these down in a given form, all mean a monument to diligence but not necessarily to knowledge.

Hence it is possible, in my opinion, to work out a plan of this kind that would be of value to the development of well-rounded, thoroughgoing graduate students who are preparing for teaching. If these things I have referred to can be done, there ought to come out of these schools, not men with doctor's degrees who have only narrow knowledge of their subject, but men who have a clear understanding of economics with a very considerable background of social, political, and industrial history. Moreover, these men would have some knowledge of educational processes, an appreciation of the problems of college and university administration, and actual practical experience in dealing with affairs. This is not a difficult program, and I see no reason why it cannot be carried out.

Certainly justice is in the criticisms that are now being made of graduate courses particularly in the direction of confounding graduate with undergraduate work, of the mixing of mature and immature men, and of diluting research with relatively elementary lecture courses to which are added special assignments as a means of raising the level of undergraduate to graduate endeavor. These so-called graduate processes are lacking in full value to the students of economics who aspire to the field of the publicist or to that of the expert; they are distinctly detrimental to the students who are preparing to teach.

The time has come for a better organization of graduate schools and the placing of them on a more professional basis than exists at the present time. To this the objection will be made that the graduate school is not a professional school and ought not to be on a professional basis. I am, however, using the term professional in the sense of developing a graduate school with the intensity of purpose that is seen in the professional school. Such progress I believe can and should be effected.

Education's Challenge to Kentucky

Summary of address at the Annual Conference of
County Superintendents, Eastern Kentucky Normal School,
Richmond, Kentucky, May 1, 1919

FROM the public platform and in private conversation, in periodicals and press, men are saying that this war means a new era. They declare that the church will undoubtedly be more liberal in its attitude, and that a new creed will be formulated as a means of religious expression. They insist that a more efficient government will be the outcome, and that education more essential and more worth while must be developed. Already signs are to be seen that the nation is settling back into the rut which it followed before the war; and unquestionably, unless we awaken immediately to the responsibilities of the hour, there will be no new creed, government will go along just the same as in the past, and the response to education will not be materially enlarged.

Moreover, the disclosures of this war show that we are not a highly educated nation. The percentage of illiteracy is great, and those who have gone beyond the sixth grade represent a comparatively small part of the population. We discovered, too, that half of the men who were called to the colors under the recent draft act were rejected because of various defects. For more than thirty years all these things have been known to the men and women engaged in education; from the platform and in books and school periodicals, they have called the attention of the people of the country to the need for larger educational facilities. If this war is to teach us anything, it ought to bring to the states and the nation the realization of the need of a greatly enlarged educational program. We spend more money on tobacco, liquors, chewing gum, and various other things than we do upon education. Education is like anything else in that we get what we pay for. And now that a national shortage of labor is threatened and young people who have gone into the field of teaching have been diverted into other channels for more lucrative compensation, the prospects which face men and women who are responsible for education in our various states are far from rosy.

It would seem time, therefore, to present a more adequate and satisfactory educational program than we have had in the past.

The educational system existing in the United States consists of the elementary school organized in eight grades, the high school of four years, the college of four years, and the professional and graduate training in addition. Supplementary to this system are the normal schools for the training of teachers. This organization of our school system is largely English in character, though modified by the French and German influences. Undoubtedly, as already seen here and there, the grades and the high schools will be organized under a somewhat different plan; instead of having eight grades we shall have six, with the junior and senior high schools of three years each. Probably a supplemental plan of junior and senior colleges will be developed.

From the point of view of an educational system, the higher education of teachers is absolutely essential and necessary. One reason that teachers have not been able to demand larger salaries has been due to the fact that they have not been qualified, both in content of instruction and in professional acquirements, for the positions that they have held. It is fundamental that any system for training teachers must demand higher educational qualifications than those of the pupils the teacher instructs. Thus it would appear that teachers in the grades and teachers in high schools should have as a minimum four years of college training. Teaching is a difficult task requiring nerve force, patience, knowledge of human nature, an agreeable personality, and ideals and aspirations. When the layman thinks that this training and these qualities, in the long run, can be had for sixty to seventy-five dollars per month, he, of course, is laboring under a delusion that is bound to become more and more apparent as time goes on. Some day we shall recognize that the most valuable crop which we have in Kentucky is not the products that we get from the earth but the children of the commonwealth.

In the management of a school system, many plans have been tried; yet, in the support of a public school system, only one plan is adequate, that of maintenance from funds raised by taxation. In the early days when the private academy was the agency of those who were well-to-do, to secure education for their children fees were paid and subscriptions collected for the support of such schools. Now, however, since we are committed to the idea of public education from the grades through the university, it is essential that such support should be from taxation. That no system of local education should be supported entirely from the state funds can be pretty clearly demonstrated. The locality itself for its own welfare and future development must bear the major part of the expense of its schools.

The majority of the states have entered upon the policy of subsidies for local schools. Our own state has maintained this method of assisting local support for a good many years, and Kentucky is now distributing a fairly large amount; in fact, it is the sixth state in rank for the money so apportioned. In comparison with this rating, Kentucky is the nineteenth state in the matter of assessed value of property and the fifteenth in rank in its wealth of agricultural products. The principle upon which this subsidy is distributed in Kentucky is that of per capita between the ages of six and eighteen. This plan is defective because it places no responsibility upon the community to insist upon school attendance. Of course, it can be said that communities where roads are inadequate would suffer in the pursuing of another plan, and yet, in the long run, the emphasis upon school attendance would probably be more productive of educational advancement.

Perhaps a better principle than distributing funds either according to the number of young people in the school community or according to the number in school attendance is the one which is accepted in some of the states and which has been followed by the federal laws in the recent legislation known as the Smith-Hughes and Smith-Howard Acts. Under this legislation, a school is given a subsidy because it encourages certain standards and endeavors to develop a high type of educational instruction. This plan is enacted in some of the northwestern states to great advantage as can be seen in the development of what are called state high schools and state graded schools. But, even in the use of this principle of distribution, the state should recognize that the main burden of support must fall on the locality and that the progress of the schools rests more upon the community enlightenment than it does upon the receiving of state money.

In the development of the program of education, the first emphasis should be placed upon teaching. This has a very close relationship to the whole problem of democracy. We are not likely to get the clear thinking that we ought to have on the part of citizens relative to the intricate and difficult problems which face us in these days unless the generations that are coming on are trained to recognize and to solve these problems. The scientific method of approach will aid our students in keen analysis. Science contains a body of material which is closely related to the law of cause and effect; the pupil can be brought to recognize this law and to apply methods thus developed to the problems of his own life and to the business of his state.

Other subjects like agriculture, domestic science, and trade would encourage the dignity of labor and give to the pupil a real power of doing things with his hands as well as with his mind. We have also discovered in this war that Americanization is not as simple a thing as we supposed. A great many of our people have little knowledge of the history or government of the United States, and practically the only way that this needed information can be supplied is through the development of more adequate training in the schools.

With this program of instruction should go a program of better school plants. We need in Kentucky for school purposes properly equipped buildings, rightly planned and adapted to the needs of the community. The problem of securing well trained and effective teachers necessitates the consideration of their living conditions. Some farsighted trustees have recognized this fact and have built what are called teacherages close to the schoolhouses. The giving of a habitation to the teacher encourages longer periods of service and brings a better type of man or woman into the teaching staff.

It can also be said that the program for better educational facilities is closely associated with the government of the educational system. We ought to have a state board of education—nonpolitical in character—that would be composed of the Superintendent of Public Instruction, representatives of the University and normal schools, a city superintendent, a county superintendent, and one or two laymen. Such a board might well take over the certification of teachers and the selection of textbooks for the schools. It is also essential that county superintendents should be placed upon a more permanent basis; they should be chosen for an indefinite period based upon good behavior and effective service. County boards of education must be established to deal with their entire counties as units and must endeavor to build suitable plants in order that all of the schools of their counties may furnish equal educational opportunities.

The program so suggested is comparatively simple. It has to do with an adequate system of taxation, a wider and more intelligent community interest in the schools, the maintenance of well equipped and well governed state educational institutions, a more competent program of studies, and some modification in the system of government now existing under the law. After all, what we are seeking in such a program is better citizens who will have intelligence, Christian character, health, appreciation, and knowledge of their duty; who will be industrious, thrifty, and filled with the purposes of a larger usefulness and greater happiness. If these things can be brought about, the state will have an opportunity of entering upon a new regime that will place it among the leaders of this country.

The Objectives of a Public System of Education

Address to the National Association of State Universities,
Chicago, Illinois, November, 1924

I HAVE turned the query over in my mind many times, read books and articles, and asked other people what they think are the objectives of a public system of education. Sometimes the answers are glibly given, but the more serious answers have been to the effect that the question is so far-reaching that uncertainty prevails. On the whole, it is strange that in view of the vast sums of money spent and of the problems of a great republic represented in education, a real declaration of these objectives has not been made. The accumulation of knowledge, the experiences of the past, and the problems of the present and immediate future still further complicate questions of education and make more difficult indeed the statement of these objectives.

James Russell Lowell said at one time, "What a lucky dog was Methuselah; nothing much to know and nine hundred years to learn it in!" Each year in the twentieth century, by the very immensity of the body of information in existence, adds to the stream of knowledge and clouds the vision. Without any doubt the growth in population, the new contacts of nations, the closer relations of the peoples of the world, and the very complexity of life itself stand in the way of a clear view of educational purposes. Then, too, we as a people have been building an educational system largely by imitation. One state follows another, and one city adds this because its rival has done a particular thing. It is indeed time to ask what is the goal of this endeavor and what has resulted from this method of accretion; not that the query is presented here for the first time and that attempts to answer the question have been lacking heretofore! Repeated efforts to formulate an answer must be made, however, until something real in purpose has been found. Therefore, I am trying to answer the question as definitely as I can.

Educational institutions may be grouped into three general classes: first, the public educational institutions, universities, colleges, schools, libraries, and museums, maintained at public expense; second, the authorized institutions, colleges, universities, and private schools primarily public in function, incorporated by the state and authorized under our scheme of education to instruct the youth that resort to them; third, the vast array of private ventures from the great endowed foundations to the schemes set up for private gain. Has the first group a special purpose that necessitates a clear statement of its objectives? If so, then, there is justification for the question I am endeavoring to answer.

Education is the process of preparing human beings for life. "It connotes," says the Standard Dictionary, "all those processes cultivated by a given society as means for the realization in the individual of the ideals of the community as a whole. It has for its aim the development of the powers of man (1) by exercising each along its peculiar line, (2) by properly coordinating and subordinating them, (3) by taking advantage of the law of habit, (4) by appealing to human interest and enthusiasm. . . . It embraces all forms of human experience, owing to the recognition of the fact that every stimulus with its corresponding reaction has a definite effect upon character. It may be either mainly esthetic, ethical, intellectual, or technical, but to be most satisfactory, it must involve and develop all sides of human capacity."

I might comment at the end of this long quotation, "Just so; education should develop all sides of human capacity." What are these, and how far can any system actually unfold every human capacity? I must frankly say that I think nobody knows at this present stage of knowledge and experience. The best that can be done is to draw from human life the results of experience and to apply the findings to the problem. Nevertheless, there is a starting point in this matter as in others for behind every system of education will be found a philosophy which makes or mars the structure built upon it. If the state is the predominant guiding factor in a nation's life, then the philosophy of the state and the theory of government determine the teachings of the school and establish the objectives of the system of education. This may be illustrated by reference to the Mohammedan state where church, government, citizenship, and religious observance are all bound together. In such a state the system of education follows naturally the theory of the religious hierarchy, and all the instruction leads to the emphasis of the religious life based on the Koran. The state enforces the laws of the Koran, and the schools teach its principles.

Under the theory of the "superstate" the educational system conforms to the teaching of obedience to the state, of the subserviency of the citizen, and of the upholding of the idea of the state as an objective in itself. The state can then do no wrong, and any means are justified to secure the purpose of the state. In the schools, all subject matter and all activities glorify the state and make the individual subordinate to the ends of the state in his life, happiness, and employments.

In the Declaration of Independence is a philosophy that may be called the basis, at any rate the point of view, of the American Republic; "all men are created equal, . . . they are endowed by their Creator with certain inalienable Rights, . . . among these are Life, Liberty and the pursuit of Happiness." Here is the emphasis upon the individual, not upon the state. This emphasis upon the individual is the very essence of democracy. In such a state every individual is called upon to do his best not as a matter of imposition by the state but for his own betterment and also for the reason that the democracy can exist only as the individual strives for the best that is in him. A despotic state can compel order by force as every state must do in the final analysis. The difference lies in the purpose of the state. One considers the existence of the state as the final good, whereas the other regards the state as the means by which the individual may do his best. Consequently, what is a comparatively simple matter in the despotic state becomes a difficult and complicated one in a republic, "where liberty must be reconciled with order and government constantly accorded with justice."

Thus education in a democracy is a real preparation for life. It is not the process of making the individual conform to the will, the purpose, or the ambition of the state; it is, on the other hand, the procedure by which the individual through himself learns to give the best in himself to the services of himself, his family, the community, and the nation. "Each person is a unit in the larger unit" where liberty exists under law. The democratic state, therefore, must emphasize the liberty of the individual and as its ultimate end must strive for the development of its citizens into men of initiative, purpose, and fullness of life.

"Education as a process of preparing human beings for life" has been used as the text of this discussion. This definition like any other is merely a starting point. Any progress in seeking objectives must be assisted by analyses of terms. So far as I know, there is no satisfactory definition of life as opposed to mere being or existence; however, it may be defined as the conscious existence of a human being endowed with spiritual and intellectual capacities in an environment of physical condition and of social and legal institutions. The child born into the world comes into it with two inheritances, one animal and the other human. The first brings him his physical and psychical nature, and the other the civilization produced by the race. Education is concerned with the understanding and training of his physical and psychical powers and with the establishing of his contact with his environment created through place and time.

Necessarily any plan of education varies not only with the theory of society in which the system exists but with the knowledge of the human being as a person and with the scientific, literary, institutional, and religious inheritance of the race. The problem of education is to give the individual an appreciation of these inheritances and to create in him some power of mastery over the conditions of life. Education is a life process. It continues in more or less direct ways from infancy to old age. It covers the whole area of life and so in fact includes any agency that teaches through experience, environment, or admonition; such agencies are the home, press, church, school, courts, legislatures, business, and any others that add knowledge or training. The entire process of education does not and cannot fall on any designated system. School procedure, however, must be based (1) upon a knowledge of child life and an understanding of the inheritances of the race; (2) upon discipline, physical and mental; (3) upon spiritual values and the dignity of human life; (4) upon the requirements of support for life in a society where each must work; (5) upon the knowledge of the limitations desirable in adaptation of the individual to life and in the adapting of life to the individual.

A public system of education must be erected on all of these fundamentals. In the United States the schools and colleges attempt an orderly arrangement of the process of fitting the individual to live in this country. Our system has been divided into primary, secondary, and higher education. Only as an arbitrary matter of administration can the dividing line be drawn for there is no actual division between the ending of one branch and the beginning of another. Education is not a matter of bookkeeping or a process that can be separated into many parts. Physical education can not be set up as a thing apart from spiritual or religious education. In fact, there is no such thing as physical education or religious education separate from education itself for the reason that instruction in one is affected by viewpoints and perceptions of the other. Consequently, education goes on in all phases of human life at the same time.

Are there not, however, some parts of the educational process that can be divided into the essential and the consequent? The essential are the divisions of the curriculum that look to preparation in the use of the tools of learning, to the securing of livelihood, and to a mastery of the inheritance of the race. The consequent, vastly more important than those classified as essential and yet dependent upon them, accompany the essential sometimes as by-products of their acquisition; such are the development of character, maintenance of health and bodily vigor, establishment of manners, comprehension of the rights of others and of one's responsibility to them, instilling of patriotism, the encouragement of religious attitudes. Everything that is incorporated in the idea of good citizenship is the consequent of education. These by-products of education are more valuable than the essential. They are the results of attitude, of the underlying philosophy of the state, and of the spirit of instruction. They are taught in any system of education through the culture, spiritual qualities, and patriotism of the teacher as these attributes are represented in hard work, honesty of mind, and spiritual understanding.

Curricula may attempt to bring these elements to the training of the students through courses of study, such as classes in direct character training and more advantageously classes in hygiene. The courses will avail little unless they are accompanied, in all classes and throughout the school, by constant insistence on honest work, fine attitudes, good sportsmanship, and formation of right physical and mental habits. Sometimes courses in character training and in patriotism, though instituted with great fervor and high ideals, clutter the school program uselessly and really accomplish little in making boys and girls ready for life. It may even be possible that too much stress has been placed upon character, service, and leadership as the direct objects of an educational system. The hope is that in the process of education these great attributes will be achieved by those who receive instruction as a result of their training.

What boy can say, "I will be a leader," and be sure that he will actually point the way to his fellows? The answer is obvious. His leadership depends upon knowledge, preparation, and a peculiarly subtle mixture of character and spiritual qualities. To place the emphasis upon what I have termed the by-products of education may end in the failure to gain the very things that are hoped will come out of an educational system. A mastery of the tools of learning, a knowledge of human inheritances, and a preparation for livelihood will, when presented in truth and honesty, produce the desired character and qualities if such are attainable by the given individual.

In the period of the first six years of the public system of education the child should be taught the use of the elementary tools of learning, such as reading, writing, arithmetic, and the preliminary phases of race inheritance in history, in literature, and in the arts. In the next six years, the secondary period, the period of inclination, the instruction in the tools of learning continues; wider knowledge of race inheritance is given; and opportunity is provided for adventures into literature, into art, and into science, both physical and social. The first two years of college must eventually be kept separate from the university by the organization of the junior college or by the absorption of the two years into the local high school. In this way the university is left to its real function which is the training in vocational or professional education; the search for new knowledge; the collection of books, objects of art, and the relics of the past; the maintenance of museums; and the general duty of keeping the torch of civilization burning.

Such an enumeration of the functions of education does not include leadership, character, or ability as matters of instruction but rather emphasizes the processes of knowledge. However, the way in which all instruction is presented brings in the real objectives of education. Truth is one of these. It comes as the result of the attitude on the part of the teacher which is reflected by the student in his approach to everything he does. "Pure religion and undefiled . . . is this, to visit the fatherless and widows . . . and to keep himself unspotted from the world"; and again we are charged "to do justly, and to love mercy, and to walk humbly with thy God." These are viewpoints—personal viewpoints—which carry over to the student through the teacher.

Character is the adjustment of mind to the world of human life, or, as John Stuart Mill defines it, "Character is a completely fashioned will." It is a by-product of what we do. Character is formed each day and hour by what we do and by the way in which we do it. And again the development of wisdom and the acquirement of judgment through the exercise of initiative, the testing of truth, and the maintenance of tolerance are the vital results of a system of education in which the character of the teacher is given the greatest emphasis because he is the agent through which the important by-products of education must come.

In other words, a system of public education must lay stress, first, upon the tools of learning; second, upon race inheritances; and, third, upon vocational and professional training; always under the guidance of truthful, honest, intelligent, diligent teachers. Through research, of course, the search for truth must go on. A state system of education cannot emphasize creed or the doctrine of religious sect; but it can, by the honesty of its instruction, by the sincerity and character of its teachers, and by the high ideals of its direction, create love of truth, belief in religious ideals, initiative, and incidentally leadership.

It should be fairly clear that there is a distinction between the means and the objectives of a system of education. The state wishes its citizens to be intelligent, first as makers of their own career and second as participants in the government of the state. The means are agencies of instruction; teachers, equipment, library, and administration. The students are to be taught to use the tools of learning; to acquire the ways of livelihood; and to understand the meaning, purpose, and ideals of the race inheritances through science, art, literature, and religion.

The public system of education is the instrument by which these standards are to be attained. Thus the elementary and secondary schools should devote their efforts to these purposes. To supplement these there should be continuation schools for those in industry, and trade schools for those who expect to become trained artisans. The university is left as a professional school emphasizing the search for truth and the viewpoint of scholarship in all of its enterprises. The state university is now called upon to carry instruction beyond its campus through extension and other agencies. These activities will doubtless in time increase until they are absorbed by the local divisions of the public schools, leaving the university proper to its real purposes of professional training, research, and maintenance of libraries and museums.

If such then are the means and the purposes of a public system of education, what are the objectives? These after all are the things hoped for, the result of things unseen. I am putting them down in an order that might be changed by any one who attempts to answer this question. The objectives of a public system of education in this country are to create the following:

First: A people sound in mind and body:

Second: An informed people in the plan, purpose, and object of the democratic state:

Third: A people who know and understand their great racial inheritances:

Fourth: A people of integrity who believe and respect the truth:

Fifth: A people who accept religion as a factor in life:

Sixth: A people who through their skill and industry make a livelihood that results in comfort:

Seventh: A people who strive for the truth and are not swayed by propaganda:

Eighth: Leaders whose initiative, obligation to duty, breadth of understanding, and adherence to truth whether in business, industry, science, education, religion, or politics point the way to a better life; leaders who comprehend the individual and social objectives of education, set forth in the words of Jesus, "For their sakes I sanctify Myself."

The objectives are attained through the means. The means produce the objectives only in so far as instruction in many fields, in many phases of human affairs, is permeated through and through with the spirit of the objectives. That spirit is truth, industry, knowledge.

Problems before Secondary Schools and Colleges

Summary of address to Kentucky School Administrative Officers, Frankfort, Kentucky, December 8, 1932

IT IS my purpose tonight to discuss with you some problems involved in the better organization of educational procedure in the secondary and college fields. In doing this I have in mind presenting to you briefly a few statistics that relate to the cost of education in this country. The consideration of statistical matters may seem to be at variance with the topic on which I speak. So much has been said, however, about the cost of education that it seems desirable to bring these statistics to you in order that we may have a clear conception of the responsibilities resting upon us as educational men and women and of the necessities to meet those responsibilities as ably and effectively as we can.

In an article in the *New York Times* of December 4, Mr. R. L. Duffus discusses the Report of the Committee on Medical Costs. These figures have to do with the year 1929 and indicate the total national income as approximately $80,000,000,000. Of this sum $16,000,000,000 were spent for food; $13,000,000,000 for rent; $10,000,000,000 were set aside for savings; $9,300,000,000 went for clothing; $7,800,000,000 were used to buy and maintain automobiles; $4,500,000,000 for house furnishings and supplies; $3,600,000,000 for education; $3,000,000,000 for tobacco, confections, etc.; $2,700,000,000 for personal adornment; and $2,600,000,000 for fuel, ice and electricity. In this list it will be noted that the whole amount spent for education in the United States is much less than that spent for certain forms of luxury.

The cost of elementary, secondary, and college education in the United States was reported in 1930 to be $2,615,068,177. The same statistical report goes on to say that the total income of the people in Kentucky in the year 1930 was $1,085,760,000. The total taxes collected in Kentucky, federal, state, and local, amounted to $119,692,888, or 7.06 per cent of the estimated income. Translated into percentages, the whole expenditure for educational purposes was 27 per cent of the total governmental costs. If we take out of the tax receipts in Kentucky the amount paid to the federal government, we find the percentage of the school costs in this state to the total taxes collected by the state and local governments is 37 per cent. In other words about one dollar out of three in Kentucky went to the support of all the educational activities carried on in the state.

These large sums have confronted the people and the state, and, not knowing how to deal with governmental costs, they have turned to the educational funds at which to direct their criticism. I think it may be said with confidence that the appropriations for education are well spent and honestly administered.

Our duty as superintendents and teachers is to use these monies as far as possible to make more adequate schools. To help in this enterprise, standardizing agencies have been created throughout the country for the purpose of requiring the institutions to meet certain criteria. Thus we have the Southern Association of Colleges and Secondary Schools. The state Department of Education for a number of years has carried on inspection of schools for the purpose of holding them to standards that apply to courses, teachers, and plants. There is also an association for the colleges of the state which maintains the level of work in higher institutions of learning. All of these agencies have rendered an important service in the past and are undoubtedly holding schools up to greater degrees of effectiveness. However, these standards are objective. They do not emphasize the importance of personal development or bring into relief a view of education as it affects the individual student.

After all, the reason for education is to help the student shape his career in order that it will be best suited to him as a person and in order that his work will bring interest and satisfaction to him. The purpose is to ascertain in the secondary school his aptitude and intelligence toward professional training or toward a vocation. We are bound to find out some time during the high school period what the student is, what his abilities are, and how desirous he is of further education.

The problem of the secondary schools in their relation to the colleges is to discover the students who will profit by advanced education. We are beginning to learn that the best bases for college admission are the students' records, their aptitude tests, and their personal histories. If these were made use of by the secondary schools and by the higher institutions of learning, many disillusionments and many disappointments would be avoided.

The purpose of both the secondary schools and the colleges is to give opportunity to the boys and girls coming into our care. In order to do this, we must pursue more eagerly the study of educational procedure, and we must be more careful administrators in our judgment and direction of students. In the long run, the justification of the cost of education to the state, the county, the city, the town will depend upon the better education of boys and girls in school today.

The Ebb Tide in Education

Address to the Southern Association of Colleges and Secondary Schools, New Orleans, Louisiana, December 1, 1932; published in *School and Society*, January 21, 1933

SINCE the days of young manhood, I have navigated small boats on inland lakes in various parts of the Northwest. This experience has not qualified me for a master's certificate or made me an authority on the management of great ships on the highways of the seas, but this handling of small crafts has taught me many things about honest workmanship, the design of boats, and the set of sails. It has taught me something of the force of the wind, the running of water, and the need of skill in guiding and protecting the boat against sudden squalls and rolling seas. It has also given to me sympathy with stranded sailors and struggling vessels in a battle against the elements. The ship of state as well as the leviathan of education labors now in rolling seas of discontent and in heavy gales blowing off the glaciers of taxpayers' debility and bankers' icy steppes that border on the seas of human misery. As I think of men and ships, I am concerned for the safety of these vessels in which we are so vitally interested.

An ebb tide is an outgoing tide. It is one that leaves exposed the sands, beaches, and marshes along the coast. It is the tide that holds ships in harbors and turns over on their sides the small boats that are not anchored in deep water. It is the tide that shows to all, great stretches of weary sands covered with the debris of the sea and the discarded miscellany of the inhabitants who live on the shore. When accompanied by winds blowing shorewards, it is a dangerous tide. This tide carries the vessel out to sea, and the wind blows it back again into ever decreasing water depths. The master is faced with the alternative of beating to sea or anchoring in water deep enough to float his craft until the tide begins to turn and reaches the full. If the navigator is a cautious man, he remains in the harbor waiting for the storm to blow over; there his craft gathers barnacles, and the owners fret because the ship is not earning its keep.

The tide of education has been running full for a generation. Great ships and small boats have put off from the harbors of their beginnings to seek the fortunes of fabled lands beyond the horizon. The cargoes brought back to the docks and wharves of human existence have been rich and plentiful. The owners have paid for new ships, for repairs to old vessels, and have furnished new gear and rigging for the ships in the service. Masters have been given their certificates with laudatory commendation and encouraging comments to push ever into the unknown. Trials and tribulations of nearly a half century ago have been forgotten; and the captains of those days have joined the rocking chair fleet on the porches of the Yacht Club of the Satisfied Sailor or have gone to their reward, "where neither moth nor rust doth corrupt," nor credits and admission problems break in to steal the time of harassed men.

This generation has seen nothing but a full tide and great ships, growing larger, carrying increasing cargoes. The trade winds blew steadily but gently; wrecks were few, insurance was low, and pay of captains and crews was certain and fair. It was a time of development in the marts of education. Men looked at problems steadily; they knew that money could be had to solve them, and that men of ability could be found to accumulate facts and bring conclusions. It was a happy time, a responsible time, a productive time, and a time of forward looking, but it was also a time of vast requirement and heavy duties to meet the needs of the day. To believe this, one has but to look at the reports of the commerce experts and statistic gatherers who reside in the United States Department of Education.

In the year 1920 there were 33,250,870 young people in the United States between the years of five and twenty. Of this number 21,373,976 were in the schools of the nation. Ten years later there were 38,387,032 persons who were listed in the census between the ages of five and twenty. Of these 26,849,636 went to school. Twenty-one out of each hundred of the population were in school. It is hard to comprehend such figures, and few of the critics of the schools do clearly perceive them. The statisticians and gatherers of facts tell us that the cost of public education in 1920 was $1,036,151,000, slightly better than 1½ per cent of the national income. Ten years later the nation was spending $2,300,-000,000 annually on public education. The value of public property used for school purposes in 1928 was placed at $5,423,-280,000, or 1.8 per cent of the national wealth of that time; that is, $1.80 out of each hundred dollars of the national holdings were in school property, and $2.80 out of each hundred dollars of national income were spent for the support of all schools.

To put it in another way for purposes of contrast, church property in the United States amounted to 70 per cent of all school property, and the amount spent by all churches was $817,214,528, or one-third of the sum used for school support. I am taking another group of figures for comparison purposes. The people of the United States in 1930 spent practically as much for automobiles and trucks as they did for education. They spent one-fifth as much for gasoline alone, or $4.00 per capita for gasoline and $20.00 per capita for education. The depreciation of automobiles and trucks, their repair costs, and their consumption of gas and oil amounted in money spent to about the same as the total cost of education in the United States.

Now the winds of adversity are blowing from the sea, stirring even the waters of the harbor. The tide is running out. What shall the captains do? Shall they stay in the harbor waiting for better weather and run with the tide; or, caught on the seas, shall they lower the anchor, batten down the hatches, take in sail, and patiently endure the pounding of the seas? These are questions of policy, and they parallel the queries raised in the minds of the captains of educational crafts who get their licenses from this association.

Perhaps the first thing to do is to go over the cargo to see if everything in the hold is worthy of transportation. The good ship *SASSY*, a name made from the initials of the Association, S.A.C.S.S., will meet the requirements of where we are and of what we are about to undertake.

After considerable discussion with the captain as to the propriety of such prying into the business of the ship's owners, he called in the mate and the supercargo to witness the searching and to prevent the purloining of anything of value while the inquiry was going on. Down in the hold were several large boxes marked "Standardizing Procedure," "Admission Methods," and "Unit Courses of Study." There were also some huge containers plainly marked "Prejudices," "Mistakes," and "Signs," indicating the direction travelers should not go. With hammer and claw the work of opening the boxes was soon accomplished, giving an opportunity to look at the material gathered in the box marked "Standardizing Agencies."

The setting up of standardizing agencies was a forward step in educational progress. The inspection of schools by tough-fibered individuals who went up and down the states complaining about hotels and meals but who spent their time listening to recitations, asking questions of principals, and peering into dark corners was all to the good. The list of secondary schools compiled by them at least separated the goats from the sheep. A new pride in accomplishment was to be noted in the secondary field, and marked improvement followed in the wake of these efforts. Gradually the secondary schools lifted their offerings, their equipment, and their personnel to better than the national average.

Although the tests of material efforts were applied with considerable vigor, the more elusive matters of course content and of student growth and accomplishment were but gingerly dealt with. The criteria seemed fixed and hard with little give to the changing views of educational procedure. Thus the standards have remained very much as they were, making but little distinction between the schools that graduated students of high quality and those that did a mediocre job. Because of the measurements that were placed in his hands with which he has had to determine the place of the school in the secondary list, the inspector has been sometimes overmuch impressed by a fine building, a good janitor, and new equipment.

The package marked "Colleges," although it was huge in size, was found to contain almost nothing about technical schools, teachers' colleges, and agricultural colleges. This material had to do with plants, endowments, incomes, expenditures, salaries, degrees, volumes in the libraries, size of classes, sanitary fixtures, numbers of students, and amounts of teaching load. There seemed to be nothing about educational results or effective teaching. Material standards when applied must of necessity give answers in terms of materials. "This was not the object," so the captain said. "The hope was that a well-trained student would be graduated, but that was not first in the minds of the framers of the regulations. The purpose of the regulations was to bring the colleges up to a point that would make competition between them more equal and fair." These regulations were much needed and had a marked effect on the colleges for a full quarter of a century.

The third package marked "College Admissions" was now at

hand. It was a bulky one and had evidently been turned over a good many times. Some of the material was new, but much of it was covered with dust and carried a burden of years. "Carnegie units" was one of the signs on the coverings. These were fifteen in number, and much difference in opinion evidently existed about what should go into the fifteen units. Some held that Latin, Greek, mathematics, and foreign languages should make up twelve of the fifteen units. Others who called themselves liberals stated that social science, natural science, and the vocational subjects should come into the fifteen. And a small group maintained that these contentions were immaterial because the real test of education was accomplishment measured by ability to do the work. Since agreement on "College Admissions" was evidently hard to get, the force of habit and the background of old methods continued to hold the schools where they had been for many years.

I have given a brief description of some of the cargo carried by the ship on which we are now traveling. It is worthwhile to ask how much of this load ought to be turned into the sea. Certainly, none of it until we have carefully examined it. So with that in mind, I wish to discuss standards, admissions, and courses. Though these items are housed in separate boxes, in reality they are parts of a large subject and have to do with the real goal of the voyage.

There had been doubt in the colleges about the fitness of students in the secondary schools to meet the mind stirring requirements of college life. The answer to this doubt brought into existence the college entrance examination board in the East and the inspection and standardizing agencies in the Middle West and the South. The examination plan accomplishes a good many things but it also raises doubts concerning its full value, as shown in the shifting in types of examinations from time to time. In the Middle West and South the certificate plan of admission to college was inevitable. The doctrine of equality in opportunity and ability was inherited from the pioneer days and was inbred in social, political, and economic life. All are familiar with the development of inspection and standardizing. Colleges and universities, public and private, carried along in the same current were forced to the certification plan and to the establishment and maintenance of requirements that were honestly and thoroughly aimed to raise the standard of both schools and colleges.

However, questions began to be asked about the certification system and also about the piecemeal and even the comprehensive examination. Suspicions cropped out that the requirements of the standardizing agencies did not touch the marrow of the problem. Sappers and miners were at work in the psychological field; personality was talked; and the war brought out the Alpha Test and with it an immense amount of new data that threw light on variant abilities in the individuals of the population. The colleges were having their problems with the hordes of students who crashed their gates. Something had to be done to satisfy the standards of education, to provide better education for those who were capable of it, and to raise the colleges from the level of the secondary schools to that of the higher institutions of learning.

"It was clear to those who faced the facts that the higher institutions were physically incapable of accommodating all those who sought admission. One way of meeting that situation was to increase equipment and another way was to decrease enrollment by higher fees or by a selective process in admitting students. Neither of these proposals met the real problem. The real problem was to find out in advance those students who were able to profit by a college experience." This is a problem that challenges all the ability and all the machinery of the educational system. The public high schools can not work out a plan by themselves, nor can the private schools go a great way without the help of the colleges. And the colleges, after they have accepted the students, are faced with the problem of guiding, eliminating, and stimulating the students enrolled in their classes. In fact, the question is boiled down to individual accrediting instead of institutional accrediting.

A number of surveys were directed toward the determination of ability to do college work and the coordination of the work the student would do after he reached college. S. S. Colvin, whom I have already quoted, found in 1922 "that of these who intended to continue their education in some higher institution, a third of the boys and a little over one-half of the girls appeared to be bad college risks with about one chance in five of doing satisfactory college work. On the other hand, one-fifth of the boys and one-seventh of the girls who did not intend to continue their education appeared to be good college material. Moreover, about one-fourth of the boys who stated that they intended to go to a liberal arts college were classified as bad risks. The corresponding ratio for girls was practically the same. Two-fifths of each were good risks."

The Commission on the Relation of School and College, created by the Progressive Education Association and financed by the Carnegie Corporation, is endeavoring to bring about changes that will permit experimental study of secondary education. The emphasis of the commission is on securing better instruction and on enabling schools and colleges "to help each student shape his course so that it will be best fitted to his needs, and so that his work will have meaning and significance for him." For our discussion the important part of the commission's statement is contained in recommendation A, in which it is stated that the high school student who is admitted to college should (1) be possessed of the requisite general intelligence to carry on college work creditably, (2) have well-defined serious interests and purposes, (3) have demonstrated ability to work successfully in one or more fields of study in which the college offers instruction.

The B part of the recommendation discusses the problem of records. The record should include a history of the student's school life, the results of tests and examinations, and other evidences of the student's aptitude and achievement during the secondary course. The committee on records is endeavoring to determine what information the college needs for wise selection and guidance of students, how that information can best be secured, and in what form it should be recorded and sent to the colleges. This is all to the good. The commission is engaged in an effective work especially if it brings about the changes in the secondary school suggested in its report. The college administrator applauds vigorously when he reads the proposed objectives. These are greater mastery in learning, more continuity in learning, the release of creative energies, clearer understanding of the problems of civilization, guidance of students, good teaching, and the revision of curriculum materials and their organization.

The schools may be able to bring much of this to pass in order that secondary education can move rapidly along the road indicated. The problem of guidance and direction of the individual pupil is still, however, to be met. I think it will be accepted by all that the secondary schools have the problem also of training pupils who are not quite capable of carrying college work. The college would be concerned in knowing that the student who entered college was really interested in college and was willing to carry the work of college classes satisfactorily. As the secondary school improves, some of the difficulties of college admission undoubtedly will disappear.

The accrediting agencies are nevertheless stressing the outward and material standards of both college and school. The colleges hopeful always of procuring good college risks should have more help from the accrediting agencies in obtaining them. At the present time the interest of the agencies in this part of the problem is largely academic. Meantime, a number of the universities have cooperated with high-school principals to use tests in finding out the weak points in their instruction as well as the kinds of pupils that are in their schools. Ultimately such tests must encourage individualizing education according to ability and aptitude.

The purpose is not to exclude students from education but rather to adapt the education to their needs. What is wanted after all is to find the most promising basis for constructive guidance. Again it is not a compact, similarly minded group of students a college should strive for, but a group, perhaps heterogeneous, who would and could profit by college education. The difficulty now is that there are many maladjustments due to failure to know and understand the differences to be found among students. The outcome of such selection and guidance would undoubtedly be educational opportunities adapted to abilities. The administrator to deal adequately with this part of the problem must have comparative material that will tell him not only what groups are doing but what individuals in that group are accomplishing.

The best present criteria for admission to college are the pupil's record, his history, and the results of an aptitude test. These taken together form a fairly satisfactory method for predicting college success and place admission on an individual basis rather than on an institutional one represented by the diploma of the school. After all, the broad highway of educational opportunity from kindergarten to college graduation should be open to every child in so far as his interest, ability, and endowment will permit. However, the possession and use of material gained from tests are necessary to fortify the judgments of principals and admission officers, not only in dealing with parents, but in discouraging some students from going to college and in encouraging others to go on with their education.

The successful working of the individual accrediting of students will depend upon the officers who carry on the organization, upon the procedure involved in the method of selection, and upon the tact and understanding with which the program is brought to the attention of the pupils and their parents. It is essential also that these officers shall be trained in the processes and philosophy behind the whole testing program. In fact, the program will advance or break down as these superintendents, principals, registrars, deans, and faculties believe in it. That many of these do not or that many have doubts about it may be observed by the comments and discussions in any educational group. The danger to the program is that the technique may advance faster than the acceptance of it by those vitally concerned, including students and parents.

The other phase of individual accreditation is just as important as the one of admitting students to college: and that is to find out what students do when in college; whether courses of study actually instruct; if the interest of students is increased; and if their adaptation and reaction to community, national, and international life are enlivened and strengthened. The sophomore and senior tests provided by the Committee on College Testing have brought out an array of valuable and astonishing results. Some sophomores know more than many seniors. Few seniors make any progress in writing beyond the sophomore year. High marks are not always indicative of understanding or correlation of interest. The college faculties must know these things. There must be something wrong with the marking system, with the content of courses of study, or with the teaching procedure. The need of comparative records of students and classes within the individual colleges and also with other institutions appears to be decidedly pressing. The problem is to be found not only in the admission of students but also in what they do and what they are given a chance to do after they enter college.

The college officer has a vast problem on his hands in the acceptance of many types of students who are to be subjected to the learning process. These students should not be dumped into a hopper as they are at present. Searching examination of courses of study, consideration of interests, and the guidance of students in finding their interests must be established. Perhaps the guidance officer will come into his own not only in numbers but in professional status.

Opposed to such a view is the laissez faire one of letting the student find his way. Much can be said for this method. On the way, however, there is a great mortality which added to incapacity leaves a burden of discouragement, disillusionment, wrong development, and loss of opportunity; these are more than a system of education can be asked to carry. The progress made here and there in the secondary field and on the college level encourages the belief that we are on the way to individualization of education through the process of finding out what the individual is and what he needs.

Certainly, if what has been outlined is the course to follow, our good ship is carrying the wrong cargo, and her officers should be aware of the drift of tide and the duration of the wind. In these times a captain must scrutinize the sky and steer his ship so that he may reach the real goal of the voyage.

The packages of prejudices and signs in the hold of our ship should be cast overboard, new freight taken on, and a chart prepared with the old maps, compasses, and rules as aids in the hands of skilled navigators. The owners are not satisfied to let the ship sail with the old cargo; they want new goods and better results. In fact, they are insisting upon reduced allowances for navigation, upkeep, and wages, not because they do not get value of a kind for what they have invested, but for the reasons that exchequers and treasury boxes no longer overflow. The old ship must travel farther, carry more lading, and bring increased dividends if the owners are to be satisfied.

You, captains, mates, and sailors assembled here, are you equal to the new task with the tide running out and the wind blowing on the shore? I think you are if clear-eyed and open-minded you are determined to throw away prejudice, cast aside intolerance, and face frankly the assignment of reloading the ship with a more valuable educational procedure equal to the needs of the times and incorporating in it the best we know. That attitude, that charter, and that kind of navigation need never fear the danger of an ebb tide in education.

Business Cycles and Education

Address to the National Association of University Schools of Business, Lexington, Kentucky, 1933

EDUCATION is the process of adapting the individual to life and of shaping life to the individual. It is indeed the means of bringing youth into contact with the wisdom of the ages and of enabling them to deal with the problems of the future. We are apt to think of education as restricted to the immature and as separated from life. We think of it in terms of schoolhouses, campuses, and books when in reality it is a part of life itself.

There has always been a system of education, going back as far as man's history on the globe. It was by word-of-mouth in the past, the elders telling the young people how to do things and passing on to them the legends of the tribe or of the clan through the bards and singers of that day. Now we are trying to bring to youth the experiences of the past and its teaching through the use of books and demonstrations. A great system of public education with buildings, laboratories, libraries, playgrounds, and highly trained instructors and scientists engaged in research has been evolved. This has been done with a purpose, and behind it is an ideal. That ideal is the development of a truly intelligent people who will be educated for constant growth. Thus education is an end and a means. It is the means of richer living to the end of bringing increased powers to the individual.

Business cycles come and go. Depression is followed by prosperity, and prosperity slowly slides into difficult times. The fortunes of individuals, corporations, and institutions rise and fall with these cycles affecting business, industry, and education. This depression in which we now find ourselves has been lasting and has exhibited various factors not present in previous depressions. Many demonstrations against the development of education and of facilities for leisure and recreation have followed in its trail. Against public education, in particular, much criticism has been proclaimed by those who are hostile to such education. That criticism has taken the form of attempts to obtain reduced taxes and appropriations. It has also brought to those engaged in the field of education new searching of heart and mind as well as careful study of the principles involved.

Educators are accused of being extravagant and of having brought into the school system a great many fads and frills. It is worth noting, however, that many of these so-called frills have been demanded by different groups of citizens. The farmers years ago asked the government in no uncertain terms to establish experiment stations and later to develop a system of agricultural education in both colleges and high schools. This agitation resulted in the passage of the Nelson, Adams, Hatch, Smith-Lever, Smith-Hughes, and the Purnell Acts. The states were called upon to pay dollar for dollar under the Smith-Lever and Smith-Hughes Acts, and appropriations were made in answer to these demands.

The business men, not to be outdone by the farmers, called for vocational education and insisted upon the placing of machines and tools for instruction in metal-work and woodwork in the high schools. They also asked so vehemently for commercial education that principals and superintendents were hard pressed at times to meet their requests.

The doctors of the land secured the passage of legislation in health and quite rightly so. Nursing service, physical examinations, and dispensaries followed in schools and colleges. The bankers then thought something ought to be done, so they procured legislation to establish "thrift week," and at their suggestion penny banks were set up with the teachers as their collectors. The lawyers in the country wished to emphasize the constitution; they believed the teaching of the constitution should be separated from the teaching of history and should be incorporated in the curricula. The women's groups pressed for home economics and homemaking, and they thought gardens should be encouraged. These in addition to the regular instruction, increasing already heavy burdens, were often times introduced against the judgment of the administrators. If we look at these matters fairly, we see that the schools have responded to the demands of the public and that the public is in large part responsible for any overdevelopment that may exist.

The fight against public education today has been joined by a new force. This group, which has not been vocal in the past, is now joining in the discussions and contentions about the schools. It is a group with incomes. With the decline of incomes, the percentage of taxes paid upon them has increased. It should be kept in mind, however, that the amount of taxes has not grown as rapidly as income and that the actual amount of taxes collected for government purposes other than for debt services is not appreciably greater over a period of fifteen years.

Between 1922 and 1929 our investments in motor cars increased 93 per cent. Expenditure for personal adornment was accelerated 81 per cent in the same period. We spend as much for recreation and fun in the United States as we do for government purposes. In one item alone, that of the management of traffic, immense demands have been made upon the local governments. Certainly money spent for good government is better used than that spent upon gimcracks and luxuries. Our people spend for gas $750,000,-000, for tobacco $1,500,000,000.

In the meantime a marked growth in the school population has taken place. In 1910, 18 per cent of the children in industry and in 1930, 4.7 per cent of the children employed were of school age. The school system absorbed the difference. Now that we move toward a thirty hour week, the employment of minors will be further cut down, and the schools will be called upon to meet a still larger obligation than they have ever met.

Meantime, what is happening to the schools? There has been a letdown everywhere, although thousands of unpaid teachers have gone on with their work with a spirit that is remarkable. Shorter terms are in evidence, and children will be thrown upon the community for longer periods of time than in the past. Institutions of learning are faced with reduced incomes; the professors, with smaller salaries. The number of students has reached a standstill in some places; in others it is smaller. Greater demands are being made than ever before. How are the schools to meet the situation?

The problem of adult education is urgent. It is quite clear that education should continue for the adult in order that his interest and an enlarged view may come into the field of public government and public management.

Many problems for the economist and the political scientist are before us. The state we have known in the past is rapidly changing; but I have no doubt that the study of government, taxation, and administration in many of our schools is based upon an ancient type of social and political organization. The economist ought to come into the picture of public education more than he does at the present time. With the facilities that he has in the great collections of books and materials together with his training, he ought to be positively engaged in envisaging the perfect pattern of the state. If he cannot point out what needs to be done, certainly the average citizen is unable to indicate the path to be followed. Since a close relationship exists between the business cycle and education, there should be a close relationship between the economist and the machinery of taxation as applied to public education.

Whose Fault Is It?

Summary of address made in 1933

IN THESE TIMES of difficulties, both public and private, people are asking who is responsible for government costs. In answer, it is stated that public officers, school men, and teachers seduced the taxpayers into an expansion of government functions when we all lived in a time of innocency. The fact of the matter is that the people as a whole called for and insisted upon the development of government functions and school programs.

There is no question that the burden of the taxpayers at the present time is a heavy one; but the attack upon education as the cause for our difficulties seems to me to be out of line with the facts. We need undoubtedly some reorganization of government, a greater concentration of schools, and a wider basis of tax support than we now have. Since the fixed charges of government such as debt service, maintenance of courts, and the like cannot be materially lessened, an attack is being made upon the public schools in the expectation that money may be saved by reducing their costs.

It is worthwhile to bring out a few contrasts in the matter of government expenditures. There were spent last year in the United States on roads and highways only ten million dollars less than the entire total spent for public education. The amount spent on veterans' relief equalled one-half of the entire bill for elementary and secondary education and was twice as much as the amount spent on higher education, both public and private. The government of the United States spent on pensions, interest, and national defense a sum greater than the whole amount spent on all education in the United States.

If these figures mean anything, we need a sense of proportion, an understanding of the problems involved, and a sympathetic attitude toward the important function of public education. In Kentucky the number of school children is 612,000. This number is 22 per cent larger than that of twenty years ago. The public high schools in the same period of time have increased their enrollment 321 per cent, to nearly 70,000 children. There has also taken place a marked absorption of children formerly employed in industry. The apprentice system has broken down, and the schools are called upon to care for this aggregation of children freed from industry.

The sum spent on public schools in Kentucky is $28,000,000. This includes the amount spent by the state and by the local communities. It cost $45.00 a year or $1.30 a week for each child. This sum includes teaching, supplies, heat, janitors, etc. The average cost per pupil per day in the United States is forty-eight cents, as against twenty-six cents per day for each school child in Kentucky. So it can hardly be charged that education is excessively expensive in our own commonwealth. In 1931 the entire amount spent by the state government for all education, including the institutions and the distribution that went to the local schools, was 28.7 per cent of the total state budget.

Taking everything into consideration, Kentucky is quite fortunate in the matter of its indebtedness. The state has no bonded debt, but it does owe a floating one of $14,000,000. The debts of the counties amount to $33,000,000; the school debt is $8,000,-000; and the city and town debts may reach $100,000,000; making a debt total of $155,000,000 for all the divisions of government in the State of Kentucky. This sum might be compared with the $225,000,000 owed by the school districts of Ohio, the Tennessee state debt of $94,000,000, the North Carolina state debt of $160,-000,000 and the obligations of its local governments of $470,-000,000 more.

Our commonwealth seems to be in fairly good condition in comparison with our sister states. Consequently, this question of education should be approached in a broad, sympathetic, and understanding way. Material reduction in expenditures for education means cheap teachers and poor instruction. It means the reduction of school advantages with a resultant breakdown in opportunities for the young people of the state that will take many years to overcome. On the whole, education is now carried on at a low cost in Kentucky, and to put it much lower will mean distinct losses to our educational system.

There are two approaches that can be made to this problem of governmental expenses. One of these is to reduce the costs of government by eliminating waste, stupidity, and dishonesty and at the same time to retain all the beneficial facilities for the protection of life and property and for the conduct of the educational program. The other means of dealing with expenses is to make a proportionate reduction in all expenditures and not to throw the burden on the greatest service rendered by the state and local government, namely, education. This is the only fair means of conducting the matter if we do not follow the first rule. To place the whole pressure on education, as is being done at the present time in some of the states, is wicked and wasteful; it is, moreover, likely to produce disturbing and disastrous results in the future.

My interest in this matter is that of a citizen of the state and of a servant of the commonwealth. The University of Kentucky is at all times a service institution. I am hoping through this opportunity to throw some light upon the matter of state expenditures and thereby to reduce some of the heat of argument. I urge upon all to deal with this question of governmental costs in an honest, sympathetic, intelligent way.

The State and Education

Commencement address, Eastern State Teachers College,
Richmond, Kentucky, June 1, 1932

I MAY BEGIN by asking *Who* is the state rather than *What* is the state because, after all, the state is a human institution composed of people living in a definite territory with certain laws which are accepted by the people as a guide for their conduct and relations. The state is not a place, or a building, or a group of people. It is all of the people with their laws, administration, institutions, business, commerce, and social organizations. The government of a state is an agency whose business is to carry out the purposes of the people, and it has an obligation to the people to hold within their control and under their direction any action of the state.

Without entering into fine distinctions, one may place the functions of the government in three general groups. The first of these is protective; for the purpose of guarding the property, lives, and health of the people, the state has established courts, police, and sanitary measures. Herbert Spencer, in his discussion of the state, insisted at the time when he wrote that its particular function is the protection of property and life; however, we in this day have gone much beyond that in our demands on the government. The protection afforded by the state to the people is for the purpose of allowing them to do many things that will advance their interests.

There is another function of the state that we may call auxiliary in that it does not add anything to the protective and constructive purposes but, through the collection of taxes and the keeping of accounts, it makes possible the work of the government to go on. The state exists not in order to collect taxes and keep accounts; but on the contrary the state does these things to assist materially the progress of the people.

The third general function of the state consists of certain groups of activities that may be called constructive. The state develops transportation facilities, it provides for the recreation and health of its people, and it sets up a system of education. The great wealth producing element of government is education; we do not produce in order to consume that we may produce still more goods. That would be an endless round of futility. The growth and care of the child are the great function of government in that the future of the state depends upon the development of its citizens.

Every commonwealth is faced with the problem of accomplishing these three purposes. The economic condition of the nation by affecting values acts upon the ability of the state to carry on its various functions. In times of depression when citizens look about to see where they can lighten the burden of government, the tendency is to place the onus on education and to take from it some of its support. To reduce the expenses that arise out of the protective element of government is difficult. In consequence, that thing not easily visualized, called education, seems to many the logical place for the reduction of expenditures although education is by all means the most important constructive phase of government.

No man would say that business, industry, and transportation are not advancing and that new ideas, quickly adopted by energetic and farseeing leaders, are not constantly appearing in these fields. Yet the impression is rather widespread that education is static, that textbooks of the past can be used in the present, and that old schoolhouses fairly efficient forty years ago are still just as satisfactory as ever. In fact, all other human agencies may change, but in the minds of many people education is education, and the provisions for it at one time are sufficient for any other. However, education today is demanding new ideas, new books, visual equipment, the use of typing machines, the organization of new curricula, and the better training of teachers. If we are to give to our citizens training, understanding, appreciation commensurate with those given in other states, it is essential that education in Kentucky shall go forward and shall incorporate all progress that is being made in this important human endeavor.

Our attitude at times seems to point to a school system as something that may be used to the advantage of individuals. The school board member and the citizen may bring pressure to secure benefits for themselves. In all of this we have largely overlooked the child and his rights. We have forgotten the future of the state and have neglected to emphasize the child's just claim to a good education. Interferences with the teacher, with the conduct of the school, and with the development of the best means of education confront the people of the state again and again. It is deplorable that in the discussions that take place in the legislature the child is entirely forgotten. We need to proclaim constantly the goals of modern education.

In the new enlightenment that is coming to students of education, the importance of early teaching stands out with amazing clearness. What happens to the child in his emotional and spiritual life between the ages of two and six has a decided effect on the kind of person he becomes in later years. Accordingly, leaders in education are directing our attention to kindergartens and nursery schools as having a significance which we have overlooked and neglected.

In secondary education lies the problem of much of modern instruction. It is found increasingly urgent that young people in the secondary period should come to have definite attitudes. If these attitudes are not established in the high school years, the whole of life may be marred by poor habits of attention, by laziness, inaccuracy, and inefficiency. Health, which in the elementary period is the result of another's care, becomes a personal matter. Command of fundamental processes and vocational facility should become habitual. Wise use of leisure has great bearing on the whole of life. Citizenship and home membership can be impressed in the right way upon the student in the secondary school with the result that he will be a happier, better member of society. Character acquires steadiness and dependability through the behavior in the classroom and on the playing field. By the student's doing his work every day, honestly, accurately, promptly, by his playing in games with good sportsmanship, and by his being trustworthy in social and club activities, he fashions his own will to do and to be. Attitudes of tolerance, of self-control, of courtesy develop in the secondary school into habits.

In higher education, problems of adjustment for students are to be met by wise counselling. The great educational system of a commonwealth is indeed a contribution of democracy to democracy. Unhampered by limitations of money, social position, or class distinction, the student may go from the kindergarten through the university just as far as his abilities and character will permit. The university is a service arm of the state and a beacon light to the people. The university is dependent on the state, and the state should in turn be even more dependent on the university.

What then is the state? All of us in Kentucky are the state of Kentucky. We are responsible for the government, for the schools, for the welfare. Therefore we can hope for Kentucky to be the glorious state we dream of, only when we realize that her children, her people, are the important consideration in the state and when we motivate that realization into action.

A poet has answered the question for us, "What constitutes a state?"

"Not battlements or labored mound,
Thick wall or moated gate;
Not cities proud with spires and turrets crowned;
Not bays or broad armed ports
Where laughing at the storm rich navies ride;
Not starred and spangled courts
Where low browed baseness wafts perfume to pride.

"No! men, high minded men
With powers as far above dull brutes indeed,
In forest brake or den,
As beasts excel cold rocks and brambles rude;

"Men, who their duties know,
But know their rights and knowing dare maintain;
Prevent the long armed blow
And crush the tyrants as they rend the chain;
These constitute a state."

Then and Now

President's address to the Southern Association of Colleges
and Secondary Schools, Atlanta, Georgia, December, 1934

No one will doubt the statement that the Southern Association of Colleges and Secondary Schools has had a notable history. It is now thirty-nine years old. Only those who were familiar with the situation when the Association was organized can appreciate in full the service which has been rendered by the Association and by the brave pioneers who organized it.

In the declaration which called for the first meeting, the committee from the faculty of Vanderbilt University stated that an organization should be created to encourage the southern schools and colleges to bring about cooperation and mutual assistance, to elevate the standard of scholarship, to effect uniformity of entrance requirements, to develop the preparatory schools, and to eliminate secondary work from the colleges. The Association did a very constructive thing and brought order out of chaos. It provided for cooperation and mutual assistance, it has unquestionably elevated the standard of scholarship, and it has supplied uniformity of entrance requirements. It has also given to preparatory schools a new dignity and a more effective place in the educational system.

In administering the standards that were set up by the Association, competent work was done, helpful not only to the colleges which were members of the Association but also to those that were endeavoring to meet the requirements. Moreover, I think a new emphasis was placed upon educational ethics, and a gradual bettering of the educational situation in the South was produced. These accomplishments from the point of view of today seem remarkable. So to those who bore the heat and brunt of battle of the early day should go thanks, appreciation, and understanding.

While speaking of the history of the Association, may I call attention to a volume devoted to the work of the organization? It was prepared by Dr. M. A. Meyer in partial fulfillment for the doctor's degree at Peabody College and is now in the possession of the Executive Committee. This manuscript has value; it should be published and placed in the hands of members in order that they may know what is the background of the Association and what are its accomplishments.

The Commission on Secondary Schools has been an active force in southern education. The high school situation, through the work done by this Commission, has been vastly improved. The Commission has shown constant evidence of life by its study of problems which faced it, and by the careful and sympathetic survey of schools applying for admission.

The Association has been busy accrediting schools and colleges, and much of the time of the Commission on Higher Education has been devoted to such purposes. However, within the last three years the Commission on Higher Education has begun to deal in a scientific way with some of the questions which confront it. Under its auspices a study of the Negro colleges is now in process. This project has been made possible by grants from the General Education Board. A year ago it began the study of teacher training under a similar relationship.

Some years ago a committee was created for the purpose of considering the marking system existent in secondary schools and colleges; this body has also attempted to show correlation between the two. Now a committee has been appointed to consider athletics; the report which is to be made at this meeting will undoubtedly prove of value in bringing order into the athletic situation in the South.

As any Association which is alive to its responsibilities must be faced with a number of problems, so the Southern Association has its fair quota. The discussion last year on the subject of membership in office and of more frequent changes in the personnel of commissions received considerable comment among the attendants upon the meetings. That discussion resulted in the bringing of the matter to the attention of the Association as a whole and in the appointment of a committee that will make recommendations at this meeting. Rotation in offices and greater frequency in the changes in membership of the commissions seemed desirable to the Association. Objection, of course, was made to any such modification on the grounds that it would reduce the effectiveness of the commissions and change the general policy of the Association. After all, however, the Association must be governed by the majority's attitude on these questions of membership and policy. Without doubt this organization has made marked progress during the past years. But, with its increased size and larger geographical area, the demand for representation becomes strong; and, having in mind the future usefulness of the Association, I think all will agree that such a request is legitimate and should be heeded.

I presume that it is unnecessary to emphasize the importance of keeping before this Association the changes that are taking place in the field of education. The influences at work everywhere tend to modify the content, purpose, and method of instruction just as various trends affect the fields of science, government, and business. It is, therefore, urgent that the Association consciously recognizes the changing, shifting character of the problems which are to be met. There is danger of getting into ruts, and this danger applies particularly to large organizations such as the Southern Association. The Association has striven to avoid routine in the consideration of all questions, but it must do more than that. It must be constantly engaged in the study of problems rather than in merely viewing them.

That the Association shall look upon education as a whole and not as a divided thing is most important. This Association has had a distinguished history and has accomplished a great many noteworthy things. It can do much more in the future. The approach, however, which it makes to these present day problems must be undivided and unbiased; it must take the scientific attitude of getting at facts, of finding out needs, and of working out plans for meeting these needs.

Questions have been raised as to whether the proceedings which now appear in a single volume should not be published in a quarterly journal. Undoubtedly, the proceedings would take at least two numbers of such a journal, and consequently there would be delay in getting the results of the meeting before the members. However, something should be said for the publication of a quarterly in that a periodical well edited tends to hold the organization together and gives the members information and knowledge of the problems with which various groups in the Association are confronted. Some standardizing agencies have publications that are regarded by the members as possessing great value particularly when they are ably edited. However, I am satisfied to leave the matter here, having raised the point.

The recognition and admission of colleges and schools to membership have been important functions of the Association. Necessarily it was essential that, in the matter of requirements for admission, certain specific criteria should be set up. These were largely of a material type and were quantitative in character rather than qualitative. That the use of such rules was of value and was practically indispensable in the earlier stages of a standardizing procedure is not to be doubted. Here and there attempts are now being made to change to qualitative tests.

If, however, material standards are continued, it is obvious that insistence upon budgetary procedure of institutions is necessary. It is said by those who ought to know that some colleges belonging to this Association do not have a budget. Moreover, careful investigation should be made of salaries paid for instruction, and scrutiny should be given to the material equipment of the colleges. The Association should look carefully at the endowment situation of some of its members. How have endowments, under the stress of conditions during the past four years, been widely dissipated, and what plans are in mind now to restore them to a satisfactory basis?

Attention has been called now and again to the movement away from these material standards that have been used in the past. This is to be seen in our own Association in the special studies and special committees that have been appointed from time to time; the emphasis, undoubtedly here as elsewhere, is upon the institutional standing and upon the character of the work done in it. "The ability of an institution to meet standards is no great assurance of the level of its performance." Thus spoke Dr. George F. Zook in his address to the Progressive Education Association meeting in New York City, November 1, of this year. Before he became Director of the American Association on Education, Dr. Zook was Secretary of the Higher Education Commission on Standards and Institutional Objectives of the North Central Association. That Association has come to the conclusion, according to the reports, that qualitative rather than quantitative results should be considered in determining the standing of an institution.

The purpose is to develop individuality in the school or college, emphasizing its specific objectives and endeavoring to ascertain the field in which it works and the success that it has in meeting its own objectives. Thus an institution under the emphasis of the qualitative rather than the quantitative standard is not compelled to adopt certain lines of procedure, to maintain certain types of classroom organization, or to follow the general trend developing in an association; it may have freedom to advance in its own way so long as it has an objective that is high in purpose.

To describe the truly characteristic colleges and universities that are worthy of public recognition as institutions of higher education is undoubtedly the first step in a policy of accrediting. To guide prospective students in the choice of an institution and to help individual institutions in various relationships, such as the transfer of students, the placement of college graduates, and the selection of faculties, are also purposes in accreditation. The heads of secondary schools are desirous of selecting teachers from, and of directing students to, qualified colleges. Finally the objective of accrediting is to stimulate improvement in the field of higher education.

In determining the basis upon which accrediting may be done, a new phrase has been brought into educational discourse. This is called "total pattern." The pattern is arrived at by attempting to find the standing of an institution in every phase of its activities. The judgment in determining the conditions must necessarily vary, but some idea may be had by comparing the pattern of an institution with the general pattern of all institutions in the Association. The purpose in establishing a general pattern is to ascertain the individual qualifications which an institution has and to deal with such questions as the capability of the faculty, the representative character of the curriculum, the effectiveness of administration, the standards of student accomplishment, and the financial adequacy.

The accrediting body does not seek uniformity in the details of institutional policy and practice but tries always to ascertain those that are desirable and necessary. Thus every institution that applies for accrediting would present statements of its general purposes and of methods used in the development of students including health and physical competence. Along with these statements there must be comments which show the institution's clientele, its geographical area, and the support which it receives from religious and other groups or, if public, from the government.

The purpose of this new approach in the field of accrediting is not to insist upon regimentation but rather to keep institutions flexible and adaptable. Educational experiments carried on may well be looked upon as evidences of vitality. These, however, must be well conceived and carefully directed.

The information needed to determine the status of an institution is extensive. Such information attempts to include an intimate study of the policy, faculty, instruction, organization, background, and equipment of the foundation. When all of these things are considered, a pattern of the school or college can be made. This pattern compared with the general run of institutions in the Association indicates whether the institution is superior, satisfactory, acceptable, marginal, or unsatisfactory. In this new accrediting program, which has not yet been established anywhere but which is in the process of examination, the word "standards" disappears and the term "tests" becomes more prominent.

In developing an educational program, every institution should have more knowledge of its students. The school or college must know what they have done and what they are doing. The purpose in such information is that the institution may shape its work and guide its policy. "Tests," as Dean Hawkes remarked the other day, "are one feature of a constantly broadening philosophy of education." Tests are not to be looked upon as possessing an infallible rule for the determination of standards to be exacted but as having value in finding out what an institution is doing; hence, although they raise many difficulties, they must come into the picture more and more. After all, tests are tools, and, if an institution is to answer the question of its place in the social organization, it must have tools for determining that position in a rather definite way.

I turn now to the junior college movement, not with the expectation of discussing it in any definitive way, but to call attention to some of the drifts at the present time. Thirty-six members of the Association are listed as junior colleges. These institutions are doing excellent work. Demands on the part of school systems and municipalities to promote local junior colleges are increasing. The proposal takes the form of creating a separate junior college under the sponsorship of a college, possibly a state university, or of extending the high school for a period of two years, the high school to carry on two years of college work in addition to the four years of secondary work. This last type of junior college has not made its appearance in this Association, but it is bound to come into existence in the near future.

A college or university that establishes in a city at some distance from the main campus a junior college under its sponsorship will eventually weaken itself in financial matters or in the presentation of unsatisfactory work. Just now with public taxation and public finances in the condition they are in, public school authorities ought to look with considerable questioning upon the extension of their program into the junior college field since the use of funds for such a purpose is quite sure to enfeeble the offerings in the secondary level. The problem should be studied carefully by those organizations that are contemplating the creation of junior colleges. For the purpose of safeguarding their own finances and maintaining the standards of the institutions, the proposals should also be studied in the light of transportation, local need, and the cost per student. This Association should not be blind to what is happening and, consequently, surprised when in a few years the consideration of increasing numbers of junior colleges presents itself in an urgent and definite form.

I wish to comment upon another problem which is facing the Association, and that is the question of graduate instruction. Many institutions are drifting into graduate work largely for the purpose of meeting competition and for the accommodation of teachers seeking to comply with the requirement of state departments or local school authorities that a teacher in the secondary field shall have a master's degree. The state departments at present make no distinctions and look upon all master of arts degrees wherever granted as meeting the requirement. The result is that we are drifting into a situation that is decidedly unsatisfactory. The offerings in the graduate field for a master's degree have greatly increased, and in many instances graduate work has become merely an extension of undergraduate courses into the fifth year. This Association may well give thought to the problems thus raised and may confer with the various state departments of education in this area to ascertain what their attitudes are on this matter.

The years of usefulness before this Association can well be measured by the past. The problems which face it now are different but no less important. If the same courage animates its membership that inspired the work of the early days, the Association can do much in advancing the cause of education in the South and in the nation. That this will be done with unity of purpose, with harmony of relationship, and with the sincere examination of all questions to be solved, I do not doubt. The Association will go on to new achievements. Presidents who come in the future will pore over the proceedings of the Association and, noting the progress made, will comment on the vision of the Association in its efforts to deal with the problems that crowd upon us in this new era. It is my hope and yours that we shall have vision and that we shall be worthy of the trust.

Why Confusion in Education?

President's address to the Kentucky Education Association,
Louisville, April, 1937

EDUCATION is a world-old process. Since man came on the earth, education has been going on. Education has always had before it the adaptation of man to his environment in order that he may look with some confidence to the future of the race. To this educational effort parents, the seers of the tribe, the elder statesmen, and daily companions made important contributions. Out of these teachings issued philosophies of education, which included inheritances of the race, practices of living, and concepts of man's place in nature. In the simpler days the doing of things, the making of artifacts, and the production of shelter, clothing, and food constituted the major elements that concerned men. The tabus of the social group and the status of the individual were fixed by rules and laws that had been proved effective in a scarcity economy and in a more or less self-sustaining society.

Through the centuries we have arrived at a very different social, political, and economic organization. Mass production, separation of man from his tools and his products, political democracy, a varied social order, and a vast system of local, state, and federal governments have come into being in what is called modern society in the United States of America. In such a social organization where men must rely upon working together, it was necessary, if political democracy was to be attained and continued, to establish the separation of church and state, to continue and hold contractual obligations in economic and political relations, and to create some agency for the dispelling of ignorance. These are enormous accomplishments. Now this society is on the edge of a great and difficult step, the attainment of economic democracy. That too is a long march requiring intelligence, knowledge, tolerance, and leadership endowed with social conscience. In this brief summary I have tried to emphasize the drift of social purpose and to lay stress upon the importance of dispelling ignorance and of establishing the place and function of the individual in the social order.

The doing of these great things is called education, a process not limited to the schools but including all agencies good or bad that affect the person in his relations to the society in which he lives. Our concern today is primarily with one of these, the schools, elementary, secondary, higher, private and public. We are told that there is confusion not only in regard to what is education but also in regard to how we are to bring it about. Moreover disagreement exists as to the general purpose of education; this may be stated as the fitting of the individual to the present and future environment in which he may live and as the preparing of him for the enjoyment of his mental, spiritual, and physical qualities so that he may live a full life.

Now in this country has been established a great system of public education supplemented by private and denominational schools. The number of youth attending these schools reaches the millions, twenty-four million in the elementary, five million in the secondary schools, and a million in colleges and universities. Nearly a fourth of the nation's population is going to school. This is a phenomenon that astonishes the world and brings to every teacher a keen sense of responsibility if he thinks about it at all. "This system of organized education, properly conscious of itself as the integrative agent of all social forces, holds the key to social stability, social decay, or social progress."

That our system of education is properly conscious of itself, that it really has more than a faint idea of its purpose, or that it is at all certain how that purpose should be carried out is sometimes doubted. Great emphasis has been placed upon organization, upon administration, and upon finance; but the real end of education seems uncertain, knowledge of the learning process vague, and the understanding of personality as a social factor barely comprehended. Since the material side of the educational procedure is more easily apprehended than the philosophical, the study of administration, the techniques of teaching, and the making of textbooks along the traditional lines occupy a major part of the time and interest of educational workers.

In addition the educational philosophers show a considerable variety of thinking about the situation. Let it be remarked that differences of all kinds are found in American life generally. Diversity of thinking is accepted as evidence of vitality and of a groping for ideals that are essential to a new age. On the other hand, a clear cut philosophy of education is necessary in order that man "may mold into a dynamic thesis his inheritance from the past and his techniques for creating out of the present a more desirable future."

From college halls, school rooms, lecture platforms, the press, and the voices of individual citizens comes the indictment that confusion exists among the educational leaders as to purpose and method of education. In some ways this outcry is a hopeful sign; in others it is evidence of failure to understand. The confusion in education is paralleled in every other field in life. There is uncertainty about the present and pessimism about the future. Men and women, however, in education are ardently striving to find the way and to clear their minds of the confusion that is undoubtedly to be found in them.

For convenience at any rate, the educational theories may be catalogued, and our conception of them may be reduced to a formula of understanding. I propose to begin with the views that may be called traditional. By traditional one means that which is customary, accepted, and derived from the past. Thus the Traditionalists maintain that the values found in the American life are essential, fundamental, and superior to those that derive from science or philosophy. Eternal values and preconceived ends are the high purposes to be attained by external disciplines. The content of education, more or less fixed, is to be placed in the minds of young people who go to school. Teaching is a process of instructing in order that the values of the present may be thoroughly grounded in the student's mind.

The Traditionalists believe in discipline, in thrift, in obedience; they do not believe that the educational motivation based upon natural curiosity can be successfully used because lack of discipline drifts into soft pedagogy and self-indulgence. Subject matter must be relied upon to furnish real motivation. Some of the members of the traditional school look upon the grouping of pupils on the basis of intelligence tests as a repudiation of the very possibility of education. Mastery of subject matter and discipline in conduct and purpose are the real objectives of education.

In opposition to the traditional philosophy is the one called progressive, which has for its center the doctrine of interest against the concept of discipline. It emphasizes the felt need of the learner and encourages the individual effort of the pupil; the school curriculum and procedure, therefore, are to be developed from day to day. The Progressives insist upon activities that parallel the growth of the child. Out of these interests and skills will flower something quite worthwhile. The function of education is to discover the budding needs, interests, and capacities of children and, having done that, to see that other tendencies develop to be used and trained later. Book subject matter and method are adjusted to the growing power of children.

In the philosophy of the Progressives both teacher and pupil participate in a constant development. From this experience emerges knowledge which comes from thinking and from the use of ideas. The discipline, so emphasized by other groups, comes from observation and from judgment attitudes that are formed in the working of the progressive idea. Society is not thought of as a fixed structure or a definite level but as shifting and seeking new ways of expression and a varied group of activities. Only by such procedure can the schools give to the new generation the equipment and the understanding needed for a changing society.

The vision of the third group who may be called the Scientists is that of a perfect social order reached through the ceaseless, minute, self-sacrificing labor of devoted scientists. What has come down from the past may be accepted, but every practice, every procedure, and every curriculum activity are to be tested by the scientific method and statistically evaluated. Nor is the theorist to go beyond the frontiers already defined by educational science. Efficiency is to be determined experimentally, and educational procedures can reach an effective stage only when they are scientifically directed.

In the opinion of this group the "Progressives worship a cult that has lost the balancing influences of history and psychology." Activities so worshipped by the Progressives cannot be substituted for language and numbers, which now and forever must occupy a central place in the curriculum. The Scientists believe that satisfaction will come to teachers and pupils through the curriculum that has systematic plans and scientific arrangement. The mental activities of pupils are directed to acting and thinking in relation to physical and social environment.

Another philosophy should be included in this summary, which

I have been able to make through the use of Normal Woelfel's book, *The Molders of the American Mind*. There is a group of thinkers who may be called Social Idealists; perhaps in the final analysis their philosophy is realistic because it attempts to pull aside the veil and look at what must be. Man is confronted by the naked facts of human experience which force him to accept today mass production and a rapidly devastating change in social life. Man's great problem is consciously to control and to master the forces of civilization. To attain real democracy, he must abandon the profit motive in industry and must adopt a rationally planned economy in the interest of all. To deal with the situation as it exists in America today is true education; therefore, the purpose of the school should be to build personalities that will create self-direction and independence.

The school perceived by the Idealists extends from the primary to adult life, closely and consistently related to life itself. The object is to create an individual and collective intelligence capable of dealing with the problems of a changing civilization. This is a noble purpose which, if actually followed, would necessitate complete application of experiences to the problems of a people and in the end would bring the Utopia desired.

The criticism of the last group of philosophers against Traditionalists and educational Scientists is severe and condemnatory. The Traditionalists have warped the educational theory to fit the status quo. Leadership in education is influenced by this static way of regarding things, which is shown in the theory and practice, the textbooks, and the administration of education. It is assumed by the Traditionalists that the present procedure will continue. No such conclusion can be drawn; the Idealists, therefore, insist upon a changing world that will relegate much that is now regarded as wise and helpful to the scrap-heap of discarded ideas. The Scientists' movement, on the other hand, the Idealists maintain, because it is allied with anti-democratic educational direction, has placed the stamp of approval upon reactionary and conservative practices.

"Hold fast to what we have; improve it if we can," says the first of the philosophic groups. "Let the pupil follow his own inclina-

tions, and encourage activities that will lead to self-expression,"
declare the Progressives. "Examine, sift, experiment, and do not
go beyond the boundary of tried theory," admonish the Scientists.
"Since the present social order is weak and unsatisfactory," the
Idealists insist, "the education of our time must produce independence, initiative, and freedom for the new world of men."

My summary is too meager, too limited, and too terse to cover
the varied views of able and distinguished men who constitute
these philosophic schools of education. Many other differences
are to be found in the definitions and uses of common terms such
as learning, study, teaching, curricula, motivation, objectives, and
so on through a long list of words and phrases.

Naturally the educational world is in confusion because it involves many fundamental matters of which a great deal is not
known. I may illustrate this by using one example. How does the
pupil learn? The answer to that simple question will lead into
depths of philosophical and psychological discussion.

Although a philosophy of education is of the highest importance,
yet dangerous portents are evident in certain kinds of philosophy
that may create in time even a totalitarian state and that may bring
about almost instantly mushy attitudes and unhappy conditions of
mind. What you and I think about education affects our own attitudes and in the long run the practice and the ultimate results of
education. To be among those whose work is in the field of education is to have a tremendous responsibility.

Because of many social changes, a greater share in personality
and character growth has been placed upon the schools. The emphasis upon subject matter in the school program too often has
pushed aside the general objectives that should be attained. The
new teaching introduces attitudes, desires, and conduct that in
themselves give an impulse to the learning of facts. Then will the
student take on new interests that lead to self-realization, the goal
of all education.

The Kentucky Education Association has accomplished much in
securing legislation for the schools, in establishing administrative
procedure, and in gaining financial support for public education. A

new turn of mind is needed so that the Association may view the work of teachers, may improve their training, and particularly may clear the uncertainties of purpose which are now apparent.

It is evident that as a professional group we must try to think our way through the difficulties of education, hoping thereby to come to a highway that leads to the right direction of an educational system. Certainly, the schools can be no better than our understanding; in the long run, therefore, the public will not be well served unless we know where we are going. Instruction in a few disciplines is not sufficient. In the pupil, the teacher must develop attitudes, appreciation, understanding, values, self-realization. The name of teacher is earned by those who accomplish this tremendous task.

There is confusion in education; there is uncertainty in other fields of endeavor. But confusion must not be continuous; it must not be permanent. It must be banished, and light must be made to prevail. That in brief is the call to the Kentucky Education Association. The members of the Association surely seek the highest attainments of good teaching and unquestionably look for that educational procedure and understanding which will best serve the state and the nation in solving their social, economic, and political problems.

Education and the Tennessee Valley Authority

Introduction to "*Adult Education—a Part of a Total Educational Program*: description of the educational and training program of the TVA"; Bulletin of the Bureau of School Service, College of Education, University of Kentucky, Volume X, Number 4, edited by Maurice F. Seay, June, 1938

MR. AND MRS. CITIZEN reading the newspaper left on the doorstep before breakfast talked of some of the day's events chronicled in the news sheet and came to the conclusion that the Tennessee Valley Authority is a giant organization set up to furnish cheap power and light to the communities of the Valley area. Much emphasis has been put upon the utility controversy, and what Mr.

and Mrs. Citizen think about it is in the minds of thousands of others.

The law establishing the Authority was intended to bring about flood control, irrigation, and conservation of soils as well as to develop power. These are inherent in the program, but down deep in the plan is a social interest that looks to the maintenance of the American way and the creation of additional opportunities for a better life in the area. To do this requires the promotion of higher standards of living which can be maintained in a land where labor and industry may receive adequate rewards. So not only does soil conservation become an important phase of the Tennessee Valley development, but also education of the people in the area is a significant purpose.

An undertaking the size of the one Valley project that has been under way since 1933 calls for a great organization and the employment of thousands of men and women. When large engineering enterprises have been entered upon in the past, little attention has been paid to the social and educational needs of the people brought to the sites of the activities. The Authority in charge of this great project perceives not only an economic but also a social challenge.

My interest in the articles edited by Mr. Seay arises out of the fact that one of the best things the Authority has done and one to which little attention has been given is the educational program. If this program were the ordinary one that is typical of town or country school systems, I should be mildly interested; but what has been done in the Tennessee Valley is a real contribution to education.

The tendency of any system, educational or otherwise, is to harden and to develop routine methods. Administration gathers a great deal of importance and is quite likely to become an end in itself. Various types of instruction are regarded as essential, and those who teach have vested interests that must be protected. Modifications of procedure or even techniques are brought about slowly. The teacher trained in an older regime does not like the new techniques that are crying out to be tried. Town and country school systems pursue their way side by side with no cooperation between them. Town libraries lend books to those who enter the doors, but the directors do not go out to the schools or attempt to serve an adult population outside the rim of circulation. These are commonplace situations known to all who have any interest in education.

A great many things that are highly gratifying are happening in schools; but practice is by no means up to knowledge and understanding of what might be done. That the Tennessee Valley Authority wisely did not follow conventional procedures in working out an educational and recreational program, not only has been of great benefit to the Authority and the people in the area, but has done much for the administrator, teacher, and citizen who are interested in education.

The Authority was faced with a real problem in its educational needs that varied with groups and communities. What was the goal to be attained? Could the program provided be a continuous one? More than that, the Authority appears to have been wise enough to see that any program imposed from above was bound to fail. Also it perceived that opportunities for progress might be strangled in the meshes of administrative units. The supposed gap between pupil and adult was bridged by unifying the whole educational process. The program had to be standard enough to meet the eyes of sceptics and sufficiently flexible to use experience gained in one place to aid a program somewhere else. I think that the Authority has accomplished this. Certainly the testimony points to results that might have been regarded as impossible in so short a time.

How was this done? First, by providing capable and effective leadership for the whole program; second, by unifying plans for the use of equipment and staff; third, by staggering programs in order to utilize staff and equipment to the fullest advantage; and fourth, by keeping the various educational programs in contact with each other through a central agency. I am enumerating the points in the philosophy since they must be a part of the educational program. These are: education is the composite of all the experiences of an individual; education is a continuous process and must be based upon the needs and interests of those for whom it is planned; in practice these principles can be made more acceptable and useful by the democratic method, and through that method the real needs of a people can be more readily met; finally, any program must possess great flexibility.

In nearly every conference held to discuss the educational procedure, the need of leadership is emphasized again and again. The Authority, recognizing this need from the first, began by acquainting the headquarters' staffs with the history, purpose, and goal of the great project. From this step others followed until by selection and training a competent staff was brought into being. The engineering problems did not vary much from dam to dam, but the educational problems varied greatly from site to site. It was evident that existing agencies must be brought into the whole of the educational program through cooperation and by agreement that the program for instruction would be modified to meet the needs wherever found. The story of what was done and what is being done is an inspiring one.

In much of the discussion of adult education found in periodicals and groups, it is evident that the writers are thinking of something separate from the general educational process. For instance, a gap between pupil and adult is supposed to exist whereas the consolidation of the processes of education makes for successful teaching. An example of the benefits of unification is seen in the fact that, although the service-in-training program was in itself worthwhile, the progress made by the trainees was pronounced when this training was supplemented by general adult education. Library facilities were carried to the men on jobs, and the selection of books was fitted to the wants of the men.

The system of interns by which leaders through practice and experience might learn the problems that they were likely to face showed highly satisfactory results. The emphasis given to internship should open the way to its use more extensively elsewhere. Graduate schools could learn a good deal from the experience of the Authority and thus help remove the stigma often laid on graduate students that they have no knowledge of field or office methods and practices.

The effect of the educational program of the Authority upon local communities and governing boards has been to increase their comprehension of the possibilities for cooperation and of the varying needs of different groups. The unifying of activities has enabled these groups to advance in the educational program. That education is a continuous process actually no longer remains a theory but becomes the recognized method of approaching community and individual problems.

This study of adult education as a part of the TVA development goes into some detail in discussing the way in which many of the accomplishments hinted at in this introduction have been achieved. It will furnish the reader important information about what is being done in the Tennessee Valley to promote an unusual and helpful educational program.

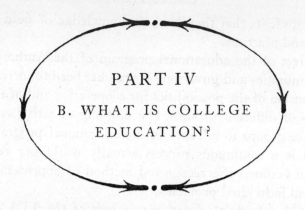

PART IV

B. WHAT IS COLLEGE
EDUCATION?

What Is College Education?

COLLEGE education is a process of growth, planning, and preparation. It is an opportunity to know what the great of the world have said and done. It should be a period during which the student learns the accomplishments of governments, the causes of disasters, the errors men have made, and the victories which have been won for enlightenment. This period of four years should bring to the student a sense of human progress, an understanding of the methods of science, some appreciation of literature and the other arts, and a reverence for God and man. It is a time when he discovers his associates, catches some idea of the working of human organizations, and begins to adjust himself to manhood's estate. During this time he ought to learn how to approach a problem, how to analyze it, and how to test its truth. Four years of college should give to the student a larger tolerance, an awakened "curiosity," a knowledge of how to work, and an acceptance of integrity of mind as the greatest of human endowments.

Now We Can Progress

Summary of address at the inauguration of President H. A. Babb,
Morehead State Teachers College, Morehead, Kentucky, May 5, 1936

THERE are times in the history of an enterprise when the ground is cleared, the plans for the future are blueprinted, and the specifications are written with some certainty of purpose. Such a time is now at hand in this commonwealth; education henceforth must be thought of in large and inspirational terms with action as the goal.

In 1932 the legislature of Kentucky authorized a commission to study the educational system and to make a report two years later. A well-considered report and an admirable code of law were handed to the next legislature. To the credit of that body the code was enacted into law. A further step was taken in 1936 by the making of appropriations for free textbooks and for an adequate per capita support of the public schools. Thus in a few years, great progress was made toward the building of a real educational system in Kentucky.

A strange notion exists that education is a stationary thing. The fact is that it changes with the times and with the variations in social organization. The teacher of today requires wisdom, knowledge, and technique, for the pupil must be related to the society in which he lives if he is to be a useful citizen. The teacher cannot do this alone; the community must have appreciation of the work the school is called upon to do. The emphasis falls upon the better prepared teacher who has vision, wisdom, and an insight into the great obligations resting upon him or her.

What the elementary school does is heightened in the secondary period where the tools of knowledge are used in the acquirement of social understanding. The colleges must go much farther since their objective is to enlarge knowledge, develop techniques, encourage thinking and responsibility.

These problems merely mentioned here must be dealt with adequately in this present time. The constructive agencies of education must work as never before in conserving and building the educational structure. This cannot be done without harmony and cooperation among us. It is for all of us to see Kentucky as a whole apart from institutions, sections, or class distinctions. With this agreement in the ranks of education, there is a chance to formulate the problems, to find the answers, and to act upon the findings. Work is here for all. Recognition of this fact is not enough; hard work must be done by the teacher and the administrator.

On a day such as this the queries I have been raising are highly important. Is this college over which the new president presides to be one more college, or is it to find new ways, engage in experiments, study problems, and perform its obligations thoroughly and well? There are many colleges, schools, and individuals that follow the conventional, expected paths as though the end of knowledge had come. If many experiments were going on in Kentucky, and all were imbued with the idea of service and the finding of better ways, progress would be rapid. The state has furnished a legal organization, authority, and funds. The teachers, administrators, and students of education are compelled to provide the leadership, find the way, and keep the vision of educational purpose alive.

The challenge is there. We have accepted it; but only a harmonious, hardworking group can win the victory. Today is a day of consecration placing upon all here and everywhere in the state the pledge of the real missionary to serve, to learn, to work, and to understand with sympathy and devotion.

Suppose we say, those of us associated with educational work in the state, that we do know what we want. Is the answer that we want better salaries, better buildings, and better equipment? Well may it be asked, when such an answer is given, to what end are these things to be provided? Exactly to what end?

In the long run, the answer must depend upon the philosophy of education held by those who guide educational procedure in the state. If this philosophy is inadequate, the education of the youth is unequal to the calls made upon it. In the main the preliminary discipline upon which training for service depends is provided by the schools. Through all the functions of teaching runs the ethical element that binds our civilization together. Moreover no such civilization as ours, based as it is on scientific appliances of great variety, can long hold together with an ignorant population. Consequently, the school as a teaching agency is of necessity the all important thing.

The great agency called the public schools has the difficult problem not only of explaining the tools of knowledge but also of orienting the pupil in his citizenship as worker and as participant in government. Since the Republic is faced with problems as well as the individual, the public schools are called upon to encourage thinking so that democracy in action may be well served. And in addition high ideals must flow through the school touching the pupil at every point.

The preparation, wisdom, and understanding of the teacher furnish the solution for the difficulties not only in the school but also in the community and state as well. So the teacher is confronted with the responsibility of comprehending these great purposes and of preparing himself or herself for these duties. Thus an important social end is revealed. The teacher through sympathetic interest should be able to fill the pupil with desire to be a real citizen of the Republic. When this great concept of the school and the teacher is clearly apprehended, the need of prepared teachers comes to be the insistent challenge to a commonwealth. That preparation is entrusted to the colleges. On them the responsibility for the preparation is placed. The charge is given directly to the leaders of the colleges to understand, to see, and to create the courses and means of providing the training for teachers. To succeed in this enterprise is absolutely necessary; but success depends on experiment, study, organization, and teaching of a high order.

The Morehead Teachers College has entered into this field of teacher education by the authority and the support of the state. Adherence to traditional methods and looking backward for inspiration will not bring to these problems of teacher training the direction that is required today. The new president comes into the administration of a state college just at the time when high hopes are entertained of a better day, a day that will impart to the service of state and nation noble inspiration, high purpose, careful direction, and skillful teaching. Nothing else will do. With his practical experience as teacher and administrator he should be a real aid to the program of preparing teachers in Kentucky. His friends and admirers think he will render this great service. To him and to the college I extend congratulations and good wishes.

Ways and Means

The Liberal Arts College in the New Social Order

Address to the Association of Kentucky Colleges,
University of Kentucky, January, 1935; published in
Journal of Higher Education, April, 1935; reprinted

F o r some years the college of liberal arts and sciences has been the subject of much criticism and of a good deal of despair. It has likewise undergone a notable amount of reorganization in an attempt to meet some of the objections made to the courses offered and to the general plan of the college. The despair of the critics has taken the form of prophecy to the effect that the college is doomed and will disappear as a part of American education.

In the effort to correct the more noticeable defects many changes have been made within the colleges themselves. Courses have been grouped so that the student no longer majors in a single subject, broad as it is, but follows his will in a flock of courses under the head of languages, arts, social or physical sciences. This arrangement is supposed to bring about a coordination in the student's attitudes and to give him a rounded training in order that he may have two wings with which to fly. Whether he will have strength enough to fly at all has not yet been evidenced. Another procedure is to be found in the honors courses; in them the student who works by his own initiative may gain much through the contact he has with the instructor who acts as his mentor. And again, individual study with liberty to follow any line of work has been used in a few colleges for specially gifted students. All of these modifications of the old methods have merit; but that merit depends upon the students and the teachers with whom they associate plus institutions that have money enough to provide more leisure for instructors and more library equipment for students.

On the organization side and in quite a different direction from the procedures briefly referred to, is the division of the college into upper and lower levels with the break coming at the end of the sophomore year. In the first two years of college the student follows set courses with few electives. He is then supposed to have gained some facility in the use of language, learned the technique of a science or two, and attained a certain background in the social sciences. When he completes the sophomore year, he is ready to enter the upper level. Here he is to follow the courses offered on a graduate basis; that is, he is expected to do independent work. In some instances comprehensive examinations must be passed before the student can move on into the higher plane. If he cannot meet such tests, he is shown the door marked, "Exit to the World."

This arrangement may be classed as a decided breakup of the college because it emphasizes the distinction between secondary-school and university processes, the very point the critics have been insisting upon, and because, if pursued as a device, it sooner or later will cut the college in two. In those institutions where the college is the only group, this division is a serious matter since it looks to the junior college and the university type of organization in which the lower two years are the preparation for the professional courses offered in the last two.

The depression for two reasons has brought a respite in the controversy over the college of arts. The first of these is that expansion can not be pushed any farther since incomes are smaller, necessitating larger classes and reduced staffs; the second reason is to be found in the change in the social situation. Leisure, adult education, and education for the fuller life are now talked about in newspapers over the land. Thus a great call has been issued to all educational institutions to enlist in the vast undertaking of educating the people in a new way. Instead of talking about the courses, the organization, and the division of colleges, the profession in the field of higher education is being asked to prepare the youth for the present social era.

In his 1934 annual report to the directors of the Carnegie Corporation, after referring to the efforts of Yale, Harvard, and Princeton to bring the students in close contact with instructors and with the courses they are following, Frederick Keppel declared: "Every year thousands of young people profit and profit richly from the opportunities which the colleges now offer, but taking into consideration all the colleges and all the students, it is a question whether the game has proved to be worth the candle."

The *New York Times*, in commenting on Mr. Keppel's courage in questioning the value of college education, said that to some the game has been profitless but to many it has been "worth the candle." To make it worth while is a matter not of tinkering with the curriculum but of dealing with the student and developing in him a love of learning. This means a different approach from the one generally followed, an approach which requires additional amounts of money. In the face of decreasing endowments, such a desirable course of action may be increasingly difficult.

I have said enough to indicate that the college of arts has been under two fires, one which aims at its organization and the other at the courses that are offered to students registered in the college. Now the third complaint, of which we hear murmurings, has to do with the question of the ability of the college to fit the student for the new social era that is apparently upon us.

There are, it appears to me, three significant phases of the problem that confronts the college of arts. The first of these relates to the incoming student; the second, to the objectives of the college; and the third, to the attitude of instructors to the first two.

It can be said, I think, that the officers know more about the students who come to the college than they did two decades ago. This knowledge rests upon the results of mental and physical examinations given to all students. That such data are considered carefully by all deans may be open to question, but the information is there for use. The records of the student from high school are more detailed than they used to be; and, if these records are accompanied by the principal's rating and a history of the student's high-school life, college officers will have sufficient knowledge of the entering. student to advise him effectively in the matter of courses and sections. Unfortunately, such information is not always asked and is not often forthcoming; so the student is just another person in the entering freshman class. The purpose of such records and of the rating that goes with them is to help the student to avoid mistakes and to enable him to adjust himself to the new environment that he discovers in college.

The present method of waiting for the student to find himself and of then bringing the wrath of the college upon him if he fails has some advantages; it is, however, expensive in the matter of mortality and in the effect on the individual student who falls short. What can be done to obviate such an outcome?

The use of tests to determine classification and student load has much to commend it. The last ten per cent may be quite as much worth saving as the middle quarter, but they cannot be saved by applying the requisites of the first ten per cent to all alike; yet that is what we do in practice. The procedure must be greater care and more scrutiny in dealing with the student's problems.

A difficulty arises at this point in following the simple requirement laid down, a difficulty that is partly financial and partly a matter of personnel. To deal effectively with incoming students demands larger staffs in deans' offices and consequently more money. To add another person to such a staff would be of little value unless that person clearly understands the problems confronting him. It is just here that much of our trouble is to be found. I put the difficulty in a formula: If an officer is looking backward to the procedure of his own college days, he cannot meet the problems of an entirely new day because he is using a technique that is too small and too obsolete. I might summarize briefly the whole matter by saying that a greater knowledge of the student, when he comes to college and after he enters, and a deeper appreciation of modern educational procedure are fundamental requisites for blotting out many of the defects in higher education.

There is also need of course adjustments from time to time.

Courses of study are set up for definite purposes but, like the tariff, they are the result of compromises made by the departments. The very fact that this is true as well as the matter of students' aptitudes raises the question of modification to meet student differences. Thus the dean should have the authority to change the courses required of a student in order to give the greatest value to the latter's work. Such substitutions would not be numerous, but the authority to make them would solve a good many student difficulties.

Discussing with the student his problems should prove decidedly helpful. If the dean could have a wider knowledge of students' errors in expression, written and oral, and if he would proceed to the correcting of these defects at once, much of the more superficial criticism of the college would disappear. To effect these corrections requires an appreciation of the difficulties by the teacher and the enlargement of the staff and facilities of the work in English.

There is a college song with the refrain, "For God, for Country, and for Yale." No doubt, the major objectives of any college are for God, for Country, and for Alma Mater; yet the attaining of these major objectives involves other purposes about which we must think. In a general way, a certain consensus in regard to the purposes of the college of arts and sciences exists. These are first, acquaintance with the tools of knowledge such as language, mathematics, science, and the use of books; second, the development of background in the minds of students through the study of the social sciences, philosophy, and literature; and third, knowledge of the actual procedure of the world in political, business, and social fields.

One of the recurring criticisms of the college is that it teaches and inculcates concepts that are those of a vanishing world. Governmental practice, as an example, is at variance with the statements of the books and with the teaching of the classroom, and so the student finds his views old and sometimes obsolete. To this it may be replied that no set of facts and conclusions remains unchanged; consequently, the great task of the college is to teach the student logical thought processes, methods of finding materials, and the need of approaching all problems in a broad social spirit. Personal habits of courtesy and right living should be developed along with these mental disciplines. Such a combination of training and attitudes is of the highest value to a nation. The question which confronts the college is how it may be achieved.

In approaching the third point, which concerns itself with the attitude of instructors to the incoming students and to the objectives of the college, may I say that there must be in a college faculty a genuine interest in liberal arts education and in the intellectual and social growth of students. I find in Dean Hawkes' report for 1934 a paragraph which fits into this part of my discussion. He wrote: "Columbia College can never deserve a commanding place in the affection and esteem of those who know her unless, combined with a flexibility that encourages contacts of the widest range in the University, there is a warmth of personal attachment to men under whom, or rather with whom, the students of the College pass from boyhood to manhood. It is to be hoped and expected that not only new appointments but the entire offering of the College will be presented with this ideal in the foreground, and that devotion to this attitude toward collegiate work will never go unnoticed or unrewarded."

In more instances than we are willing to admit, have the difficulties of the college of liberal arts been cabined and confined by unmindful, unenthusiastic instructors. The college needs men and women well trained, socially minded, and full of the power to teach. We have seen enough of the great teacher on our campuses to know what leaven, not one, but several inspired teachers would be in a college.

The problems of this present era cannot be solved by any college. The solution of social problems is not the business of the college. But the business of the college is to train and guide its students to intellectual and social purposes. The college is justified only when its students, taking on the duties of citizenship and of leadership in business and government, bring clear unfettered minds to the meeting of every situation and to the settlement of every question.

The admission of students and the direction of their studies are definite obligations that rest upon the officers of the college. How to meet these assignments has been worked out and is available in the literature of education as well as in the practice of some colleges. The weak part of the procedure is to be found in the dearth of adequately trained, forward looking officers.

The problem that rests upon the colleges is not to be solved by creating more courses of study with names that have a relationship to present day government experiments. In some colleges, courses need to be reduced in number and increased in interesting subject matter. If reviewed and restated every now and then, many a course that has been left too long in a moldering condition would come to life. Again quoting from the report of Mr. Keppel: "For the most part, advance cannot be looked for through large expenditure for physical change nor by such modifications in the institutional set-up as will break up the personality of the college itself, but rather by an effective study as to the application of what we now know regarding individual differences, interests and motives, mental hygiene, the technique of continuous record, the uses of comprehensive and other examination. It will involve building on the personality of the existing faculty. Though such changes require study rather than money, nevertheless, particularly in these days, some money is needed for experimental equipment, possibly temporarily for salaries."

The definite steps therefore to be taken by a college that hopes for a more effective influence on the life of today are these: first, a careful study of students admitted to college; second, a continued scrutiny of the work and progress of students after they have entered college; third, the adjustment of students to their work and programs in the light of such knowledge; fourth, examination of courses of study as to content and number and consideration of their value for the training and stimulation of students; fifth, vigilant selection of staff so that men of ability and social outlook may be assured for teaching posts; sixth, review and restatement of the objectives of the college. To put the matter broadly and bluntly, what are needed today in our colleges are better jobs of teaching, of supervision, and of direction.

The liberal arts college has much to contribute; it is a valuable factor in the social organization and will continue to live so long as its administrators and teachers have vision. The process of experimentation must be used in dealing with its problems, subject to and aided by knowledge and professional skill.

The future of the college depends upon the constant alertness and increasing information about the students who are in the college. The tendency in days like these is to sit down and try to hold what we have. That too must be done, but there must be advance in administering and instructing through knowing the purposes of the college, the individuality and ability of the students, and the trend of the social organization. Progress will come indeed by a series of trials and errors under the guidance of good sense, knowledge, and vision.

Progress and Problems in Higher Education in Kentucky

Address to the Kentucky Association of Colleges and Secondary Schools, University of Kentucky, October 29, 1937

AN AMAZING change has taken place in the state of Kentucky in attendance upon high schools and colleges. The figures for the year 1916-17 show 22,025 pupils enrolled in Kentucky high schools, a ratio in population of one to one hundred. Twenty years later the figures given by the state Department of Education on high-school attendance are 94,000; the ratio has risen to one to twenty-seven of population. Or to be more specific the growth in the twenty-year period is a quadruple one.

In 1916 the state Department of Education reported 2,468 high school graduates. This was a ratio of one graduate to nine pupils in attendance. In 1936 there were 12,017 graduates, or one to seven and nine-tenths pupils attending. What will the ratio be in 1940? My guess is one to six and five-tenths.

During this period of twenty years, attendance in the colleges of Kentucky increased nearly four times. It was reported by the state Department of Education that 4,576 students were in college in 1916, or one to each five hundred of the population. In 1937 there were 16,980 students pursuing higher education, or one to one hundred and fifty-five of the population. The nation's ratio for college students is about one to one hundred and thirty of population, and for high-school students one to twenty-four of population. The figures for Kentucky are somewhat less than those for the nation both in high-school and in college enrollments.

It is important to know in planning for educational programs what the general trends are. So I am guessing again by saying that the peak in high-school attendance will be reached in the next ten years. The colleges will lag behind the schools, reaching their high point in fifteen years. After that we are quite sure to see some decline in college attendance and a more or less fixed attendance in high schools. There are now in the state thirteen four-year colleges, eleven two-year colleges, and two universities; all of these are affected by changes in enrollment, in wealth of the state, and in other conditions. It is quite possible that the number of four-year colleges will decline, accompanied by an increase in the number of colleges engaged in two years of college work.

In the early history of the liberal arts college, the emphasis in the establishment of curricula was placed on the preparation of students for the law, for the ministry, and for teaching. Since the beginning of this century, liberal arts colleges have moved in the direction of specialization, both professionally and functionally, and they have been busy promoting pre-professional courses for the preparation of students in law, medicine, and other vocations. It was natural that the distinction between the first two years and the last two should be emphasized and that two curricular divisions called upper and lower should be created. During the last two decades, various survey and orientation courses have appeared in the lower division.

Along with this movement in the four-year colleges a rapid increase in the number of junior colleges has occurred. The arguments for the creation of this type of college can be summarized as follows: first, it makes the transition to college, especially to the larger college, much easier; second, the two-year period whether it is college, junior college, or lower level provides a natural terminus for secondary work and at the same time furnishes a more personal approach to the needs of students; third, the junior college enables the student to engage in exploration, during which time he has an opportunity to look to his future and to establish the means of testing his own interest; fourth, it gives an opportunity to profit by guidance facilities that are coordinated closely with the period of exploration.

That the number of junior colleges will increase seems to be quite apparent. Separated from the four-year colleges as they are in many instances and not associated with secondary schools, these two-year colleges face problems of attendance. The inclusion in the junior college curriculum of the last two years of the high school will probably in the near future solve various difficulties of numbers and organization. There is danger always that the junior college will continue the tradition of the secondary school and fail to attain the college attitude.

In some institutions special colleges have been organized to provide instruction in the two-year period for those who do not have the interest and inclination to go into professional and graduate fields. One of the best examples of this procedure may be found in the General College of the University of Minnesota. In the analysis of the purposes of that institution, an attempt was made to find the areas of human needs. I am paraphrasing the statements of the director: first, the student must be trained for the job in which he will have satisfaction; second, it is essential that the student shall understand values, those that apply to himself and those that apply to the community; third, he must develop the ability to face both the triumphs and disasters of his job; fourth, he must learn to evaluate the work of the world as well as his own job. Thus it will be seen that in the opinion of the director the drift is away from the fixed course toward an orientation of the student in terms of himself and his environment in order that he may have an understanding of home, family, and community in their importance and relation to each other. Given this course, the student is expected to develop a real philosophy of life and finally to become socially and politically sensitive to the needs of the social group.

In the liberal arts colleges a considerable breakdown in departmental isolation is to be noted; in the place of departmental offerings we find an association of courses in the curricula which lead into larger fields of study. This integration gives to students more freedom than they have had in the past, and from this movement graduate study may begin at a lower level than it can at the present time.

With this separation of the upper and lower levels and the widening of fields, comprehensive examinations have made their appearance for the purpose both of testing the progress of students and also of eliminating, or saving, students who might not be able to continue into professional or graduate work. There are in the development of these programs a great many problems such as the administration of examinations so that they will be not only fresh but also constantly abreast of the developments in teaching procedure.

As the enlargement of fields goes on, the method of instruction is generally modified. Here and there may be seen the seminar method for undergraduates even in the lower level with emphasis upon materials in the course and upon discussion of problems arising in the use of these materials. Individual study under the guidance of instructors has been tried with rather marked success. An interesting feature in instruction, coming gradually into use, is the visual procedure. It may be said that the projector and film have great possibilities both in developing effectiveness of instruction and in extending the range of a course.

Another drift appears in the modifications and changes that are taking place in the liberal arts college in the effort to aid the entering students in their adaptation to the tasks that confront them. The recognition of individual differences and the classification of students by testing have created an understanding of the necessity of guidance and supervision. Students who are not as well prepared as they might be or who have not the interest or ability to continue are helped to find their places either in college or out of college. The limitation of the amount of work which a student is allowed to carry under a program of guidance and tutoring may be called crutches for the lame. The elimination of this burden on the colleges would be possible if the high schools would undertake testing and guidance programs during the four years of secondary instruction.

For approximately forty years, standardizing procedure in the field of college education has been going on. There are some indications that this program has reached its climax. In the southern area the Association of Colleges and Secondary Schools was established in 1890. At that time great differences existed in the entrance requirements of institutions. Some colleges were allowing students to come into college work at the end of the high-school sophomore year, some at the end of the third year, and some colleges were insisting on four years of high-school work. Courses required for admission, moreover, varied greatly.

The Southern Association of Colleges and Secondary Schools instituted standards such as class numbers, minimum salaries, minimum library facilities, minimum endowments and incomes, certain requisites for teachers, and certain essentials regarding the plant. This procedure began in 1890 and gradually moved in the direction of specific regulations that were hard and fast. The emphasis of the Association was at that time placed on material things as a means of getting at spiritual and educational values. Meantime, the Association has moved slowly toward the study of problems and research in educational matters. This is to be seen in the committee appointed for analyses of secondary-school curricula and in the recent discussion of graduate work.

In our own state of Kentucky some progress has been made in a testing program. The hope is that the work of the Kentucky Testing Bureau may be extended to all the high schools in order that the more important questions relating to admission may be answered before the student receives his diploma from the secondary school. Undoubtedly, additional ground will be gained in the next ten years; the emphasis will fall upon the ability, the character, and the record of the student who wishes to go to college. There are many difficulties in such a procedure which cannot be easily overcome; however, unless these difficulties are met in this state, we shall continue in the same position in which we are at present. My belief is that the wider interest in the purposes of this program can bring a solution to the matter of high-school graduation in relation to college admission.

I have referred to the recognition of individual differences in students. This is a concept that points to a considerable departure from the mass procedure that has been followed for many years. A recent experiment based on the idea of individual differences was organized about four years ago in the establishment of New College by the Teachers College of Columbia University. This college has as its objective the preparation of teachers for nursery school, kindergarten, elementary school, and high school.

The principle involved in the program of New College is found in the purpose to set up a personal program for each student whereby it is possible to take the student from the place that he now occupies to the higher ground of personal and community interest. Such a program requires a careful selection of students for the work that is carried on in the cooperative group. The purpose is to meet the problems of living; first as an individual, second as a member of the social group, third as a teacher. The curriculum looks toward answering the needs of the student; this may be attained by independent study. In the plan there are no credits and no grades. It is hoped that the whole body of experience at the college may be coextensive with life and as education may be related to the conditions of our time. Consequently, the instruction and activities deal with the personal and the important community problems. Emphasis is placed on the larger social implications found in them. The course deals also with professional aspects and attitudes involved in teaching. The college does not regard the curriculum as a fixed entity but emphasizes understanding as opposed to subject matter alone.

Four major areas of knowledge are considered: first, health and home relations; second, natural sciences; third, arts; fourth, philosophy. The whole is integrated through the seminar where views, facts, and conclusions are brought out and tested. In the development of the procedure the college requires the student to pass through an orientation period which is followed by resident study in the college, then by working in industry, and later by rural living. An examination follows when the faculty believe that the student has attained the scholarly attitude. The final steps are an internship and an apprenticeship under supervision.

I have described at length the program of this college because it is an example of a new educational process as well as an attempt to find a way to bring the student face to face with actual living problems. We must all realize, therefore, that, while the liberal arts college has been engaged for three hundred years in attempting to train students for citizenship and the professions and at present in pre-professional work, many ways and methods of accomplishing the goal still must be tested and understood.

In considering the problems and progress of higher education in Kentucky, we are assured that the state will be confronted by an increase in high-school attendance followed by a larger number of students going to college. These events place upon the secondary schools and the colleges a great responsibility which must be reflected in what they do in meeting the problems in education, such as changes in curricula, guidance programs, and instruction based upon the principle of individual differences. It is quite evident that the number of junior colleges will increase and that, if they are not interrelated with secondary education, they are likely to find the going rather hard. On the other hand, there may be a decrease in the number of four-year colleges due to the difficulty in financing them.

The fact that some changes have taken place in teaching procedure and content of courses during the past twenty years indicates that more experimentation will follow which should bring definite conclusions of value in conducting both secondary and college courses. I have the impression that the colleges with some exceptions are following traditional procedure, and undoubtedly these institutions can continue to do so for some time to come without raising too many questions in regard to their effectiveness. In the long run, however, courses of instruction will have to be changed to meet the situation so that students may adapt themselves more effectively to social and economic conditions.

The problem of preparing teachers for the elementary and secondary schools of Kentucky has been met by the creation of teachers' colleges, by better certification laws, and by more careful administration of the educational program. The teachers' colleges have reached a point where they will move on paths that take them away from the traditional four-year courses of the liberal arts colleges. I look to see them place increased emphasis upon their function as institutions for the training of teachers. The near prospect of a decided shortage of prepared teachers indicates that the work of the teachers' colleges should be in their designated field. This is a very large order; and, judging by what is being done under such conditions as those at New College, we can be sure that the teachers' colleges, without going into what may be called university functions, will have all that they can do to meet the demands upon them.

I can see that the two universities of the state are moving steadily in the direction of graduate and professional work and are emphasizing the philosophy and content behind these courses. It will be a long time, however, before the universities in Kentucky can give up the first two years of college and enter upon distinctly graduate and professional organization.

A good deal of gain has been made in the application of standards to schools. The hard and fast procedure that has prevailed in the past is being modified with less emphasis upon the system now in vogue and with more attention to the results of instruction as the bases of classification and standing.

Guidance and personnel programs in our schools and colleges are in their early beginning. Some experimentation is going on, and some progress is being made. These programs, however, depend for their success and for their effectiveness upon trained leadership with an understanding of technique. As yet the schools have not been able to provide the financial outlay necessary for securing thoroughly trained and highly intelligent direction. In the long run, admission of students to college must be on interest, ability, and character. At present the use of tests by the colleges is almost entirely limited to the classification of students and the sectioning of classes. I look to see an expansion of interest in the testing programs on the part of the secondary schools and the colleges and an increase in the use of tests for guidance and counselling.

If the doctrine of individual differences is accepted, and undoubtedly it must be, the procedure followed in our schools and colleges at the present time will be modified materially. It may be said that consideration of the attitude of the students toward their problems in their relation to matters of importance in a social world will make a marked difference in educational methods. The approach can be made first, on the basis of testing and guidance; second, by opening the way to students to develop their own interests; third, by the construction of courses of study upon a community and social viewpoint rather than upon a group of facts unrelated to the students' lives and interests. In our colleges if this attitude is to become important and effective, we shall have to provide new methods, new direction, and a larger organization. The essential problem is as always the guidance and development of students. The colleges will struggle with this fundamental matter during the next twenty years and, I think, will move forward to new heights. I sincerely hope that they will produce graduates who will take their places with distinction in the social and economic world.

I believe that I can see a pronounced growth in attempting to meet the educational problems of the state not as individual institutional considerations but as needs of the state. We are trying to view these problems as a whole, and we do not find the process easy. A friend of mine in commenting on this question said, "The greatest need in education is the deflation of the ego." This deflation may well apply to institutions, departments, and individuals in order that all may give thought not merely to their institutions, their departments, themselves but also to the educational urgencies of Kentucky.

Determined cooperation in striving to understand and to solve the problems involved in the development of education in Kentucky is demanded of us. Worth while results will reward our efforts if we all pull together instead of moving in different directions. Progress can be attained only by frankness, understanding, knowledge, and good nature. The results of our educational procedure are so important that we must keep always in mind the real reason for the existence of our schools, colleges, and universities. The reason is that Kentucky may have a better trained youth, a better citizenship, and that Kentucky may be a better state.

The Keystone of Higher Education

Address to the Institute of Colleges,
University of Minnesota Center for Continuation Study, July, 1940

T H E college of liberal arts was once, and its adherents hope that it will be again, the keystone of higher education in the United States of America. There are many who think that it is and will always continue to be the arch that supports all advanced educational endeavor. The truth of the matter is, however, that subversive influences have been at work within the walls of the college for the past forty years, and parachutists have managed to get within its boundary, all unsuspected of their intent to use the college as the basis of their operations. This sounds like an excessive statement that needs some proof. In view of the complacency of many of the advocates of the college program, the evidence should be given as fully as possible.

The curriculum of the liberal arts college has been called outmoded by critics who say that it does not meet the demands, in fact, the needs of students. Special courses were set up, largely pre-vocational and pre-professional in character, such as the pre-medical requirements called for by the medical schools. Courses for teachers, journalists, social workers, chemists, and nurses and courses in business subjects which were frankly vocational in character were introduced. In many instances the prerequisites carried down into the freshman year.

In the universities these special lines of study were removed from the college of liberal arts and were established in the institutions as separate schools or colleges. Where the institution was a four-year college under one organization, the original purpose of the college was lost in the multitude of requirements for the vocational courses. These subjects had been put into the curriculum to meet the demands of students and to appease the fears of the authorities that, through falling off of attendance, the income of the college and its prestige as measured by numbers of registrants would be affected. There were some critics who said further that the athletic prowess of the college would suffer if the vocational offerings were not liberal enough to provide for the kind of education that athletes in the main felt that they should have. Thus was lost the real purpose of the college of liberal arts, namely, to furnish the students with perspective and background which are the essence of a liberal education. The subversive influences have undermined the college of liberal arts.

If the educational historian goes back in the story of the founding of universities in this country, he will find that the college of liberal arts was either the only college in the beginning or, when this was not the case, the center of the organization. With the appearance of other courses and professional schools, the liberal arts college ceased in some universities to be the outstanding unit.

Professional schools and courses that had a professional or vocational end in view compelled the college to give preliminary instruction in languages and sciences which were regarded as necessary to the successful pursuit of the specialized lines of study. As this process went on, the liberal arts college became a service agency in the university organization. The instruction in the college, no longer having the liberal education in mind that had been its primary objective, conformed more and more to the demands and the needs of the professional courses. Even in the matter of time, the newer courses claimed a larger share of the student's hours and in consequence created a situation that worked both above and below the middle years of the four-year course. In the first two years the student was expected to follow the line of study required by the preliminary preparation needed for the pursuit of the work in the last two years, and in the second half of his college course he was shut off from the liberal courses that might have been open to him as a junior or senior.

There were students who wanted the liberal arts courses and who had an interest in the perspective and background that are supposed to constitute the real reason for the existence of the college. However, since the college had become a service agency for the professional schools and the vocational courses, the liberal emphasis had been subordinated to the needs of the newer schools and colleges. The situation in the separate four-year college was even worse in that liberal education and the preparation for vocational pursuits were carried on in smaller departments manned by a few instructors who struggled courageously to meet the double demands placed upon them.

While the influences so far depicted were at work, there was another portentous factor gathering increasing power that threatened the very existence of the four-year liberal arts college. This was the movement to cut the college in two by establishing junior colleges in the towns and cities and by creating in the universities and in the colleges themselves upper and lower divisions often under separate deans. That the junior colleges have value, surely in the minds of the people who are willing to support them, is shown in their rapid growth during the last decade.

The advantages seem to be that the local junior college is near the students who wish to attend it; the cost of the first two years of college, therefore, is not large; and the students are not thrown into unknown difficulties and pleasures of the college miles away from their homes. In addition, the junior college hopes to set up a curriculum free from the overwhelming influences of the professional schools. Usually such colleges are mere adjuncts of the high schools, and, assuming the qualities and procedures of secondary education, they thus defeat the purpose of college training. Examination of the curriculum of the two-year school shows the same trends at work as in the four-year college. In fact, such trends are more pronounced in the junior college because local demands for vocational training are more likely to manifest themselves.

In the universities lower and upper divisions were established in the college of liberal arts for the purpose of providing a broad curriculum in the first two years and a specialized one in the last two years. In the lower level the student was expected to receive instruction in the basic courses that would acquaint him with the elementary phases of science, mathematics, languages, literature, and the social sciences. In the upper division he could follow some special lines of work that he might be interested in or that were of value in a professional career.

It is important to keep in mind that the work done in the upper two years tends to move in the direction of graduate instruction both in the material offered and in the method of conducting the courses. The results that follow are the entering upon the graduate work at an earlier period in the life of the student and the separating of the college from the graduate school at the beginning of the junior year, thus inaugurating the European system of university organization. If this form of university organization prevails in the conduct of an institution, the college of liberal arts ceases to exist as an entity. Although the autonomy of the college does not suffer as much where there is only a separation in the conduct of upper and lower divisions, nevertheless the college cannot have the unity that has always been one of its strongest points and has given it the opportunity to carry through a general purpose in the educational program.

Experiments have been tried in the college of arts to meet the needs of a large group of students of fair ability and with no great interest in any special field. These young people do not expect to enter any profession and have no wish to become scholars or teachers; yet certain advanced educational opportunities are desirable for them and for the state on the ground that they with some college experience may prove to be happier and more useful citizens. A general course of broad interest involving instruction in the social sciences may hold them in the college and may give them a valuable background. There is much to be said for this point of view. When, however, the plan is introduced into the college of arts, the traditional purpose is gone because the liberal arts college has for its foundation the encouragement of scholarship and the development of some expertness in library and laboratory techniques as well as the giving to the students social and historical background. These fundamentals along with the general courses of broad interest surely cannot be given in two short years.

Finally awakening to the condition of the arts college and recognizing the distance it has drifted down the stream, those who are vitally interested in the continuance of the college as a factor in the intellectual and cultural life of the people have been undergoing a good deal of stock taking and have manifested searching of purpose to find out what has happened and what can be done about the present situation. Various plans for honor courses, the use of the seminar method, guidance, the organization of groups, and even the establishing of special colleges that will emphasize the liberal tradition have been worked out in order to stay the decline and to check the subversive influences that have brought the liberal arts college to its present state.

Ships and Captains, Crews and Passengers

Commencement address, Berea College, Berea, Kentucky, June 5, 1939

IN ADOPTING the title, "Ships and Captains, Crews and Passengers," I am committed to a metaphor. There is always danger in using this figure of speech because the writer or speaker, before he has completed his literary effort, may add confusion by mixed applications. Thus the orator, probably not a member of the House of Commons, declared, "The British lion, whether he is roaming the deserts of India or climbing the forests of Canada, will not draw in his horns or retire within his shell." With this terrible example of a would be eloquent speaker before me, I shall try to maintain the comparison of ships with colleges, captains with presidents, crews with staffs, and passengers with students, alumni, and the public.

For ages, century upon century, men have gone down to the sea in ships. Ever they have sought to improve their crafts so that they will carry more cargo, hold the sea, sail better. The navigators have studied the heavens, thereby slowly working out the principles of navigation, that they might reach distant lands and return in safety to their ports.

Men have sung of ships:

> "I must go down to the seas again, to the
>   lonely sea and the sky,
> And all I ask is a tall ship and a star
>   to steer her by."

Poets have written of the state in words of the ship,

> "O Ship of State! . . . O Union, strong and great!"

Ships have been likened to the souls of men reaching out into the unknown. In "A Sea Spell" Fannie Stearns Davis says,

> "Once I was a ship with glorious sails
>   That leapt to the love of the wind."

In figurative language Kipling has told of the workaday craft and the great liner:

> "The liner she's a lady, and 'er route is cut
>   and dried;
> The Man of War 'er husband, and 'e always
>   keeps beside;
> But, oh, the little cargo boats that 'aven't
>   any man!
> They've got to do their business first, and make
>   the most they can."

The student of ships and voyages has an interesting time as he pursues the story of the building of vessels. Early steamers appearing in the first quarter of the nineteenth century were built of wood and took nearly a month to cross the Atlantic. The *Savannah* on a voyage in 1819 ran out of fuel when eighty miles on her way across and finished the voyage under sail. The *Sirius* sailed from Liverpool to New York under her own steam in 1829, reaching her port in thirty days. The Dutch are said to have built the first steam vessels that sailed on the ocean. The clipper ships, famous in song and story, made such swift voyages that they were able to hold their own against the steamers until the middle of the century. The Civil War emphasized iron vessels, but their future was hampered by the heavy engines and boilers then in use. Today the great vessels equipped with steam turbines cross the ocean in less than five days. On board are such numbers of passengers and such heavy cargoes that the crafts of a hundred years ago are mere boats in comparison with the steamships of today.

The commanders and crews underwent many hardships in the early days of the merchant marine when crafts with inadequate power tried to sail the seas. The men who navigated the vessels of that time had to know the sea and wind because they went on long voyages with strange ladings and often mysterious passengers.

I have thought of colleges as kinds of ships; there they are upon their campuses in a region that shifts like unto the sea. These colleges are subject to the winds of public opinion and the calms of indifference. They were small and inadequate in the early days. Their equipment was meager indeed with small libraries and poor laboratories. Like the ships they have passed through various stages, from sail to steam, from small to larger campuses, and from small student bodies to numerous groups, natives of many states and foreign countries.

You will recall Captain John Smith, who set out from Jamestown after the founding of that colony to study the coast of the country to the north. He sailed with a few men in a pinnace and went as far as Capawuck where he found some fishermen. Christopher Columbus, who came across the ocean, had three vessels none of which was more than 200 tons. Then the Pilgrims landed on Plymouth Rock in 1620 from a sailing craft called the *Mayflower*. Examples like these might be cited again and again—the movement of men in small ships to strange lands.

One important thing about Berea College was the embarking upon the sea of learning back in an early day when it was necessary to lay the keel right. You will recall the work of Rogers and Fee and Fairchild, which was interrupted by the Civil War, for these men launched a considerable educational ship.

When President Frost came to Berea, he brought with him new ideas and larger purposes of service. He was here at a time when ports of call were infrequent and the difficulties of navigation in the educational field were considerable. In an era of changing structure such as is brought about by shipping, iron was superseded by steel with stronger engines and more powerful boilers. Cargoes were carried to many different parts of the world, and there was an increased demand for more extensive voyages. Much the same thing can be found in the parallel of the colleges when Frost navigated his Berea through many storms.

Then William James Hutchins came on the bridge as the commanding officer of a larger craft. The builders of ships lay them to plan from keel to top deck with nothing put down in the blueprints that is not thoroughly worked out before the builders begin; but a college grows and varies with the passing of every day. The shores and depths of the sea constantly shift and demand a considerable knowledge of charts, ships, and cargoes. In the educational field changes too take place.

Like the previous commander President Hutchins was Oberlin nurtured and Oberlin tested. He had had a long experience in the pastorate and in the professor's chair. He came to this new ship wise in the ways of man from long experience. He found his craft sailing on a different sea from the one that the earlier ship traversed. The ship was now bigger, the crew larger, the cargo heavier, and the passengers more numerous. The calm, wise attitude of the new captain assured all that he had qualities as a navigator on the sea of education. Friendly, kind, ready to lend a hand in all the tasks of his colleagues, he enabled the ship to proceed on a straight and true course.

On the seas in the ancient days wives occasionally accompanied the skipper; on the land the wife of the commander of a college becomes a very important personage in the navigation of the academic craft. She must be gracious, tactful, intelligent, discreet, courageous. She is hostess to the many who come to her door. There are times when the captain wonders about his course, the loyalty of the crew, and how the declining funds in the ship's treasure box may be replenished. Then it is that his companion brings him comfort and a new determination to carry on. Happy is the ship that has such an aide whether she is on sea or shore. For the past two decades Berea has possessed such a lady to help in the navigation of her husband's ship.

The new commander of some twenty years ago found the vessel well prepared and working in a satisfactory way for a time that was past. The conditions of navigation which confronted this worthy captain when he came on the bridge were not wholly the same as those known to former masters. More was required, more money, more plant, larger staffs, and an understanding of what was happening in the world. In the earlier day labor and conventional education, largely elementary and secondary in character, together with religion formed the main portion of the Berea procedure.

In the change of commanders the old was not discarded; religion was held important, labor was dignified, and the educational processes were strengthened. The change to the new was seen in the wider use of music, painting, and plastic arts; in emphasis on health; and in a more liberal knowledge of the ways of life. These were all introduced into the discipline of crew and passengers.

The ship owners painted their ships, changed rigging, installed new boilers, modified the angle of propellers to give more speed and power. They knew their vessels must be kept in good condition to be able to battle the elements. But the use of the paddle wheel and engine to take the place of sails was opposed by the old-timers. In educational institutions objections oftentimes are made to changes. There are, on the other hand, those who want change for various personal and departmental reasons.

Another captain, now the President of Oberlin, Dr. Ernest H. Wilkins, has a paper on "Change" published in *School and Society*. In this we are told that some declare there ought to be change. Many of those who favor it are advocating change for personal and departmental advantages. Again, they say that change ought to take place because other institutions are modifying their procedure and because alterations in the social order must meet with response. There are those who believe that change is desirable for itself and that, if institutions are to maintain prestige, they must make changes from time to time. Undoubtedly much experimentation in education is desirable, but it should be based upon a real understanding of the purposes of the experiments. There are those who oppose change because of the effect upon their personal positions. Others set themselves against the advancement of departments other than their own. Some oppose change because a weary inertia, personal and institutional in character, holds them back. And others think the place, method, and organization so perfect that any change is unnecessary.

As in the days of shipping there must be a real knowledge of the navigation of a ship, so in the days of educational development in an institution there must be a real understanding of objectives on the part of all if the voyage is to be a purposeful one.

The commander of an educational ship is concerned about many things. If he is compelled to depend upon endowments for the support of his institution, he finds himself faced with declining interest rates that reduce the amounts coming from investments. New security programs on federal and state bases will undoubtedly affect educational maintenance in the future. What will be the result in the final analysis, and how will the financial assistance to schools be altered?

Again many theories of educational procedure must be considered. Shall the emphasis for those who come to college be placed upon learning and the development of it or upon the provision of vocational and trade experience? According to recent figures

4,000,000 young people have left high school and have never had a job or attended college. Perhaps increased thought is needed to be given to the development of vocational and trade schools.

The commander on the bridge of the ship has occasion to feel anxiety. Just as the ship commander has instruments for the guidance of his ship and radio warnings against ice and fog, so also the wise educator knows where he is going. The commander who has brought his vessel into port and has turned it over to a successor, however worthy, is concerned about the new shoals and obstacles to navigation. How will the crew respond, and will the merchants continue to do business with his ship? He knows that there is no danger that the ship will discontinue its voyages with his going because he remembers that the north star is the true compass, that the sea moves with the tide in rhythm, and that now as in ages past men sail the sea. So the educational ship moves on under the guidance of its star and the navigation of its commander.

These graduates who face us today, the passengers, and also the crew have had the advantages of sailing in a modern ship under a great commander. It is their obligation to believe that the ship that has carried them so long will continue to sail. It is the duty of all to see that the ship's gear, hull, and engines are kept in repair for years of voyaging under the commander soon to come upon the bridge.

President Hutchins, who retires in a few months, is a personal friend of mine, and I have found help in his wisdom and knowledge. He has been a calming force in educational and industrial affairs of this state. We shall miss him indeed. I feel in closing this address that I may add to the figure of speech, which I have tried to carry through from the beginning, the words of McAndrews as he gave up his ship to live on shore for the rest of his days:

> "Ye've left a glimmer still to cheer the Man—
>   the Artifex!
> *That* holds in spite o' knock and scale, o' friction,
>   waste an' slip,

An' by that light—now, mark my word—we'll build
    the Perfect Ship.
I'll never last to judge her lines or take her curve—
    not I.
But I ha' lived an' I ha' worked. All thanks to
    Thee, Most High!
An' I ha' done what I ha' done—judge Thou
    if ill or well—"

Interpreting and Teaching Democratic Ideals in Colleges

Address to the Kentucky Education Association, Louisville, April 14, 1939

IN THE minds of many Americans, democracy is associated with
the form of government. In fact, however, democracy is not merely
a form of government. It is something more, a something that includes the spirit, mind, and good will of a people. We are likely
as a people to insist that the United States is a democracy because
the government is republican in form.

The city state of ancient Greece is referred to as a democracy;
that state undoubtedly had freedom for the upper classes, yet,
since it was based on slavery, it was not in truth a democracy. Nor
is a particular type of economic organization a democracy even
though the purpose of economic ideas in use may have the benefit
of the whole population in mind. The centralization of government or the decentralization of processes does not necessarily carry
with it the great purposes of a democracy, nor does a scheme
of representation based upon a geographical area or the recognition
of crafts and professions in legislative bodies qualify as a democracy. The doctrines of Rousseau or of Jefferson may not function
in such a state.

This ideal we call democracy is based upon fundamental assumptions. These have been well presented by Professor C. E.

[291]

Merriam in an article appearing in the *Political Science Quarterly* for November last.

The first of the assumptions is the essential dignity of man in that he has a life to lead toward a higher ideal which involves his relations to his fellows and the need of opportunity to serve and live with his fellow man. There is, too, a belief in the perfectibility of man in that he can grow to great heights toward excellence. It is assumed that the gains made by a democratic society should be equalized since these gains are mass gains. In a society of this kind the decisions made on social policy and direction are, and must be, popular decisions. The accomplishment of social changes comes about through consent rather than by violence.

Many objections are made to a democracy based upon any such assumptions. These objections are in part that it is expensive to operate, inefficient in bringing results to pass, and slow in reaching decisions; that democracy of the people carried on through popular vote is subject to pressure groups; and that in selecting its agents and officers, the mediocre man gets the place. The opponents of democracy declare, so Merriam informs us, that individual differences and personalities are crushed and that government is kept weak in order that privileges may be maintained.

These are severe strictures upon the procedures of democracy. The most ardent believer in democracy will admit its seeming weaknesses, its slowness, its sometime inefficiency. The tremendous advantages in the development of man, however, far outweigh any disadvantages resultant as they are from humanity itself with all its vagaries.

In a land where a democracy exists, great freedom gives to each one the right to speak, to write, and to think those things that are in his heart and mind. This freedom also enables the individual to act as he pleases so long and so far as he does not injure the well-being of others.

Again let me repeat, democracy is not simply a form of government. It is something that must reside in the hearts of men; it is in large part love for the people, a respect and consideration for our fellows. These are the working forces of a democracy.

Some government there must be, but the success of democracy rests on the fact that the people accept the assumptions on which it is based and carry them into government itself.

In the practice of democracy men must sustain in their daily lives these assumptions. The meaning of this statement is very broad indeed. If democracy should come to be a part of everyday life, in business small practices and the use of coercion between labor and capital would cease; in government men would give their best, and dishonesty would no longer make men traitors to the welfare of all. If democracy really held sway in our hearts and minds, our democratic government would be effective, and the people would live purposeful lives in peace and contentment.

Having thus far presented the assumptions of democracy and its meaning in the organization and conduct of society, I now turn to the topic under discussion this afternoon, "Interpreting and Teaching Democratic Ideals in Colleges."

First of all, a spirit of democracy must be in the institution and in the hearts and minds of the people who conduct the instruction. Such democratic ideals should appear in the administration of the institution, in the conduct of student affairs, and in the application of the general understanding of what democracy is to the everyday business of the college and its activities. That this is a difficult thing to bring to pass must be admitted. Lip service may be given to the general ideal of democracy at the same time that practice is departing very far from the real spirit of democracy. I am quite sure that the teaching of courses in various fields in which democracy is stressed does not have the weight that we ordinarily suppose it to have. Nevertheless the study of comparative governments and of present-day political philosophies is highly important.

The spirit of democracy in the teaching of all courses, whether in the social sciences or in other fields, will finally inculcate the ideal in the minds of students. I can think of literature as being taught from the viewpoint of the freedom of the mind, or from the philological point of view, or from the value of the great men idea, or from the social history attitude, or from the standpoint that literature reflects life and shows the struggle of mankind; and I can see the spirit of democracy emanating from each method or from a combination of several or of all. As always we come back to the preparation and attitude of the teacher.

In the upper level of student groups the largest freedom should be given to them to find their way and to express themselves in the classroom and on the campus, the only restrictions being those of decency, courtesy, and good will. Colleges should have in their libraries books, magazines, papers, pamphlets that are helpful and inspiring for the understanding of democracy. The student thus gets some of the approaches that can be threshed out in the classroom. Again, the breadth and wisdom of the teacher are the essential part of democratic interpretation.

A fixed course of study on "The History of Democracy" or "The Processes of a Social Organization" cannot be depended upon to furnish democratic leaders; nor can we feel, when we have initiated such a course, that our duty is done toward teaching democratic ideals in our colleges. These courses may be of some value, even of great value, if properly taught. They may sum up for the students attitudes and activities found in the whole curriculum of the institution. If badly taught, they may even influence the student in the opposite direction from that intended. The emphasis should rest upon the spirit that exists in the institution; the character, wisdom, and training of the teachers; and the open policy of a larger freedom of discussion in the classroom and on the campus.

Democracy, however, carries heavy responsibilities, and it is here that we fail in part in our institutions. If students are to have freedom in organization and expression, they must also assume the responsibilities that go with such freedom. This again requires careful direction and instruction and also organization with the broadest kind of understanding on the part of administrative officers.

Again I come back to the essential points of the whole matter; the attitude and spirit in the institution itself, in faculty, and in administrative officers; the breadth and wisdom and viewpoints of the teachers of all subjects; the freedom of students in discussion in the classroom and in their own organizations. All these interpret and teach democratic ideals in college.

PART V

A. REMEMBER
KENTUCKY

Remember Kentucky

From an address at the banquet of the Kentucky Society in Chicago
honoring alumni and students of the University of Kentucky;
broadcasted from the Edgewater Beach Hotel, October 20, 1928

THIS is a glorious month in Kentucky. The hills in the distances
are intensified in their purple garments by the flame and golden
foliage of the trees along the roads, in the valleys, and on the up-
lands. Everywhere nature vies with the artist in making a memor-
able colorful picture. It is the Kentucky that has enchanted its sons
and daughters all through the years. Much the same life goes on
as in the old days. The charm of manner and of living holds a
people in loyalty to Kentucky wherever they may go. They remember Kentucky. Such an affection is a great factor in the life of
a state; it molds opinion and holds tradition, keeps a people to the
memories of the past, and creates a great love for the commonwealth.

Some there are, both at home and abroad, who would not alter
Kentucky in any way. None of us, whether native son or daugh-
ter or adopted citizen, would care to see courtesy, leisure, and
good will pushed aside in the competition of modern life; however, in this day of advancement Kentucky changes whether we
wish the change or not. Progress is now a vogue in Kentucky. A new
spirit rests upon the state. Modern roads are being built throughout the commonwealth; each year the people place $12,000,000

[295]

in the hands of the Highway Commission with which to build highways and to maintain them.

The people of the state are greatly interested in their teachers'
colleges, and in the last ten years they have recognized the need
for a modern state university which they are steadily building
at Lexington. Ten years ago the University had an enrollment of
one thousand and forty-seven; today there are two thousand five
hundred students in daily attendance. A decade ago it had no campus plan and no building program. This year it is erecting six additional buildings. These are evidences of the spirit of the state. High
schools, too, have grown in number until they total eight hundred.
Consolidated schools are increasing with the coming of improved
roads. It is indeed a Kentucky to remember with its story and romance but also a Kentucky that now holds aloft the banner of
progress.

Many there are who think of the old state as backward in
education, transportation, and business. But Kentucky is going
ahead. Listen to some of the comparisons that make Kentucky a
modern commonwealth along with her sister states. In size it is
thirty-sixth, and it is fifteenth in population. Agriculture looms
so large that the state is ninth in farm population and twenty-first
in dairy products and twenty-sixth in wealth. It is nineteenth in
net personal income according to income tax returns and twenty-
seventh in manufactured products. The mineral resources place
the state in mining activities among the first seven of the union.
In the matter of homes owned without debt, Kentucky is nineteenth.
Tax burdens are not heavy compared with other states in that
Kentucky is forty-fourth, and forty-second in state debt. These
are figures and comparisons that show Kentucky among the first
half of the states in progress and at the same time among the lowest in tax and government costs. The state needs leadership and
it needs truthful publicity.

Opportunities must be opened to the youth of the state. Of the
people born in Kentucky during its one hundred and thirty-six
years of statehood, more than a quarter have lived elsewhere.
Kentucky is giving generously of its resources to other states, and

now it wants to return to the people within its own border some of the experiences, advantages, and progress of the modern state. It is a notable ambition and one that every true Kentuckian hopes to see realized.

Remember Kentucky, you who live elsewhere. Remember it for its beauty, its kindly living. And more than that give your voice, your interest, and your purse to its forward movement in present day industry and education.

Some Problems for Kentucky to Solve

Address at a conference called in 1919
at the University of Kentucky to consider the problems of the state

LOOKING backward over periods of history, men are able very
definitely to mark certain epochs in the progress of mankind.
Curiously enough most of these are indicated by wars largely due
to the fact that the historian has given his time and effort to a
study of the doings of princes, potentates, and sovereigns rather
than to the activities of the common people. So it is that we look
on the year 490 B.C. when the Battle of Marathon took place as
one of the eventful periods in the history of Europe. A little band
of Greeks was able to keep the Persians out of Europe and to
hold for that continent the Grecian civilization with all that it
meant. More than eight hundred years afterwards at Adrianople
in A.D. 378 the Huns defeated the Romans and were able to make
their way into Southern Europe. Fortunately enough, however,
they were absorbed by the Southern European civilization and did
not have the modifying effect that would have taken place if a more
advanced people had won the contest. In Spain during the eighth
century the Saracens had built up a considerable civilization that
was Moorish in character. In their attempt to force the Franks
into submission they were defeated, and once again Europe was
saved for the western civilization.

Again, in 1066 the Normans won the Battle of Hastings, pressing upon England their mode of living, their architecture, and
customs. Then came the great event of the Magna Charta. Other
epochs followed: the Thirty Years' War, the Seventy Years' War,
the American Revolution, the Napoleonic War, our own Civil
War, the Franco-Prussian contest, each with resultant changes.
And now has come the World War.

It may be expected, therefore, that men see in this last war something more than a contest of arms. Certainly the press is filled with
discussion of the far-reaching consequences of this event. It is
clearly manifested that, if out of the World War comes a League
of Nations making possible the maintenance of permanent peace,

the conflict will not have been in vain. Men see in the present era important historical significance. Many of them believe that a church with larger liberality of view, new energy of purpose, and higher spiritual aims will emerge. Others see visions of a wider democracy in which education shall be adequate, effective, and efficient and in which every citizen shall have increased opportunity, more leisure, and a broader viewpoint. Some people expect that greater understanding and sympathy will come into being as a consequence of the needs that have been shown to exist. Many believe that better, more enlightened citizenship will be born in us to meet the urgent wants of our country.

It is more than an academic question surely then to ask if these hopes and ideals are to be realized. It is true that we can fall back into the old rut; we can let the church go on as before, democracy blunder along as in the past, and the government more or less inefficiently carry on its work. But, if these hopes are possible of realization, it is worthwhile to try to attain them. The meaning of this conference lies in the fact that there is a feeling that these things can be brought to pass if an earnest endeavor in the right direction is made. All of us are anxious to have Kentucky in the vanguard, and, in spite of the handicaps under which she labors, it is possible to place her there. If we can visualize the needs of the commonwealth for the next quarter of a century and if we can discover the steps necessary to meet those needs, then a very definite task is ours and one that can be accomplished.

This conference has been called for the purpose of discussing Kentucky problems. It perhaps is desirable at the beginning to ask, "What is a problem?" A problem is subject to solution; it is an attempt to relate cause and effect and to determine how the two are associated and connected. It is then important to discover the specific difficulties that lie before us in Kentucky. In a general way these problems concern individuals, the community, and the state.

The individual is concerned in so far as the conditions of his heredity and the conditions of the heredity of his children are affected and in so far as the environment in which he lives and in which they in the future will have to live is good or bad. When we turn to a community, we find here a group of individuals acting more or less together in the everyday conduct of life. The tendency has been for these units to plan alone and to act selfishly. When a community has grasped what it can do when all act together, it will have taken a long step toward the accomplishment of many things. The state occupies a much larger area and is affected by a broader sweep of economic, sanitary, and moral agents than influence individuals and even communities. In the matter of commerce and trade, in the transportation of the products of industry, in the conduct of the state's business, and in the management of its affairs, many factors must be considered. In the final analysis all of these problems may be solved by education of the citizens of the commonwealth.

The difficulties facing Kentucky have been suggested in general. There are, however, specific problems some of which may be at least considered briefly. We should surely bring before us for consideration at this conference such matters as education, public health, industry, efficient government, and community organization.

It is generally conceded that everywhere and particularly in our own commonwealth we need a better school system. The citizenship of this state is gradually becoming aware of the fact that more attention must be paid to education. We find that our children are handicapped when they come into competition with children from other commonwealths, and we finally are realizing that we must attack the problem of education, not as a private, but as a public question.

In Kentucky about five hundred thousand children are of school age; to meet the needs of these children as they come from the grades into the high schools, there are but two hundred and fifty high schools, public and private. Probably twenty-four hundred seniors complete the high-school course, and from this number the state must depend for its leaders. Instead of a few more than two thousand, at least seven or eight thousand boys and girls should be graduating from high school each year. By the failure of these young people to finish the secondary courses, the state is affected in its larger intelligence, in its better government, and in its attempt to secure the necessary leadership.

We have discovered too that the program of the schools should be modified. The results that are now being obtained in our schools do not seem always to insure the ends that are desired. More emphasis should be placed upon the sciences, and the application of the arts to practical life should be steadily maintained in school courses. It is true that the Federal Government is attempting to introduce these emphases by the new legislation that is being provided and by the Federal Board for Vocational Education. Schools everywhere should take into consideration the necessity of scientific attitudes in order that students may develop accuracy of thought. When these students trained in mind and hand are charged with the responsibilities of carrying on the affairs of the commonwealth, it is believed that they will perform their duties in a clear-headed way instead of in a mushy and sentimental manner.

We know too that the making of citizens is a process much more difficult than we had supposed. The World War brought to us clearly the fact that a great many people living in America are woefully unaware of the government under which they are living. Too many of them have so little knowledge of the history and ideals of the United States of America that they fail to appreciate their heritage and are therefore lacking in good citizenship. The schools are certainly in large part to blame for this want of understanding. New emphasis must be placed upon the making of real citizens.

Another problem of education looms large and deep in America. Throughout the United States of America the average child does not attend school beyond the sixth grade, and, shameful to admit, many children are unable to read and write. The percentage of illiteracy in the whole country is said to be 7 77/100 per cent, whereas in our own State of Kentucky illiteracy reaches the alarming figure of 11 per cent. Regardless of the reasons for this illiteracy, I say to you that it nevertheless constitutes a dangerous thing. Appeals to the superstitions and ignorance of a people unable to inform themselves in other ways are made possible. Hence, one of the problems which our commonwealth must face is the elimination of illiteracy at as early a date as possible. We must have better schools, better teachers, more money for the support of education, and we must insist upon the enforcement of the compulsory educational law.

The publication of the facts relating to the personnel of the army brought forth an amazing number of important matters. In the first place, it was found that a very high proportion of the men called to the colors were physically unfit. The older the community, the larger was the percentage of deficiency; and for the whole country, practically forty men out of every hundred could not qualify under the standards established by the War Department. Such shortcomings in the physical qualities of the manhood of the country are alarming and must be corrected. We had assumed that the number of unfit could not be very large. We know now that we must undertake the correction of this defect in our national life and attempt to build healthier citizens than we have had heretofore.

It is also noted in the publications of the army that venereal diseases had reached an alarming percentage. For our own state the number was 3 77/100 per cent, which was about the average for the country at large. The percentage is too high. The War Department has clearly insisted that measures must be forthcoming to bring information, instruction, and medical care for the checking of these diseases. They will not be checked if we simply stand aside and consider that individuals will see to their own care. The prevention and cure of venereal diseases are a public question and must be accepted by the state as such to be carried out with all the vigor which the commonwealth can bring to bear upon such a problem.

During the recent influenza epidemic we were found to be by no means prepared for such a widely sweeping disaster. All of us have read with interest the effect of the black death in the fifteenth century, but, devastating as that was, it did not begin to carry off as many citizens as the recent influenza epidemic in the year of our Lord, 1918. The experience with this epidemic indicates that an effective program for sanitation must be instigated and that better and more extensive educational institutions for the training of large numbers of nurses are necessary. The American Red Cross now has in mind the establishment of a Home Service that will attempt to meet the situation in some degree, but the American Red Cross is unable to do this alone. It must have the cooperation of the state government, of the local governing bodies, and of the schools. With all of these combined, provisions for future difficulties can be made, and a large staff to take care of epidemics and disasters can be trained. But even this is not sufficient. It is necessary to go further and to establish in our state adequate public health organizations by which facilities for the care and prevention of disease may be maintained and through which the physical well being of all Kentucky's citizens may be encouraged.

The basis of any commonwealth's development is, of course, its industry. Out of the ground men must take wealth, and from nature they must find the materials and the means for supporting and sustaining life. The earliest of these industries associated with the soil is agriculture. We have now reached a stage in the development of population where greater measures of conservation of the earth's surface must be undertaken. Agriculture has been pursued for thousands of years, but a method of farming is arriving which will yield larger production. If we are to have an independent people within the borders of Kentucky, our policy must be constant renewal of the soil because any type of agriculture which tends to reduce the soil fertility simply points to the fact that we are not only wasteful and ignorant but also unmindful of future needs. Probably more progress has been made in the field of agriculture than in any other industry, but much remains to be done in bringing about better methods of cultivation, in marketing the product, and in securing the proper distribution of the wealth which comes from nature.

Our mining, lumbering, and oil industries need strengthening by the right kind of legislation. Through legislation we should grant encouragement to them in the matter of proper taxation, in better transportation facilities, in better roads, and in low rates for the movement of freight in order that they may find adequate and satisfactory markets.

But beyond these important considerations is another that calls for still greater emphasis. I have reference to the relation of capital and labor. In our system of society, capital now from all sources is conducted in corporate form while labor tends to be more and more organized as units for the purpose of securing its rights. Left alone, the conflict between these two great factors is bound to arise, and, unless understanding between them is brought about, disaster is sure to result. It is necessary that labor shall have acceptable conditions to work under and a livable wage, a wage that will give leisure and opportunity for better living. On the other hand, capital must be assured of continuity, an opportunity to work without interruption. These are the conditions, and it is possible to work out a cooperative relationship between the two that will remove many of the difficulties that now exist. One of the great problems before a conference of this kind, as well as before representatives of capital and labor, is the establishment of a plan by which all can work together to their own mutual benefit and to the best interests of the people of the commonwealth.

The history of the centuries has shown again and again that ineffective, despotic government places a heavy burden upon industry and brings disaster after disaster upon the people who may be attempting to make progress in their civilization. We should know that local, state, and national government must be effective and free from graft in order that the communities, the state, the nation may prosper as they should. The men who are in administrative positions must be farsighted and able to visualize the future. We are reaching a stage in the United States of America where men in high places in community or state who are conducting government for their own advantages must be replaced by new types of government officers who will have before them the purpose of service.

The state can be helpful to the local government by insisting that local officials be men of vision and integrity. By careful systems of taxation, well organized and developed on right principles, the state can encourage rather than discourage the development of industry. By watchful oversight and by helping educational institutions, the state can bring about an increase in leadership. And by proper care of defectives and dependents, the state can prevent the development of parasitic groups that are likely to be a burden upon the people. The state must have, as already suggested, an adequate system of taxation.

State government from this viewpoint becomes something more than a contest between parties; it becomes a matter of vast importance to the commonwealth as a whole. Certainly the constituents of a commonwealth must realize sooner or later that the kind of government which they have is a help or a burden to them, and in realizing this fact they must decide to do something about the matter. Behind all of these problems is the great question of organization. What is nobody's job is never accomplished. No one individual is going to take upon himself the correction of these difficulties. It is only by organization beginning in the communities themselves that we can hope to get results and a superior pattern of living.

The World War has shown that in every community is an ardent patriotic spirit that, when aroused, can be called upon to do the necessary things. Times of war bring this fervor to the front; when the ordinary routine of peace comes, however, this spirit of patriotism declines with the consequences that the community continues to move along in the old way without becoming the noble, enlightened place it could be. A new obligation is before us. This war has shown to us our shortcomings. Responsibility must be recognized and accepted by the leaders in the various communities. It is not within the scope of my discussion to point out how this community organization can be accomplished. It is necessary, however, that such an organization be brought to pass at an early date if we are to accomplish the results hoped for.

Certain it is that these conditions made apparent to us signify the need for new and responsible citizenship. That democracy rests upon her citizenship is a commonplace saying. If we as believers in democracy make no effort to produce better citizens, then democracy is bound to fail. We have had our imaginations aroused by this great war. The man in the street sees that a marked change has come in the affairs of the world. In some countries he has forsaken the old regime entirely and has turned to an irresponsible or violent type of government that fails to understand the practical problems of life and that does not bother to maintain the rights of individuals.

It is essential that we in this Commonwealth of Kentucky recognize the turning-point in the history of the world and that we benefit from the great awakening that has taken place. We should take steps quickly to bring about some of the desired results. For the sake of our own future and our own necessities, we must assume the responsibilities that the conditions of modern life demand.

United We Stand

Memorandum of speech at the Kentucky Good Roads Luncheon, Lexington, May 29, 1924

BEFORE the world Kentuckians are first, last, and all the time for Kentucky. But at home they are town and county men first; Mountaineers, Blue Grassers, Penny Royalians and Purchasers second; and Kentuckians last. Our allegiances historically and romantically are to Kentucky, but economically and politically our ties are local. Perhaps the various soils, the distribution of minerals, the lines of railroads, all contribute to the division of the state into sections. At any event those who are in the least familiar with the situation know that Kentucky is divided into areas that do not have very much to do with each other because the means of communication are largely rudimentary. Such a situation hinders the growth and development of the commonwealth. Mental and physical accessibility of all these parts to each other will produce a bigger and better Kentucky.

There are two fundamental means by which this closer relationship can be brought about; one is a thoroughgoing public school system, and the other is the development of roads.

Our public schools are good and poor. In many communities the schools are excellent; in others quite unsatisfactory. Some of our counties have no high schools at all, and in others the schools are not extensive enough. It has been found that the state must supplement the school efforts of the less advantageously situated communities. In any thoroughly worked out educational system, provisions for higher education as well as for primary and secondary public schools should be made. Since education in a state can rise no higher than its source, a university and normal schools must be maintained. Kentucky has all of these; however, their financial support has not been sufficient to permit them to do what the people and especially the children and young people should have done for them.

In the matter of roads, no system exists in Kentucky. It is impossible to get from one part of the State to another by any means of transportation. Our Kentucky people have not yet recognized that the automobile has ushered in a new means of transportation that is even more far-reaching than the construction of railroads was in the last century. In refusing to build roads now, we are failing to provide one of the important elements in modern transportation. For the first time in the history of the state, an effort is being made to give the commonwealth, the whole commonwealth, an adequate school system and modern roads. If Kentucky succeeds in having good schools and good roads, we can look forward to a period of prosperity that will encourage capital, keep the young people in the state, and give them the training and the opportunity to build a great Kentucky.

Kentucky Is All of Us

From an article: *How the Expenditures Arose*, written in 1932

I T M U S T be remembered that Kentucky is all of us who live within the boundary of the state and the government is some of us selected to carry on the business of the state. The officials at Frankfort do not authorize the expenditures for the state, though they may have something to do with securing the legislation creating them. In the constitution certain departments of state are specified. Later legislatures, elected by the people, add to these and appropriate the funds to keep all departments going. The people do these things through their representatives and in consequence are responsible for the maintenance, continuance, and effectiveness of government.

As an example of this statement, let us consider roads. When the automobile made its appearance, the people demanded roads. Legislation was enacted, setting up taxes to provide funds and creating a commission to administer the funds and to construct the highways. Also when adequate schools were demanded, laws were passed and a better system was established. So the growth of government agencies continues. The people can find the answer to the expenses of government in the requirements made by the state, that is, by all of us.

If all of us are uninterested, and only a few are solicitous about the affairs of the state, naturally the government drifts about because we who should be especially concerned do not give the time or make the effort to take our parts as citizens. Groups of people are always on the job to see that they get what they want. All of us, unfortunately, let things slide along, optimistically thinking that someone will take care of us. Kentucky can be great only if all of us who are Kentucky are vigilant, alert, and interested citizens.

Kentucky in Statuary Hall

Explanatory remarks by the chairman of the commission to select
two Kentuckians, on the occasion of the unveiling
of the statues of Henry Clay and Ephraim McDowell in Statuary Hall,
Washington, D.C., March, 1929

WE HAVE met today for the purpose of unveiling the statues of
two of Kentucky's great men. It is an occasion for rejoicing and
congratulations; but one of regret also in that Isaac W. Bernheim,
the donor of the statues, cannot be present to see them unveiled,
accepted by the state, and given to the national government to
adorn Statuary Hall in the Federal Capitol. In 1925 Mr. Isaac W.
Bernheim, a former resident of the city of Louisville, offered to
give to the state of Kentucky statues of two of the notable men of
the state if the legislature would appoint members of a commission to designate their wishes in the matter. At the legislative
session of 1926, an act was passed appointing a commission consisting of George Colvin, President of the University of Louisville; William J. Hutchins, President of the Berea College; and
Frank L. McVey, President of the University of Kentucky. This
commission was asked to nominate two Kentucky citizens and to
report its findings to the next legislature.

In due course of time the commission met, discussed the situation, and decided to ask the teachers and school children of the
state to choose those whom they would wish to represent Kentucky.
Notices were sent to the county superintendents and to the superintendents of all city school systems calling attention to the matter
and asking for their cooperation in securing suggestions. The result
was interesting. Many names were proposed; however, again and
again the names of Clay, Davis, Breckinridge, Carlyle, Lincoln,
Boone, McDowell appeared. Henry Clay received more nominations than any other Kentuckian. In another meeting the commission canvassed the material that had been brought together,
discussed the purposes of the representation, and came to the conclusion that Kentucky should be represented in Statuary Hall, not
by warriors, not by statesmen and politicians alone, but rather by

two exponents of the state's attitude of mind. To that end the commission was unanimous in the choice of Henry Clay and Ephraim McDowell.

These men, Clay and McDowell, represent the spirit of Kentucky. Clay saw clearly the needs of the Ohio Valley and the Mississippi basin. He voiced the thought of the people in this extensive region and carried to Congress through his own vision the wishes of this people. Henry Clay was a great Kentuckian. Dr. McDowell was a pioneer in medicine. Highly trained in the best schools of his day both in this country and abroad, he brought a rich experience and superior preparation in medical science to the people. Ephraim McDowell was a great Kentuckian.

When Mr. Bernheim received the decision of the commission, he asked the well-known sculptor, Mr. Charles Henry Niehaus, to undertake the creation of the statues of Clay and McDowell. At the session in 1928 the legislature received the report of the commission and adopted it.

In this brief presentation of the story of the statues, too much praise cannot be given to Mr. Isaac W. Bernheim, nor can our thanks be too great for the gracious way in which he has given these statues to the state and to the nation. Although Statuary Hall has had a long history, Kentucky has had no part in it. Through Mr. Bernheim's generosity, Kentucky today is unveiling the statues of two distinguished sons in this hall where the other states have placed their representatives who have attained national fame. Mr. Charles Henry Niehaus has caught the spirit of these men and has presented in an unusually effective manner Henry Clay, statesman, and Ephraim McDowell, scientist. This occasion is one of rejoicing, one of thanks to Mr. Bernheim, and one of congratulations to ourselves for the happy and delightful conclusion to an interesting episode in Kentucky's history.

Foreword to *Kentucky, a Guide to the Bluegrass State*

Introduction to Kentucky Guide Book, compiled and written
by the Federal Writers' Project of the
Work Projects Administration; sponsored by the University of Kentucky;
published by Harcourt, Brace and Company, 1939

THE American Guide Series, including a guide book for every state in the Union when completed, will be a monument to the idea of the United States of America and also a source of information and help to the people of this country and to visitors from other lands. As each state compiles its special interests, attractions, and history, the many diversities in peoples, customs, scenes, and ways will become apparent; at the same time those qualities in mind and life that bind the states together in understanding will be revealed.

These guide books of the forty-eight states will find their way into every school and college, into the public libraries, and onto the shelves of private book collectors where they will be consulted again and again for items, facts, comments, and ideas. General readers will enjoy the books; students will find therein information; and travelers, native born as well as from other states and nations, will carry the guides with them on their journeys to learn of the things they should see in the various parts of this country.

Although many historians have attempted to investigate the origin of the name, Kentucky, yet no explanation has been acceptable to all readers. However, the account of its settlement and the adventures of Kentucky's great men have brought romance and charm to novels, poems, and stories which have carried the name of the state to all parts of the world and have endeared it to many who live beyond its borders.

Readers of stories, articles, and books about Kentucky have had emphasized for them some one particular aspect; they have been harrowed by details of poverty and hard living or they have been soothed by picturesque ornaments of fantasy. In this guide book, readers will find interesting things about the state that will bring a new picture to their minds. Here in Kentucky is a culture a century and a half old, enriched by the inheritances from other ages and other lands. Kentucky was the crossroads of the trek from the seaboard and from Europe as the pioneers went farther West or moved into the South. People bringing with them books, papers, pictures, furniture flowed into the state—some to remain and some to continue on their journeys. The traveler through the state today not only will find evidences of the older culture and of the progress that has been made in the past one hundred and fifty years but also will discover evidences of prehistoric inhabitants.

For many years I have been thinking about a book on the subject of "Why are Kentuckians as They Are?" I have thought of the early pioneers, of their contributions to Kentucky, of the settlements that were established, of the houses they built, and of the civilization that was erected on such foundations. It is a complicated and fascinating subject. This guide book furnishes for the reader a broad basis for knowing the state that every Kentuckian loves so devotedly; moreover it suggests again and again the courtesy, the graciousness, the charm of living that prevail indigenous to Kentucky.

The writers of the articles in this book have portrayed Kentucky scenes, resources, and attitudes. Photographs and maps strengthen the written word. The traveler will rejoice that touring routes mean something, and his journeys into the state will be greatly enhanced by the ownership of the book.

While the reader turns the pages of the book, let him remember that it is impossible to say everything that he would wish said or to say it as he would wish it said. Anyone who knows the difficulty of bringing unity to a guide book will be pleased by the accomplishment of the state director and of the various writers. We are thankful that the Kentucky Guide Book is a reality, and we are grateful to all those who have contributed their time and talents to add to our enlightenment, our pleasure, and our understanding.

PART V

B. THE ART SPIRIT

The Art Spirit

APPRECIATION of the beautiful is a great possession, possible for anyone with eyes to see, ears to hear, a heart to understand. The teacher who points the way to this comprehension of beauty has given untold riches to the student. Entered into at any age, knowledge of the arts and practice of one or more of them are enlightening and enriching; begun at an early age, they are of inestimable value in bringing to life zest, understanding, and worthwhile interest.

The Art Spirit in Life

Address at Founders' Day celebration, Randolph-Macon Woman's College, Lynchburg, Virginia, March 12, 1931

A CENTURY has passed since the founding of Randolph-Macon College. For nearly forty years this institution in Lynchburg has contributed so well to the education of women that its students and graduates portray the best traditions of college training and its name is highly respected throughout the nation. It is a pleasure to me to be present on this Founders' Day and to extend the good wishes of the University of Kentucky to the students, faculty, alumnae, and friends of Randolph-Macon Woman's College.

Since the consideration of what may well be expected of college graduates seems to be suitable to the time and place, I shall discuss the reasonable expectations a college has for its students and I shall emphasize in particular the spirit that I believe college students should have in meeting the problems, opportunities, and interests of life.

In a recent book Professor Giddings of Columbia University has set forth his views on some of the present day social problems under the title of *Mighty Medicine*. In one chapter he enumerates what a college senior ought to know. A senior should have a knowledge of English so that he can use his own language accurately and effectively. To use English well requires hard study and constant practice. The senior, however, should know his own language and should be able to use it in a way which carries his meaning in writing and speaking. He should have an appreciation of literature, especially English literature. In his four years at college he should have developed some taste for good reading and should have acquired a critical outlook on the meaning and standards of literature. He should also be able to find his way among the books and materials of modern scholarship. If he has any training at all, he should know how to use a library; he should be able to investigate references that will start him on any piece of work he is doing.

And again, if he is to have an influence upon the political concepts of his time, he should understand the meaning of history and have such judgment of it that he is able by checking and measuring to guard against the easy acceptance of the many panaceas offered today. He ought also to know what science is. He should comprehend the aim of scientific men and women and should appreciate the methods of science as those that must be applied to every type of problem. These methods include the gathering of facts, the application of statistical formulae to the distribution of facts in order to ascertain general tendencies, and finally the checking again of the facts and conclusions arrived at.

To this list of Professor Giddings' I should add as necessary for college seniors the inculcation of manners, the development of courtesy, the acceptance of tolerance as an attitude of good sportsmanship, and the habitual confirmation of intellectual honesty.

After four years of college the student should have made a beginning on a philosophy of life. He should have come to some conclusions about his attitude toward living. He should, in fact, have a concept of religion and of its relationship to the interpretations of life. As a matter of course, it is hardly to be expected that a young man or woman in the early twenties can have formulated a complete philosophy, but, if his years at college have been worth anything, he has come into something of a viewpoint concerning the meaning of life.

In our activities from day to day, as important as they are to us, we miss the beautiful because we are not ready to accept it as a part of life. The word art expresses our relation to the beautiful. Too often art is regarded as extraneous and something outside of us, not something to live by; and yet nothing is more lasting than art. "All passes. Art alone enduring stays to us." And what is this art spirit? It is a real understanding of things, their order and their balance. It is a grip on life. The artist in the broader sense of the term teaches the meaning of life. To catch his inspiration is important to all of us. In this spirit of art, dwell harmony, form and beauty, and the ultimate expression of truth. The art spirit in its application means the removal of drudgery and the pushing aside of meanness. Toil takes on a new dignity when the spirit of art is applied to what we do.

The art spirit is illustrated by the painter who tries to put on canvas as beautifully as possible what he sees. It inspires the poet to express his thought in words that have form, rhythm, and beauty. If he is a great poet, his songs live on forever because they are beautiful, artistic, and spiritual. The musician brings harmony and beauty out of sound and symbolizes the great truths of life in his compositions. The architect by design, mass, color, and proportion pictures to mankind a revelation of what art is and what beauty can bring to life. These are among the great who show men the art spirit. In every man, though, there is the longing for the expression of himself, which longing is the very essence of the art spirit.

In these days of increasing leisure the art spirit must prevail, or we shall fail to get out of life any considerable part of its meaning. When we understand that we can carry the art spirit into the houses we live in, into the clothes we wear, into the furniture we use, and into the human relations of everyday, life brings a great gift to us. In our communities yards and lawns may be made beautiful, and roadways, parks, and countryside can express the art spirit of man. But this is not all. A renowned philosopher said, "The mind of man makes his world." With the God given gift of thought man clothes his world with beauty. But he cannot know beauty nor can he see it unless he has caught the spirit of art. Beauty is here to see. When man grasps the harmony of the world, his heart and his mind are filled with beauty. When the art spirit claims him, a new attitude appears in man's relation to his fellows, and his own heart responds to the doing of everything he sets his hand to do with thoroughness, honesty, and care. He does it because he wants to do it. He glories in the work and in the result. He is an artist. Living is thus freed from drudgery. Life becomes worth while because it can be lived beautifully.

An obligation rests upon the college and the university to show the meaning of the art spirit and to point out the way whereby a community may be lifted to higher levels and may be endowed with an appreciation of beauty. It is the duty of the college to invest the students with this spirit so that life may have excellence and value. When the art spirit becomes dominant and men are filled with it, pessimism disappears, and the machine age has no terror for men living up to their highest possibilities. This way of looking at life under the influence of the art spirit is given to us in a poem entitled "Colors" by Phoebe Crosby Allunt:

"I am so glad of the colors of things
    Night, of course, is blue,
And morning red and yellow, like a tulip.
    Babies are blue, flecked with white,
Because of their eyes.
    A voice I know is the green of a breaking wave.
Callers that outstay their time
    Get a shiny brown.
Church going is purple,
The dull, flat purple of a prayer book marker.
There is another purple, though,
Radiant, rosy.
I have only seen it once, in northern lights,
I think it must be Religion.
Adventure is golden,
Because of the sun on brass helmets.
Love is white, glowing.
I know what I'll do!
I'll gather them all together
And make a stained glass window of them
Inscribing it thus:
    To the glory of God
    In loving memory
        of
    My days on Earth."

The buildings of the college mean much. They mean more than stone and mortar. They mean the dominating of the art spirit in their construction and the entrance of that spirit into the ways of life. The whole college should be and often is an expression of the art spirit.

When the people of a state are imbued with this spirit, a state wonderful indeed to live in will be developed. College men and women should be apostles of this new, this old, art spirit and should carry its truth to their fellow men into every part of the commonwealth and into every walk of life.

Painting for Pleasure

Published in *Journal of Adult Education*, June, 1930; reprinted

THERE is a response in every man's heart and mind to beauty. Great national monuments have been erected through patriotic ardor; if they are beautiful, the citizen is aroused along with patriotism to an appreciation of what the artist has tried to do. For centuries the traveler across the valley of the Tiber has seen the dome of St. Peter's glistening in the sun. The picture has not only filled him with enthusiasm for his religion but has also deeply moved him by the massive magnificence of the building. Poets have told and men have dreamed of St. Paul's in London. Whistler made an etching of it as he saw it through the channel of the streets. The traveler from abroad as he comes up the harbor of New York is amazed by the beauty and impressiveness of the skyline of our largest city. In his heart is a thrill not only because of its material greatness but because of the design and form that tell a story of artistic creation. So the visitor to Washington who sees the memorial to Lincoln and the monument to Washington catches something of the inspiration that filled the artists when they undertook to put into stone their dreams.

The men who have looked upon these great monuments and others elsewhere have without question been affected by them. They have caught a bit of the meaning expressed in harmony and design, and in an unconscious way they have translated these qualities into their living.

Now that we have achieved leisure for all classes of our people, what are we going to do with it? Of course it can be filled with games and collecting, but it may also be enhanced by the practice of the fine arts. Through this experience an individual now and then may grasp something of the art spirit and realize the beauty of life.

What is it that we mean by the art spirit? It is primarily the doing of things well. The artist is constantly teaching the world the idea of life. The art spirit is really a grip on life, in fact an understanding of things in their order and balance. Through it one comes to the meaning of harmony, form, and beauty. It is essential that the painter shall have an appreciation of beauty, but it is likewise necessary that he shall learn the meaning of design, shadows, line, harmony, and color. The painter endeavors to express in a picture what he, himself, sees. An artist, not a photographer, he must eliminate and arrange the objects before him. He puts into the picture his own emotion and belief. The poet expresses beauty in thought by means of words, form, and rhythm. The musician finds beauty in sound, and the architect embodies in great masses of stone and brick his ideas of form, mass, color, and proportion. This art spirit is incorporated into our own living; it finds expression in our houses, our clothing, our roadways and parks. The art spirit should dominate our lives in our relations to others and should enable us to use our increased leisure in ways that will give added significance to life.

The ordinary concept of art is that it is something apart belonging in practice to the few and possessed in form by the rich. We say it is difficult to understand and a futile thing to know. But the artists tell a different story. A painter friend of mine once said to me, "There is too much *talk* about art. I can tell all I know in an hour." And he is an excellent painter. In a lecture the other day Rockwell Kent said, "Art is an intensification of all the things we all are." Just so! It is only through art that we come to a larger fruition of our powers, interest, and appreciation.

For many years I had a desire to do something in the field of art. I have used a pencil in an amateurish fashion since boyhood days. When I expressed this longing to a friend, he urged me to try to paint. Looking back over the ten years of my efforts to paint, I can see a considerable growth as a result of my reading of books, of my study of the work of artists, and of my actual application of color to canvas. Because of the fear of ridicule, I began with some trepidation. But after all, what does it matter what other people think if painting means joy and interest? And so the plunge was made. I bought Birge Harrison's *Landscape Painting* and East's *Landscape Painting* and read them many times. I attempted to understand how a flat surface can show form, distance, and tone. I wrestled with the variations of color and the meaning of values, and I became so enthusiastic that I went to art school each summer for three years. Out of these experiences have come self-development and a great amount of joy as well as some accomplishment.

The benefit I have derived from the study of the fine arts has given me a genuine interest in art as an avocation. As soon as I face a canvas with brush and color, I am confident that my mind will be relieved of all worries except those that have to do with the picture I wish to paint. My work in art has made me see things more clearly and has given me a larger conception of the meaning of life. Rather interestingly it has brought into our family an understanding of art that we did not have before. It has given us an appreciation of artistic things and beautiful surroundings. It has led me to look forward to an increasingly interesting life.

I have referred to the effect that imposing buildings have upon the traveler. Too often he looks upon them as the work of a genius who is different in kind from the rest of us. The fact of the matter is that the art spirit is in every one of us; through its influence we can in everyday living be dissatisfied with the mediocre and shoddy in accomplishment and can determine to do all things with thoroughness and honesty.

To leave the matter here would be to abandon it on the doorstep of the average individual. There must be some means of bringing the art spirit into the life of the adult, and it seems to me that the proper agency is the college. It is true that colleges ordinarily deal with young undergraduates. Nevertheless, here are great numbers of adult persons who need direction and who have an interest in using the fine arts as a means of satisfaction. If the colleges will throw open their doors to adults and teach them by unacademic methods the history of art, art appreciation, the theory and practice of art, these colleges will find adult education a vital process. This statement is not based on theory only. In the United States at the present time many groups of business and professional men and women are painting once or twice each week. Organization, direction, and a sympathetic attitude on the part of the colleges will encourage those groups already established and will enable many other individuals to find inspiration, broadening interests, personal joy, and sometimes real accomplishment from *painting for pleasure*.

Practice of the Fine Arts

Summary of address to the Adult Education Council of
Metropolitan Cincinnati, April 10, 1932

THE topic that I am to discuss in this symposium of the afternoon is the "Practice of the Fine Arts." The people who live in a city such as Cincinnati are fortunate in having a museum of fine arts, an art school, and a very high order of direction in many art activities. The majority of people in America have no such opportunities. How may they have a part and a place in the fine arts?

The sales of artists' materials, paints, brushes, indicate a widespread interest in the practice of the fine arts, and this interest on the part of the people is manifested because of a desire for self-expression. After all, the real purpose of the fine arts including the works of notable artists is to secure two things for which we all have a vague longing, self-expression and appreciation of beauty.

The difficulty is to bring to the people this second gift, which I should have mentioned first, namely, the appreciation of beauty. Yet it is something that is open to every person if the way is shown. Looking out of this window for instance, you will see against the blue sky a tree with its spring buds and soft leaves. It is a beautiful thing. No payment is required; you have only to look at it.

[321]

When traveling by train I have occupied myself by studying faces to note the relationship of the different parts and planes. All you need to do to increase your pleasure and your appreciation is to observe that light and shadow, form and outline, in nature and in people make pictures that are interesting, sometimes very beautiful, and sometimes odd.

The general problem of the appreciation of beauty is always before us. The art museums are encouraging the quest for beauty by bringing together the best painting and the best sculpture that can be obtained. In the field of music the orchestra is endeavoring to raise musical appreciation. The radio is taking part. How to develop understanding of the arts is an important question.

The great mass of people are coming into a larger leisure, which may be a very helpful or a very dangerous thing. How can this leisure be well used? If leisure means idleness, inertia, if it means being swayed without purpose to whatever comes, then leisure is dangerous. If leisure can give opportunity to people of seeing beauty in cloud formations or in other natural phenomena, of observing the beauties of art and life, then leisure is helpful.

Beauty is at hand everywhere. Our towns and cities with their great piles of buildings display shadows and forms of amazing interest. Art exhibitions furnish enlightenment and happiness to people who have appreciation of beauty. In kindergarten and on through the grades efforts are being made to enable the child to know the elementary principles involved in the arts and thereby to help him to incorporate them into his life. The adult should have a wider opportunity to understand their meaning.

One reason that greater appreciation of beauty is found in some of the foreign countries than in our own is that the children even in the villages have a good piece of sculpture in the square or a fine painting in a church. They see these beautiful objects and so learn to appreciate form, color, design.

Nearly all of us want to express ourselves somehow through the arts, through painting, sculpturing, music, writing, or some other art form. There is a delight in making something with our hands. The land is full of medical men, lawyers, and business men who are engaged in painting, in etching, in making furniture, in producing all sorts of things, many of them exceedingly well done. Those who practice the arts find relaxation and, moreover, they may reach a kind of exaltation. However, I must add that this attachment requires resolution and effort. The purpose of art to me and I think to most of those who express themselves about it is to enable people to live in the world of spirit, in the world of mind, and in the world of beauty.

Frank criticism is good for the soul of the would-be artist. Something has been gained all the way around, and that gain is a greater appreciation of art, of the difficulties of art, and a better understanding of beauty.

All of us are looking for self-expression. Such expression can be found in whatever we do if we do it in the art spirit. However, the practice of the fine arts is essential to the free enjoyment of beauty and self-expression. That practice will be more effective if it is associated with museums, with exhibits, and with courses of study in the field of the arts. The end is enjoyment and the expression of self, which are great contributions to the making of interesting people and of interesting lives.

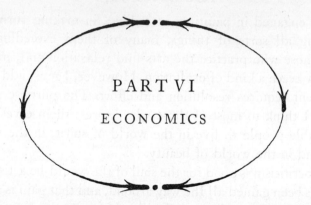

PART VI
ECONOMICS

Modern Industrialism Looks Ahead

From *Modern Industrialism,*
D. Appleton and Company, Second Edition, 1923, pp. 346-348

BUT the discussion of modern industrialism cannot end at this point. It must go beyond the confines of national life to the international tendencies of today for the World War raised a query of great importance. It was this: is the state the supreme form of political institutions? German emphasis upon the state as the superior power did not reassure the advocates of democracy throughout the world, nor did it hold out to the small states much of a guarantee that their autonomy would be secured if their fortunes carried across the path of the great state. Without doubt, nationalities must survive under the principle of kindred relationships shown in languages, institutions, and history. But, on the other hand, the right of a state to dominate the world for its own ends is at variance with the principles of democratic life.

The World War stressed the international mind, much as we may think it opposed internationalism. . . . The Allies learned that there was strength in unity. They learned that to win the war a "give-and-take" policy must be accepted by them. They learned also that no state can hope to be supreme in a human world. The story of past centuries points to nations unified against the aggressor, and so it will continue to be. Nor can the commerce and the trade of the great powers grow on the basis of force. Cooperation of the nations is the only fundamental basis for world trade. Such cooperation cannot be limited to a small group of powerful nations for immediately the contest of the weak against the strong is awakened. A League of Nations, in one form or another, is the next step in man's progress providing it is a league of all the nations of the earth.

Standing astride the arteries of trade, holding to the resources of the earth, cannot bring commercial results or prevent war. No nation is sufficient unto itself. Men of science know fairly well what the earth has in its treasure box. Trade and industry grow with the development of the peoples of the earth. On the other hand world anarchy, like the anarchy in national life, lays violent hands on the powers of a people, their resources, and their communications. Some organization of world agencies becomes necessary. Modern industrialism has burst the bonds of national life. It is international, and the great nations must recognize that fact.

The Nation's Call for Thrift

Published in the *Annals of
the American Academy of Political and Social Science*, January, 1920

IN THE older days of railroading a sign stood guard at every crossing on which were the words, "Stop, Look, Listen." Evidently this positive command has been forgotten in railroad circles, and elsewhere for that matter, for the traveler is now informed that it is a railroad crossing which he is approaching, the "Stop, Look, Listen" being taken for granted as part of the functioning of a reasoning human being. On the whole the same attitude appears to be the rule in other departments of activity. Everywhere are advertisements setting forth the attractiveness of goods and knick-knacks as the desirable things to exchange for money. So the world goes on piling up consumption goods, and the people buy without thought of the future. It is in reality high time to put up the sign "Stop, Look, Listen" over every door in the land.

Perhaps such a statement needs explanation. It may even appear dogmatic—it probably is—but the purpose of an opening paragraph is acknowledged if attention has been attracted to the real import of the statement. In the face of the demand for higher wages, more rents, larger prices, and all the rest of the phenomena now familiar to all, every citizen is requiring more income in order that he may meet the cost of everyday living. This in itself is the natural way out of personal difficulties, but, when multiplied by thousands of instances, the mass of people are no nearer the end of their troubles than before. In fact, new demands leave the problem just as unsolvable as before.

It hardly seems necessary in the year of grace 1919 to set forth the simple principle that production of goods for human needs is the only way in which human wants, and as a consequence higher wages and better living, can be met. Yet all the evidence points to the conclusion that the principle has been forgotten. Since more wages in money will help one person, why not the same for all?

When Robinson Crusoe sat in his cave making an inventory of

his possessions, he came upon a bag of gold in a great sea chest. Looking at the gold sovereigns so worth while in civilized England, he gave utterance to the remark, Defoe tells us, "Sorry, worthless stuff." And it was to him. He could not buy anything with it; he could not use it in any way that he thought worth while; there were no human beings who were willing to exchange it for goods. So it lay in the chest forgotten for years. Our civilized societies are in the reverse condition. Men have money, but the goods are not there in the quantity necessary for the needs of the world. Strikes are not likely to produce more goods, and extravagance in the consumption of goods will not bring them into existence. Where then are we?

The agencies of production are labor, capital, land, and management. No prolonged endeavor can go on for any great length of time without all of these agencies. Labor must have food, but food requires labor, land, and capital for its production. Only in the last one hundred years has the world accumulated any great quantity of capital, and no inconsiderable amount of that has been wiped out by the Great War. The disasters of nature dog the steps of man and place heavy burdens upon him. Pests destroy his crops, and winds drive his fleets on rocky shores. Against all of these, he struggles bravely and hopefully. The war has swept some countries bare; billions of capital have been destroyed, and millions of lives were given over to the god of war. The impress of all of this has not yet been made upon the world. We must come to thrift, economy, and hard work to restore the world to the place where it was in the year 1914.

With some danger of repeating what has already been said, it is worth while to rub the lesson in. We must grasp the idea that man is not free to go on indefinitely consuming; he soon encounters powerful influences which work against the increasing of product without augmented labor, added effort, more capital, and better organization. "The more food and clothing, fuel, and other material goods we require, the farther we have to go for the material, and the harder it is to get; we must plow inferior lands yielding smaller crops, we must sink deeper shafts for our coal and iron.

As our population grows ever larger, and this larger number wants more and more pieces of the earth to feed its machines and turn out the increased quantity of goods, the drain upon the natural resources is constantly increasing. The material world is limited; in time, nature will become exhausted, and long before this happens, the quantity of human labor required to raise the increased supply of raw material in the teeth of the Law of Diminishing Returns will far exceed the economies attending large-scale production."

The population of the United States is now more than 100,-000,000. From the point of view of consumption and the supplying of wants, this means an ever increasing demand for foodstuffs, higher land values, smaller exports of food products, and larger imports of materials for manufacturing. Progressing at this rate the growth of population in the United States will necessitate the taking up of the waste places and the introduction of an era of intensive cultivation with higher efficiency in production. Conservation of natural resources also must reach the stage of an economic necessity, and interest in that subject will no longer be deemed a fad as is often the case at present. But against this necessity of labor are the constant retarding forces of nature and the foolish tendencies of men to fritter away their patrimony.

From time to time a vast amount of wealth is destroyed by storm, fire, and flood. A tornado on the Great Lakes and the east coast of the Atlantic not long ago drove hundreds of vessels ashore, drowned many men, and destroyed valuable cargoes. In 1913 a storm on the Japanese coast accompanied by a volcanic eruption killed thousands of people and laid waste the property of many more. The report of the engineering division of the War Department states that the annual loss from floods in the United States averages $50,000,000. In the Ohio flood in 1913 the damage suffered by railroads, cities, and private individuals amounted to hundreds of millions.

Losses by fire add to the appalling aggregate of wealth destruction. In the year 1916 the fire losses in the United States amounted to $168,905,100. Despite the efforts of the insurance companies and other agencies to limit the size and frequency of fires, the absolute amount of waste has declined but slightly. The newness of some parts of the country, the absence of regulations for building in many places, and the failure to provide first-class protection against fires give the United States a per capita fire loss which is from five to six times as large as that of any of the leading European countries.

Irving Fisher in estimating the cost of the annual charge against the country for illness places the figure at $1,000,000,000. Probably $660,000,000 of this cost is attributable to tuberculosis alone. Dr. L. O. Howard, Chief of the Federal Bureau of Entomology, says that malaria costs the country $100,000,000 annually; and Dr. George M. Kober of Georgetown University thinks that $350,000,000 is a conservative estimate of the annual toll from typhoid. Diseases of plants and animals cause losses of millions of dollars every year by destroying products or impairing their value.

It is essential that some comment be made upon the acts of men themselves which affect the consumption of wealth, as distinguished from the acts of nature. The World War furnishes the most apparent instance in all history of the destruction of wealth through force. Among the direct costs of the war are to be enumerated damages of property, cost of the army, seizure of raw materials, and other direct detriments to governments and cities. The indirect costs amounting to billions of dollars include losses of agricultural and industrial production, of interest on investments, of earnings from shipping and banking, and of profits of insurance and mercantile houses. The deficiency throughout the country caused by the injury and death of young men just coming into their productive years can hardly be estimated.

An economic depression due to the destruction of capital and wealth invariably follows war and causes a scarcity of food that brings about more deaths than the actual fighting. The fact is that even in civilized lands the resources of many are so scanty that an increase in the price of bread falls heavily upon the population.

In direct contrast to the expenditures for war are the amounts which are spent by governments, individuals, and private associations for social amelioration and betterment. These comprise two classes, compulsory and voluntary expenditures.

The first class includes the appropriations for the general conduct of government and the outlay for expenses incurred by the different divisions of the government for services such as the salaries of civil servants, police, soldiers, and judges. Military and naval defense is included in this group. Postoffices, telegraph lines, and railroads, when owned by the government, supposedly pay for themselves since the users return the cost of service.

Voluntary expenditures include the outlay for countless social and philanthropic agencies both public and private. At one of the meetings of the American Academy of Political and Social Science, according to the American Year Book for 1913, the art of giving was discussed as an exact science. It was declared that in 1912, perhaps the most notable year, gifts totaling nearly $267,000,000 were reported by the press and that, for the twelve years preceding, the annual total of outstanding gifts had exceeded $100,000,-000. This statement tells something of the extent to which consumption for social purposes may be carried voluntarily.

The latest estimates of the yearly consumption of liquors and tobacco in the United States reach the enormous figure of $2,830,-000,000. Of this sum $1,200,000,000 is spent for tobacco and $1,630,000,000 for malt and spirituous liquors. The total gives an almost incredible per capita figure of $28.00. In the fiscal year 1916, there were withdrawn for consumption in the United States 136,000,000 gallons of distilled liquors and a little more than two billion gallons of fermented liquors. Our consumption of coffee, tea, and sugar has come to surpass that of any other nation, and they have been made a part of every family's diet. By unthinking individual consumption the magnitude of the social burden is materially increased. When a goodly portion of the individual's consumption is governed by habit, the charge becomes practically fixed.

The nation's drink bill is often compared with the cost of government, and the nation's tobacco expenditures, while not so large as the liquor cost, were four times the amount spent on the army and navy before the World War. Then, too, through the carelessness of smokers, thousands of dollars in property are destroyed each year. The amount spent annually for tobacco is three times the cost of the Panama Canal.

Social customs are also responsible for consumption. What is termed fashion has come to set standards of living in food, clothes, and housing. Conformity to these criteria is looked upon as a test of social standing, and thus modern society is bound in many ways by the restrictions and limitations it places upon itself, which in turn affect individual expenditure.

For several years the public prints have been filled with comments upon the cost of living. The cartoonists have exercised their skill in depicting in humorous fashion the ideas in vogue about the ascending scale of expenditures. The increased cost of living as compared with earlier days is due to a rising standard in the common life of the people seen in better housing, more attractive clothing, higher qualities of food, and the larger variety of amusements demanded by every class of the population.

In addition to the rise in the standard of living, there is another and more immediate cause for the increase in the cost of living; this is to be found in the pressure of the population upon the food supply. Agricultural products have not grown in quantity commensurately with the needs of the population. The number of cattle has decreased not only in proportion to the population but absolutely; in the past five years the increase in tilled acreage was 9 per cent and the increase in population 14½ per cent. The United States, once a great wheat exporting country, now uses in normal times practically all of its grain for home consumption. These facts point to an enlarged demand without a corresponding growth in product. The result is as a matter of course higher prices.

Besides the influence of underproduction upon supply, there is another factor in the higher cost of living; that is the money standard, which during the past twenty years has been changing in value under the influence of increasing supplies of gold and securities. In like manner an enlarged credit due to the material growth of the basis of credit, gold, has had its influence upon the purchasing power of the dollar with the result that the dollar is not now able to command in return so great an amount of commodities as formerly.

Viewed in the light of the present, this is an overwhelming category of consumption in a civilized society. It is bad enough in normal times. To it have been added individual prodigality, the refusal of labor to work as of old, and the very discouraging burden of war expenditures.

In a recent speech before the House of Commons, Lloyd George explained the matter: "The aggregate direct cost of the War was $200,000,000,000. If 40,000,000 able-bodied young men were to take a holiday and be withdrawn from the task of production for four years, and if during that period one thousand pounds were placed at the disposal of each, you would have some sort of notion what a war on this gigantic scale means." Dr. Rowe, formerly Assistant Secretary of the Treasury, moreover has said: "It is evident to every student of the world situation that the sum total of productive goods, raw materials, tools, implements, machinery, etc., is today insufficient to meet the pressing needs of mankind. The amount of available capital at any one time is limited and at no period in the life of this generation has it been limited as at the present moment." "The fate of Europe is balanced on a knife edge," wrote Mr. Frank Vanderlip recently. The only way out is to save and with the capital so created to produce, produce, produce.

The world is poorer, much poorer, than it was in 1880. The generation now coming on faces a less pleasing prospect than the one that is passing. What is more disturbing is the lack of habits of hard work and thrift in the new generation. The hope for the solution of these serious problems is to be found in a productive people who know how to produce, who appreciate the great power of thrift, and who are willing to forego the pleasure of the present because they know that capital is the result of saving and that labor without capital is a blind man groping in the dark. The times call for all of us to "Stop, Look, Listen" and, having heeded the warning, to work and to save.

Economic Adjustments during the Next Decade

Summary of address to the Association of
Grain Commission Merchants, Chicago, Illinois, February 6, 1936

To TRY to tell about economic adjustments during the next year is a large order. To forecast the next decade is almost impossible. We are in great confusion in this country and as a people have little understanding of economic fundamentals. Because of our tendency to define wealth as money, we propose various schemes for the distribution of national income and we lose sight of the fact that the only way to raise the standard of living is through the production and increase of economic goods.

Most of the next decade will be doubtless taken up in learning what can and what cannot be done. Various plans will be offered, and probably changes in our money structures will be made by which some of the chaos of distribution will be straightened out and the value of money fixed.

The recent decisions of the Supreme Court appear to many people to have wiped out the program of the New Deal; however, an examination of what has been done shows the organization of at least five groups of governmental activity. The first has to do with what may be called the building up process such as conservation, housing, rural rehabilitation, and the prevention of soil erosion. The second division provides for an economic policy in price determination, the financing of markets, and the establishment of gold and silver monetary values. The third relates to regulations dealing with securities, bank deposits, motor carriers, and utilities. The fourth applies to various credit facilities for rural communities in particular. The fifth has to do with opportunities for young people, with security for the aged, with unemployment, and with public construction. Out of this list practically all the provisions for bettering conditions will stand, I believe, except certain matters of economic policy.

Agriculture has been in a serious condition for years. Only within recent times has any financing agency been established by the government to care for its needs. Agriculture in losing its foreign market has accumulated a lot of surpluses. Thus to wait on economic forces to clear the situation would entail enormous suffering and losses. Since the farmer working alone cannot develop a self-made plan of salvation without damage to the good of all, surely some plan of agricultural control will continue. Moreover, the recognition and valuation of rural life as a way of living will be vitalized.

For the decade as a whole it would seem that agriculture will be better ordered, economic policy will be slowly improved, and, I trust, inflation in money values will be controlled. In this decade adjustment of monetary systems should take place by international agreements. Progress in the balancing of the budget should be made during the next three years, and the national debt should be taken seriously with a definite attempt to reduce it. Foreign markets will be widened, and tariff walls will be broken down; an evidence of these processes we have in the Canadian reciprocal trade agreement.

Within the country I am quite sure that the consumer will appear as an important force with much better organization than he has had in the past. Also planning by government agencies will be more extensive, and the movement toward centralization with the breakdown of small local units will be accelerated. Perhaps a most important forward step will be the adjusting of taxation between the state and the federal government. These economic processes, dependent as they are on many events, will continue successfully if national understanding and solidarity are existent and if world peace is maintained.

An Economist Looks at the World

Some Major Events
in Foreign Countries and the United States

Radio talk over WHAS, March 28, 1938

T H E police theory of government is rampant in the world today. "Let us reason together" had reached a fair degree of effectiveness before the World War, but it is no longer a factor in world politics. Force used at the right time, whether within the boundaries of a state or against a weak neighbor, produces immediate results though it may be the cause of a whirlwind fifty years later. The Versailles treaty was most unjust in Germany's eyes; it was a devastating treaty, so the Austrians say. Thus the poison of 1918 continued to work. Moreover the widespread depression weakened the financial and industrial strength of the world. When force, armed force, was brought to play in such a world, it triumphed; and the pay-off was large. Witness what happened in China a year ago and in Europe on the sixth of March. The continuance of war in Spain is due to outside aid given by interested nations who look to some reward in the future. It is a topsy-turvy world, a discouraged world, but still a hopeful one.

On the seventeenth of March before the National Press Association meeting in Washington, Mr. Cordell Hull, Secretary of State, made a distinguished speech that may well be regarded as the program of the United States in the field of foreign affairs. He asserted that this government will protect its nationals wherever they may be. This the United States has always done and will continue to do. Nor can the United States look with indifference upon what is happening in other parts of the world and remain within its own boundaries an isolated nation hugging the delusion of the hermit who lives alone, a solitary man of no value to any one. It is necessary to maintain strong armed forces to resist encroachment upon our possessions and those of our neighbors and to protect our nationals in other lands. Secretary Hull stressed the foolishness of tariffs, quotas, exchange restrictions, and all the machinery instituted by a chauvinistic people aspiring to become wholly self-sustaining. He pointed the way toward the removal of economic barriers through the use of trade treaties that will encourage commerce between nations and so set men to work. It would be a happier world, no doubt, if such agreements might be reached.

The seventeenth bilateral trade treaty was signed with Czechoslovakia during this month. There was protest from many of our manufacturers, especially from those who make shoes. The New England factories were loud in their opposition, claiming that they would be ruined; yet the treaty gives them considerable protection.

At the same time negotiations have been going on with Great Britain. The complications in this case are much greater than those with a single country since the Commonwealth of Nations includes in its membership all the British Dominions. This agreement must satisfy a number of enterprises not only in the United States and Great Britain but also in Canada, Australia, South Africa, and India. On the face of the problem, to reach a satisfactory agreement seems practically impossible. However, it is very important that the democracies shall concur in trade treaties. At the present time the experts gathered in Washington are at work on the details of the diplomatic contract.

Unless nations come together in trade relations, breakdowns in trade, in industry, and in exchange will surely follow. It is said that the United States can get along alone without difficulty; but experience shows that our fortunes go up and down with those of other lands. Thus continued depression abroad will be reflected in the United States, and, if the economic crisis persists long enough, this country is dragged down too. A statement of this kind if it is true, and I think it can be regarded as true, throws a great flood of light on the necessity of building up trade relations and establishing them in treaties. The success of our negotiations with Great Britain is an important force in the continuance of the democracies and in their understanding of each other.

The demand for a large navy and increased army personnel has been markedly stimulated by the happenings in Europe and in Asia during the past year. In his message to Congress, President Roosevelt urged the enlargement of the navy by many battleships, cruisers, and submarines. Congress was sympathetic and added to the original amount an additional 20 per cent, bringing the sum to be spent in the next four years to more than a billion dollars.

The hearings held by committees on naval affairs and on appropriations brought out a number of interesting things. One of these was the value of a battleship when bombing machines may be used in naval battles. The officers of our navy insist that the plane is not a great menace to properly constructed battleships. In other admiralties there is more doubt on this point. The committee was evidently convinced of the rightness of the admirals' opinion and accepted the commitment of more battleships whose tonnage was to be raised from 35,000 to 45,000 tons. The other contention was that the United States should have two fleets large enough to protect the east and west coasts. Admiral Readly declared that such a policy would cost several times more than the proposed expenditures. There was a rather formidable opposition to the navy bill, but the House voted the $1,100,000,000 by a majority of 150 members.

Railway transportation in the United States arises now and then as a major problem for the people, the legislatures, and Congress. Government regulation has grown with the years as indeed has the question of rates and finance. If the arguer takes the side of the railroad, he becomes not eloquent but indignant over the hamstringing of a great industry by heavy taxes, government regulations, high wages, and union exactions. The opposition points to the backwardness of the railroads in meeting the needs of the public, in the failure to face the competition of automobiles, and in the gigantic financial structure erected by the corporations.

Whatever the cause, the railroads of the country with three or four exceptions are sick, and many of them are in bankruptcy. The railroads have asked for higher rates, hoping thereby to increase the companies' incomes. After considerable delay the Interstate Commerce Commission ordered a 10 per cent increase of rates that may produce an additional $240,000,000 of income. The advisability of such a policy of rate raising is very much in question since the railroads need more tonnage resulting from a revised industry. Higher rates burden business. The President recognizes the situation and has recommended consolidation of lines and the reduction of operating costs. This may help, but in the long run the financial organization of transportation companies will have to go through the wringer so that the water may be pressed out of stocks and bonds.

The Tennessee Valley project, vivid in the imagination of many people, has fallen into controversy within the Authority itself. For some time it has been apparent that the members were not in harmony on many of the questions that came up for decision. The chairman evidently believing himself wholly responsible for leadership and policy forming held that the other two members were to support him. Differences of opinion upon power questions made this one man direction impossible. The gulf between members had reached an acute stage when the chairman charged his colleagues with dishonesty and with violation of the purposes of the TVA act.

Since such a public statement could not pass unnoticed, the President called upon Arthur E. Morgan to substantiate his charges. This he refused to do, saying that it was not the place or the time for his statement to be given and holding to this position through the three meetings held in Washington. On Monday the President removed the former chairman and sent to Congress the order, a report of the meetings, and General Cummings' opinion on the power of removal. The President is not opposed to a congressional hearing and leaves the ordering of the hearing to Congress. The effects of the Morgan episode are already to be seen in the failure of the House to pass the appropriation for the Gilbertsville Dam. The enemies of the TVA are rejoicing in the row going on in the Authority, and meantime the progress of a great enterprise is checked.

One more news item may be included in the remaining minutes of this broadcast. Again President Roosevelt figures in this bit of news. More than a year ago he appointed a Committee on Education. This committee under the leadership of Dr. Floyd Reeves has finished the report and given it to the press. The report recommends the support of public schools in the different states by the federal government. If the recommendation is adopted and if Congress makes an appropriation, the public schools of backward states will be brought up to the national standard. The document containing the report should be read carefully by parents and school people.

Is There a Mountain Problem?

Address to the Southern Mountain Workers Conference,
Knoxville, Tennessee, April, 1935

THE territory called the Appalachian area is limited geographically to some 17½ million acres extending 600 miles diagonally northeast to southwest from 87 degrees to 78 degrees longitude and 33 degrees to 37 degrees latitude. In this area, about 70 per cent the size of the state of Kentucky, 1,665,907 people live. Of this number 147,154 are engaged in mining, 148,813 in agriculture, and 54,987 in manufacturing. This Appalachian region is not to be confused with the southern highlands in which 6,000,000 people live.

An old belief persists that the people in the Appalachian region are a marooned people held there by geographic and economic conditions. This view, presented in books and periodicals, is quite generally believed. A recent study, however, indicates that the presence of the inhabitants in this mountain area cannot be accounted for in that way. It will be recalled that the trek from the east to Kentucky was through the Cumberland Gap. Much f the immigration into the state came over this route. As time went on this trail was the scene of considerable activity. There were inns, settlements, and blacksmith shops along the way. Probably the easiest access into the "great meadows" west of the Alleghany Mountains was by this path until the coming of the steamboat and the railroad, which shifted travel to other routes.

It appears from the study of land titles and other records that some of the people who had sought locations in the Blue Grass region of Kentucky, and possibly of Tennessee as well, returned to the Appalachian area. They settled in the valleys, built houses, and developed comfortable communities. Because of the confusion of titles and the competition for land in the more fertile tracts, they chose to live among the mountains. What forces, natural and economic, have combined to isolate these people in the hills of Appalachia?

At least half a dozen reasons are to be found for their condition. The first is the shift of travel to the Ohio River when the steamboat was introduced and later to many places by the railroad; where once was extensive travel, newer methods of transportation left the entire area off the beaten paths. Another reason is to be found in the increase in population which forced the people into the hills from the adjacent valleys. Meanwhile, the continued abuse of the land and forests practically destroyed the timber in less than a century. The tendency to divide the patrimony into smaller and smaller parcels of land augmented the difficulty of living. Because the industries of mining coal and cutting timber were highly unstable, periods of considerable prosperity were often followed by times of poverty. In this century the process of biological and economic selection has gone on with the result that the more enterprising groups have moved to better sections, leaving a lower type of population.

The whole situation has been more and more affected by isolation, poor roads, low educational standards, inferior schools, and decreased intelligence. How marked is the influence of population in causing these results is to be found in the statement that in the period of 1900 to 1930 the increase in the number of people in the Appalachian counties was 55 per cent as against 33 per cent in the other counties of the eight states. At this point I want to say as emphatically as I can that these statements do not apply to all of the so-called Appalachian region but to some parts of it. Some of the area is as good as any land, and the people are as industrious and as prosperous as they are in the most favored parts of the United States.

To apply the word mountain to the problems found in the area is questionable and perhaps unfair for the difficulties are the same that are found elsewhere when population has outgrown economic resources. Moreover, conditions that exist in the Appalachian region are closely related to those seen wherever people are living on land of low fertility. The birth rate can explain many things. In this area 676 children under 5 years of age exist to each 1,000 women of 15 to 44 years of age. For the remaining portion of the United States the data show 391 children under 5 years of age to each 1,000 women of 15 to 44 years of age. Large families have tended to reduce per capita value, and this in turn has made difficult the maintaining of schools and public roads.

Ill health is more prevalent than in some other parts of the country. The usual diet is not productive of robust health, and the death rate from typhoid and tuberculosis is too high. The situation in the Appalachian tract in regard to crime is due to the conflict of a people unacquainted with new methods and codes. They regard these as a menace to their own social order and an effort on the part of the world to break down their customs. Not understanding the newer social organization, they try to combat it. The lack of educational facilities prevents their comprehension of other ways of life and tends to keep them from progressing. Because of their inability to sustain schools and roads, they are more and more cut off from new ideas and modern life.

In the United States Department of Agriculture bulletin on *Economic and Social Problems and Conditions of the Southern Appalachians, Miscellaneous No. 205*, some interesting data relating to schools and churches are given. In the year 1926, 171 counties had 14,423 churches. In order to see this picture a little more clearly, we reduce this area to square miles and find 187 churches to each 1,000 square miles of territory or one church to each five square miles. The Baptists prevail to the extent of 34 per cent and the Methodists to 33 4/10 per cent. According to this bulletin 98 denominations have churches in this tract. The preachers in most instances are engaged in other occupations, and only 1/6 of them live in the counties in which their churches are located. Of their training, this bulletin states that 4/5 attended neither seminary nor college.

In making these statements about the Appalachian area, one should keep in mind that many excellent farms are in this region and that in the fertile valleys living standards compare favorably with those in other places. Conditions are by no means static and are constantly changing. In fact it should be pointed out that a whole area has been done an injustice by being lumped all together.

The question arises in regard to what can be done to meet the conditions which spring out of this region. Certainly the efforts here and there to better the educational and living circumstances of small groups have been productive of good results; however, the problem in the large remains. It is essential that war be declared upon the situation. I use this phrase merely to cover a procedure. We have started campaigns which have persisted for short periods; war, however, is always continued until its objective is won. The tactics in a campaign and in a war are considerably different. The former requires a short, quick push. War attempts to coordinate economic, political, and military forces to bring the affair to an end. If we apply this principle to the problem before us, we find certain things that can be done. These I divide into material efforts and into uses of intellectual and spiritual forces.

The first material benefits that ought to be projected are roads into this isolated region. Some there are who oppose this view because they think the people should be allowed to remain in seclusion; the fact is that these people are going down hill while this isolation continues. Construction of roads would bring employment to a number of people, would open the way throughout this scenically beautiful area to tourists and to tourist business, and would also provide an outlet for local products.

Another purpose in this war would be to launch an energetic and sympathetic movement by the combined strategy and forces of the various state boards of health. Distinct efforts should be made to assist materially the work of the doctors by establishing hospitals where hospitalization can be carried on for the population. Such concerted endeavor by the eight states would result in remarkable betterment of sanitation and health.

It is quite evident to those who have studied the situation that forests will have to be enlarged by state and federal agencies for the simple reason that the stand of timber in this area is largely of low grade and of such slow growth that for a long time lumber cannot become a source of livelihood. An extended study of the region has been made. Present plans include an acreage of six million or about one-third of the area for reforestation. There is also some plan for the conservation of streams and lakes. Another material thing that can be done is to build dams in many of the present streams for stopping floods, conserving water, and establishing fishing preserves. This would, moreover, give employment in caring for the streams and in providing boats and supplies for fishermen who visit the area.

For a number of years now the coal industry has been in a low state financially and economically. With new inventions and discoveries, however, the use of steam will undoubtedly be greater, and coal will be in more demand than it has been in the immediate past. The fact remains that the coal industry needs to be reorganized. Competitive agencies are embattled, coal is overproduced, miners are often idle, and great misery is experienced in the mining districts. Efforts are being made to ameliorate these conditions, but they are slow in attaining the goal. A wider distribution of workers is necessary in order that large groups will not be concentrated in places in which are insufficient opportunities for employment. Certainly in these areas where the coal industry prevails, public works should be planned so that better schools, recreation, and other opportunities may be provided for the population. The large sum of money recently appropriated by Congress should point the way by which this can be done. So much for the material efforts that can be carried on by concentrated and purposeful planning.

In regard to the uses of intellectual and spiritual forces much can be said. The first of these is a careful consideration of an educational system that will meet the needs of the people in the mountains. In these schools the right emphasis on diet, on sanitation, and on the maintenance of health should be stressed. A program of training in the operation of the farm and of the home should be a part of the schools. Instruction should be given in first aid, in nursing, and in personal and community hygiene. As simple as is this program, many difficulties stand in its way. An entirely new group of teachers will have to be trained in the processes that point in this direction. The rural schools need new procedures and attitudes which can hardly come into being before teachers with advanced methods of education are found. The only way to obtain these teachers is through the colleges; the hope is that the colleges will see the need of a wider training for rural teachers. The influence of the person with really adequate training and broad vision would be wonderful indeed.

Along with development by an educational program should go an active search for increased opportunities. The people need guides in finding these opportunities. Having been held back by the experiences and outlook of the past, they find now not enough occupations for them to follow in the old way and insufficient knowledge of new pursuits. One of the important matters is to discover additional callings. This is a difficult task, requiring new techniques and knowledge. No doubt many things need to be done, but the average teacher knows nothing about them; the colleges, therefore, must undertake to provide better qualified teachers with a wide knowledge of rural needs and rural conditions.

Another intellectual and spiritual force needed in this war upon conditions in the Appalachian region is the maintenance of, in fact the insistence upon, church unity. The bulletin to which I referred noted 98 different denominations in the area. They have no united program, and they do not understand each other's field and each other's purpose. In the main they do not appreciate the economic problems with which their people are confronted. Emphasis must be put on unity and understanding and the educational program required. The setting aside of denominational prejudice and the making of an honest effort to understand each other would go a long way in bringing about not only church unity but the solution of other problems as well.

"Is there a mountain problem?" I asked in the beginning of this discussion. I think I can say that the mountain problem is not indigenous to the people of the Appalachian region. It is the problem that exists in many parts of the country. Wherever is concentrated a combination of poor land, low per capita wealth, isolation and its resultant ignorance, disease, and poverty, the same situation is apparent. The difficulties with which the people are faced must be understood and appreciated.

In only one way can the problem be solved, and that is by study and perseverance until the end is attained. In doing this we must have a long view which takes into consideration national trends and national problems. Much has been done by churches and organizations, but the improving of general conditions can only be brought about by an overall endeavor in which many agencies will have a part. The suggestions I have made point to some of the ways in which these changes can be accomplished. The successful outcome of such an effort rests with time, with understanding, with the cooperation of all factors, and with a public opinion awakened and determined to solve the problem.

Rural Statesmanship in the South

Address to the American Country Life Association, University of Kentucky, November 31, 1938

T H E American Country Life Association was organized because of a wide interest in rural problems and a purpose to render constructive, helpful aid to the solution of them. It was therefore with a great deal of pleasure to us that the invitation of the University of Kentucky was accepted to hold the national meeting here in 1938. For nearly twenty years the members of this Association have gathered in convention in various parts of the United States to discuss with interest and understanding the problems of rural

America. That the Association should meet in Lexington, the seat of the University of Kentucky, is indeed appropriate for interest in country living has been one of the first objectives of this institution.

I have been thinking about "Rural Statesmanship in the South" for some time, and I have read a number of books and reports dealing with the subject. These range from Jonathan Daniels' *A Southerner Discovers the South* to government reports and a large volume brought together under the leadership of Howard Odum and entitled *Southern Regions of the United States*. I have read periodicals, magazines, and papers, hoping to get a satisfactory background for discussion. I recall also that, since I have been in every state in the Southeast not once but many times, I know something of the picture. Perhaps the thing that impresses me most about these books in the face of travel and observation is the fact that they make sad reading, doleful reading, and leave one with a feeling of helplessness in regard to the situation in the southeastern states.

The conclusions of the different authors and reports are very much at variance, but without exception certain fundamental difficulties are pointed out by all of them. Among these is the regional and personal poverty of the South. Another is the dire effect of the "King Cotton" regime; another is the devastating influence on the South of the industrial credit procedure; another, the presence of fascism in some of the states and the use of a depressed people by political leaders; another, the play upon prejudice clearly related to a background of the historical past.

Perhaps I should answer briefly at this point the question, "What is the South?" Answers have been made many times, and volumes of statistics have been presented regarding the South; however, in order to have a starting point in this discussion, perhaps a few facts should be given.

In reality no line can be drawn to delimit the South. The boundaries are dependent always upon the people who are discussing them. For my purpose the South consists of twelve states, four of them located on the west and east banks of the lower Mississippi and all lying south and southwest of the Ohio and Potomac rivers. The State of Texas was a member of the Southern Confederacy, but the problems of that state are wholly different from those of the Southeast. The oil and citrus industries and the widespread use of machinery in the production of cotton have brought prosperity to the state. Texas does not enter into the consideration of the problems of the South.

In these twelve states 22 per cent of the nation's population have their habitation. The area contained in the southeastern section aggregates one-sixth of the nation's land. For two hundred years the area has been engaged in agriculture based largely upon a one crop system. It was a type of agriculture that exposed the soil to excessive erosion. When the Civil War was over, no money was to be had for the establishing of industrial enterprises, nor was any considerable capital available for the conduct of agriculture. It was therefore natural enough that the share-cropper system should be used to bring land and labor together. The white landowners had land but no labor and no money. The Negroes and the poor whites had no land and no money, but they had labor. Sharecropping was the inevitable result. This system which was created to meet an emergency has continued for seventy-five years. It places a heavy burden upon agriculture and takes away from the farmer and the share-cropper an undue proportion of what they produce.

The use of southern lands for the production of one or two crops kept the area under the agricultural regime, forced the farmers to export their crops, and compelled them to import the goods they used. Thus the South came to be bound down to an order not unlike the type of colonial policy pursued by imperial nations. The scheme resulted in high prices for imported articles and low prices for exports. The credit system moreover brought constant pressure to maintain the one-crop type of agriculture. In a region of heavy rain this kind of agriculture resulted in vast erosion that has given the South, in return for its labor and fertilizers, great acreages of marginal and submarginal lands.

In order to show something of the condition of these twelve

states in relation to the rest of the nation, resort must be made to statistics on a basis of per capita wealth. The use of per capita wealth as a means of comparison is a theoretic one, but it does help to create a picture of the problem. Without attempting to go into this phase of the matter to any considerable extent, I shall give a few facts gathered from some of the reports. A larger percentage of population engages in farming in the South than in any other section of the country. Unquestionably the increase in wealth elsewhere is dependent upon industrial development and urban civilization. No great cities of the second class and comparatively few of 100,000 or more population are in the South. Whether this is a result of the failure of agriculture to be carried on profitably or a result of the diversion of industry to other parts of the country has been debated again and again. Whatever the conclusion may be, the South is poor.

The per capita wealth of the twelve southern states according to the figures of 1929 is shown to be 39 per cent below the national average, which would indicate that the rest of the country is twice as well off as the Southeast. The farm population of the Southeast is about 2/5 of the total farm population of the nation, and those 2/5 have only 14 per cent of the fixed capital used in agriculture and 20 per cent of the nation's farm buildings. It is pointed out that Iowa with about the same farm population is twice as wealthy as Virginia. North Carolina and Indiana are about the same size and have about the same population, but Indiana is twice as wealthy as North Carolina. It may be observed that the ratio of the wealth of the people of the South is less in proportion than the ratio of wealth in the North. The farmers of Virginia receive 22 per cent of the state income, but they have only 12 per cent of the wealth of the state. The farmers of Illinois receive 8 per cent of the state income and yet have 15 per cent of the wealth of that state. The proportion of income to total wealth was 3 to 10 in Illinois; and in Tennessee, Virginia, and Kentucky it was 5 to 5. Such figures cause concern in their translation of the meaning of the situation.

Many would turn to legal action to change these conditions and so call upon statesmen to act. No region has had more men interested in the political scene, but little has followed their activities. It is said that a statesman is a politician in a Prince Albert coat. In the minds of the people there is a good deal of truth in this popular definition. A census of so-called statesmen would show that Prince Albert coats have adorned only a few but have been a disguise to many who had no claim to such a designation.

Rural statesmanship in the South is a widely used topic that covers two centuries of political, economic, and religious discussion. In broad terms it might be said that there have been four periods in which statesmanship has attempted at one time or another to deal with the problems of the South. First is the period of the country gentleman, a period that lasted until the War Between the States; then came the regime of the "carpetbaggers"; these were followed by the politicos dwelling on the wrongs of the people; now you can see occasional statesmen who may be called social economists and social workers and who are attempting to get at the facts and the problems of the area.

The statesmen of the first group were prominent in the history of the United States; several of them were Presidents of their country, and all of them looked at the problems as country gentlemen largely interested in better farming, better living, better markets, and more production. They were not confronted with many of the difficulties of the present. Lands were not worn out, though in their writings reference is made to the erosion of the soil. They rather looked upon the situation as more or less permanent since the political problems did not reach the point of a social sore. We have but to name George Washington, Thomas Jefferson, James Madison, James Monroe, Patrick Henry, and later, Andrew Jackson to understand the attitude of these men toward the problems of the time. Andrew Jackson was the only one in the group who coped with what might be called a social revolution. His emphases were not upon erosion and low levels of income and of living but rather upon the domination of a great financial institution over the property and lives of the people.

The second quarter of the nineteenth century was given over to a controversy in which "king cotton" and the slavery system were dominant factors. This system with its implication of states' rights and with its determination to maintain itself brought on the Civil War and fastened upon the South a continuance of cotton planting. A result was the breakdown of the plantation arrangement, which in turn caused the share-cropper method of agricultural production.

The invasion of the South by a group of men termed "carpet-baggers" drove the people of the area into many a defense mechanism, a kind of digging-in process, that held them to the devices which they invented to keep themselves going on a meager scale. Through this period the South groped almost in darkness for some way out. Finally a better price for cotton brought with it a kind of revival hampered, however, by poor transportation and indifferent markets. The depression of the seventies and of the nineties, holding the South in the grip of old procedures, made difficult the creation of a capital structure that could enter into manufacture in the area. So the South, still bound to an old type of agriculture with considerable indifference toward industrial development, drifted along; population increased; and lands were giving up more and more of the top surface to rivers and the sea.

Then the South began to be conscious of its difficulties and actually to listen to the siren calls of a new group of statesmen who emphasized the wrongs of the people and suggested a means of remedying them by political action. Amazing men have been among those who have held the reins of government and have directed the political activity of the South. It is unnecessary for me to mention their names because you all know them and their methods of winning political victories through massed factions and machine organization. These were built upon a foundation of prejudice, and their appeal was made to the people on that basis. In several of the states of the South this prejudice created an opportunity to set up a form of fascism that enforced the wishes of the leaders through compulsion, through punishment, through reprisal, and through other dictatorial methods.

The South is a great seed-bed of singlemindedness, of prejudice, of sense of wrong, of futile living that gives to any group of men who cultivate it a tremendously dangerous power. It is no longer necessary to use the age-old slogan of white domination; now it is possible to appeal to the absence of opportunity, to the long and binding poverty, to the feeling that something must be done through force to bring justice. This great mass of people, who are often subservient to the wiles and machinations of political groups, revolt against the effort to keep the lower classes in servitude. Even the cry to "keep the Negro in his place" has been modified in the interest of a common wrong. It is this sort of thing that the so-called statesmen of the twentieth century have utilized for the purpose of gaining political power.

Happily one can see a change in attitude in the people of this great area. In the universities and colleges, in the churches, in the editorial offices, men have begun to speak about the problems of the South more freely and more intelligently than they have in years gone by. The information that has been gathered by Howard Odum and Rupert Vance, and that is in the studies of other men and women, has placed in the possession of the people knowledge of the problems and the desire for some adequate solution in the very near future.

It is said that the South is the last frontier of the industrial revolution. In the South old types of agriculture still prevail. Industrial development, except in the case of the tobacco factories and some textiles mills, lingers or has not grown at all. There is a conflict in the mind of the South in regard to whether it is worth while to go industrial if the burdens of mass production are to come along with industrialism. The price which must be paid may be too heavy. Is it worth the change and trouble to be industrialized?

Still the southerner is not averse to being rich. Until now, however, he has not been willing to sacrifice a way of living to possess the wealth that supposedly comes from industry. Tradition, prejudice, and strong individualism work against any program that may interfere with his way of living. He has an emotional feeling for the Negro and possibly fears the poor white, but in both cases he is not willing to give them a place. The share-cropper system holds the white to continued poverty. A mobile and free population constitutes an important factor in any industrial development. The possibilities are there, but the mind to direct them in the right channels remains in doubt as to the course to pursue.

No agency can solve the problems of the South other than the South itself for the reason that attitude of heart and mind is fundamental to the success of any great undertaking. Consequently, the doubt expressed by the new schools of thought in the South makes an outside attack upon the problems well nigh impossible. Here and there something can be done with federal money under southern leadership. In the long run the South must make up its mind as to where it wants to go and, having done so, must work out the solution if it wishes to control its own future. I do not propose to leave the ox in the ditch, but, rather than call by telegraph and cable for those from far away to come to assist, I do say that the neighbors must do the job of extricating the ox from its difficulties.

The soil is the basis of agriculture and industry. It is the greatest possession a people can have. The first problem then that confronts this region is the stopping of erosion and the preservation of the soil. That some progress is being made is shown by the changes in methods of agronomy. One evidence is the use of contour cultivation in place of the square type so long in practice. Indifference however to the welfare of the future generations who will cultivate the soil continues in too many instances. A speeding up of the procedures now known may stir indifference and result in building up the land. I have hope.

With this matter of soil preservation is the closely associated share-cropper system, which involves land uses, type of crops, credit, merchandising, and banking. The use of cash in the place of barter would help solve many of the injustices now existing in the system and would give money for purchases. The whole agricultural situation would be improved by such a change. But the accustomed methods of long standing put obstacles in the way when business men give their minds to the task of reformation. A greater variety of crops with more gardening and self-sustaining agriculture would go far to relieve the farmer from the burdens of the present order and would give him a better standard of living.

What can be done to bring a greater share of health to a considerable body of the population in the South? The organization of the public health agencies on modern lines with well-trained staffs could do much to eliminate malaria, hook worm, and pellagra from the area. A report given this week at Chapel Hill, North Carolina, on the occasion of the meeting of the National Academy of Sciences was heartening. Nicotinic acid, the audience was told, can cure pellagra. What a boon that will be! The South needs a sturdy, industrious people. The burdens of low standards of living can be lifted if the people are in vigorous health. Only a few of the states in this area have modern departments of health. For many years the work that was being done in these southern states was wholly inadequate, with the staffs largely political in their attitudes. Marked improvement can be seen in five of the states. The training of public health officers in some of the universities of the South holds out a promise of new leadership in this field of medicine. Again I have hope.

In most discussions of the South, education is given the first place in the list of problems. Here I have dropped it to third because we need in the South to use what is already known. With leadership and money we can use our educational facilities. The continuance of the program and its understanding, however, rest upon an intelligent people who can read and write and so make their own judgments. Education does not have a chance in the South to do what it might do. The states struggle manfully and tax themselves extensively beyond any tax in the North to support schools, but it is not enough. The way out may be through federal aid for school enterprises. Even then the thought of the South regarding the share-croppers' children and those of the Negroes must be enlightened and progressive. It must look to giving these people opportunity. As a part of education wholesome recreation should have a place because of its importance as an adjustment agency. Recreation is vastly needed in the South in order that the dull monotony of the lives of those who work in mill towns and who till the soil on tenant farms may be broken by healthful pleasures. A program of recreation need not be costly, but whatever the cost the returns would be great in wholesome play and in pleasant amusement.

The church has a part to perform in the matter of recreation because in it is a group that will respond to leadership. Too often play and recreational enterprises are regarded as evils and therefore to be frowned upon by church members who forget that the devil finds mischief for idle hands to do. The church can and does furnish means for emotional outlets and provides a way to give stability of mind. However, because the world in some instances is looked upon as a vale of tears where future rewards are the only recompense for living, some southern church leadership will have nothing to do with any outside activities. Real religious statesmanship should recognize the need and the dilemma and meet the call not only for worship but also for happier, healthier living.

The people of the South have not answered the question of either factory or land. In some places it is being answered, but no considered program of industry is in operation. Until a definite attitude is taken, certainly no real progress can be made. There are many things to be done. A more aggressive banking and credit policy should take the place of the one that rests so largely upon the cotton regime and should look to the development of industry for its future profits. Bankers satisfied with the present organization of agriculture and industry will continue to think in terms of cotton and of the barter system of distribution. One banker cannot meet this new need. The railroad rates prevailing in the South are based upon the thesis of an agricultural people living in a land of long distances and meager local traffic. The rates are higher than in the northern area, and they are discriminatory against manufactured products that would find markets outside of the area. The South sells at wholesale and buys at retail.

A writer in *The Saturday Evening Post*, October 8, of this year declares that "the South acting under the sting of economic disparity obliges itself to think northern: deeper than its thinking that way is its feeling southern." The federal government cannot do a great deal for the South until the South develops a conscience about its problems. This is not an easy thing to do in the face of heritage, of the conditioning element of climate, and of the Negro. Class distinctions persist, and the will to keep the lower classes in servitude is still too often present in the southern gentry. However, conflicts which press hard upon the traditional culture arise between the old plantation system and the new situation. In view of all these conditions, one is forced to say that the science must be southern and the social reform must be southern if real things are to be accomplished. The invasion of the twentieth century carpetbaggers, even though well disposed, cannot gain the confidence of the people of this area.

Because of the problems and the story of the South, which still affect thinking and attitudes, rural statesmanship in the South must be southern. Such statesmanship is making its appearance. The approach seems to me to be sensible, wise, and inclusive. Can the South become aware of what it must do in order that the labor of these awakened men and women may avail much? The matter is beyond the question stage. There is a definite movement to create leaders and to furnish the facts and processes. The land-grant colleges and universities have labored diligently to learn the procedure. The older leaders are gone or worn out, and new leaders must come forward to replace them. This is a long process.

The problems are known; something of the technique is understood; but the man power and the brain power must be found, and that right speedily. Prayers are needed, earnest prayers. Action is needed, right action. Thought is needed, wise thought. Leaders are required who are imbued with the missionary spirit. All of these are the essence of statesmanship. There are signs of a better day. May it not be long delayed.

The Interest of Agriculture
in Wealth Production

Summary of address to the Farm and Home Conference,
University of Kentucky, January 24, 1939

IN THE course of three hundred years the western world has moved from a scarcity to an abundance economy. Before that time food was hard to come by, and commodities produced by hand had a value of rareness. Now through the development of wealth there is plenty of food in the world, and many commodities supply the needs of people. In the struggle during the middle ages between the kings and the lords of the manors, the crafts came into power and influence in the cities; with their growing skill and enlarged production, wealth increased. With the progress of trade, capitalism made its appearance and, with various devices for its organization and development, it has created great plenty.

During these recent two hundred years of the growth of capitalism, the attitude of government has been that of letting alone and of allowing a man to do what he wished on the supposition that his interest and the general interest would coincide. While this theory allowed great latitude, it was hampered in many instances because monopoly tendencies prevented the actual working out of these mutual interests. The emphasis which in the early day had been placed upon consumer need was now put upon production. It has taken a considerable length of time to see the effect of this emphasis, but today we find the result in technological unemployment, in increased numbers without jobs.

Proceeding to omit a great deal of history and interesting development, we come to our own time when we find ourselves faced by a great national problem. That problem may be stated simply in the form of a question, "How can this country sustain a reasonable standard of living for its people?" Here are great resources, tremendous organizations of capital, aggregations of machines, and remarkable technical knowledge. Because all of these are present, every individual in our land should have a decent basis of living.

We find ourselves surrounded by uncontrollable forces and running against a stone wall which we appear to be able neither to climb over nor to go around. If we produce more, prices go down, and employment declines; continued production results in commodity surpluses, and we are brought to the problem of how to remove this abundance. All that we have been able to do recently has been to wait until the surpluses have been reduced by gradual absorption. Employment then begins again, wages rise, prices go up; in turn demand falls off, and we return to reduced employment. The problem is how to break this circle.

The laissez faire or let alone theory which prevailed in the first century of the factory system was only a theory. It maintained equal liberty in production and consumption; however, it never became a fact because monopoly triumphed over free competition. With a change in emphasis, man was sunk in work, the life of man was given over to labor, and consumption was subordinated to production. When this happened, men became subject in turn to machines, and the purpose of machines was to produce more goods. Thus the world moved toward national monopolies; and some of the national states attempted to hold this movement through autarchy, through commercial warfare, by tariffs, by subsidies, and by other devices. Nations began to arm, and the competition has gone to such a point that the inevitable end is military conflict.

The excuse given for the development of all this is that national necessity has been created by economic necessity. Because more land is needed to feed populations, war has resulted in order to take the land of neighbors. Because more people within the territory must be provided in order to have an abundance of soldiers, more land is needed. The natural way to meet this situation and national necessity is through the predatory process; it is primitive, usual, and almost habitual because it goes back to animal instincts. This procedure is not in reality based on national necessity or well being, and it produces consequences which affect every country in the world. True national necessity and well being require thought and leadership and long-view planning.

Reference was made to consumption as being in fact the larger requirement of man. It is quite certain that unless consumption uses what is produced and sold, then under existing circumstances production stops. The purchasing power of the consumer is in the form of wages; however, as nations produce more, wages are reduced although demand is governed by purchasing power. When the price which is limited by demand outdistances wages, as it often does, employers cannot sell, and workers are discharged. Prices fall, wages go downward in the hope that buying will follow declining prices, but the purchasing power is not there. A delusion that high prices and prosperity are associated seems prevalent.

This in part is something of the problem which has come upon us here in the United States. We turned to a procedure by which production would be limited by the granting of quotas. We also set about redistributing the national income by the process of taxation and by giving through various national agencies employment to those who had none. I think no one claims that we have solved the problems that confront the United States; we can say, however, that certain experiments have been followed by sufficiently convincing results to lead to the hope that these may point the way to answers to some of the questions that have been raised.

Our national attitude is against communism; we do not want it. We are against any enlarged socialism. We wish to retain the individualism of the person so that he may have freedom to do, to work, and to enjoy. Various alternates to socialism and communism have been suggested. One of them is the gradual growth of consumer cooperation. Others suggest modifications of the capital system such as regulation of profits, control of financial organization, reduction of the cost of marketing, and the establishment of markets that will be fair to producer and consumer; these changes are considered essential in meeting some of our problems.

Suggestions are made, moreover, that we should have better and more reasonable transportation; that the government must provide information on drifts and trends in prices; that the system of taxation both federal and state should be modernized and equalized; that small owners and small producers should be provided credit to meet their obligations; that adequate housing should be provided for the population;, and finally that education for culture and for the acquirement of the skills and crafts of industry should be much more widespread than it is at the present time. All of these suggestions have value. The answer to the problem of how to provide an adequate standard of living in a land of plenty is by no means easy to find. The farmer has a profound interest in the solution because of his importance in production and in consumption.

Past and Present Sticking Points in Taxation

Address to the
Mississippi Valley Historical Association, Iowa City, Iowa, 1910

IN THIS Athens of a notable commonwealth we stand in almost the geographical center of the northern Mississippi Valley. Here in a basin filled with productive fields and remarkable natural resources has been gathered from the four corners of the world a high type of democracy composed of citizens firm in their adherence to the principles of representative government and well trained in habits of industry. Everywhere are to be seen the evidences of enlightenment. On the hilltops arise the centers of education; in the towns and villages are located schools, libraries, and newspapers. Over this democracy hovers a spirit of social advancement. Every face is turned toward the future. The belief in cooperation and in wider governmental interest gives forth evidence of further progress.

Such a movement forward demands government of a high order, clear-sighted intelligence, and hopeful courage, thoroughgoing and militant. Back of it all is the hard problem of means to accomplish the ends desired. Out of it, as in the case of the sinews of war, appear the question and the principles of taxation.

As citizens in this democracy, the thing which checks our progress and keeps us, a great people, from moving forward to new accomplishments in the field of social endeavor is a matter of vast importance. Hence, in discussing with you for a brief period the past and present sticking points in taxation, I have the feeling that I am bringing to your attention something worthy of your consideration and a matter that is vital to us all.

A glance at the industrial organization of the different commonwealths in the Mississippi Valley accompanied by some examination of their constitutions and statute books reveals the fact that there is a close similarity and in some instances an actual identity of language and principle in the taxing systems in vogue. We are all hung, as it were, upon the same peg. We are all sticking at the same point. When it is kept in mind what the sources of the institutions, governmental and social, have been in this Valley, it is little to be wondered that such adherence has been given to the same system and the same methods of raising revenue.

The effect upon the social organization is marked by the instance of tax laws; where departures have been made from the old system from which we as Mississippi Valley states have derived our laws, there have been advances toward a more modern type of social enterprise. What fitted us in the early days no longer suffices for the solution of the larger and more complicated problems of the present. Education demands larger facilities; charitable institutions have ceased to be penal and are now social; mud roads, always inadequate, will no longer be tolerated. As a democracy we are face to face with the question of how to meet the new social demands of the day. What holds us back? The answer is lack of revenue and an inadequate system of taxation. My duty is done if I trace the source of our present difficulties and point out how we may progress toward better things.

Three streams of immigration passed into the new territory opened to settlement after the Revolutionary War. One came through the Mohawk Valley into New York and later moved into Ohio; a second, proceeding by way of the mountains, entered finally into the valley of the Ohio through the opening at the headwaters of the Allegheny and Monongahela rivers; and the third group made their way westward over the great pass which separates the Allegheny Mountains from the Blue Ridge. The first group was composed largely of people from New England; the second, from New Jersey, Delaware, New York, and eastern Pennsylvania; and the third came from Virginia, North Carolina, and South Carolina.

The group that entered by the northern passage found their way into Ohio; the same was true of the second group; and the third traveled into Kentucky and Tennessee. Ohio was the region through which the population in its westward movement passed. East, north, south, west, whatever the direction, the stream moved into this great valley; much of it stopped for a time, absorbing thereby the customs, laws, and ideas of a common people. Thus Ohio became a great territory of amalgamation where the ideas brought from the more eastern settlements were mixed and molded into constitutions and statutes.

The constitution of Ohio reflects this view. On the subject of taxation it provides that all property, personal and real, shall be taxed equally and uniformly. The Kelly Act of 1846 set forth in more definite terms than the earlier laws the nature of the general property tax. Under its provisions, while some exceptions were made, the test of ability to pay taxes was the amount of property owned by the individual taxed. But, more than that, the law provided that under the sanction of oaths the taxpayer should tell about his property and that all men should make returns according to the exact truth. The legislators believed that it would be possible to compel the rich people of the different communities to pay taxes on intangible wealth through this plan of self-assessment.

What proved to be true, however, was that the law permitted avoidance of taxation rather than enforcement; and as society grew more complicated, the law became less and less efficient. This general property tax, nevertheless, fitted to a degree the pioneer conditions of the day. The property which men held consisted of lands, buildings, tools, and stock. All were to be seen and all were open to inspection so that a rough sort of justice could be maintained under the provisions of the law. This system, however, instead of being modified to meet conditions and instead of legislation being enacted for the establishment of appropriate tax methods elsewhere, has been copied in the states that have been formed to the westward. In Indiana, in Illinois, in Iowa, in Minnesota, in Wisconsin, and in the Dakotas, the same provisions are to be found in almost the same language as were formulated in the earlier laws of Ohio. The Ohio constitution states that "laws shall be passed, taxing (1) by a uniform rule all moneys, credits, (2) investments in bonds, stocks, (3) joint stock companies, or otherwise; and also all (4) real and personal property, (5) according to its true value in money." (ART. XII, Sec. 2.)

The constitutional provisions of the other states mentioned are in intent the same as those of Ohio.

Minnesota (ART. IX, Sec. 1): "Taxes to be raised in this state shall be as nearly equal as may be, and all property on which taxes are to be levied shall have a cash valuation to be equalized and uniform throughout the state; and laws shall be passed taxing property according to its true value in money."

Illinois (ART. VIII, Sec. 20): "The mode of levying a tax shall be by valuation, so that every person shall pay a tax in proportion to the value of the property he or she has in his or her possession."

Indiana (ART. X, Sec. 1): "The General Assembly shall provide, by law, for a uniform and equal rate of assessment and taxation; and shall prescribe such regulations as shall secure a just valuation for taxation of all property, both real and personal, excepting such only for municipal, educational, literary, scientific, religious, or charitable purposes, as may be especially exempted by law."

Wisconsin (ART. VIII, Sec. 1): "The rule of taxation shall be uniform, and taxes shall be levied upon such property as the legislature shall prescribe."

South Dakota (ART. XI, Sec. 2): "All taxes to be raised in this state shall be uniform on all real and personal property, according to its value in money, to be ascertained by such rules of appraisement and assessment as may be prescribed by general law, so that every person and corporation shall pay a tax in proportion to the value of his, her or its property."

North Dakota (Art. xi, Sec. 176): "Laws shall be passed taxing by uniform rule all property, according to its true value in money."

This similarity is not to be wondered at when it is remembered that, as new frontiers were established, the customs, the institutions, and the methods of the older communities were transferred to the newer territory and established there. An examination of the first legislatures of several of the states reveals the fact that the men who composed them were born and reared in New England or in the central states; as they moved westward and took part in the creation of new states, they turned naturally for guidance to the pages of the constitutions and statute books of the commonwealths from which they came. In consequence there has been built up in the states of the northern Mississippi Valley a code of law which reflects the point of view together with the errors of the early legislators of Ohio. In so far as this statement applies to the general property tax, the legislatures had an honorable example in the transmittal of the idea from England to the soil of Massachusetts Bay Colony; this concept they in turn revived and mixed in the Ohio crucible to be molded later into constitutions and laws.

Occasionally attempts have been made to depart from the long established general property tax and to create a system that would be more conformable to fundamental economic principles and the changing conditions of industrial life. In 1871 David A. Wells, fresh from his experience as Commissioner of Revenue for the Department of the Interior of the federal government, was called to the leadership of the tax commission of New York. This body had been created by the legislature for the purpose of securing an investigation of the tax situation in that state. After careful study the commission made a report containing a number of recommendations. The discussion of the methods of taxation was conducted with keenness and analytic power; however, upon presentation of the report to the legislature, no action was taken. The commission, being a temporary body, passed out of existence with only its admirable volume as its record.

Ten years later the state of Maryland, confronted by many of the same questions that puzzled the members of the New York legislature, created a temporary commission which was to investigate and report to the legislature. The commission under the direction and leadership of Richard T. Ely presented an excellent report, thoroughgoing and worthy of consideration. The suggestions in it were pointed; but, here too strange to say, the legislature of Maryland refused to adopt any of the suggestions made by the commission.

In Massachusetts in the year 1872, a temporary tax commission made a report, and again in 1894 and in 1908. The last commission analyzed the personal property tax, showed the way in which the decline in assessments came about, and made some practical suggestions to the legislature. Still, because of constitutional difficulties, no essential parts of the report could be adopted.

A step forward is to be noted at this point. Just as the temporary commission was an advance, so the permanent commission was a step in the direction of a better system of taxation. Beginning with the year 1894, a departure is to be noted from the temporary commissions of the earlier days to the establishment of permanent state tax commissions. These continuing bodies had power and authority over the making of assessments and were given instructions to investigate and to report to the legislatures.

In 1905 Wisconsin reorganized her tax commission, which had been established in 1899. The new commission began at once the important work of reassessing the railway properties in the state and attempted to obtain information concerning the true value of the real estate in the commonwealth. A system of supervising taxation by commission has now been in existence in Wisconsin nearly 12 years. In that time considerable progress has been made in assessment under the provisions of the general property tax. The assessment reached 70 or 80 per cent of the total value of the real estate. Since the establishment of the first Wisconsin commission in 1899, a number of other states, notably New York, Indiana, and Minnesota, have created permanent tax commissions. These bodies, after a history of from one to four years, have dropped back into assessing and valuation boards without attempting to do very much in the way of reform.

Some reference to the experience of the tax commission of Minnesota will bring out more clearly the statement just made. This commission was created in the year 1907 and took office in May of that year. It had an annual appropriation of $30,000, and its first attempt was to procure information regarding the actual value of real estate in the commonwealth. Its second purpose was to obtain some idea of the values existent in the iron properties in the northern part of the state.

The first problem was met by what is called the sales system of valuing land. The method followed was to take the sales of land in a given community and compare them with the assessment made against this land. In this way the relationship between the two was established. After determining the ratio of assessment to the value of the land, the commission was able through the total assessment to ascertain the value of the real estate in a community. This was done both in Wisconsin and in Minnesota. In Minnesota the results of the work revealed the fact that the assessment of real property in and about the state including the cities averaged about 42 per cent of the actual value as disclosed by sales. But it was further discovered that, outside of the northern counties, property in the country was assessed at a lower figure than that in the cities. In St. Paul the assessment on the average was about 57 per cent, in Minneapolis 50 to 51 per cent, in Duluth about 44 per cent, and in the city of Winona about 50 per cent. Here was a situation that was well worth noting; wide variations were found between the cities themselves and also between the cities and the country.

The second problem mentioned above was the assessment of the iron properties in the northern part of the state. The different types of mines were classified on the basis of the value of their ore, the difficulty of getting at it, and the cost of mining. Out of this situation were designated five distinct classes of mines and three separate kinds of prospects. The various mines were given values in accordance with the classes to which they belonged. On account of the thoroughness with which the ground had been explored by the

companies, it was possible to ascertain rather accurately and somewhat scientifically the amount and value of the iron ore. The result
of this proceeding was that the commission placed an assessment
of $194,000,000 on the iron properties in the state. The next
year, because of the amount of ore that had been mined, this value
was somewhat reduced. And last year, on account of new tonnage
discovered through new explorations, the assessment was increased
to $205,000,000.

The two things, therefore, which the Minnesota Tax Commission has accomplished in the three years of its history are first,
the valuation of real estate and the determination of the percentage
of the assessment to land values, and second, the valuation of the
iron ore properties in the northern part of the state. In 1909 a
constitutional amendment was declared adopted under the provisions of which the legislature was enabled to create any kind or
type of tax law; the constitution now maintains that property may
be classed and the tax fixed in accordance with the class. Under the
old system all classes of property had to be taxed in the same way;
under the new provisions of the law it is possible to tax any class
in any given way so long as the tax applies to the entire class.

The result of this amendment was that the legislature was
flooded with a mass of bills on all phases of taxation. As a consequence of the situation thereby produced, no legislation of any
importance was effected that dealt with the tax problem. The
tax commission had recommended a number of things in its report
to the legislature. Among these were the establishment of the county assessor system and the taxation of public utilities. But none of
the legislation asked for was passed, and the session closed with
no seeming advance over the previous two years. The legislature
upon its adjournment left with the commission the request to investigate the income tax and to report the findings to the next session. It also authorized the commission to act as a board of appeal
in case local assessors wished to protest the assessments made by
county commissioners.

The history of the Minnesota Tax Commission, therefore, seems
to follow the trend in other states except that during the time of

its existence it has actually accomplished more than most commissions. In its dealings with the legislature, however, it has failed to obtain any more than the other state taxing bodies. Here is the second sticking point in taxation. Some progress may, however, be noted in the movement away from the earlier forms of laws generally adopted.

You will remember that the temporary commission of 1871 in New York, of 1881 in Maryland, and of 1872, 1894, and 1907 in Massachusetts failed to secure any results. When the permanent commissions were established, practically no advance legislation was gained in conformity with their efforts to better the situation. The permanent tax commission is unquestionably an improvement over the older system in that it centralizes assessments. But we are again stalled at just the same point at which we were before. The legislatures refuse to change the system of taxation.

Of the two dangers which confront the permanent tax commission, one is that in the transition from the temporary to the permanent body the initiative which created the latter will grow less and less in the matter of reform legislation; the other is that the commission will gradually become little more than an assessing board with somewhat larger powers, with somewhat more initiative possibly, and with perhaps a more scientific way of making assessments.

It is the common opinion that our tax system should be reformed, but for some reason we are not going forward as rapidly as we should. Out of the economic conditions which have existed in the Mississippi Valley, a marked individualism is manifested in the attitude of men toward industry, toward government, and toward the modification of legislation; also a firm belief in states' rights has been created. The states in their relation to the federal government have had the emphasis placed upon the local problem with the result that our whole system of taxation has grown from a local to a state system, the state system having been modified to meet the previously existent local forms of taxation. These two things—individualism and states' rights—stand in the way of a modern system of taxation. Income and property can no longer be localized. The attempt to tax every man on all of his property must give way to the idea that property must be taxed in accordance with its earning capacity. This may mean direct or it may mean indirect taxation. Therefore, the entire philosophy of taxation as it has been developed in our history, particularly here in the Middle West, must be changed.

We used to adhere to the doctrine, and it is still held by many, that the state is the best governed that is the least governed; however, the passage of many laws that have produced great social betterment has in a measure placed this political theory in the background, and we are beginning to recognize that the social aspect of government is more important, more essential, than the individualistic phase. In view of this consideration it may be said with a good deal of emphasis that our failure to advance toward larger reform in matters of taxation may be due to some fundamental conceptions that have arisen out of our earlier history.

The fiscal problems that are confronting us today have their origin within recent years, and our concern in meeting these has gradually brought us to a realization of the fact that some change in the attitude of legislatures and in administrative methods must be secured in carrying on the work of taxation. As in many other social problems, we have begun at the wrong end and have attempted to reform from the top downward rather than following the reverse method. The first step toward betterment must be in the field of administration; and this means that, with greater care in the selection of officers and with some modifications of the law, the present system of taxation can be administered with more efficiency than in the past. This, coupled with the work of the permanent tax commissions, will slowly produce results to meet the increasing demand for greater income for social purposes; and in time these changes will require modification in the legislation itself.

Before this can be done, however, it is necessary that a larger appreciation shall exist in the matter of the relation of the system of taxation to social welfare. Constant vigilance and insistent education will in time bring us to the solution of our tax problems; but, before we can get anywhere even on that line, we must by all means come to some agreement as to what taxation really is. If the single-taxers agree upon one form and other tax authorities upon another, each group having its own strong body of adherents, we shall obtain adequate and satisfactory legislation only after a long period of time when some common ground has been reached from which demands for tax reforms may be made.

If we could come to definite conclusions relative to taxation—for instance, that there ought to be separation between state and local taxation; that the state, except on extraordinary occasions, ought to levy a tax not upon real estate but upon securities and other corporate business enterprises within its boundary; and that the local bodies should have the choice of collecting their taxes from real estate—we should be in a position to give up some of the present forms of taxation. For these less satisfactory methods of taxation could then be substituted not necessarily a uniform income tax but some form of taxing securities, bonds, stocks, and the like that would to all intents and purposes be a modified income tax.

Such a program carefully worked out and elaborated would in time carry us beyond the sticking points that have held us fast during the last fifty years. A new crucible must be found in which these ideas on taxation can again be molded into a system. The materials for the crucible must be created through the medium of education and then carried from the state where the experiment is being tried to the newer and younger states farther west thereby repeating the history of the last century.

In some measure two states appear to have lighted the fires under the crucible, in fact to be engaged in placing materials in it. Wisconsin with her contribution of the tax commission, railroad assessment, and better administration and Minnesota in her gross earnings tax, taxation of iron ore properties, and centralized assessment of property throughout the state are furnishing important ingredients to this melting pot of fair and helpful taxation. When these ideas have been formulated into definite and clear-cut laws and other features have been added, the various states will again be ready to copy the systems that have been tried successfully.

A Rational System of Taxing Natural Resources

Address to the second annual
Conference of the National Conservation Congress,
St. Paul, Minnesota, September, 1910

IN ORDER to clear away any misapprehension regarding the adequacy of the general property tax as a fiscal policy, it may be said at once that the difficulties involved in the taxing of natural resources exist to an even greater degree than in the case of other property. As a matter of fact a rational system of taxation has not been attained in any field, nor are the efforts now being made likely to produce the hoped for results. Revamping the old system by adding to or taking from it seems to be the method of tax lawmakers.

Economic conditions in America have changed materially in a quarter of a century, and these changes have forced upon the whole country a reorganization of procedure not only of manufacture and of transportation but also of administration, government, and social organization. Such conditions of affairs are seen today in nearly every state, and attempts are being made to meet them. In the specific instance of the fiscal problem the old system of taxation is being added to by special levies on corporations, inheritances, royalties, and incomes. In reality so far as natural resources are concerned, we have no principle existent in the general scheme of taxation that can be used to meet the situation that has arisen in our efforts toward conservation. Just as the problems of industrial organization have come upon the states, so now we are faced with the problems of our natural resources.

Sometimes in discussing this question of natural resources, a great deal of emphasis is placed on the statement that their taxation is the far-reaching cause of the depletion of timber and mineral lands. I think it may be said at the outset that the taxation of natural resources can be at most only one of many factors in their depletion. The extent to which this contributes is impossible to be known; but the fact remains that taxation may or may not hasten the destruction of forest lands, the exploitation of minerals, and the ruthless utilization of the soil.

Where lands bearing timber are owned, interest charges with each year of ownership are piled up, and the same is true of the taxes. Where, on the other hand, lands are held through a royalty contract, the lessee is in a position to carry the lands without special cost to himself except that of the taxes. The consequence is that it is impossible to apply the same principle of taxation to agricultural lands, timber lands, minerals, and water power. There must be a differentiation between them, and a differentiation that will clearly meet the various uses to which they are put. Without question, the general property tax as it now stands upon the statute books of the different states does not meet in any true sense the usual economic conditions and the special needs of mining and lumbering. The principle of taxing the product when it is placed upon the market applies particularly to mineral and timber lands; the same principle in the case of farming lands by deterring their use would probably fail to meet the needs of revenue and would work to the discouragement of the agricultural industry.

The single-taxers have insisted that the taxation of land hastens its use and forces the owner to develop it. This method of taxation may be just the thing that is needed in the special instances of agricultural lands and of town lots, but the same principle cannot be applied to the other resources of the nation.

It is possible for the owners of timber lands by following the principles of forestry to modify the product and to keep the land in producing condition indefinitely. Taxation of such land, therefore, should have in view the maintenance of this condition. It must be clearly understood, however, that the fear of fire, interest charges on investment, and the cost of management will act quite as surely toward the rapid destruction of forests as will taxation. These difficulties must then be recognized by the state in the establishment of a fire warden system and the encouragement of forestation through some plan of bonuses.

Where forestation is not practiced, the taxation of timber products under present conditions, whether on stumpage or in transit to the sawmills, is a serious problem; serious to the local governments because under existing laws logs in transit are taxable where they are owned, and serious to the owners of the timber lands because the fixed charges on their properties increase each day without any income from them. As nearly as can be ascertained the annual taxes on timber vary from 1 cent per 1,000 feet to 50 cents per 1,000 feet with an average tax of about 15 cents per 1,000 feet. Interest charges are probably about 23 cents, making a total annual cost of something like 38 cents per 1,000 feet. In ten years time the tax on each 1,000 feet of standing timber will amount to $1.50, which compounded with interest makes a total of $2.37. Added to the other charges this tax probably compels the owner of timber under modern conditions to realize at least $13.02 per 1,000 feet on his logs delivered at the mill if at the end of ten years he is to have a profit of 6 per cent.

The suggestions which have been made from time to time regarding the taxation of timber have as their fundamental principle the separation of the value of the land from the value of the timber. This plan meets the criticism of the local assessing officers by providing a basis of taxing annually on a part of the valuation and of producing some income for the local government. If we understand then that the land may be taxed annually and the timber product when it is cut, we have under this plan a simple scheme of taxation which will unquestionably meet the difficulty that is now urged against the general property assessment of timber lands. Under the old plan of valuing annually the property, to secure an appraisement that was satisfactory to anybody was almost impossible; and, moreover, as the years went by, the local governments found their assessed values decreasing and the burden of government materially increasing with the decline in amount of standing timber. The annual taxation of the land upon which the timber stands meets this difficulty whereas the taxation of the product at the time of harvesting provides a plan that is fair both to the local government and to the owner of timber.

On the other hand, the taxation of mineral properties differs from the taxation of timber lands in that it is not possible for the

owner to increase by any plan of conservation the amount of tonnage that he has in his possession. The conservation which he
might practice is the simple procedure of saving for a future
time. From the point of view of the state the problem is largely one
of getting a share of the value of the minerals in the ground. The
method that has been generally followed is that of making an appraisement of the mineral lands, which may be very far from
or very near the truth.

The same principle which is applied in the case of timber lands,
namely the taxation of the land and of the product, should be
applied to mineral properties. There is no question that the easiest
way, and the most satisfactory and acceptable for all concerned, is
a tonnage tax varying possibly with the character of the ore and
the cost of mining but always depending for the rate and the
amount upon the ore that has been mined. It will probably be
argued, as it has been in other instances, that the local governments
are compelled to rely largely for their support upon the taxes
paid by the owners of mineral properties, and consequently a tonnage tax would deprive them of the regularity of their income.
There is much to be considered in this point; but the taxation of
the surface on some such basis as that seen in the case of the timber
tax will provide a regular income supplemented by the amount
at the time of mining.

The rate of tonnage tax is not likely, as in the case of the appraisement under a general property tax, to hasten the utilization of the ore. That would be determined entirely by the demand
for it in the fields of manufacture. The real essence of the tonnage
tax lies in the fact that wealth found in the ground is distinctly a
product of nature, which an ad valorem tax cannot recognize; that
the state's right to a share of the earth's products is considered; and
that the diminishing value element involved is not overlooked.
The protection of the local government and often of the mineral
owner demands a combination of the tonnage tax and of the local
land tax.

When we come to the taxation of water power, we are face to
face with a problem that contains even more difficulties than are

found in the case of the timber and mineral lands. The thing here implied is so illusive, so difficult of measurement, and requires such expensive administration that quite probably many years must elapse before an adequate plan for this kind of taxation can be developed. Because water power is perpetual, it differs from timber and mineral properties and is more comparable to farm lands. It differs from the latter, however, in this particular; the work in harnessing water power is done once for all and does not demand continued effort as in the case of the farm. Nature, having been harnessed, is able to accomplish the work that is demanded of her.

The first step in any adequate system of taxing water powers must be their survey. This means listing, locating, and measuring. Unquestionably the legislature should assume at the beginning that all water powers belong to the state and that the acquirement of them must be through lease as in the case of mineral lands in the state of Minnesota for example. Several plans have been suggested for the taxation of water power. One is the measurement of the water flowing over a dam, and another is the taxation of the actual horsepower developed. The latter plan is subject to many criticisms.

The development of horsepower depends so largely upon the skill of the engineer, the capital invested, and the way the water is handled that the better method of taxation is, after measuring the capacity of the dam under proper engineering authority, to determine a fair rate for the amount of power produced by the water passing over the dam. Of necessity many refinements of this plan would be required such as the determination of the movement of the stream, the height of the water, the difficulties of harnessing the power; but it is possible by taking into consideration the general expense of operating a water power plant to work out a rate which will be fair to the users as well as to the state.

In no instance of conservation does a greater need of proper taxation appear than in the case of water power. Nature provides a perpetual force with but little expense after the necessary fundamentals have been arranged. If the state is to receive no compensation of any kind for the utilization of such a large wealth-producer, the greatest possible injustice in the matter of taxation is allowed to exist.

It will therefore be seen that rational taxation of natural resources does not depend upon difficult and intricate formulas but upon regulations that are comparatively simple. That the taxation or agricultural land, of minerals, of timber, or of water power must differ in many respects and that a principle of taxation applied in one case may not work in the others should be definitely understood. But if we keep clearly in mind the purposes for which all natural resources can be utilized and perceive that the primary taxation of land as such can be made annually and that the assessment on the products can be levied at the time of their harvesting, we have in the three instances of agricultural, mineral, and timber lands a principle that may prove satisfactory when put in the form of legislation. The same idea can be applied to the water power sites; taxation of the land at a nominal value and of the water power on the basis of the power produced by the amount of water passing over the dam gives us again a rule for fair dealing.

The states have reached a point in their fiscal affairs not only where more revenue is needed for the purposes of general social advancement but where better administration of money matters is essential and necessary. An administration bureau must be provided in all of the states to furnish the required data if we are to reach some practical basis of conserving our resources through taxation. Tax commissions must be given sufficient authority and in addition must have expert advice and assistance to furnish significant information.

To my mind a rational system of taxing natural resources depends largely upon administration based upon a few fundamental principles of legislation. A rational system is not a difficult matter; it is largely a question of willingness to meet the problem. If, however, the experience of the past has any light to throw upon this subject, we must expect that legislation will be slow. The various interests involved, through fear of some possible advantages likely to be gained over them, will cling to the old methods until any results to be produced through adequate taxation will perhaps be lost. Here as elsewhere broad views will aid in solving the problems; little and narrow prejudices will prevent progress.

The Conflict of Administrations

Published in *Popular Science Monthly*, February, 1912; reprinted

IN A LETTER to the governors of the states at the close of the Revolutionary War, Washington fervently prayed for four things which he humbly conceived as not only essential but actually vital to the existence of the United States as an independent power. These four things were an indissoluble union of the states under one federal head, a sacred regard for public justice, the adoption of a proper peace establishment, and the prevalence of a civic and friendly disposition among the people of the United States. This attitude of harmony would induce them to forget their local prejudices and policies, to make those mutual concessions which were requisite to the general prosperity, and in some instances to sacrifice their individual advantages to the interests of the community.

None of the revolutionary fathers could see difficulties other than those of a seacoast commerce policed by many petty sovereigns. The problem of cooperation between the federal authority and the states would, in their opinion, arise only when brought to the surface by a state jealous of its prerogatives, never through the action of the federal authority. A hundred and twenty-five years have passed, and many things naturally not anticipated in earlier days of this country have happened. Moreover persons and corporations engaged in commerce seek the extension of federal power at the expense of state authority, if need be, in order that commerce may go on unhampered and free from restrictions of a territorial character. Thus at the beginning of the twentieth century in the United States of America has arisen a new type of problem in the conflict of administration which can be solved only by a process of cooperation.

Men rang the bells in steeples and gave utterance to their jubilation in loud hurrahs when the fleet of King George III left New York Harbor. They had forgotten that a nation did not exist, that effective cooperation had ceased when Washington disbanded his army in 1783, that the union which was then dissolved lived only as a tradition, and that the states were thirteen independent sovereigns who were jealous of each other and open to the abuses of foreign intrigue.

Writing to Duane in 1780, Alexander Hamilton declared: "The fundamental defect is a want of power in Congress . . . it has originated from three causes; an excess of the spirit of liberty, which has made the particular States show a jealousy of all powers not in their hands . . . a diffidence in Congress, of their own powers, . . . a want of sufficient means at their disposal to answer the public exigencies, and of vigor to draw forth these means. Congress . . . should have considered themselves vested with full power to *preserve the republic from harm.* . . . But the Confederation itself is defective and requires to be altered. It is neither fit for war nor peace."

The problem confronting the people of America in 1783 was the conversion of a voluntary league of states into a firm union. They needed to be first awakened to the necessity of organization and the adoption of a national policy. After this awakening they had to draft the instrument of agreement and establish the government. It is not necessary at this time to discuss the detailed story of the making of the Constitution of the United States of America.

From the very inception of the Constitution, men took opposite views in regard to the rights of the individual states and the nature of the powers that should be given to the central government. Those who upheld the idea of states' rights feared in their hearts the rule of the people. They argued for state representation in the national Congress while maintaining that federal authority should be reduced to a minimum. The federalists on the other hand insisted upon a broad interpretation of the powers of the national government, thereby creating a controversy which furnished the basis of modern party relations. These relations were materially modified by the tendency which was brought about by the Civil War to discuss the import of questions rather than the functions of government. The same motive, however, which caused men to turn to the states in the earlier day now causes them to look to the federal government; they are hoping, as they hoped at the beginning of the Union, that control by the people may be checked and regulated.

For a period of nearly thirty years after the Civil War, government in the United States, both federal and commonwealth, was used largely as an agency for the promotion of wealth. Special privileges came to overshadow common rights, and many problems were left untouched because in the opinion of the courts of the day the federal government had no authority over them and the states by the Constitution were not authorized to deal with such problems. As industry has grown in immensity and has spread its organization from commonwealth to commonwealth, producing a series of new situations in the movement of commerce from state to state, friction and questioned authority have increased between state and federal government in the United States.

The Constitution of the United States provides that the states shall have all the rights of government with the exception of the right of secession, which was implicitly determined by the results of the Civil War, and with the exception of those powers which the Constitution expressly confers on the federal government and such other powers as the Constitution withholds from the states. Not many years elapsed before shrewd lawyers discovered that a "twilight zone," as it has been picturesquely described by one of America's party leaders, existed between the powers of the federal government and those of the several states as interpreted by the two court systems.

The specific powers of the federal government were determined broadly, while the general powers of the states were interpreted specifically. There arose, as a consequence, certain types of problems, certain species of acts, to which no special law seemed to apply; these left their authors in the possession of concerns working in a no-man's land. To meet this serious difficulty, it has been proposed on one side that federal authority to deal with all such problems shall be markedly increased and on the other side that the sanctity of the Constitution shall be preserved, the sacredness of the judiciary upheld, and the doctrine of the division of powers kept intact.

Those who believe in an increase of centralization have maintained that the Union is a federal one, that the sovereignty of the states never existed, and that with their present authority and power they are merely nuisances clogging the way of the federal government. There is no question that a series of difficult problems have arisen which demand a wider interpretation of federal jurisdiction, but the attitude just mentioned would result in the reduction of the states to local administrative units with no more power and authority than a county or township possesses. It is declared that the conservation of resources is so important that state lines ought not to be taken into consideration in dealing with this matter. Moreover, if we are to be a great commercial nation, interstate commerce and the questions that are associated with it prohibit the recognition of state authority over commerce and trade within certain boundaries.

Such, briefly stated, is the controversy in regard to the theory of American government. In the course of this discussion it will be necessary to examine some of the experiences and outcomes of federal legislation and to present, if possible, a program of co-operation between the two branches of government whereby neither will be subordinated to the other and both will continue their usefulness and dignity.

Probably the one problem of national character which is most important from the point of view of the public is that of interstate commerce. The legislation and various attempts at legislation in this connection cover a period of forty years. In the year 1872 Mr. Regan, a Congressman from the state of Texas, presented a bill regulating interstate commerce conveyed by railways. The bill was the outcome of grievances and difficulties arising from the attempts on the part of the various states to obtain betterment of transportation facilities, improvement in the matter of lower rates, and efficiency in methods of carrying on business. Annually for more than fifteen years this bill made its appearance in Congress; not until 1887, however, was the Interstate Commerce Act passed with its regulations of railroads and railroad rates. Despite the complaints that were made regarding the inefficiency of this law and the difficulty of bringing under it many of the problems that arose, no other interstate commerce legislation took place until the year 1903. The law was again modified in 1907 and in 1910.

If we turn to the National Bank Act, which has been referred to many times as one of the most beneficent laws that the federal government has put upon the statute books, we perceive that it had its origin in the necessities of the Civil War and that it was developed as a revenue measure in the hope of forcing the banks of the day to buy the bonds of the distressed government. The principles which were recognized by the Secretary of the Treasury at the time as essential to the establishment of a banking system were taken in part from the experiences of Massachusetts and New York. Out of these experiences as important parts of the National Bank Act came the right of free banking, the principle of the redemption fund, and the issue of paper money upon a bonded security.

Passing in quick review the federal legislation relating to pure foods, we find that not until 1906 was any legislation secured which authorized the inspection and examination of foods by federal officers and the placing upon adulteration an adequate penalty. For seventeen years the people of the nation had urged Congress to pass a bill that would meet the many abuses that had arisen in the adulteration of food and dairy products.

Tariff legislation by Congress has certainly not been always wise. The tariff bills that have been enacted since the Civil War for the purpose of protecting manufacturers in the United States have steadily increased in number and have steadily augmented the burdens in the form of customs duties regardless of the conflict of interests and the necessities of the consumer. Under the provisions of the McKinley Bill, the tariff rate stood at a higher percentage than at any time in the history of the nation.

Nor is this all. The encroachments upon the financial strength of the states in the form of added taxes have come with the growing activity of the federal government as might well have been expected. In the year 1909 the federal corporation tax was laid upon all corporations engaged in interstate business in the United States. Some benefits promised from this levy were the large revenues to be obtained and the greater control over the many corporations of the country whereby their bookkeeping and accounting systems would be reorganized along the lines of the best principles of accountancy.

The law, which has now been in existence about two years, has shown clearly that it lays a heavy burden upon corporations in the impossible demands of the accounting methods required; whereas the principle of self-assessment, unchecked by government examination, practically permits the corporations to determine what they will pay. But the worst side of the corporation tax is that the fiscal systems of those states that have developed such a plan of taxation are materially affected. These states find that their own sources of revenue are cut into because the corporations subject to this federal levy are provided with an argument of double taxation against proper state taxes. This phase of the corporation tax has been regarded by many economic authorities as unfitting the tax for use by the federal government, and its application has been denounced in many quarters as an invasion into the proper field of state taxation.

In the efforts now being put forth to establish a federal income tax the same tendency is to be seen. Although it cannot be denied that the federal government should have the power in time of need to levy a federal income tax, yet the wisdom of such a federal tax in time of peace is distinctly questionable. The problems which confront the states at the present time are indeed serious. Upon them fall all of the burdens of maintaining local governments; and these, with the development of broader ideas regarding obligations to society, constantly tend to increase rather than to diminish.

The states are now called upon to promote extensive educational systems, to care for the insane, to punish criminals, to maintain courts, to preserve order, to build roads, to support the poor, to erect public buildings, and in the municipalities to provide water, light, paving, and the other necessary improvements of modern towns and villages. To have the federal government, therefore, reach out into the states for additional funds for federal support means interference with the states' fiscal systems and in the long run the weakening of their financial powers. In the customs duties and the internal revenue, the federal government has every facility to provide sufficient support for the conduct of its business.

What has already been said regarding the history of federal legislation in connection with the Interstate Commerce Act, the National Bank Act, the pure food and dairy enactment, and the tariff indicates the slowness with which Congress meets the problems of legislation and the difficulty of obtaining modification of a law by that body. In nearly every instance the states began the legislation and carried it forward to a point where it was necessary to look to Congress for some wider interpretation because of conflicts between the states. The work which Congress has done, commendable as it is in many cases, shows clearly that the federal government cannot act effectively in every instance because of its distance from the problem; moreover, since it follows general lines of action, it cannot by the very nature of things be expected to meet local needs.

Sixteen years after the introduction of the Regan bill came the Interstate Commerce Act. For sixteen more years no modification of the law was made despite the insistent demands for certain changes. The National Bank Act remained practically unchanged from the date of its passage until the year 1900. Examples of this kind go to show that federal legislation is attended by many disadvantages. Undoubtedly Congress can deal with large problems on general principles; however, when Congress attempts to work out experiments and changes in the law, delay and confusion sometimes are the result.

It is just here that the states come to play an increasingly important part. They are in fact laboratories in which industrial and political experiments can be worked out on such scale as to determine the value of the experiment. The states can relieve the nation as a whole from many of the pangs necessary in the growth of democracy. The national government has the opportunity of utilizing the best that comes from such experiments and of being saved in disappointment and in loss of time for large enterprises. The states have, as a consequence, an important governmental function to carry out. They are not to be regarded as mere administrative units, subject to the direction and domination of a federal authority thousands of miles away, with no autonomy such as is found in the case of the departments in France; but they are rather constituent parts of the Union, self-directive and capable of maintaining their own autonomy and of carrying on their own functions within their own boundaries.

To the state in which we live we intrust our daily welfare; to the United States of America we commit our collective interests. Nevertheless, the state and the nation are one and the same government, each a part of the whole; separately organized, they work together and are mutually dependent. To substitute one for the other is to violate the whole principle of the federal scheme.

The conflict between the federal and state governments is more apparent than real. The difficulties of the situation have been materially exaggerated not always without a purpose. In the early history of our nation, many of the believers in states' rights took that position because of their feeling that the government should not be in the hands of the people but should be only representative; today that same attitude exists in the demand that the federal authority be enlarged and the states reduced to minimum power in order that again the authority of the people may be hampered and limited.

The laws of the nation and of the states, founded as they are on the common law of England, will be discovered by the diligent inquirer to contain within them greater uniformity than diversity. The extent of this similarity is marked. Although much confusion of detail and of procedure clouds the issue, the principle of action in both state and federal government is the same. From one state to another have been handed the principles of legislation and forms of government. In one state is initiated some new phase of political organization; its preparation is carried on into another community; and little by little over the land an increasing uniformity of legislation moves constantly.

Whereas it may be said that as a nation we are confronted with serious industrial problems over which we have no central authority, nevertheless the nation has made some progress under present constitutional provisions and the states are diligently seeking legislation that will meet the difficulty. Any danger to the government is not likely to come from our failure to solve our problems in a fairly satisfactory way through the utilization of both state and federal governments but from a tendency seen now and then towards excessive centralization. Excessive centralization is dangerous to us not from the point of view of tyranny, as we might suppose, but rather from the fact of breakdown within an organization too extended to be capable of effective operation.

There can be no question in the minds of students of political history that the future of the nation depends upon the cooperation of the governmental units rather than upon the exaggeration of one of them. Instead of attempting to magnify the federal government, the citizenry should be engaged in an effort toward the equalizing of the functions of both nation and states.

Because of the extent of its authority over a large area, the federal government is in a position to obtain information on all topics for utilization in the various states. An instance of this function is found in the collection of data already undertaken by the various bureaus at Washington. With the authority of the national government behind them, the departments are able to bring together an immense amount of information that throws light upon many questions. To limit the functions of the United States government to the mere assembling of materials is not the desire of any one. The accumulation of data should be supplemented by specific investigations of various matters of interest to the public welfare. Again this is not sufficient. Such information must be made available. The federal government has sufficient prestige and power not only to make widely known its own actions and the results of any investigations which it carries on but also to insist upon publicity on the part of all interstate agencies and corporations.

Because of the conflict of authority in the field of commerce, many suggestions have been made from time to time that the federal government be enabled to take over full control in the matter of incorporation. In behalf of this movement is cited the conduct of many of the states now permitting incorporation under peculiarly satisfactory provisions for the companies. The result of this method is the inability of other states to control these corporations which are operating also within their boundaries.

Although there is considerable truth in this position, yet the matter could be comparatively easily settled if Congress would pass an act setting forth the conditions under which corporations may engage in interstate commerce. These conditions would have reference to capitalization, publicity of accounts, and responsibility for any statements regarding the business of the corporations. Such a law would in no way necessitate incorporation under the federal government or disturb the incorporation of companies by the different states. But like the tax upon bank currency passed in 1866, this law would have a marked effect in forcing corporations to comply with the federal conditions and would at the same time allow the states to enact laws that were pertinent to the conditions of their own territories.

Many other instances might be cited in which the same relationships are to be found as in interstate corporations. The more one studies the situation, the more one is impressed with the fact that the relations between the states and the federal government can be strengthened rather than weakened by the passage of laws on the part of Congress which will establish the conditions whereby business concerns can enjoy the privileges of carrying on their traffic between the different states and which at the same time will allow the regulations to be developed by the commonwealths. It may be argued that this method will still retain the worst features of present conditions without discrimination and with lack of uniformity.

An examination of the laws of the states will confirm the impression that the states are rapidly taking over the regulations and laws which have been proved by the test of time to be satisfactory and efficient. Any limitations of the authority of a state like Wisconsin would be unwise; here under the direction of an underlying public sentiment, much progress has been made in working out a number of highly efficient methods of dealing with serious questions. It is indeed doubtful if the same progress could have been made by the federal government through the medium of legislation by Congress.

The people of this country are interested in efficient administration. They are not insistent upon either federal or state authority as such. What they want to see is progress in dealing with some of our momentous national problems. But history proves that, when a nation tries to cover too large a field and through its national legislative body to deal in detail with local questions, it fails to accomplish the result that was expected. In America we have a fortunate separation of functions which, though perhaps weak at some points, makes on the whole a satisfactory division of authority. To push the states down into the position of mere administrative units would result in the enfeebling of the whole plan of government. Moreover because of the distance from central authority, governmental matters without any legal powers in the states would probably be inefficiently handled.

Our attitude on this significant question of the conflict of administrations should be that of seeking for the full utilization of both federal and state authority, for the elimination of friction between them, and for the securing of an adequate working plan by which both can be used to the best advantage. We are a nation of one people believing distinctly in the federal form of government. It remains therefore for us to insist upon a clear understanding of the functions of the federal government. We should appreciate the fact that the states are carrying the burden of the expense and difficulties of local problems. And we should realize fully that interference on the part of the federal government is likely to result in an increasing weakness of authority rather than in a strengthening of government.

A century and a quarter have passed since the creation of the Republic in 1787. The indissoluble union so fervently hoped for by the father of this country is now achieved. Though the regard for public justice can hardly be referred to as sacred, nevertheless, the nation is making progress steadily toward more efficient courts. Our peace establishment meets the needs of the nation. Great advance has been made toward the civic and friendly disposition among the people of the United States, which attitude is sufficient to induce them often to forget their local prejudices and policies. Thus are the four desires of George Washington either accomplished facts or well on their way to fulfillment. We have still to solve the problem of federal versus state control and to decide wisely in regard to what and how far the government shall by central authority attempt to rule. The question is of vast importance; its determination will have much to do with the perpetuation of the Republic.

Taxes and the County Tax Commissioner

Address to the County Tax Commissioners of Kentucky;
Louisville, June, 1940

THE gathering of the county tax commissioners of a state is an important event among the happenings of the year because these officers have in their hands the welfare of citizens and by the conduct of their offices affect the business of government. Consequently, I am honored to be invited to address this company on some of the problems of the taxing of property in Kentucky for government purposes.

Many years have passed since I was intimately associated with the questions that confront you today. At one time I was the chairman of the first state taxation commission created by legislative act in the state of Minnesota. The commission of three was appointed by Governor John A. Johnson then in his third term of office, a Democrat in a Republican state. He did not designate the chairman but asked the commission to select its own head and to determine the terms that the members were to serve. This was done by the simple method of drawing straws. I pulled the short one and by that chance became the first chairman of the commission.

At the initial meeting the commission appropriated one thousand dollars for books on taxation, subscribed to a clipping bureau for articles and news, and arranged to employ a librarian who would help to keep the members informed on tax matters both in this country and abroad. These were good investments. The second step was to visit all the tax commissions located in the states east of the Mississippi. This trip, lasting about two weeks, put the commissioners in touch with what was being done by these agencies and, still more important, enabled them to talk with experienced people about the problems and difficulties that were common to all states in the assessment and collection of taxes.

The main reason for the passage of the legislation leading to the creation of the commission in Minnesota was the dissatisfaction of the people with the assessment of the iron ore properties in the northern part of the state. Public opinion demanded that something be done to remedy what many thought was a gross discrimination that favored the mining companies and gave them advantages. The duty of the commission under this popular mandate was to waste little time in dealing with the problem of assessing ore properties.

It was decided to make an inspection of the mines in order to learn as much as possible of the types of mines, character of the ore, and methods used to get the ore to the surface. To do this the commission undertook to cover the whole iron range, which extends a hundred miles. Arriving at the western end of the range about the middle of July, the commissioners began the journey in a buckboard wagon drawn by two sturdy horses. In the course of the trip more than a score of mines were visited, and the workings of twenty-two were explored. Returning to St. Paul, the members were faced with deciding upon a method of taxing the properties. After considerable study a plan was devised that has stood for years as the procedure of arriving at the valuations for tax purposes. I shall not go into the details of the scheme on this occasion for you are already asking, "Why does the speaker tell us this story of taxation in Minnesota?" I have brought to you these activities to show how essential it is to gather facts and to study them if the work done by the taxing authorities is to stand the test of time and the actions of complainants in the courts.

The assessment of real property is one of the important functions of the assessor if money to run the town and county governments is to be found. To let the owner make his own valuation is surely to result in great inequalities between different pieces of real estate. The assessor may make quite as great errors if he does not fortify his judgment with all the facts that he can get in the matter of location maps, of property sales in the district, of insurance valuations, of construction costs, of dates of buildings, and of obsolescence charges against the value of the property. The up and coming assessing officer must have this information in available form, which means the use of charts, indexes, and maps in his office. Now that aerial photography has been developed to a high degree, there is no reason for each county's not having a complete set of maps which will cover every farm and town within the boundaries of the county. It is true that the cost of making the maps will amount to a considerable sum, but the expense is justified in the better assessments that will result.

Although the law requires the assessor to make his assessments at full value, this is seldom done. He must settle the questions of the equality of assessments throughout his official area and of his being fair and just to all land owners in the county. Here again it is necessary to resort to the facts which are to be found in the sales of property over a period of years. When he collects this information, he can by comparing it with the estimates placed upon property for taxing purposes arrive at a valuation. Without doubt the assessor will discover considerable differences in the assessment ratio, for the tendency is always to assess a small piece of property at a higher rate than a large one because the assessor can more easily judge the value of small properties. Thus, the small owner is discriminated against almost automatically. Such results from the operations of assessments are unjust and lead to great dissatisfaction. If justice is to be rendered, the assessor must find the ratio for the whole county by tabulating and keeping up to date the records of sales of all properties over a period of years.

A real headache for the assessor is to be found in his valuation of personal property. Every assessor knows the great variations and absurdities of the process and the devastating results. In some counties there may be a watch or two, no diamond rings, and no valuable jewelry. Libraries are assessed by law; however, there are so few books that the impression might prevail that the population is highly illiterate. Moreover, since the assessing officer has a hard time evaluating rugs and other household possessions, he usually accepts the values placed by the owner. In fact, there is little else he can do. In spite of exemption of two hundred and fifty dollars, which helps some in determining whether anything should go on the assessment books, every county has valuable personal property on which no taxes are levied.

Most authorities advise that the personal property tax laws on tangibles as well as on intangibles be rescinded. Still, because the tendency is to cling to anything that will add to the state's income, we go on in the old way. The wise state should be willing to give up both real and personal property assessments in lieu of a levy upon income because through a well worked out income tax the state treasury will be more prosperous than it can be through attempting to find the small possessions of the many. However, whenever the state gives up the property tax, real and personal, the majority of the citizens lose interest in the costs of state government, and state expenditures are not given the attention by the constituency that they should have.

In our state there is much opposition to any move the Kentucky Tax Commission may make to equalize assessments on the grounds that, since local matters alone are involved, each county should determine its own estimates. This is a shortsighted policy because business and social activities are not confined within the county but cut across county lines. A brick plant for example in a county sells its products over a considerable area. If a competitor in another county has a lower valuation on his plant, then the plant in the first county, because it is carrying a larger fixed charge, finds difficulty in competing with the prices of the other plant. If this sort of thing goes on for some time, the county may find it has lost an industry that paid a noticeable sum in taxes. What is said here regarding the brick plant applies as a matter of course to other commercial enterprises. The assessor has in his hands important control which, if used wisely and well without fear or favor, contributes to the growth of business and farming in the county and in the state.

I am led to say at this point that the assessor ought to be a student of his community in order that he may be in touch with the economic trends in his county and in adjoining counties as well. He of course can follow a sedentary life sitting in his office from day to day and letting the taxpayers come to him at all times. If he does that, he must rely wholly upon personally interested individuals to tell him what they are doing. To get out in the field takes time, but it is time that, if well used, will bring valuable results. At present the assessor no doubt depends upon the state tax commission's field men for information about values; but this information is often concerned with the shortcomings of some individual.

The assessor should know the general trends in the county. This knowledge is illustrated by a few questions. Is the population going up or down? Are the towns doing real business? Do the farmers really try to farm and are they fairly well versed in the best practices? Are the children well taken care of? Is there a feeling that the county is a good place in which to live? After all, the assessor may say, "These questions are matters that should interest every citizen, especially the local boards of commerce, and are not really a part of my business." However, these matters are the business of the assessor because the valuation in the aggregate is not an individual but a community affair and as such must include the entire situation in the county.

To equalize values between individuals as well as between communities is a significant phase of the assessor's work. In our practice the assessor can act as an advisor to the county board. Nevertheless, since the members of the board may be intent on holding down assessments in order that the county will pay as little of the state tax as possible, the assessor's advice may not be asked or heeded. This attitude is not one that can be called scientific; it is rather a sort of hit or miss policy that is used largely for protection of classifications of property and of individuals.

The status of county assessors has little opportunity for improvement except through the support and help of the state tax commission. This support can come only when the local assessors see eye to eye with the state authorities, both having in mind the larger service to the local county and to the state. They then are determined to follow the law and to make the best assessments that can be made in spite of the handicaps of tradition, of practice, of ability, and of funds to be had for the work. There is a tendency on the part of local administrators to blame the state authorities for any disturbances that may arise in the local assessments. Complete frankness and full cooperation on the part of all are essential to the administration of the law. In the long run such procedure is good politics.

Our taxing system is made up of many conflicting features and old processes. It may be a long time before we reach the almost Utopian situation of tax laws that will be completely coordinated and adjusted to the activities and business of the people. However, thinking about these problems and discussing the issues involved will bring results in time.

Since 1917 there have been at least six practically complete changes made in our Kentucky tax laws. In the year 1917 a special session of the legislature considered for more than a month the ably presented report of a commission appointed to bring in a tax code. The main features of this report were adopted and were made a part of the law. The tinkering which began two years later has continued. To recognize now what was considered a very good law at the time of its passage is almost impossible. The state has practically given up the real property tax, but despite an income tax it still taxes personal property in the form of household goods, equipment of the farmer, and small possessions. In fact the taxes of today tend to discourage thrift and industry by placing undue burdens upon enterprise.

Such discussions could continue indefinitely; but the point I have in mind is that the county assessor must have some knowledge of the tax problem and should try with the help of the state commission to develop a real understanding of the tax question. I can see little chance for betterment of the taxing process until the hand of the state tax commission is strengthened and until the county tax commissioners are taken out of politics. A merit system based upon ability, knowledge, and administrative capacity which includes of course getting on with people would bring the desired results. Also taxation must eventually be administered as a state rather than as a merely local matter. We have a long way to go, but progress is being made.

In another ten years we should see county commissioners on the merit system, a fairly satisfactory code of tax laws enacted, and the state commission strongly intrenched as an administrative agency. Since the state will then be out of debt, taxes will be adjusted to the business and lives of the people. When these things come to pass, Kentucky should move forward rapidly. The citizens of the commonwealth will then rejoice in many social accomplishments; a real educational system, well built roads over the whole of the state, and a penal and charitable organization that will be the equal of any in the United States will be theirs. When these benefits come to pass, the tax commissioners of the counties, if they have been alert and intelligent and conscientious, can truthfully say that they have had an important part in the great forward movement of our state.

The Tax Commissioner, Yesterday and Today

Address to the National Association of Tax Administrators,
Lexington, Kentucky, June 9, 1941

T H E change in attitude and viewpoint in regard to many political and governmental questions in the nation, the state, the county, the city, the town is apparent to all of us. It is difficult to reconcile the position of twenty-five years ago with the situation of today. An increase of at least 300 per cent in the cost of present government over that of thirty years ago—and in some of the states the increase is even greater—confronts us with the problems of more revenues and higher taxes and of the necessity of spending the money effectively.

A different concept of our obligations has appeared because we have learned the possibility of doing things cooperatively that cannot be done individually. For instance, we are beginning to recognize more fully than we have heretofore our duty to the wards in our state institutions, to the blind and the indigent persons, to the matters of education and of social adjustment. Moreover, our natural resources and agriculture are organized today and are accepted as national responsibilities. For years funds for the support of education and of the wards of the states have been in our budgets. Now certain other budget expenditures appear for practically the first time. Take the questions involved in government pensions, in expansion of the social welfare activities of the state, in the obligation the state owes to the underprivileged children; all of these claims are now accepted, and the people are accordingly called upon to find the necessary funds to meet the cost of providing for them.

One might say that in a group of tax commissioners the attitude and the effort look to the raising of revenue. Naturally with a good deal of relief new sources of revenue are welcomed wherever they can be found. The problem of finding more money grows constantly with the development of expenses of maintaining government. Where will additional revenue be discovered? The situation requires an increasing amount of study and careful analysis of the structure of government. The danger is that the tax administrator will be so intent on the production of revenue that he will overlook the fundamental social adjustments that must come with any added taxing procedure.

In administration of taxes the drift is toward specialization. In many state departments one person devotes his whole time to inheritance taxes; others are concerned with licenses, income taxes, corporation franchises, and the like. Because many of these men have never made a study of the whole tax problem, the larger phases may be overlooked unless there is some way to bring the knowledge of the specialists into a pool. From this reservoir taxing officers may draw information in regard to the various taxes and also in regard to the effect of the tax payments upon the community and state.

I make bold to suggest that the state taxing departments should hold seminars frequently to discuss the theoretical principles of taxation. Otherwise, tax administration tends to bog down and so fails to adjust taxes to changing social conditions.

When a lawyer comes before a tax commission, he reflects the view of his client and expects to show that his ideas are correct in the matter of placing a tax on the property of his client. The lawyer is an important citizen who wants to do the right thing; yet in the position he occupies as the representative of another person, he urges the narrow interpretation of the law in the hope that a decision favorable to him will be made. The business man particularly in the field of manufacturing regards taxes as a personal matter because his business may be hampered by the amount of taxes he pays. Then, there is the politician who tries to make the government a going concern under the two party system; he too has his view. His object is to get the money by taxation in order that his party can produce results and please the public. Here are four groups of men who are concerned with the welfare of the state and who, because their interests are opposed, become farther and farther apart in the serious consideration of tax problems.

It is essential that there shall be a broad understanding between men in business and in government in order that the social philosophy and practices of the state—the things important to be done by the state—will be recognized and accepted by all. Those who follow the pursuit of the law, those engaged in business, those who administer the law, and those who keep the political organization going must contribute to each other their interpretations of the functions of a state and of taxation within that state. With such an understanding the tax commissioner will not be regarded as a parasite or as a person interfering with the best interests of business but will be looked upon as a social agency who produces results beyond compare in the growth and development of the state.

When I was on the tax commission in Minnesota, I remember talking with a group of men about the matter of taxes. One man who had a clothing store was obnoxious in his attitude, maintaining that the tax authorities were "robbing" him. After a good deal of such comment by the merchant, I turned to him and remarked that he did not pay any taxes. He was as mad a man as I had seen in a long time and of course demanded that I tell him how I reached such an outrageous conclusion. "The taxes you pay are included in the price of the clothing which you sell." And I asked him if that was not true. He reluctantly answered, "Yes," and admitted that he tried to incorporate taxes as well as the rent and clerk hire into the price. His ability to do this depended upon competition and upon his competence in handling the business he was carrying on. This merchant passed the tax on to the consumer; if he paid an income tax, that tax fell upon him as an individual, but in his business the tax was paid by the buyer.

What are the implications of the whole matter of taxes? What is the tax? Where does it rest? Who pays it? Unless the tax is placed in a fair sort of way, discontent which may lead to rather serious consequences later on will surely arise.

My feeling today is that tax administrators must be students of taxation. Although in their busy lives to give the theory of taxation the attention that should be given may be nearly impossible, nevertheless the finance officers must understand and know the results of work done by students in the field of taxation. By their understanding of the problems, and they are many, the wise tax administrator can reduce the difficulties and can bring the practices to a scientific and impersonal procedure. In the days of huge public expenditures, as of the present, the careful administration of taxation becomes highly important because of social effects that follow in its train.

What do we know about income? What is income? Is it the cash one receives? Is it the book income? Does it involve what is called personal consumption? Or does it simply mean a book cash account? Whether it is income, inheritance, or property tax, the question of the relation of the tax to income arises inevitably. Yet amazingly little about income is considered in the larger field of taxation. We have much difficulty in defining the meaning of national wealth. Is it three hundred billions, or what is it? When we talk about national wealth as the basis of taxes, we forget that any material thing is a part of national wealth; a house across the street, a public park, lamp posts, and sidewalks, all are a part of national wealth. What function have these things in the matter of income?

In Kentucky we are paying in taxes to the federal, state, city, and county governments approximately two hundred and fifty million dollars per year. About one hundred and sixty million dollars go to the federal government, and the remainder is divided between the state, cities, and counties. What is the income of the people of the state of Kentucky? Does it have a proportional relationship to the amount of taxes being paid? How far can the tax be laid on the total income of the people of the state? Is that income fairly adequate? How is the income distributed? Although these questions appear to many people to be theoretical and academic, the answers are important in showing the ability or inability of the people to support the tax bills. Do the taxes at present tend constantly to reduce the amount that goes into production? If they do, unfortunate indeed are the results. On the other hand, do the national and state taxes which are distributed in wages actually produce increased income to the people in the form of service, recreation, and other activities? These are perhaps theoretical questions; the answers, however, are exceedingly significant.

As I recall my first year as a tax official in 1907, the commission spent that twelve months trying to do four things. The first of these was to acquire a social and economic understanding of the state of Minnesota, the kinds of industries, the incomes and outgoes, and the costs and methods of government. Another consideration was to reassess properties in the state so that a greater equality in the tax burden might prevail. A third goal was to provide a more effective administration of the assessments and collection of taxes in the state. And the result of all the foregoing was to formulate a law by which personal property, money, notes, and mortgages might be taxed at a regular rate of three or four mills on the one hundred dollars.

When the commission presented its report to the legislature, fifteen different recommendations were on the list. The legislature in the kindness of its heart passed two of them.

Looking back at that first year, I have come to feel that the legislature was right. At each session after that as the members of the legislature acquired more confidence in the taxing machinery, other suggestions were adopted and accepted until today Minnesota has a good system of taxation understood and upheld by the people of the state.

To look at the future is a prophetic procedure limited by time and by ability to understand. We may expect, it seems to me, a decrease in incomes due to heavy taxation and higher prices, an enormous increase in federal and state taxes, and a movement to make the federal government the responsible agency for the collecting of many of the taxes now collected by the states. This latter procedure will result from the advisability of having the same methods of administration over the entire country. Moreover, we may anticipate a marked increase in governmental activities such as the TVA and an advance in cooperative movements making possible the wider distribution of agricultural products throughout the land. Along with these changes I think that there will be a decided trend towards an improvement of the taxing machinery.

If I were Governor of a state—and I hasten to proclaim that I have no desire to be Governor—I should say, "The first thing I want is a thoroughgoing, honest, just administration of taxes in order that the income of the state may be as regular and as effective and as plentiful as it can be in all fairness." I should place in the finance department the best men I could find; and I should hope by so doing that the staff would be continued on from year to year as long as the personnel was effective because the business side of the state should not be disturbed with each administration. A depleted treasury and a mortgaged state do not make for successful government. Kentucky, as you doubtless know, will soon be entirely free from debt. To Governor Chandler, to Governor Johnson, and to their finance departments go the praise and gratitude for this at one time seemingly impossible achievement.

The trend is decidedly, I believe, in the direction of bringing into government faithful, well-trained men and women who are students of taxation, of administration, of other affairs of the state. From these effective and honest men and women will come better government and, as a result, a more enlightened and enlivened citizenry. In the hands of you as tax administrators rests a large part of the success of this hopeful enterprise.

PART VII

DEMOCRACY—OUR
HERITAGE

Democracy—Our Heritage

Excerpt from speech to the Paris, Kentucky, Rotary Club,
February 26, 1936

OURS is a land of democracy. The faith of the founders placed the emphasis upon equality of opportunity. For one hundred and fifty years the Republic has lived under the Constitution with belief in its citizens. Mistakes have been made, and our government has not always been efficient; nevertheless, the individual has continued to enjoy freedom.

Criticisms of democracy are more frequent today than they were at the beginning of the century. Our form of government is charged with being ineffective, cumbersome, and expensive. In spite of whatever handicaps it may have, it has attained many important results. To the credit of democracy are beautiful buildings, extensive parks, monuments, art galleries, museums, roads, sanitation, health, and, as a crowning evidence of the democratic ideal, a great public school system. Above all these tangible values, democracy has held the gift of liberty for men.

Now and then we hear some blusterer assert, "what this country needs is a dictator." The advocate of this outrageous suggestion, making the usual charges against democracy and criticizing public officials, berates our government on many points. Meanwhile, complaining bitterly he remains inertly indifferent to any obligation of citizenship.

[400]

Dictators have arisen in other lands. Their tribe has increased throughout the world. In each of these countries liberty as we know it has ceased to be, and the individual is subordinated to the government. His end is no longer personal; he is the tool and the means of the state.

In this land of ours we have the great heritage of the Anglo-Saxon given to us by a thousand years of struggle. To surrender to a dictatorship, which may mean for a while a little increase in efficiency and an almost total loss in personal liberty, is to lose the results of our heritage. The right to "life, liberty, and the pursuit of happiness" is gone when the dictator comes. He is a poor American who says, "what this country needs is a dictator."

Coming and Going

Address on Columbus Day, October 12, 1925,
Frankfort, Kentucky

FOUR hundred years after the discovery of America by Columbus, the world Columbian Exposition was opened in Chicago
with pomp and ceremony. The only evidence there of the part
played by Columbus in the drama of world exploration was the
presence of three ships, replicas of the *Santa Maria*, *Pinta*, and
Nina, that had been sailed to America from Portugal. Proof of
four centuries of progress, however, had been gathered from every
part of the globe. Nation vied with nation to show its greatness to
the millions who came to see and marvel.

In four centuries from an America of savage people, sparsely
inhabited, a continent had been conquered; great cities had been
built; communication by rail, water, and wire established; governments evolved; and nations created. These were accomplishments
worthy of the wonderful exhibitions housed in beautiful buildings,
buildings that were the materialization of the dreams living in the
minds of the architects and artists of the land.

The year 1893 stood midway in the course of time between the
Franco-Prussian War and the World War. It was still five years
before the Spanish-American conflict and ten years before the
Boer War would disturb the British people. The time was one of
peace; however the unrest due to economic conditions, the battle
over monetary standards, and the wrangling of nations in the contest for world commerce were the beginnings of the great revolutionary upheavals of the twentieth century. The achievements of
the era were truly marvelous. Indeed it was a fitting tribute to
the progress of four centuries that the exposition in 1893 placed
before the people of the world almost unbelievable evidences of
the works of art and science.

Not very far from the city of Genoa in the spring of 1446,
Christopher Columbus was born. In many ways the century in which
Columbus appeared was in its spirit not unlike that of the nine-
teenth. It was a period of awakening. Leonardo da Vinci had

painted, made discoveries, created inventions, pried into the mysteries of nature, and stirred the minds of men. Copernicus looked into the heavens and formulated the idea that replaced the Ptolemaic theory of the universe. The Turks by the capture of Constantinople in 1453 closed the eastern trade routes and made the Mediterranean an Ottoman lake. Men of the West turned to the Atlantic for an outlet to the East. Marco Polo had visited China. The world was no longer flat. It was a sphere, and the way to the East was by the West.

In this thrilling fifteenth century Columbus was born. Serving a short time in his father's business of carder and weaver of wool, he became a sailor, visited the southern ports of the Mediterranean, and made voyages to England and Iceland. His interest centered more and more in maps and globes; in his mind he dreamed of an Asia beyond the seas to the West. The story of his disappointments and voyages is known to the schoolboys of today.

We are gathered here in his honor to commemorate his deeds and to glorify his courage and vision. Four hundred and thirty-three years ago he discovered America. Since then the spirit of Columbus marches on, and America has steadily come into the heritage of a vast continent with its stretches of fertile land and enormous treasures of minerals. The days of discovery, of exploring, and of pioneering have passed; it is no longer a new land in which we live. Columbus came and is gone. America is built, and the beginning time has been written down in history. Mindful of the past we turn to the future to ask the question, whither is America going?

Perhaps somewhere in America a new Columbus, a new leader, has been born who will point the unknown way to the reorganization and the rearrangement of the world. In the swamps of Germany a thousand years ago the "folk moot" evolved the first principles of representative government; and it is not for nothing that a League of Nations and a World Court have been established in the twentieth century. Beginnings there must always be. Columbus had the perception of a spherical world. He saw the coasts of America, but he could not see a Republic of more than a hundred millions of people governed by the people themselves. Just as Columbus had a dream of a new world of fabulous wealth, so we can visualize this hemisphere great and powerful in the centuries to come.

Are we failing to see, beyond that power and greatness, the spiritual and intellectual part America must play in international affairs? Are we realizing that the world cannot again be as it has been in the past four centuries? It has become a different world even in the thirty years since the Columbian Exposition. Events move fast, and inventions open the way to new accomplishments. Because of steamship, cable, radio, and railroad, it is a smaller world than Columbus' world. It is more difficult than his world, more complicated, and more intricate. It is a world in which men must see as they have never seen before, a world in which thought and vision must rule, a world which must banish savagery and learn to govern itself lest the great Frankenstein of scientific discoveries which it has made fall upon it and destroy it.

Columbus came. He knew not to what his journeys might take him. The goal to which we are moving may also be infinitely greater than that which we anticipate. However, the qualities of vision, courage, persistency, and intelligence that led Columbus in his day are just as necessary now as then. Said the Proverbs of old, "Where there is no vision, the people perish"; so too America must have vision as she goes into the future.

The Fourth of July

Radio address over WHAS, July 4, 1929

I sat the other day in a grandstand overlooking a parade ground. In the middle of the field a great flag staff supported the stars and stripes lazily floating in the air. Now and then the wind extended the flag showing the thirteen stripes and the forty-eight stars and the red, white, and blue of our national colors. High in the sky the clouds, tinted with cerulean blue, purple, pink, and even red, formed and marched in gorgeous processions.

This magnificent view of the flag as it floated that afternoon in the sunshine seemed to parallel the place of the United States of America in the affairs of the world. A mental picture formed in my mind of the progress, the hopes, the ideals, and the accomplishments of a people.

This is the Fourth of July, the anniversary of the beginning of our national life. One hundred and fifty-three years have passed since the day, now celebrated as the birthday of the nation, had its origin. Much has happened in that time. The territory of the country has expanded to the Pacific Ocean and into the islands of the seas. The people have grown in number from three millions to one hundred and twenty-five millions. The government, begun and administered in a feeble way, is now vigorous and strong, accepted by the people, and respected abroad. The growth has been amazing, interesting, vital.

To us, a great power today, the little beginnings of the United States in 1776 may seem small indeed, but they were freighted with importance. Celebrations for one hundred and fifty years have modified the intensity of feeling that accompanied the earlier times when noise, hilarity, disorder, and oratory were plentiful. Then it was the day of days, but now the Fourth of July is a national holiday quietly celebrated by the individual rather than by the community. It is still important, but the story is forgotten; as the sons and grandsons of those who lived in the days when the nation was in the making have died, the romance and the picture have become less vivid and impressive.

There is then justification in telling what happened when the Declaration of Independence was adopted by the Continental Congress and the United States of America was born. The situation in the colonies in political relations with the Mother Country had been under criticism and sharp condemnation for several years. Early in 1776 the legislatures of North Carolina and Virginia had proposed a resolution calling for separation; it remained, however, for Richard Henry Lee to move the session of the Continental Congress "That these United Colonies are, and of a Right ought to be, Free and Independent States." John Adams of Massachusetts seconded the resolution. This was on the seventh of June, 1776. Debate followed. The conservatives were astonished, and the proponents, sensing the necessity of agreement, accepted the postponement of action for three weeks.

Meantime, a committee consisting of Thomas Jefferson, John Adams, Benjamin Franklin, Roger Sherman, and Robert R. Livingston was appointed to draft a resolution; and Thomas Jefferson was asked to write the statement. Jefferson thus became the author of the Declaration of Independence. Without waiting for the committee resolution, Congress voted on the second of July, 1776 the Richard Henry Lee motion, "That these United Colonies are, and of a Right ought to be, Free and Independent States." Ten states voted affirmatively. New York did not vote and Pennsylvania and Delaware cast divided votes. The Jefferson resolution being completed, the report of the committee was presented to Congress on the fourth of July. The resolution was adopted on that day, but the vote was not finished until the ninth of July when the New York legislature voted yes. However, delay in carrying the record to Philadelphia held back the announcement of the acceptance of all the states until the fifteenth of that month.

No signatures were attached to the document on the fourth of July; and it was not until the second day of August, 1776 that the instrument we call the Declaration of Independence was signed by the representatives of the colonies. There was one exception in the case of Thomas McKean, who did not sign on that date. His signature was not attached until 1781 when by act of Congress he was allowed to sign the famous resolution because he had been present on the second of July.

Jefferson's draft and the resolution when it was adopted in its final form were practically the same. The Declaration of Independence consists of three parts: a statement of the political principles upon which the new nation was founded; a long list of charges against the King of Great Britain; and the declaration "That these United Colonies are, and of a Right ought to be, Free and Independent States" with the closing solemn statement that "with a firm reliance upon the Protection of a Divine Providence, we mutually pledge to each other our Lives, our Fortunes and our sacred Honor."

By this Declaration of Independence "a state for the first time in history founded its life on democratic idealism, pronouncing governments to exist for securing the happiness of the people and to derive their just powers from the consent of the governed." The American Revolution was a democratic movement, and this document was the instrument which set forth the principles of the Revolution. It gave the people recognition equivalent to promises which, as fast as the new government was instituted, were converted by the written Constitution into rights. All these principles are set forth in the first part of the second paragraph of the Declaration of Independence. It has been read and repeated many times, and it should be learned by every American.

"We hold these truths to be self-evident, that all men are created equal, that they are endowed by their Creator with certain unalienable Rights, that among these are Life, Liberty, and the pursuit of Happiness. That to secure these rights, Governments are instituted among Men, deriving their just powers from the consent of the governed. That whenever any Form of Government becomes destructive to these ends, it is the Right of the People to alter or abolish it, and to institute new Government, laying its foundations upon such principles and organizing its powers in such form, as to them shall seem most likely to effect their Safety and Happiness."

Many things have been said about the Declaration of Independence. It has even been called "a document of platitudes." In reply to this comment Madison said the object of the instrument was not to discover truths but to assert them and to implement the purposes for which the people were striving. The fathers of the Revolution having in mind economic and political changes gave to the people of this land an ideal principle for the government of the nation.

The formulation and adoption of the Declaration of Independence were received with enthusiasm throughout the colonies. When the news was announced, the Liberty Bell, which is now a sacred emblem enshrined in Independence Hall in Philadelphia, rang out the good news. The rejoicing was widespread; the militia paraded, bonfires were made, and feasts were held to honor the occasion. The contrast of a Fourth of July today with the celebrations of an earlier time is indeed apparent. To make a noise and to have much oratory are not necessary; however, we can and should keep in our own hearts the significant truths set forth in the Declaration of Independence.

The Greatest Sin in America

Chapel talk, North Carolina College for Women, Greensboro,
November, 1931

THINKING about what I should say to you on an occasion like this, I decided that I should talk to you about the greatest sin in America. What in your own mind is the greatest sin in America? Some of us might say that it is the disregarding of the prohibition law. There are others who would say that the violation of that law is much like the violation of the colonial act which taxed tea in America and that they are bound by duty to break it. That viewpoint I do not concede or accept. There are others who would say that playing cards is the greatest sin because it is associated with gambling and that when you bet upon racing you are committing one of the chief sins of America. Others might say that profanity and the debasing of the mind by the use of obscene words may be the greatest sin. One might say, too, that theft of money and of property by officers high in the public confidence of the community or the stealing of money from orphans and widows is possibly the greatest sin.

Without elaborating further upon these viewpoints, may I say that I have fixed in my own mind that the greatest sin in America is disloyalty, not disloyalty to country in the usual sense because most Americans are loyal to their flag and to their country. Most of them are loyal to the Constitution in so far as they know anything about it and understand it. Most of them are law-abiding in the main. Nevertheless there is a spirit of disloyalty running through our American people.

A man is disloyal who accepts a public office and debases it to selfish interests or to the interests of a special group at the cost and at the expense of the people of the commonwealth. Wherever that man may be, that man is disloyal to his own conscience, to his country, to his oath of office, and to his fellow citizens. He is disloyal to the posterity that is to come in that he has not fulfilled his trusts and his obligations.

And the man who as head of a great business concern uses that position for the purpose of grinding the poor, of taking advantage of his competitors in an unethical way, of doing things within his power that are not good for his community or for the nation or for his fellowmen is disloyal. He has discredited his own heart and mind and the best of the training that is in him in order to bring about that fundamentally selfish and unethical thing.

We may proceed further to say that the teacher is disloyal who in his capacity as a leader of youth fails to give to youth all that he possibly can, who fails to be a student of his subject, who fails to take into consideration the lives and purposes of those who come to him. He is disloyal to the best that ought to be in his profession and his calling and to the ideal that has always been held in regard to the responsibility, the opportunity, and the obligation of the teacher.

The student is disloyal who coming from home accepts her parents' money to pay her expenses, who wastes her time, who fools along, and uses her time and money for purposes other than those for which she came to the institution—that student is disloyal to herself, to her conscience, to her heart, to her parents, to her commonwealth. We are all disloyal when we fail to meet the obligations, the requirements, and the purposes which we ought to have before us.

As we think of the problems here in America, of a people faced with questions and difficulties and opportunities, we realize that loyalty in heart and purpose to the things we are trying to do is required of all.

The lawyer, for instance, who accepts his client's fee and who abuses his confidence debases the law. He is disloyal to his client, to his community, to the state, and to himself. The legislator who, accepting the obligations of representing his community and of legislating for his state, fails to carry out by the use of his mind, the use of his conscience, the use of such abilities as he possesses the trust imposed in him is disloyal. Because he has failed to do the very best for the state, to push aside venal things, and to work for the accomplishment of his commonwealth, he has committed a great sin.

To me the greatest sin of our time here in America is not the violation of this or that law, though there is disloyalty associated with such violation, but rather the feeling that we as individuals may have personal advantages, that we may get certain results from our failure to meet the obligations of the community in which we live. We hope to obtain some sort of selfish benefits in the form of money, of prestige, of standing, or of whatever it may be through our deficiency in coming up to the requirements that are placed upon us.

In all of these American colleges, a thousand or more scattered throughout the land, are a million and a quarter students who, if they were filled with the spirit of loyalty, could bring to pass in this great nation of ours almost any result that might be desired. Here in our commonwealths we have difficult problems. These problems require that we shall think, that we shall use our minds, that we shall be informed, and being informed that we shall try to do the best we can by our attitudes, by our influence, and by our purpose to bring about the highest good of our communities. If the college students, for instance, are not to have that high ethical viewpoint regarding their responsibilities, then the colleges have not met the situation for which they were created. Yet it is not in the colleges alone that this loyalty can be brought about but also through the community, the church, the home. It is necessary for the student to bring into her relationships everywhere as a student, as a member of a community, as a member of a family this sense of loyalty. Then she is a loyal citizen of her commonwealth and of her nation.

The other day one of the newspaper editorials in my state deplored the fact that a constitutional amendment had failed to pass because it had not received the minimum number of votes required by law. In one city out of a hundred and twenty thousand voters, some thirteen thousand voted on the amendment. The amendment concerned a constitutional convention. The paper went on to say that it was depressing indeed to realize that, in a time like this in regard to a matter so important, only one-tenth of the voters in that city should express themselves either positively or negatively.

I think that one reason for this seeming inertia is that we no longer have fervent discussion of politics in America. In the days of the Revolution and of the formation of the Constitution, every man was discussing the question of the Constitution: What it meant? How was it to work? How it was to get on? How it could actually be established? For many, many years before and after the adoption of the Constitution, political discussion of a high order was prevalent in America. The Missouri Compromise, the Louisiana Purchase, the problems leading to the War Between the States, all these were occasions for constant argument, North and South. In these differences in regard to the various constitutional obligations and difficulties, in matters involving economic, social, and ethical problems, the discussions created an enlightened and an energetic public opinion.

Since the beginning of 1900 and even as early as 1890, no constitutional questions with the exception of the eighteenth and nineteenth amendments have arisen as subjects for heated controversy. We have stopped talking about political organizations and purposes. The state is taken for granted. We have become a people of acquiescence, of merely accepting "what is," and of allowing government to go along as it is without change or modification. We allow certain groups to control the town, the commonwealth, and the nation with a consequence that the people take what is given to them without thinking very much about it. No democracy can continue on such a basis.

One of the obligations of college students is to know something about the history of their country, to understand the Constitution both of the states and of the nation, and to keep in mind their rights, privileges, and liberties. To do this involves the real responsibilities of citizenship. Where and when we have failed to meet those obligations, we are disloyal in principle, in heart, and in conscience to the fundamental purposes that make us a nation.

So I say that the great difficulty which confronts us here in America today is the sin of disloyalty. Other sins may not touch us, or, if they do, we may have no part in them. To the extent that we are indifferent to our business obligations, to our standards as professional men and women, to our opportunities as college students, and to our duties as citizens of the nation, we have failed in our responsibilities and we are disloyal to the best principles that ought to prevail. Our hope is as time goes on that in this American life may develop a more enlightened conscience, a loftier attitude, a higher ethical purpose that will make us not disloyal but loyal to ourselves, to our fellowmen, to our state, and to our nation.

The Engineer and Society

Summary of commencement address, Chrysler Engineering Institute, Detroit, Michigan, June, 1934

T H O S E things that we think of as typical of the twentieth century, such as great inventions, modern machines, and the medical accomplishments, had their beginnings in small ways centuries ago. The clock was the forerunner of the great machines of today. Only through perfection of gears, pinions, and escapements have the motors of the present become a reality.

Behind these machines are to be found the scientists whose work the inventors have made into a practical whole. The radio owes its realization to Clark, Maxwell, and Hertz. The dynamo required the principles developed by Faraday before it could reach the possibilities now inherent in it. Out of such beginnings came the great industrial age of which we speak in terms of awe.

Social and economic attitudes and adaptations have not followed the enormous mechanical advances. We still have slums, and poverty raises its head among us. Everywhere men are using a social organization produced by earlier ages and not adapted to the time in which we live. The automobile is hampered by roads built for old usage. Our towns still cling around centers making living difficult and a satisfactory life for the mass of mankind almost impossible. Our tax systems adhere to methods in use hundreds of years ago. Town building is measured by the size of lots and by real estate ventures. Everywhere vested interests in things hold us back. Somebody or something stands in the way, and we go on trying to fit new techniques to an old order. The techniques of today are way beyond our most extensive use of them. The engineer is thus fettered by an old and outworn system. He cannot use the techniques he knows to their full power because they are unable to function efficiently in the social and economic conditions under which we live.

The great engineer is by nature a dreamer. He ought to see the need for a better order because the free play of his technical knowledge and the utilization of all that such knowledge promises depend upon the application of understanding, imagination, and work to the world of today. Progress is deterred by politics, governmental procedures, social organization, and education. If all these look backward instead of to the new day, the dream of the engineer and of the industrial planner cannot come true. The day of miracles may again come to pass when men will see a world that is equipped not only with the technical facilities which will bring them more leisure and less drudgery but also with the intelligent minds, the spirit of adventure, and the social attitudes that will enable them to use these facilities wisely and well.

If the engineer is interested only in gears and pinions of machines, he as the wise one of his generation can expect from his efforts much less than he would hope. When the engineer realizes fully that the conditions of society make possible the use of his machines, he must of necessity do his part in the leading of the mass of mankind to the understanding of the present day with all of its implications. The old obstacles of outgrown conditions must be pushed from the way of progress. Men must look to an order that goes along with the new techniques. Otherwise the engineer is merely cluttering the world with machines and remains a mechanic and not an engineer.

We Must Know National Trends

Address to Semicentennial Anniversary Convocation, Rollins College,
Winter Park, Florida, November 4, 1935

DURING the last five years, four words have appeared with increasing frequency in the daily press and in the periodicals. These words are fascism, socialism, communism, and regulation. Behind each word is a definition and a philosophy.

Fascism has been defined by a student of the subject as the maintenance of capitalism by force. Socialism looks to the direction and ownership of large industries by the state. There are, however, many phases of socialism, and it is to be found in one type or another in nearly every land on the globe. The conduct of the government by the proletariat is the essence of communism, which is established for the benefit of all without profit and which requires state production and state distribution of the production of the country. Regulation is a policy that frankly recognizes the continuance of the profit system with the use of government regulation so that industry will yield a profit, will serve the people, and will give scope to individual enterprise.

Under the principles involved in fascism, all classes, all organizations, and all the people are enlisted by compulsion in the service of the state. Looked upon as an organism, the state in its actions transcends the individual or any group. The state is in fact not only an economic unit but also a political and a moral entity. The moral law is the state law, and the interests of individuals are subordinated to the interests of the state. Under fascism political liberty as we know it cannot exist. Private enterprise, although recognized, is directed by the government in regard to organization, capital, management, labor, and output. The labor union disappears, and labor is organized under a system of guilds.

The fascist movement in Italy was in its beginning directed against the socialists and syndicalists who were attempting to control the political situation of the state. The purpose was to freeze the capitalist structure of society so that the older vested interests might be safe and might be protected against the seizure of their property by the proletariat. Because the example of Russia was before them, the leaders in this effort of the fascists had at least the nominal support of the capitalist group.

Germany is another example of the fascist movement. What is going on in that country attracts the attention of the world, and what the future will be is a matter of concern to all of Europe. From 1871 to 1914 Germany advanced from a group of small states into a great world power. Germany is a country with poor resources but with a gifted and industrious population. She has been compelled to import raw materials used in making the finished goods for export, and she knows that her very existence depends on foreign markets. Before 1914 German goods were desirable but hardly necessary; consequently, the nation was distinctly dependent upon the international situation. Although the World War upset her foreign relations, yet the country had made such substantial recovery of its losses from the war that in 1924-1928 Germany had become again a considerable factor in world trade.

The world depression, however, brought a great decline in international commerce and caused living conditions in Germany to become almost intolerable. The attitude of the Nazis, emphasizing their own narrow interests, made the situation still worse. Credit declined, sales went down, and Germany was faced with an unfavorable trade balance. Moreover, unemployment had been steadily increasing since 1928. The proletariat dissatisfaction was becoming desperate; the conflict between peasant and junker disturbed the agricultural situation; and under the resulting economic conditions the great middle class lost both capital and security.

Following the World War, Germany had established the Weimar Constitution and the Republic. The democratic group lost control of state affairs in part because they did not assert themselves and displace the old regime; the socialist party broke down; the conservatives disintegrated; and students in the universities who could not find employment opposed the Weimar Constitution and the Republic. The unfairness of the Versailles Treaty, as interpreted by Germany, was blamed in that country for the general breakdown in government and morale. The Nazi organization took advantage of this situation and outmanoeuvred the conservatives and the socialists. Since from time to time there had been threats of communism, the reaction was toward the support of the Nazi group led by Hitler. Hitler in turn used nationalistic ideas to stir the people to accept the fascist state. In Germany a dictatorship rules the nation.

Fascism in Italy, as well as in Germany, is at the crossroads of a new development. Will fascism move in the direction of an economic democracy with wider interest in the affairs of the state by the people, or will it move in the direction of a new feudalism in which the people will become serfs of an industrial state?

Socialism, speaking broadly, has two particular principles upon which it stands. The first of these is that a national minimum standard of living to apply generally is to be enforced in order that there will be no underprivileged people in the state. The second principle of socialism is the common ownership of the means of production and the democratic control of industry. Those who produce are to have a part in the direction of the industries; the means of transportation and communication, as well as the raw materials required for production, are to be nationalized; and capitalistic enterprises where they exist outside of state ownership will be controlled by constant audits of accounts and by supervision of the business.

In England a modified form of socialism has been in existence for a number of years; it has steadily grown in its power to influence the purposes of the state. Great Britain has learned through its long years of experience that much can be done in modifying institutions while allowing the name of such institutions to go unchanged. Perhaps the English situation can be told briefly by citing their governmental endeavors. They, like some of the other peoples, are attempting to establish a fair standard of living. Private property and private industry are to be regarded as a part of the national organization and to be carried on as cooperative enterprises to the extent that unfair practices regarding wages, prices, and methods will no longer continue and excessive profits will go to the state. The social provisions for the care of the people are to include old age pensions and insurance against ill health and unemployment. Taxation is to be used to bring the social surplus under the control of the people as represented in the national government. And, finally, the causes of war are to be removed, and peace is to be maintained through national cooperation.

For sixteen years now the present regime has continued in Russia where is to be found the longest and most complete attempt to bring into existence the extreme form of centralized government called communism. There is also the attempt to make an agricultural nation into an industrial one. Classes in society must be obliterated, and the proletariat must be organized to deal with a new Russia. Adaptations have made the plan much more suited to the world situation and possibly to present day human temperament than it was in 1917.

In Italy and Germany where the fascist system has been successful, a strong middle class stood between the proletariat and the control of the state. In Russia where this bulwark was missing, the weak middle class of the nation was easily shoved aside. The communist party took over the revolution and thereby obtained complete control of industry.

The problems, however, of the new Russia were by no means easy of solution. When the farming peasant refused to give up his surplus to the state, although this refusal brought on a conflict of authority, the national economic policy was adhered to. The early control of industries by workers was accomplished. Later money came back into use, and now the worker is paid on the bonus and piece system. In 1927 in order to stem the movement toward private industry, a new social offensive was set up in which greater emphasis was placed on state farming. Extended discipline and control over economic life were effected by a complete system of price fixing and by various taxation schemes.

Russia, in this period when she was moving from an agricultural nation to an industrial one, was confronted with ineffectual workmen, a lack of skilled labor, and the deterioration of machinery; naturally the country suffered from a poor quality of output. Within the last few years the industries have become more efficiently run and are producing a fair quality of goods. Whatever may be our attitude toward communism and the experiment in Russia, we are forced to admit that much of interest and of accomplishment has come out of that land in the past sixteen years.

In an article in *Foreign Affairs* for April, 1934 Trotsky asks, "How may the economic unity of Europe be guaranteed while preserving the complete freedom of cultural development to the people living there? How may Europe be included within a coordinated world economy?" The attempt now, he says, is to subordinate that economy to the outdated nationalistic state.

Fearful of other states and confused by the intricacy of the world depression, statesmen all over Europe are closing the doors, pulling down the blinds, and developing the isolationist attitude. The spirit of self-preservation rules in the council chambers with emphasis on the domination of the political body. Communism faces, it thinks, a hostile world that in the end must come to the acceptance of that philosophy. Trotsky's comments look far into the future where there must be economic unity in Europe with the preservation of the cultural heritages of the centuries.

The spread of reactionary nationalism goes beyond the confines of Europe. East of Russia on her Siberian border is Manchukuo, a land under the protectorate of Japan. With fifty million people in a group of islands that possess little arable land, Japan has sought an outlet on the mainland; this she has acquired by seizure. The process of expansion goes on, with possibilities of conflict with the Soviet Republic on the border of Manchukuo. Japan has had until recently a monarchy with a constitutional parliament; but the rights of parliament have been subordinated, and Japan is now a fascist state with domination by army and navy groups. Fascism there has not been carried to the limits that are to be observed in Italy and Germany since the capital structure continues to have freedom as before and the organization of labor has not proceeded to great lengths. However, from the point of view of the condition of the people, Japan is distinctly fascist. A conflict between fascist and communistic states appears to be in the making in Asia.

Regulation is used to define what is taking place in the United States. In this country we are attempting to retain the framework of our accustomed social and economic life and to build within it a stable and progressive country. We desire equality and justice in economic life. The National Recovery Authority program with all of its different ramifications, with perhaps here and there some of the phases of socialism, and with procedures that are strange and untried here shows no definite indication of putting the nation under a dictatorship. We hope to produce recovery by control through the processes· of studying and of analyzing our problems and through the cooperation of labor and capital, of the government and the people. It is, in fact, a social planning process and does not mean dictatorship or fascism or communism.

Under the emergency powers of the NRA an attempt has been made to bring about cooperative action among trade groups, to produce united action of labor and management, to eliminate unfair practices, and to regulate prices and hours of labor in order that there may be a profit for the employer and a reasonable wage for the worker. In considering regulation in the United States, one must necessarily call attention to the purposes and the necessity of bringing the nation to a status of recovery and of furnishing greater opportunities for all the people. Progress has been effected in both purposes. Moreover, revolution by violence may be said to be an academic question in the United States and probably will remain so for the simple reason that the determination of national policy rests in the final analysis with the people.

It is true that, although some of the factors which appear in a revolution may be found to exist in this country, they are not in sufficient force or sequence to produce a violent governmental upheaval. Of the five phases in revolutionary procedures—first, discontent leading to revolt; second, the consolidation of the revolt by a central group; third, the maintenance of the central group by force and the elimination of the discordant factions by stringent methods; fourth, the centralization and unification of the revolution so that the controlling agency is in full power; and fifth, the setting up of a program of action—may it not be said that in the United States we have arrived at the last point without going through the disorganizing, bloody stages of the earlier periods?

We have reached a program of action in the United States. We are analyzing and formulating in an attempt to establish a normal procedure for dealing in an effective way with the problems of the nation. The important part of this whole movement is the adequacy of the program which must in the final analysis be placed upon sound economic and ethical bases.

The two bases—that of economics and that of ethics—are not necessarily coordinate. A sound economic organization might be based on slavery with economic security but without freedom. The capitalistic system provides for freedom of individual action but does not sustain in itself a security of livelihood and of maintenance. The problem, therefore, becomes both an economic one and an ethical one. How are the forces that work for production and the forces that operate for justice to be included at the same time in the framework of our government?

That hazy and indefinite thing called the national income is a very important factor in the well-being of a people. This income is affected by tariffs, wars, strikes, taxation, philanthropy, extravagance, and government expenditures. In fact, the welfare of a people depends upon their work, labor, savings, and habits. The distribution of the national income is affected by many influences such as laws of inheritance, systems of taxation, banking provisions, monopolies, distributive methods of trade, labor unions, education, and standards of living. Many of these forces work automatically;

others are enforced through the power of government; and others by the control of organizations determine where the national income shall go. Admittedly no central wisdom conceived by man can govern all these forces at one time; however, a resolution to understand and to guide the general movement of national fortunes must exist if a people are not to fall by their own devices.

The important point now is the fact that the desirability of such a purpose is generally recognized and that the effort is being made to find the procedure that will open the enigma of national and world economic conditions. Although the method of trial and error is costly and disappointing, yet in the absence of accepted methods it may be all that can be hoped for now. Dependence in these changing times upon a formula that may have worked well in the past will spell failure because both ethical and economic considerations are in the present problem.

Vast numbers of the population of this great nation are underprivileged, ill fed, and badly housed. The underlying cause of unrest is the horrid uncertainty of wage payments which in turn brings on makeshift devices to keep life going. The nation, therefore, must enforce housing regulations, sanitation, safety of life and provide means of caring for the unfit, the incapacitated, and the old. These are ethical considerations on an economic basis. The government must also see that justice is done and that fraud and dishonesty are eliminated in order that the national income cannot be raided by those who are not entitled to the shares that they take. This is a tremendous program, ethical in intent but dependent squarely on the solution of the economic problems of the United States.

Various proposals for realizing this course have been made, such as the raising of wages, the staggering of work, the creating of employment, and the placing of withdrawn laborers on the dole. The New Deal in part is based upon the notion that high wages and high prices will produce prosperity; however, there must be a profit for the producer and security for the worker. Wages are fundamentally related to prices. It is impossible to pay more than is produced, and nothing can set this economic law aside. Capital will not be accumulated, nor will it operate, without a profit. The accepted way out is to open the means of production and maintain the idea of a fair wage that will not be subjected to the uncertainties of the old procedure. How to accomplish this is, as I think of it, the problem of our country. Neither fascism nor communism is the answer. Only guidance, hard thinking, careful action, and patience will solve the difficulties.

In Italy, in Germany, and in Russia a certain group seized the power of government and used that power to bend the economic organization to the wishes of the group. Thus fascism is a group capitalistic movement, and communism is a group proletarian one. The United States of America in her desire to maintain the original structure of democracy is not willing to permit the government to fall into the hands of any one group. Through modification and regulation the United States of America hopes to realize that ideal of the founders of our nation, "Equality of opportunity for all," and that belief of a later American, "Government of the people, by the people, for the people."

Drifts in National Living

Address to the National Council, General Federation of Women's Clubs, Miami, Florida, April 29, 1936

IN THE book, *The Bridge of San Luis Rey*, by Thornton Wilder, Brother Juniper is left disconsolate and greatly disturbed when the bridge falls carrying with it some of his friends and acquaintances into the chasm below. He cannot understand why God has punished these friends of his, and he feels that there must be something behind the tragedy which can only be explained by the secret sins of those who were destroyed. Firm in his belief that God acts only for reasons, he begins a careful investigation of the lives of the people who were killed when the bridge fell. He follows the story of the great lady and her maid, looks into the life of Uncle Pio, and searches out the history of the others even to the comings and goings of the muleteer who lost his life when he started to cross the bridge.

At the end of his investigations he finds that none of these people had committed great sins; they had their peccadilloes, and some strayings from the path of righteousness were all that he discovered. They were a rather kindly group, friendly, courageous, and on the whole helpful. Why then did God destroy them? The only conclusion that he could come to was that some things were beyond the understanding of human knowledge and that there was some purpose that the individual mind could not see. So he came to the conclusion that God acts in mysterious ways unknown to man.

In our own land the bridge across the economic chasm which lies between prosperity and industry fell in the great depression. It carried with it many persons, fortunes, and possessions. It was a catastrophe that cast the nation into gloom, slowed up its activities everywhere, and brought a feeling of chaos and uncertainty to millions of people.

Some asked why this calamity had been brought upon us. We are on the whole a God-fearing people, they said; we have tried to do right. We have followed to the best of our knowledge the purposes of national life. Others knew pretty well what the reasons were for the difficulties and why the disaster had fallen upon the nation. They pointed out the errors that had been committed, the mistakes that had been made, and the follies that stood in the way of understanding. They showed the nation drunk with wealth-getting. Some prescribers went farther and said the only way out of the situation was to bring in a powerful, competent man who could tell the people what to do. The type of government which we have and the ideas that we possess, the whole attempt to rule the nation by a debating society, they declared, had failed; and there was need of direction. They spoke of dictators and proclaimed that democracy had broken down and had covered itself with graft and misdirection.

There were those who turned the pages of history and looking through the letters of Lord Macaulay found one to the Honorable

H. B. Randall of New York. Bearing the date of May 23, 1857, this letter of warning written nearly eighty years ago pointed out clearly what Macaulay prophesied would happen to us. In this letter Lord Macaulay declared that in his opinion the placing of the supreme authority of the state in the possession of the majority of the citizens is to put it into the hands of the "poorest and most ignorant part of society"; moreover, he maintained that "institutions purely democratic must sooner or later destroy liberty or civilization, or both." He specified that in France the Revolution of 1848 attempted to establish a pure democracy. "During a short time there was a strong reason to expect a general spoliation, a national bankruptcy, a new partition of the soil, a maximum of prices, a ruinous load of taxation laid upon the rich for the purpose of supporting the poor in idleness . . . Happily," he wrote, "the danger was averted; and now there is a despotism, a silent tribune, an enslaved press; liberty is gone, but civilization has been saved."

He was writing in 1857, it is to be remembered: "I have not the smallest doubt that if we had a purely democratic government here, the effect would be the same. Either the poor would plunder the rich, and civilization would perish, or order and property would be saved by the strong military government and liberty would perish." Continuing, he said, "You may think that your country enjoys an exemption from these evils. I will frankly own to you that I am of a very different opinion. Your fate I believe to be certain, though it is deferred by physical cause. As long as you have a boundless extent of fertile and unoccupied land, your laboring population will be more at ease than the laboring population of the Old World; . . . But the time will come when New England will be as thickly populated as Old England. Wages will be low, and will fluctuate as much with you as with us. You will have your Manchesters and Birminghams. Hundreds and thousands of artisans will assuredly be sometimes out of work. Then your institutions will be fairly brought to the test. Distress everywhere makes the laborer mutinous and discontented, and inclines him to listen with eagerness to agitators who tell him that it is a monstrous iniquity that one man should have a million while another cannot get a full meal."

In England, he wrote, "The supreme power is in the hands of a class, numerous indeed, but select of an educated class . . . deeply interested in the security of property and the maintenance of order. Accordingly, the malcontents are firmly yet gently restrained . . . The bad time is got over without robbing the wealthy to relieve the indigent . . . I have seen England three or four times pass through such critical seasons as I have described.

"Through such seasons the United States will have to pass, in the course of the next century, if not of this. How will you pass through them? I heartily wish you a good deliverance . . . It is quite plain that your government will never be able to restrain a distressed and discontented majority. For with you the majority is the government, and has the rich, who are always a minority, absolutely at its mercy. The day will come when . . . a multitude of people will choose the legislature . . . On one side is a statesman preaching patience, respect for vested rights, strict observance of public faith. On the other is a demagogue ranting about the tyranny of capitalists and usurers, and asking why anybody should be permitted to drink champagne and to ride in a carriage while thousands of honest people are in want of necessaries. Which of the two candidates is likely to be preferred by the working man who hears his children cry for bread?, I seriously apprehend that you will, in some such season of adversity as I have described, do things which will prevent prosperity from returning; that you will act like people in a year of scarcity, devour all the seed corn, and thus make the next year a year not of scarcity but of absolute failure. There will be, I fear, spoliation . . . There is nothing to stay you. Your constitution is all sail and no anchor. As I said before when society has entered on its downward progress either civilization or liberty must perish. Either some Caesar or Napoleon will seize the reins of government with a strong hand, or your Republic will be as fearfully plundered and laid waste by the barbarians in the twentieth century as the Roman Empire was in the fifth; with this difference, that the Huns and Vandals who ravaged the Roman Empire came from without. . . ."

This letter has been given rather widespread circulation in the United States during the last four years. Many people believe the letter well describes the conditions in our land, and so they look to the strong man to preserve us and hold together such civilization as we have. They know that liberty will be lost if the dictator comes; however, they are willing to give up liberty for the maintenance of civilization and more probably of special privileges.

These persons turn to the record of democracy and see in it only incompetence, cumbersome government, and lack of effectiveness. They point to the waste of public funds, the making of unholy contracts, and the pillaging of the people by those in the possession of power. The cynical and mean picture that they draw undoubtedly loses sight of many fundamental things and forgets the story of democracy and what it has accomplished.

There are evidences in this world right now of what the dictator has done and what the people have lost when he comes into power. My purpose at this time is not to discuss the reasons for the appearing of dictators in many lands. To point out that they are here is sufficient. One may turn to the story of Italy, the land of much sunshine and shadow, a land that has contributed to the beautiful in art, music, and literature and to the enriched memory and happiness of the world. But now it is a land under a dictator. Trains run on time in Italy, the streets are cleaner, beggars are banned from the public squares, and obscene language and profanity are forbidden; but freedom does not exist in Italy. All that one has and is must be contributed to the state. Whatever a man says or does depends on the action of the state. The state fixes the moral and the civil law and tells the citizens when to come and to go.

And again in Germany a dictator rules. One may speak of a people discouraged, whose self-respect is gone and who are distressed by the economic conditions existing in the land, as a justification for a dictatorship; and it may be that Germany must pass through such a period in her history, but liberty is gone in Germany in the democratic sense. Men are told that their lives and property belong to the state. The state is the ultimate end of all that is. The philosophy that the highest development of the individual is the hope of civilization has no meaning in Germany. Music, philosophy, science are subordinate to the state. Religion is tolerated only as the instrument of the state. Liberty has disappeared.

And if we turn to a smaller country nearer our own shores for another example of the dictator, we find there a nation that has also been forced into the surrender of its land and its rights. In the Dominican Republic a dictatorship exists. It may be on the whole a benevolent one, but it is in full control of supplies and has taken over monopolies of light, power, and food. All the revenues from these sources go into the coffers of the dictator. The citizens cannot protest lest they lose what they have but must wait patiently for better times.

In other lands dictators rule, as in Japan where the people under a fascist government have little liberty in the modern sense of the word.

We do have difficulties in this America of ours. We are careless of our citizenship and indifferent to its obligations. We have forgotten our history and the long heritage that has come to us. Yet we have in America a constitutional government. We believe that the happiness of the individual is the end and that the purpose of the state is to forward the well-being of all the people. We have freedom to speak and to write; we have freedom of religious thought and freedom of assembly. These are precious possessions that have come to us through a long history.

For a thousand years our Anglo-Saxon ancestors struggled for parliamentary government. Little by little the right of the people to have a part in the government was secured by hard endeavor. Now the obligation is ours to preserve constitutional government and parliamentary representation. The founders of this nation had faith in the institution they had established. They believed that it pledged to the people human rights and that, if the citizens cherished and appreciated these rights, all would be well.

I do not agree with the strictures which are placed upon democracy. I think its accomplishments surpass those of other governments, whether monarchies or dictatorships. Democracy has given us much that we can be proud of, beautiful buildings and cities, parks in countryside and congested areas, monuments to be found everywhere, as well as paintings in galleries and halls. Roadways that extend from one ocean to the other, sanitation, and health provisions that become more efficient with the passage of each year are among its achievements. It has founded a public school system which guarantees to every child an opportunity to have an education, and it has safeguarded that opportunity in many ways. It has given men liberty, it has given them inspiration, and it has given them hope. What more can any government or any system of government give to men than these benefits?

But we have been indifferent to the obligations of citizenship; we have allowed crafty persons to steal the power of the people. We have ignored the management of our affairs, and at the same time we have criticized public officers who have tried to do the best they can. Failing to give them any meed of appreciation, we have fallen into the bad habit of belittling our officials and our government. The superficial person who becomes habitually fault finding is an enemy of our most cherished possessions. We ought to hold to the freedom that we possess and to the rights that are ours. And in turn we need to remember that the purpose of the United States of America is not an end in itself but that it is an organization created to advance the happiness of, and opportunities for, a larger individual life. The lesson in all of this carries over into our relationships in church, school, and the press. We need to keep before us the lasting good, the great ideals, and the heritage of the nation.

May we indeed

> "See future sons, and daughters yet unborn,
> In crowding ranks on every side arise,
> Demanding life, impatient for the skies."

So wrote Alexander Pope in 1712. Alexis L. Wolfe made these words into a hymn in 1838. America should be the hope of her children. We should cling with tenacious grip to the ideals of the founders who believed in equality of opportunity for all in order that every man and woman might live a full life in the United States of America.

It is unavailing to leave the matter here. To do so is to invite the dictator, the man on horseback, to take charge. Democracy cannot be maintained by lip service or by prating about its values. Democracy must be tried. It must be used. It must be lived. Our government is called a representative government. The will of the people is carried out by those who are chosen to take their places in legislative halls and administrative offices. Here is the center of the whole enterprise. Once conscious of the importance of representation, the people must choose their representatives and their officers on the basis of character, ability, and beliefs. So long as people take their heritage and their obligations lightly, so long will politics be a game of control for place, salary, and advantages that may be turned into cash and into personal or party power. In time the dictator will come if that is the attitude. I have faith in our land, in our people, and in our institutions; however, we can not any longer take our blessings for granted. Democracy must be worked for, prayed for, and thought about. It is worth having. It is the hope of men in our time.

In the letter of Lord Macaulay from which I quoted extensively it is stated that our government is the majority. If that majority is imbued with false ideas and foolish concepts, then democracy will fail. In a democracy we strive for an enlightened, high-minded citizenry. This is the challenge, and with this challenge the methods and purposes of materialistic living must vanish for those who love liberty.

In the book, *The Bridge of San Luis Rey*, Brother Juniper completed his investigations only to have the manuscript fall into the hands of the Inquisition. The little padre died at the stake for committing a heresy. Our country departs from its history and its hope if it gives up its heritage and allows any group to seize its birthright of liberty, of self government, and of equality of opportunity for all. No such consequence can follow if we believe in democracy and practice reasonable procedure in carrying it on. Our hope is in our purpose, in education, and in the continuance of our ideals. These rest with us. In no other way can our great Republic continue.

A Messenger from the Skies

Summary of commencement address, University of Louisville,
June 6, 1941

WHEN Rudolf Hess came down from the skies and landed on a Scotch meadow more than eight hundred miles from the point where he had set his plane in motion, the world was astonished and agog over a nine days' wonder. Since then the comments from him and the silence of his captors have not disclosed the mystery surrounding this adventure. The Germans declared he was idealistic and mildly insane; Hess said he brought with him a peace plan, hatred of Communism, and suggestions for a world organization; whereas Ernest Bevin, Minister of Labor and National Service in the British Government, told his countrymen that Hess was a gangster who out of step with his colleague had fled the country to save his skin. Whatever may be the reason for this amazing event, it is worthwhile to examine the statements made by Hess.

We gather from his peace plan that Britain should stop fighting in order to save the lives of Englishmen and Germans and in order to inaugurate the new regime without the delay occasioned by continuance of war. That Britain might stay in her island with part of her Empire intact and that she should refrain from any dominance over Europe and from any amount of trade with the continent were apparently the assumptions of Hess's plan. A proud people were to taste to the full the dregs of defeat; they were to keep their houses and their bodies but not their pride. This messenger from the skies declared that he was a foe of communism and that he opposed it as a menace to the German way of living and to the German ideas. Germany must bring about a world system.

World associations have been proposed long before the days of Hitler. The Roman State, the Holy Roman Empire, and the great efforts of Charlemagne were early examples of what might be called world orders. Twenty-five years ago Woodrow Wilson proposed and was able to inaugurate an international organization based upon the idea of free peoples consulting together. By their combined power the nations of the world were to prevent war, to maintain freedom of the seas for the trade of the nations, and to work toward a gradual righting of the inequalities and wrongs in the world. We can now see what might have been accomplished by the League of Nations. Many of us are realizing that our participation in that world order might well have saved this generation of Americans thousands of lives and billions of dollars.

Hitler's world order is first a domination of Europe, West Asia, and Africa in which will be three classes of people, the lords of rule, cooperating nations, and vassal folk. These last will include the British, Norwegians, Dutch, Finns, Poles, and the whole population of Africa with the exception of the areas of Libya, Morocco, and French West Africa. The rest of the world is to be brought into subjection by Germany's control of trade. Commodities produced by the vassal folk under a system of enforced labor will flood the markets of the world at a price so cheap that the remaining free peoples will be economically powerless to compete. Not at first is there to be world conquest by arms and by naval power. The invasion is to be by infiltration, by propaganda, by restricted trade, by barter agreements. The one great nation outside the new world order is to be slowly strangled.

Against the strangulation and compelled isolation, the forces of Britain stand alone in this war. We as a nation are now in a state of emergency. Our nation has loosed its strength to assist with materials, supplies, munitions, and ships the beleaguered British in their fight for the rights of free peoples. The situation, unparalleled in world history, calls for all that we can give and do.

In such a world you, my young friends, are to receive degrees tonight from the hand of your distinguished president. It is a time of confusion and fear. These we must banish from our minds and hearts. Confusion about the future and fear that what we have may be taken from us, that our mode of living may be lost, cause us to stumble and to hold reservations that hamper action. Uncertainties and all reservations must be dismissed. Our duty is to know our country and what our way of life means to each of us. If we renew our knowledge of the United States of America, we can but believe in this institution of freedom and good will. We have forgotten our heritage and the blessings that we have had in such generous proportions through the years. May I urge you to recall these blessings, to clear your minds of confusion, and to eliminate fear. Then you will give to your country as your country needs, and you will deserve well the appreciation of your countrymen.

Democracy is worth all that we can do for it. Democracy is the only hope for the world you will live in. Believe in it, live it, work for it, and fight for it as our fathers did in the past. May this country of ours, our ship of state, weather the rough seas ahead and arrive safe in a glorious haven.

Defense of Democracy

Address to the Southern Association of Colleges and Secondary Schools, Memphis, Tennessee, December 12, 1940; published in *Southern Association Quarterly*, May, 1941; reprinted

THE academic voice amazingly, if not a little disconcertingly, waited until there was general talk about the perils to democracy before it too took up the cry "Defense of Democracy." Could the colleges, feeling a security in the idea of democratic procedure, have fallen into the error that, since our fathers had once and for all won freedom for us, the following generations did not need to think or do anything about the matter? Unquestionably departments of history and political science have taught the procedures and the story of the way in which freedom was won and the methods of attaining and holding democracy at the beginnings of our national life. In our colleges democratic forms have been followed by faculties and student organizations teaching some tolerance and a considerable amount of parliamentary law. But something has been wanting.

The enthusiasm of the men of an earlier day for the democratic forms of government is not so much in evidence as it once was. The recent election, in which nearly fifty millions of our people took part, demonstrated that there was sympathy with the democratic procedure; however, the extent of fervor for, and belief in, the democratic way and its results is wholly a matter of conjecture. A lack of confidence in democracy is shown in speeches, editorials, articles, and books which voice cynicism or downright pessimism about the future of the American state. This doubt has attained magnitude and significance in the twentieth century and has been reenforced and intensified with the decline of the democracies in Europe under the iron heel of the fascist states. It was encouraged moreover by the disillusionment following the World War.

That state may be called democratic in which the majority rules without the coercion of minorities. The form of government is not the important factor in the definition of democracy whether it be the Greek city state, the Swiss republic, or our own federal government. The significant element is that the people rule and by their action control the purposes, objectives, and spirit of the state; if that is the case, the state is then a democracy in the political sense. In our own government, based as it is on the ideal of the rights of every individual to life, liberty, and the pursuit of happiness, we can have democracy only when those rights are maintained in cultural and economic as well as in political relations.

The democratic government that we have today has been long in the making. Nearly a thousand years is the story of the Anglo-Saxon growth and development of the democratic idea; and years before the Anglo-Saxon took the first steps toward self-government, the Greeks and the Hebrews made valuable and lasting contributions to this great ideal. In England as long ago as 1215 the knights and barons wrested from King John the Magna Charta. That document, the keystone of English constitutional law, established no new guarantees of rights and liberties but restated the old laws and liberties. It placed limitations upon the power of kings, denied the right to imprison without legal cause, protected the property of subjects, and guaranteed speedy and fair trial. The Magna Charta was in fact a national declaration of independence.

The Petition of Rights was exacted from the Stuart king in 1628. This step toward larger English liberties made forced loans and gifts to the crown unlawful, forbade billeting of troops, again emphasized that no freeman could be imprisoned without cause, and prohibited the use of martial law in time of peace. The excesses of Charles II brought a restatement of law regarding the detention of prisoners, culminating in the Habeas Corpus Act of 1679. Another Stuart king tried to carry on as had his predecessors, but the Revolution of 1688 replaced him with a new king, and in 1689 an act known as the Bill of Rights was passed by Parliament. Under this act the King without the consent of Parliament was not able legally to set aside laws, levy taxes, or maintain an army in time of peace. The act provided also that members of Parliament should have freedom of speech in Parliament without question elsewhere. Furthermore, to guard the liberties of the people the Bill of Rights made unlawful the holding of special courts, the requiring of excessive bail, or the interfering with the selection of jurors. Through the years was developing a body of Common Law, which the King was compelled to recognize as greater than his own will.

With this background of liberties gained by degrees through the centuries, the English colonists brought to the new land the Common Law, the Bill of Rights, the writ of Habeas Corpus, and the determination to have the rights of assembly, freedom of speech, and freedom of religious worship. These principles had to be maintained in the new land against variances of opinion and aristocratic heritages from the old country. Colonial government in this country with the final emergence of representation in the business of government, of control of taxes, of establishment of courts and rules of law is a long struggle that reached its climax in the Declaration of Independence and the Constitution of the United States. Since the colonists insisted upon having all the rights of Englishmen and since they desired safeguards for the future, they were agreed that the Constitution of the United States of America should not be approved until it contained the Bill of Rights. Before the rights could be generally accepted, much suffering, many valiant efforts in behalf of personal freedom, and some persecution endured by colonial men and women were of necessity to be undergone to the end that freedom of speech, freedom of worship, and right of assembly should be established. In the first eight of the ten amendments to the Constitution, the writ of Habeas Corpus, the prohibition against bills of attainder, the opposition to any law that went back of the time of its adoption, freedom of speech, freedom of worship, and the right of assembly were affirmed.

Moreover, no citizen could be punished without trial, and the right to bear arms was asserted. The government in the enforcement of its decrees was forbidden to enter the homes of the people without a search warrant; and no citizen could be deprived of life, liberty, and property without due process of law. Thus was established the procedure described by Daniel Webster as that "which hears before it condemns, which proceeds upon enquiry and renders judgment only after trial. The meaning is that every citizen shall hold his life, liberty, property, and immunities under the protection of the general rules which govern society." The ninth and tenth amendments to the Constitution defined the rights of the states. The accomplishments of a thousand years of history are summed up in the Bill of Rights of these United States. We have in our Constitution the evidence of the spirit of democracy. This ideal should be kept burning in our hearts and should be made to dwell in our minds so that nothing can smother the spirit or erase the memory.

Neither the Declaration of Independence nor the Magna Charta, however, provided the groundwork of democracy. For democracy a great foundation was necessary. That basis is Christianity. Without the teachings of Christianity men could not have formed the kind of government that was fit to control the affairs of men. The substance of democracy is spiritual. Let there be no misunderstanding about that because democracy like Christianity is based upon the essential dignity of man, who is a being susceptible to truth, beauty, reason, and excellence.

If man possesses an inherent dignity, he is capable of ever greater perfection. It may be assumed therefore that in the concept of democracy one must think of man's power of growth. So Jefferson insisted in his comments on democracy that the education of the people must be a matter of right since it was a determining factor in the development of democracy. In the long run, popular decision can not function in all of its far-reaching influences without education on a generous scale. The people through education must be taught constantly to stress tolerance, to insure rights of minorities, and to refrain from violence in dealing with minorities who do not agree with the decision made by the majority. As George Woodberry wrote in his essay on Democracy in *The Heart of Man*: "Men must be persuaded of justice and expediency before democracy can impose itself as the will of the people."

Another American, William Littell, writing in 1814 in a book called *Festoons of Fancy*, said: "Governments founded on false principles and consequently producing immoral results eventually deprave whole nations beyond the possibility of reformation. This has been the case with many nations who have been swept from the face of the earth, and will be the case with many now existing, which are in the highway to perdition."

Men can not be persuaded of the desirability of democracy and the wisdom of supporting it unless they believe in their hearts as well as in their minds that democracy offers a larger way of life than any other form of government and social organization. Accordingly, the gains made by society, the so-called mass gains, should after all inure to the well-being of the whole people. These gains are the advantages that arise through the years from the progress of a people expressed in better standards of living, sanitary and convenient housing, opportunities for culture and recreation, maintenance of health, education for children and adults, and a consistent growth in mind, spirit, and body. If the benefits, the result of the work of a people, continue to be the heritage of the democratic form of society and to enrich the lives of a nation, then democracy will persist and the people will grow in happiness and effective living. Under these conditions of life citizens should be staunchly patriotic, ready to defend their land with their lives and property in every national emergency be it one of short or long duration. The spirit of a people is the supreme creative power capable of holding all to their course and to their purpose.

No doubt a democracy, slow in developing and yet young in comparison with human existence, displays many weaknesses in the conduct of its affairs. These weaknesses show more conspicuously in the complicated society in which we live than in the simple way of life that was largely agricultural. In the early days of this country men were free to do as they pleased to a greater extent than they are in the industrial, urbanized, and mechanized age in which we live. Restrictions have of necessity increased. Along with centralization of population, economic opportunities have materially changed; and social forces at work in the land are intricate and difficult to understand. Nevertheless, there is no reason for a democracy's not meeting the challenge of this more difficult age if the people become increasingly aware of the dangers with which they are confronted and if they are determined to deal with these hazards purposefully and courageously.

Democracy, say those who are distrustful of it, will always be slow in making decisions, so slow in fact that the time of action may well have passed, and the emergency may have developed into a completed act or have become a cause of future disturbance, before action is taken. Yet again and again in the course of history, a democratic people have arisen in courage and in might to combat this view. In everyday action undoubtedly a democratic government may move slowly or even be guided not by national purpose but by the ambitions of individuals. In fact, it is stated that in a country like our own large groups of people do not want a strong government but prefer one that is weak in order that they may pursue their individual interests without opposition. There is nothing new about a charge of this kind. However, such an attitude on the part of various groups may be itself an important reason for working toward a strong alert government that will assure equality of opportunity for all.

It is further said in criticism that the drift of the democratic form of government is toward the mediocre in performance and personnel; this tendency arises out of the ambitions of numerous individuals without training to attach themselves to the people's payroll and out of indifference on the part of the electorate. The awakening of the United States to the importance of good government is surely on its way if not here now. Much of the inefficiency of government will disappear when the people realize not only their dependence upon government in the conduct of their affairs but also the benefits both spiritual and material that come to a nation from good government.

The democracies have large accomplishments on the credit side of the ledger. Holding always to the belief in the importance of the people and in the knowledge that government in a democracy is for the benefit of the people and not vice versa, the democracies have established and fostered extensive mediums of education based on the value of the individual and on his need of enlightenment. This belief in the value of the individual is the fundamental difference between the democracies and the states now instituted on the fascist basis where the state is all in all and superior to the individual. The democratic state has taken the place of kings, princes, and potentates who gave to the people what the rulers wished them to have in order to keep them in a subservient condition of mind. The kingships of other days have given way to the sovereignty of the people who determine for themselves what they may do in their own behalf. Now the democratic states have built for themselves huge auditoriums, libraries, museums, art galleries; they have supported orchestras and maintained parks, recreation areas, and play centers.

Great highways extending from one end of the country to the other are the visible evidence of the ability of a democracy to build means of communication that bind the people together in intimate relations arising through trade and social intercourse. Beyond these achievements is the public school system from the pre-kindergarten through the university, a manifestation of belief in equality of opportunity for all. Moreover, a steadying influence that protects the individual citizen in freedom of speech, of worship, of assembly and in freedom to work in his own right has grown up in our democracy. These are great accomplishments often overlooked in the hectic unsettled days of the present. These rights and responsibilities should be dear indeed to the citizen of the United States of America for they are a noble heritage won through difficulties by those who have gone before us.

Thomas Jefferson, often spoken of as the father of democracy in this country because of the part he played in the writing of the Declaration of Independence and of the Virginia Bill of Rights, championed throughout his life the democratic way. He stamped our national life with the concept of rights and of freedom that belong inherently to the individual. In his attitude toward the people he did not fear their ignorance because he believed in their honesty of purpose. He had a large faith in the common sense of the whole people and he believed that education, basic in the continuance of a democracy, could eliminate mass ignorance.

In his day free land was an important economic, social, and political factor in the life of the people. In truth the democratic idea rested on free men in a free land, and always the western frontier promised in those days new homes and new opportunities. Access to lands was to be supplemented by the opportunities provided by free education. Also Jefferson maintained that there must be in the new republic the right to free enterprise under which men would be entitled to the results of their labor. Competition under such conditions would appear as a matter of course in the business of the nation, and each man would find his place through the opportunities that were open to him. The government was not to check the individual's enterprise by heavy taxes; moreover, it was to protect his legitimate undertakings from being curtailed by greed and organized monopoly. With free land and with free enterprise the man of that agricultural society had his fate in his own hands so long as there was a frontier that allowed him to seek his fortune wherever opportunity showed a chance of success.

The frontier of land and resources is no longer a geographical entity. With the spread of population from ocean to ocean the natural resources have long been taken up, and with this acquirement of ownership the old basis of a democracy is gone. New frontiers must be found if democracy is to continue in the land. Let there be no mistake about this; men will fight for their own homes and firesides. The problem in America is to find new ways to provide men with opportunities that carry the hope for future betterment in homes, in living, and in meeting their cultural needs. Unemployment, therefore, bears heavily on the nation's conscience. In too many instances doubt about the nation's future arises because democracy is indeed a falsehood if men are but puppets and chattels.

Are opportunities to be found now and in the future that can spell, in letters large enough to be seen by all, the ideal which men had when the nation was founded—Democracy?

New frontiers in the field of science sufficient to challenge the best minds and extensive enough to employ men in the activities of industries and inventions are surely ours for the seeking. The arts too can make contributions in the beautifying and dignifying of life; the products of industry by the artist's touch are today replacing in homes, offices, stores the often ugly in design and poor in material. With the growth of responsibility and the enlargement of the idea of social justice, a great frontier emerges that will require trained people to direct and to carry on its manifold functions. A hope for security in job, in sickness, and in old age has gripped the imagination of the people. This hope of security always with us has found a new expression in our day. The United States of America, enterprising and forward looking in many respects, has been slow in undertaking the program of security and welfare, a program the results of which will steadily improve as we learn how to administer it. Two important considerations appear in regard to social security; it will raise national standards of life and will furnish in its administration opportunity for adequately trained young people to find employment.

Numerous frontiers of mind and spirit are calling for us today. Many things are to be done in this country as we move from the horse and buggy age to the electrical and metal one. Highways, towns, houses, equipment to meet the needs of a new time are required in the days that are ahead.

The horizons of our own country seem none too bright at the present moment, reflecting as they do the wars east of us and west of us. Are we as responsible citizens of this great democracy prepared for the challenges that are coming to us now and that will continue to face us? Intelligence, education, training are needed to make their contributions. In reverence, in sincerity, and in deep emotion we ask ourselves if we are ready to meet the requirements of today and of the days to come. Are there a sufficient number of adjusted persons with the requisite skills to answer the calls for help that are upon us? If democracy rests in the main upon the chances a man has to use his abilities, then unquestionably a sufficient number of opportunities are present today, for the man prepared in mind and heart and hand, to assure us of its continuance. In the early history of the nation a strong back, courage, industry, and a few skills enabled the pioneer to win a home and some distinction in that less complicated society. But now the simple man of the earlier day must be superseded by the man who knows and who has skill enough to use the machines, devices, and social organizations of his time.

Lowell in his *Literary Essays,* written almost a hundred years ago, reveals a condition resultant from our commercial life: "In proportion as man grows commercial, does he also become dispassionate and incapable of electric emotions? . . . On the whole I . . . find myself surmising whether a people who, like Americans, put up quietly with all sorts of petty personal impositions and injustices, will not at length find it too great a bore to quarrel with great public wrongs." The founders of this nation had beliefs and convictions. Now men, in ceasing to think of their country except perhaps in regard to their own small grievances and inconveniences, have lost much of the faith that counted so much in the days of the past. This is a calamity of the first order. It is in offsetting this lack of faith that church and school can make their greatest contribution; first, in teaching anew the perfectibility of man; second, by instilling into the minds of the children in the land the cause and purposes of democracy; and third, by consistently practicing democratic principles in the conduct of the institutions. Nor can adult education in a democracy be neglected by church, school, and press.

Can men once again catch the real meaning of self-government by a people so that it becomes a genuine faith that can not be shaken by any winds of misfortune or by any mental quakes that tend to disrupt secure foundations? The need of the present hour for all of us in this country is a great revival in the spirit and purpose of democracy. The pressure from without that comes from the wars now waging in the world drives us to think seriously of our heritage. The future for us is to be safeguarded only by the deep conviction in regard to the worth of democracy and by the possession of a faith in its ultimate ends that nothing can destroy.

But even such faith can not long endure unless men see a future for themselves and their children. In the economic organization men must find opportunities in order that there may be a place for each to use his abilities and his knowledge. The totalitarian states guided by fascist rule say that under the democratic form of government where every man goes his own way such economic opportunity for all is impossible. They maintain that only the totalitarian states, in which the national purposes are recognized as requiring complete subserviency to their causes, can give economic security. Here is the challenge. It is more than theoretical; it is real.

In a democratic society man must accept his responsibilities as well as seek his opportunities. New attitudes, intellectual integrity, additional techniques and skills, better vocational training to equip for a mechanical and metallurgical age, and vitalized subject matter are needed in our educational system. Adjustments are needed in business and in government to the end that real democratic living may be ours and that this government of the United States of America may continue and grow. A marked acceptance of these principles by those who direct in the business world may well bring a day of industrial peace if in the same spirit labor accepts also its responsibility to the public. The recognition of the problems of distribution on the basis of national needs will go far in removing the discriminations in market and store that are so noticeable now. A careful and scientific system of taxation that will not hamper industry and yet will adjust some of the discrepancies in fortunes that irritate the public mind may well bring also greater freedom of enterprise.

Many of these changes in the educational, the business, and the governmental fields are going forward at the present time. Through such variations, social barriers are reduced. Men educated in heart and mind who feel their responsibilities and enjoy their opportunities are working enthusiastically for the continuance and the constantly growing procedures of democracy. Love of this country then follows because the people believe in and understand its heritages, its purposes, and its destiny. Men grow in grace, demonstrating the infinite perfectibility of mankind, when they give their minds, hearts, and strength to the flowering of democracy.

May God give us wisdom to persevere in our destiny and in the destiny of the United States of America.

Books, Reports, Surveys, Articles
By Frank L. McVey

I. BOOKS

The Populist Movement. Economic Studies. Vol. I, No. 3. Published for American Economic Association by the Macmillan Company, New York, N.Y., 1896

Modern Industrialism. D. Appleton Company, New York, N.Y., 1904. Second Edition, 1924

The Government of Minnesota. Macmillan Company, New York, N.Y., 1908

Railroad Transportation. Cree Publishing Company, Chicago, Ill., 1910

The Making of a Town. A. C. McClurg & Company, Chicago, Ill., 1913

Economics of Business. Alexander Hamilton Institute, New York, N.Y., 1914

The Financial History of Great Britain, 1914-1918. Carnegie Endowment for International Peace, Washington, D.C., 1918

II. EDITORSHIPS

The Minnesota Academy of Social Sciences. Vols. I, II. Minneapolis, 1908-1909

Social Science Series. Twenty-five Volumes, A. C. McClurg & Company, Chicago, Ill., 1914-1923

III. REPORTS

Minnesota Tax Commission, 1907, St. Paul

Minnesota Tax Commission, 1909, St. Paul
Prepared in part—statistical tables by staff

President, University of North Dakota, 1910-12-14-16. Published in Bulletin of University, Grand Forks, N.D.

President, University of Kentucky, 1918-20-22-24-26-28-30-32-34-36-38-40. Published in Bulletin of University of January of the year. Lexington, Ky.

University of Louisville, Organization, 1927, Louisville, Ky.

Central University of Venezuela, Reorganization and Location, 1943, 1944, Caracas, Venezuela, S.A.

IV. MEMBER OF SURVEY COMMITTEES

North Dakota Higher Education, 1915
Oklahoma, Education in State, section on Higher Education, 1923
Indiana Higher Education, 1926
Florida Higher Education, 1927
University of North Carolina, 1932
Education in Kentucky, 1934
State University of Louisiana, 1940
William and Mary College, 1940
Rhode Island State College, 1940

V. ARTICLES IN THE FIELD OF ECONOMICS AND GOVERNMENT

"State Banks of Issue," *Gunton's Magazine*, New York, N.Y., March 1894

"State Aid to New York Railroads," *Gunton's Magazine*, New York, N.Y., May 1894

"The Quality of Money and Wages," *Sound Currency*, Reform Club, New York, N.Y., September 1895

"The Populist Movement," *The Independent*, New York, N.Y., September 1896

"Various Financial Views," *The Minnesota Magazine*, St. Paul, October 1896

"The Contest in the Maumee Valley," *Midland Monthly*, Des Moines, Iowa, October 1896

"Some Suggestions Concerning Strikes," *Year Book of Society of Engineers*, University of Minnesota, May 1897

"No Dividend Argument," *Bibliotheca Sacra*, Oberlin, Ohio, June 1898

"The Tin Plate Industry," Two Articles, *Yale Review*, New Haven, Conn., November 1898, August 1899

"Religious, Political, and Economic Freedom," *Self Culture Magazine*, 1899

"Work and Problems of the Consumers' League," *American Journal of Sociology*, University of Chicago, May 1901

"Recent Books on the Trust Problem," *Dial*, Chicago, Ill., May 1, 1902

"Ships Subsidy, Frye Bill," *Yale Review*, New Haven, Conn., May 1902

"Social Effects of the Eight Hour Day," *American Journal of Sociology*, University of Chicago, January 1903

"Problems of Industry and Society," *Dial*, Chicago, Ill., May 1903

"The Government of Minnesota," *Gunton's Magazine*, New York, N.Y., May 1903

"Subsidizing of the Merchant Marine," *Journal of Political Economy*, University of Chicago, June 1906

"Modern German Merchant Marine," *World Today*, November 1909

"Taxation of Mineral Resources," *International Conference on State and Local Taxation*, Toronto, October 1908. Published, Columbus, Ohio, 1909

"Past and Present Sticking Points in Taxation," *Proceedings of Mississippi Valley Historical Association*, 1910, and reprinted

"A Rational System of Taxing Natural Resources," *Quarterly Journal of University of North Dakota*, January 1911, and reprinted

"The Conflict of Administrations," *Popular Science Monthly*, New York, N.Y., February 1912, and reprinted

"Syndicalism and Socialism and Their Meaning," *Quarterly Journal of University of North Dakota*, April 1914, and reprinted

"The Evolution of America" (Address at University of Oslo, Norway, 1912). *Quarterly Journal of University of North Dakota*, July 1915, and reprinted

"Recent Social and Industrial Tendencies in the United States" (Address at University of Oslo, Norway, 1912). *Quarterly Journal of University of North Dakota*, January 1916, and reprinted

"The Nation's Call for Thrift," *Annals of the American Academy of Political and Social Science*, Philadelphia, Pa., January 1920

"The Tax Commissioner, Yesterday and Today," *Revenue Administration—1941*. Published by Federation of Tax Administrators, Chicago, Ill., 1942

VI. ARTICLES IN THE FIELD OF EDUCATION

"Teaching Economics," *Educational Review*, Columbia University, New York, N.Y., March 1908

"The University and Its Relations," Inaugural Address. *Quarterly Journal of University of North Dakota*, Inauguration Number, September 1910

"Admissions to Universities," *Proceedings of National Association of State Universities*, 1911

"The Quality of Service," *Survey*, New York, N.Y., February 1912

"College Entrance Requirements," *Popular Science Monthly*, New York, N.Y., September 1913

"The Net Cost of Higher Education and Monetary Waste of the State," *Proceedings of National Association of State Universities*, 1913

"Participation in Politics by University Professors," *Science*, Lancaster, Pa., March 20, 1914

"What Is Education?", *School and Society*, Lancaster, Pa., September 4, 1915

"The Relation of Universities to Public Service," *School and Society*, Lancaster, Pa., March 28, 1916

"Graduate Work in Economics in Preparation for Teaching," *Journal of Political Economy*, University of Chicago, January 1917, and reprinted

"Has University Extension Fully Justified Itself?", *School and Society*, Lancaster, Pa., February 24, 1917

"Report on Secondary Education and Its Relation to the Colleges," *Proceedings of National Association of State Universities*, 1918

"The Spirit of the University," Inaugural Address, University of Kentucky, *School and Society*, Lancaster, Pa., June 22, 1918

"Research as a University Function," *School and Society*, Lancaster, Pa., June 21, 1919

"The Office of University President," *Quarterly Journal of University of North Dakota*, April 1920, and reprinted by the University of Kentucky

"Teaching as a Calling," *School and Society*, Lancaster, Pa., June 12, 1920, and reprinted

"The University and the Development of Agriculture," *The University and the Commonwealth*, University of Minnesota, Minneapolis, May 1921

"The Critical Attitude of the Public toward Higher Education," *Proceedings of National Association of State Universities*, 1923; *School and Society*, Lancaster, Pa., August 1924

"The Objectives of a Public System of Education," *Proceedings of National Association of State Universities*, 1925

"Who Should Go To College?", *School and Society*, Lancaster, Pa., October 1, 1927

"Administrative Relations in Colleges," *School and Society*, Lancaster, Pa., December 8, 1928

"The Art Spirit," *School Executives' Magazine*, June 1929

"Financing the State University," *Proceedings of National Association of State Universities*, 1929

"Going to College," pamphlet illustrated by the author, University of Kentucky, 1930, 1934, 1935, 1938

"Painting for Pleasure," *Journal of Adult Education*, New York, N.Y., June 1930, and reprinted

"Education in Relation to Industry," *Kentucky Progress Magazine*, Frankfort, Ky., April 1931

"The Superintendent of Buildings and Grounds," *Educational Business Manager and Buyer*, Chicago, Ill., December 1932

"The Ebb Tide in Education," *Proceedings of Southern Association of Colleges and Secondary Schools*, 1932; *School and Society*, Lancaster, Pa., January 21, 1933

"Consideration of Admission Requirements," *Proceedings of National Association of State Universities*, 1933

"Individual and Institutional Accreditation," *Educational Record*, Washington, D.C., January 1933

"The University of Kentucky Station at Quicksand," *Mountain Life and Work*, Berea, Ky., January 1934

"The Registrar and the Next Step," *Bulletin of American Association of Collegiate Registrars*, July 1934

"Publication and the Tax Program," *Proceedings of National Association of State Universities*, 1934

"Then and Now," *Proceedings of Southern Association of Colleges and Secondary Schools*, 1934

"The High Obligation of the Land-Grant College and University," *Proceedings of American Association of Land Grant Colleges and Universities*, 1935

"Ways and Means of the Liberal Arts College in a New Social Order," *Journal of Higher Education*, Columbus, Ohio, April 1935, and reprinted

"Message from President of K.E.A.," *Kentucky School Journal*, Louisville, May 1936

"High School Commencements," *Kentucky School Journal*, October 1937

"Education and the Tennessee Valley Authority," *Introduction to Adult Education, a Part of a Total Educational Program*; Bulletin of the Bureau of School Service, edited by Maurice F. Seay, College of Education, University of Kentucky, June 1938

"The Value of ODK to Colleges and Universities," *Silver Anniversary Brochure of Omicron Delta Kappa Fraternity*, 1939

"Universities in Critical Times; Experiences from the Past," *Proceedings of National Association of State Universities*, 1939

"Turning the Page," Commencement Address, June 6, 1940, Published by University of Kentucky, Kernel Press, 1940

"Defense of Democracy," *Southern Association Quarterly*, May 1941, and reprinted

"Land-Grant Colleges and Universities," *Higher Education in English-Speaking Countries*, Twentieth Educational Yearbook, Bureau of Publications, Teachers College, Columbia University, 1943

VII. OTHER ARTICLES AND ESSAYS

Review of *Deep Channel* by Margaret Prescott Montague, Awarded First Prize by *The Atlantic Monthly*, 1925

"On Hotels," Informal Essay, *Scribblings*, published by Scribblers Club, Lexington, Ky., 1926

"On Collar Buttons," Informal Essay, for Scribblers Club, 1928

"Two Flies Do Not Make a Summer," Informal Essay, for Scribblers Club, December 1931

Foreword to *Kentucky Guide Book*, Harcourt, Brace & Company, New York, N.Y., 1939

Book Reviews, Editorials, Occasional Articles, Essays

Index